Environment and Society

Critical Introductions to Geography

Critical Introductions to Geography is a series of textbooks for undergraduate courses covering the key geographical subdisciplines and providing broad and introductory treatment with a critical edge. They are designed for the North American and international market and take a lively and engaging approach with a distinct geographical voice that distinguishes them from more traditional and out-dated texts.

Prospective authors interested in the series should contact the series editor:
John Paul Jones III
Department of Geography and Regional Development
University of Arizona
jpjones@email.arizona.edu

Published
Cultural Geography
Don Mitchell

Geographies of Globalization
Andrew Herod

Geographies of Media and Communication
Paul C. Adams

Social Geography
Vincent J. Del Casino Jr

Mapping
Jeremy W. Crampton

Research Methods in Geography
Basil Gomez and John Paul Jones III

Political Ecology, Second Edition
Paul Robbins

Geographic Thought
Tim Cresswell

Environment and Society, Second Edition
Paul Robbins, Sarah Moore and John Hintz

Forthcoming
Cultural Landscape
Donald Mitchell and Carolyn Breitbach

Environment and Society

A Critical Introduction

Second Edition

Paul Robbins, John Hintz and Sarah A. Moore

WILEY Blackwell

Library of Congress Cataloging-in-Publication Data

Robbins, Paul, 1967–
    Environment and society : a critical introduction / Paul Robbins, John Hintz, and Sarah A. Moore. – Second edition.
        pages   cm
    Includes bibliographical references and index.
    ISBN 978-1-118-45156-4 (pbk.)
1. Environmental sciences–Social aspects.   2. Environmental protection–Social aspects.
3. Human ecology–Social aspects.   I. Hintz, John.   II. Moore, Sarah A.   III. Title.
    GE105.R63   2014
    333.72–dc23
                                                                          2013032142

A catalogue record for this book is available from the British Library.

Cover image: Tourists in boat watching penguins on an iceberg, Antarctica. © DreamPictures / Getty Images
Cover designer: Design Deluxe

Set in 10/13 pt Minion Pro by Toppan Best-set Premedia Limited
Printed and bound in Malaysia by Vivar Printing Sdn Bhd

6   2016

Contents

Contents

List of Figures

List of Tables

List of Boxes

Acknowledgments

The book would have been impossible without the impeccably polite prodding of Justin Vaughan at Wiley Blackwell, an editor whose creative interventions extend beyond editing and were key sparks in imagining the book and setting us writing. He also sprang for dinner that time in Boston. Many thanks too to Ben Thatcher at Wiley Blackwell for his patience and hard work.

Paul Robbins and Sarah Moore would like to thank the School of Geography and Development at the University of Arizona for the stimulating environment in which to think and write, and especially John Paul Jones III, Sallie Marston, and Marv Waterstone. They would like to thank the students of their Environment and Society classes for slogging through early performances of some of the material presented here. They owe a debt of gratitude to their current and former graduate students who embody and convey much of the plural thinking in the book. The University of Wisconsin-Madison has become an equally invigorating home, including both the Department of Geography and the Nelson Institute for Environmental Studies. Paul and Sarah would also like to thank Marty Robbins, Vicki Robbins, and Mari Jo Joiner. Special thanks to Khaki and Onyx the Great Danes, who are profound society–environment problems in their own right.

John Hintz would like to thank his colleagues in the Department of Environmental, Geographical and Geological Sciences (EGGS) at Bloomsburg University for helping keep the stresses of academic life to a minimum. Innumerable thanks also need to go to his incredibly supportive family (Michelle, Lyell, Claire, Theo, Carolyn, Mom, and Dad).

1

Introduction
The View from a Human-Made Wilderness

Source: Oostvaardersplassen, a nature reserve in the Netherlands.

Keywords

- Anthropocene
- Political ecology
- Reconciliation ecology
- Rewilding

Chapter Menu

Environment and Society: A Critical Introduction, Second Edition. Paul Robbins, John Hintz, and Sarah A. Moore.
© 2014 John Wiley & Sons, Ltd. Published 2014 by John Wiley & Sons, Ltd.

News headlines from forests, fields, rivers, and oceans suggest we are in a world of trouble. Storms ravage the coasts of Asia and the Americas, with more looming as sea levels slowly rise. Fresh water is increasingly scarce around the globe, owing not only to heavy water use but also widespread pollution; there is not a single drop of water in the Colorado River in the United States or the Rhone River in France that is not managed through complex dams and distribution systems, or affected by city and industrial waste along their paths to the sea. Agricultural soils are depleted from years of intensive cropping and from the ongoing application of fertilizers and pesticides in the search for ever-sustained increases of food and fiber; in North India, after decades of increasing production, yields of wheat and rice have hit a plateau. Global temperatures are on the rise and, with this increase, whole ecosystems are at risk. Species of plants and animals are vanishing from the Earth, never to return. Perhaps most profoundly, the world's oceans – upon which these global systems rest – show signs of impending collapse. The accumulation of these acute problems has led observers to conclude that the environment may be irreversibly lost or that we may have reached "the end of nature" (McKibben 1990).

And yet in Flevoland, a province in the Netherlands, wild species are thriving as never before. Red deer roam the landscape, feral horses travel in herds, and an ecosystem of foxes and wild birds has arisen, including egrets and wild geese. Aurochs – the massive wild cattle of Europe – have been extinct for centuries, but their human-bred cousins, Heck Cattle, graze the landscape, their long horns and hairy forms rumbling across the marshland (Figure 1.1). This 15,000-acre wilderness, called Oostvaardersplassen, is filled with wild

Figure 1.1 Heck Cattle. *Source*: Roel Hoeve/Foto Natura/Corbis.

life. Remarkably, all this wildlife is thriving in one of the places on Earth most densely populated by people. For safari visitors, who pay 45 dollars for a visit to the park, there is no question that the place creates a great sense of wonder, as visits to wild places do for most all of us in a world that is increasingly encroached by human activity, pollution, and influence.

But if this place is a wilderness, it is by no means a natural one. Envisioned and created by biologists in the 1980s, this park had previously been little more than muddy lowlands devoid of wildlife. Over time, and with the careful introduction of various animals and plants, the landscape has been crafted to produce these animals. Most notably, the very ground upon which the park sits was reclaimed from the sea, as much of Dutch land was long ago. In the time of the Aurochs, Oostvaardersplassen would have been under meters of water! Though intended to mimic a late Pleistocene (10,000-year-old) ecology, therefore, the place is artificial. It is the product of **rewilding**, where long-lost ecosystems are crafted by people from whole cloth, in order to reclaim – or create – landscapes as they might have been before human influence (Kolbert 2012).

> **Rewilding** A practice of conservation where ecological functions and evolutionary processes, which are thought to have existed in past ecosystems or before human influence, are deliberately restored or created; rewilding often requires the reintroduction or restoration of large predators to ecosystems

The wonderful landscapes of Oostvaardersplassen therefore raise as many questions as they answer. Which animals are introduced and which are not? Who says this state, devoid of people, is the natural one? Where some animals like the Aurochs are extinct, is a human-bred substitute ecologically acceptable? Given that the Heck Cattle were in fact bred by the Nazis in their effort to restore "pure" European nature, are such introductions socially acceptable? In a world desperate for the protection of existing wilderness (to say nothing of clean water and air), are expensive efforts at creating new wildernesses practical, or elitist?

This view from the Netherlands makes our global situation easier to understand, though perhaps no simpler to solve. The contradictory proposition – dramatically transforming the environment in ways that may preserve the environment – is a metaphor for the condition of our longstanding relationship to the non-human world. From this view, Oostvaardersplassen is in no way unique. Yellowstone National Park in the United States, though heralded as a wilderness, was created through the violent extirpation of the dozens of native tribes who lived in the region, transformed its landscapes, and relied on the resources of what would become a park devoid of people. Coffee plantations throughout Asia and Latin America, though regarded purely as economic and artificial landscapes, often teem with wild birds, mammals, and insects, all beyond the intent and control of farmers, conservationists, or anyone else for that matter. Everywhere we seek some place beyond people, the marks of human creation and destruction confront us, and wherever the works of humans are in evidence, there are non-human systems and creatures, all operating in their own way.

Decisions made in places like Oostvaardersplassen, therefore, cannot be made solely on the basis that the region is a "natural" one, nor a "social" one. The area is simultaneously neither and both, with animals, plants, and waterways springing from human interventions, creating altogether new habitats and environments. Wildlife parks and coffee

Anthropocene A metaphoric term sometimes applied to our current era, when people exert enormous influence on environments all around the Earth, but where control of these environments and their enormously complex ecologies is inevitably elusive

plantations are *both* landscapes of the **Anthropocene**, therefore, one term for our current era, when people exert enormous influence on the Earth, but where control of these environments and their enormously complex ecologies is inevitably elusive.

If decisions about what to do (and what not to do) are to be made, and the larger complex puzzle of living *within* nature is to be solved, we need tools with which to view the world in fresh ways and assess possible routes forward. For example, viewed as a problem of ethics, the creation of a Dutch wilderness becomes one of sorting through competing claims and arguments about what is ethically best, on whose behalf one might make such an argument (that of people with competing claims on the scarce resources required in this undertaking or that of the animals themselves?), and over which criteria we might use to adjudicate "good" policy. From the point of view of political economy, by contrast, one would be urged to examine what value is created and destroyed in the transformation of these muddy lands, which specific species are selected and why, whose pockets are filled in the process, and how decisions are controlled and directed through circuits of expert power and conservation authority. Indeed, there is no shortage of ways to view this problem, with population-centered considerations competing with those that stress market logics, and arguments about public risk perception competing with those about the romantic social construction of the park.

What Is This Book?

This book is designed to explain these varied interpretive tools and perspectives and show them in operation. Our strategy is first to present the dominant modes of thinking about environment–society relations and then to apply them to a few familiar objects of the world around us. By environment, we mean the whole of the aquatic, terrestrial, and atmospheric non-human world, including specific objects in their varying forms, like trees, carbon dioxide, or water, as well as the organic and inorganic systems and processes that link and transform them, like photosynthesis, predator–prey relationships, or soil erosion. Society, conversely, includes the humans of the Earth and the larger systems of culture, politics, and economic exchange that govern their interrelationships.

From the outset we must insist that these two categories are interlaced and impossible to separate. Humans are obviously environmental beings subject to organic processes. Equally problematically, environmental processes are also fundamentally social, in the sense that they link people and influence human relationships. Photosynthesis is the basis of agriculture, for example, and so is perhaps the most critical environmental process in the history of civilization. More complex: human transformation of carbon levels in the atmosphere may further alter global photosynthesis in a dramatic way, with implications for human food and social organization. Obviously, it is difficult to tell where the environment leaves off and society begins. On the other hand, there is not universal agreement on these relationships and linkages. The perspectives summarized in this text present very different views about which parts of society and environment are connected to which, under what conditions these change or can be altered, and what the best courses of action tend to be, with enormous implications for both thinking about our place in the ecosystem and solving very immediate problems like global warming, deforestation, or the decline in the world's fisheries.

In Part I, we lay out some of the dominant ways of interpreting the environment–society relationship. We begin in Chapter 2 with a perspective that is foundational to the history of both the natural and social sciences: population. Here we describe how human population has been viewed as a growing threat to the non-human world, contrasting this with views of population growth as a process that not only consumes, but also potentially *produces*, resources in the world. In Chapter 3 we consider economic ways of thinking about the environment. These views stress the power of markets – a category in which we include systems of economic exchange – to respond to scarcity and drive inventive human responses. This is followed in Chapter 4 by approaches that stress institutions, which we define as the rules and norms governing our interactions with nature and resources. Institutional approaches address environmental problems largely as the product of "common property" problems that are amenable to creative rule-making, incentives, and self-regulation. Chapter 5 examines ethics-based approaches to the environment, with their often radical ways of rethinking the place of humans in a world filled with other living and non-living things. The view of the environment as a problem of risk and hazard is explored in Chapter 6. That approach proposes a series of formal procedures for making the best choices possible, given that environments and environmental problems are inherently uncertain and highly variable. This is followed by a description of political economy approaches in Chapter 7, which are those that view the human relationship with nature as one rooted in the economy, but which insist that the economy is based in, and has fundamental implications for, *power* relationships: who gets what, who works for whom, and who pays. Contrary to market-based approaches, these point to the environmentally corrosive impacts of market economics. Chapter 8 closes this part of the book by describing approaches to environment and society issues that stress social construction, which we define as the tendency for people to understand and interpret environmental issues and processes through language, stories, and images that are often inherited or imposed through systems of media, government, education, or industry. These stories are not harmless, since they can encourage or overlook very real actions, impacts, and behaviors with serious environmental and social consequences.

Within these several ways of seeing are many others, of course. Within political economy, for example, issues of environmental justice are critical to understanding why some people are more heavily exposed to hazards than others. We have nested many of these perspectives within larger categories of thought, though without pretending we can do more than introduce many important concepts. Of particular significance are issues related to gender. These are so important, indeed, that we chose not to set them aside in a separate chapter, but to thread them throughout the book, amidst themes as varied as population and political economy.

Part II presents a set of nine critical objects, and examines each of them in turn using a sample of these approaches. Each chapter begins with a "short history" of the object followed by a discussion of ways in which the characteristics of the object present a puzzle or conundrum, and then presents divergent ways of thinking about the object from competing points of view. In Chapter 9, we introduce carbon dioxide, a curious gas with a complicated history on Earth that shows it to vary widely over time, with enormous implications for the forms of life dwelling here. As one of the most important greenhouse gases, moreover, CO_2 has become an increasingly contested object, with competing views about its control, regulation, and circulation. In Chapter 10, we discuss trees. These plants have been companions of human civilization since the beginning, though the long relationship has been marked by dramatic ebbs and flows. In this chapter we take the opportunity to introduce varying theories to account for deforestation and reforestation, as well as a startling ethical proposal for trees to legally represent themselves. Chapter 11 is dedicated to wolves, a species with which humans have a current love–hate relationship and whose return throughout North America and parts of Europe and Asia represents a dramatic change in the way humans and animals relate. This chapter stresses diverse cultural understandings of the same animals, and the implications of our ethics and institutions for the many animals that share the landscape with humanity. Chapter 12 addresses uranium, a natural element that has been harnessed for extraordinary power and benefit, but which has a history rich in danger, injustice, and environmental harm. The tuna takes center stage in Chapter 13, and with it the profound problems faced by the world's oceans. Here, human economics and ethics collide in a consideration of how fish production and consumption are regulated and managed in a complex world. Chapter 14 discusses lawns and the risks posed by the artificial chemical inputs required to maintain them. Chapter 15 addresses one of the world's fastest-growing commodities, bottled water. This object has the rare dual role as a solution to problems of water supply in some parts of the world, while being a clear luxury item – with attendant environmental problems – in others. We next examine French fries (also called "chips"!) in Chapter 16, a culinary invention that connects the complex centuries-old history of the transatlantic "Columbian Exchange" with the health controversies and industrial food economies of the twenty-first century. We close by addressing e-waste in Chapter 17, all the hazardous trash from cell phones, computers, and other electronics that continues to build up in landfills around the world, but which has also become a source of "treasure" for people and companies who mine it for recyclable materials.

Quite intentionally we have selected *objects* for exploration, rather than *problems*. We do this for two reasons. First, while many objects are obviously linked to problems (trees to deforestation, as we shall see in Chapter 10, for example), *not all human relations with non-humans are problems*. Second, we intend by this structure to invite people to think seriously about how different things in the world (giraffes, cell phones, tapeworms, diamonds, chainsaws . . .) *have their own unique relationship to people* and present specific sorts of puzzles owing to their specific characteristics (they swim, they melt, they migrate, they are poisonous when eaten . . .). This is intended as an opportunity to break away from the environment as an undifferentiated generic problem, one universally characterized by a state of immediate and unique crisis. While global climate change is a critical (and sprawling) suite of problems, for example, the long and complex relationship of people to carbon dioxide itself provides a focused entry point, filled with specific challenges and opportunities. We do indeed face enormous environmental problems, but we believe them to be best solved by exploring the specificities and differences, as well as commonalties, of both people and things.

We do not pretend to have provided an exhaustive list of socio-environmental situations, interactions, and problems. Instead we provide a few key examples to show how objects are tools to think with, and to demonstrate the implications of divergent ways of seeing environmental issues.

We have also provided boxed discussions throughout the text entitled: "Environmental Solution?" Our use of the question mark is both intentional and provocative. All the examples we describe have been considered, by someone, to be a solution to environmental problems. We invite readers to consider whether these solutions make sense but also to interrogate the theoretical assumptions that underpin each such solution, using the tools we have provided in the text to think critically about what constitutes a sensible way to address environmental challenges.

It is also important to note that this is not an environmental science textbook, though it is a book that takes environmental science seriously. Several key concepts and processes from a range of environmental sciences are described and defined, especially in the latter half of the book, including carbon sequestration, ecological succession, and predator–prey relationships, among many others. These are described in terms detailed enough to explain and understand the way human and social processes impinge upon or relate to non-human ones. Throughout we have drawn on current knowledge from environmental science sources (the report on global climate change from the Intergovernmental Panel on Climate Change, for example), but we intend a book that requires no previous knowledge of such sciences or sources. We believe this book might reasonably accompany more strictly environmental science approaches, or be used in courses that seek to bridge environmental ethics, economics, or policy with issues in ecology, hydrology, and conservation biology, or vice versa.

The Authors' Points of View

Finally, we provide many points of view in this volume that directly contradict one another. It is difficult, for example, to simultaneously believe that the source of all environmental problems is the total population of humans on Earth, and to hold the position that population growth leads to greater efficiencies and potentially lower environmental impacts. Even where ideas do not contradict one another (for example, risk perception in Chapter 6 might be seen as a sort of social construction in Chapter 8), they definitely stress different factors or problems and imply different solutions.

With that in mind, it is reasonable to ask what the points of view of the text's authors might be. Which side are we on? This is difficult to answer, not only because there are three of us, each with our own view of the world, but also because, as researchers, we often try to bring different perspectives and theories to bear on the objects of our study, and to foster a kind of pluralism in our thinking.

Nonetheless, we do collectively have a point of view. First, we are each urgently concerned about the state of natural environments around the world. Our own research has focused on diverse environmental topics, including Professor Hintz's work on the status of bears in the western part of the United States, Professor Moore's research on the management of solid and hazardous waste in Mexico, and Professor Robbins' investigation of the conservation of forests in India. From these experiences, we have come to share an approach best described as **political ecology**: an understanding that nature and society are produced *together* in a political economy that includes humans and non-humans. What does this mean? To keep it as straightforward as possible, we understand that relationships among people and between people and the environment are governed by persistent and dominant, albeit diverse and historically changing, *interactions of power* (Robbins 2012). This means that we have some special sympathy for themes from political economy and social construction.

> **Political Ecology**   An approach to environmental issues that unites issues of ecology with a broadly defined political economy perspective
>
> **Reconciliation Ecology**   A science of imagining, creating, and sustaining habitats, productive environments, and biodiversity in places used, traveled, and inhabited by human beings

When Hintz examines the conservation of bears in Yellowstone, for example, he thinks it is critical to examine how bears are *imagined* by people and to know what media, assumptions, and stories influence that imagination, since these prefigure how people do or do not act through policy, regulation, or support for environmental laws. When examining solid waste in Mexico, in another example, Moore thinks the crucial question is who *controls access to and use of* dumps, since this determines, to a large degree, how waste is managed, whether problems are addressed or ignored, and where the flow of hazards and benefits is directed. When examining forests in India, Robbins wants to know how local people and forest officers *coerce one another*, in a system of corruption that determines the rate and flow of forest-cutting and environmental transformation. People's power over one another, over the environment, and over how other people think about the environment, in short, is our preferred starting point.

We also share an assumption that persistent systems of power, though they often lead to perverse outcomes, sometimes provide opportunities for progressive environmental action and avenues toward better human–environment relationships. We are stuck in a tangled web, in other words, but this allows us many strands to pull upon and many resources to weave new outcomes.

As a result, we also stress throughout the volume a preference for some form of **reconciliation ecology**. As described by ecologist Michael Rosenzweig (2003), this describes a science of imagining, creating, and sustaining habitats, productive environments, and biodiversity in places used, traveled, and inhabited by human beings. This point of view holds that while many of the persistent human actions of the past have stubbornly caused and perpetuated environmental problems, the solution to these problems can never be a world somehow bereft of human activity, work, inventiveness, and craft. Such a point of view does not deny the importance of making special places (conservation areas, for example) for wild animals, sensitive species, or rare ecosystems. But it does stress that the critical work of making a "greener" world will happen in cities, towns, laboratories, factories, and farms, amidst human activity, and not in an imaginary natural world, somewhere "out there." As Emma Marris describes the possibilities of such a world, she invokes the metaphor of the Earth and its ecosystems as a "Rambunctious Garden," a hybrid of wild nature and human activity (Marris 2011).

For all the weight of our own views, however, we strongly believe in the analytical challenges presented by *all* of the approaches described here. It is our intention, therefore, to present the most convincing and compelling arguments of the many and diverse ways of viewing society and environment. We insist that, while it is impossible for us to present a fully unbiased view of the many ways of thinking about nature, it is possible to present fair characterizations of many points of view, characterizations without caricatures. Only the reader can judge our success in this regard.

References

Kolbert, E. (2012). "Recall of the Wild." *The New Yorker*, December 24.

Marris, E. (2011). *Rambunctious Garden: Saving Nature in a Post-Wild World*. New York: Bloomsbury.

McKibben, B. (1990). *The End of Nature*. New York: Random House.

Robbins, P. (2012). *Political Ecology: A Critical Introduction*. Oxford: Wiley Blackwell.

Rosenzweig, M. L. (2003). *Win–Win Ecology: How the Earth's Species Can Survive in the Midst of Human Enterprise*. Oxford: Oxford University Press.

Part 1

Approaches and Perspectives

For all the weight of our own views, however, we strongly believe in the analytical challenges presented by *all* of the approaches described here. It is our intention, therefore, to present the most convincing and compelling arguments of the many and diverse ways of viewing society and environment. We insist that, while it is impossible for us to present a fully unbiased view of the many ways of thinking about nature, it is possible to present fair characterizations of many points of view, characterizations without caricatures. Only the reader can judge our success in this regard.

References

Kolbert, E. (2012). "Recall of the Wild." *The New Yorker*, December 24.

Marris, E. (2011). *Rambunctious Garden: Saving Nature in a Post-Wild World*. New York: Bloomsbury.

McKibben, B. (1990). *The End of Nature*. New York: Random House.

Robbins, P. (2012). *Political Ecology: A Critical Introduction*. Oxford: Wiley Blackwell.

Rosenzweig, M. L. (2003). *Win–Win Ecology: How the Earth's Species Can Survive in the Midst of Human Enterprise*. Oxford: Oxford University Press.

2

Population and Scarcity

Source: Vladimir Wrangel/Shutterstock.

Chapter Menu

Keywords

- Birth rate
- Carrying capacity
- Death rate
- Demographic transition model
- Ecological footprint
- Exponential growth
- Fertility rate
- Forest transition theory
- Green Revolution
- Induced intensification
- Kuznets curve (environmental)
- Neo-Malthusians
- Zero population growth

Environment and Society: A Critical Introduction, Second Edition. Paul Robbins, John Hintz, and Sarah A. Moore.
© 2014 John Wiley & Sons, Ltd. Published 2014 by John Wiley & Sons, Ltd.

A Crowded Desert City

A trip into Phoenix, Arizona on almost any day of the week is a journey into a dense haze of exhaust fumes, ozone, and blowing dust. This desert metropolis of four million people is the tangled conurbation of 10 separate cities, together planted squarely in a low desert depression: "The Valley of the Sun."

The city effectively did not exist at the turn of the twentieth century. In a place that receives seven inches of rain a year and where summer temperatures can exceed 120°F for many days in a row, it was a largely overlooked site for settlement during the period of American Westward expansion, though a range of native peoples had adapted and thrived in the area in small numbers in the centuries prior.

Starting in the 1950s, new people began to arrive in the area, bringing with them new demands for land and water. Going from a half million people before 1960 to its present size, the rate of growth in the valley has been on the order of 40 percent per decade. In the 1990s, the population grew by roughly 300 people per day, as a sun belt economy mushroomed in the region, driven by high tech production, service industries, and retirement communities. As of 2012, Phoenix is home to 1.5 million people, making it the fifth largest city in the United States.

With each new person comes more demand for limited available water, the production of mounds of garbage, and the disturbance of large areas for new home construction. Given weeks on end with temperatures above 100°F (more than 38°C), summer demands for air conditioning are constant. The hundreds of thousands of cars in the region (two automobiles per household) each emit roughly their own weight in greenhouse gases per year, contributing seriously to both local air pollution and global climate change. The dramatic rate of population growth poses obvious questions about the limits of the land, water, and air to support the city.

Still, there is more than just the *number* of people to concern us here. The average person in Phoenix consumes more than 225 gallons of water per day. This compares poorly even to nearby municipalities like Tucson, where an average individual uses around 160 gallons a day. Where does all this water go? To dishwashers and toilets, among other things, but also to green lawns and vast green landscapes in the desert. Given that by best estimates the minimum amount of water required for human survival is perhaps five gallons a day, it is clear that the affluence and living conditions of people in Phoenix are as important contributors to water use as the overall number of residents.

Either way, the human pressure on resources in the region is tremendous and that impact is by no means limited to water. As new home sites devour land across the valley, the habitat of rare and important desert species (like Gila monsters – rare and fabulous local lizards) declines as well, with implications for global biodiversity. Dense human habitation and activity also encourages the arrival and spread of invasive species and increases the risk of fire hazards across the region. There is a growing human footprint in The Valley of the Sun.

To what degree do the explosive numbers of people in Phoenix represent an environmental crisis? How have affluence and lifestyle influenced this impact? Is there enough water to allow such a city to survive? Many explorations of the relationships between environment and society typically start right here, asking a basic question: Are there simply too many people? Can the world support us all? If not, can human numbers ever be expected to stop growing? How and when?

The Problem of "Geometric" Growth

These questions are by no means new either to the field of ecology or to the examination of society or policy. The concept of overpopulation is indeed ancient, though its most prominent modern adherent lived in the decades spanning the late eighteenth and early nineteenth centuries: Reverend Dr Thomas Robert Malthus. His assertion, in its clearest form, was that the capacity of population to grow is greater than the power of the Earth to provide resources. Given the procreative capacity of humanity and the inherently finite availability of the Earth's resources, in this way of thinking, human population is the single greatest influence on the status of the Earth and its resources. Conversely, the Earth's resources provide the most definitive and powerful limit for human growth and expansion.

In more careful phrasing, Malthus was clear to describe the mathematical underpinnings of this relationship, stressing that population growth is effectively "geometric" ("**exponential**" in today's terms), since the multiple offspring of a single mating pair of animals or people are each capable of producing multiple offspring themselves. Assuming six children from every mating couple (a family size typical in Malthus' time), for example, means a growth from two to six in the first generation, 18 in the

> **Exponential Growth** A condition of growth where the rate is mathematically proportional to the current value, leading to continued, non-linear increase of the quantity; in population, this refers to a state of increasingly accelerated and compounded growth, with ecological implications for scarcity

second generation, 54 in the third, and so on. That growth, when graphed, takes the form of a curve, much steeper than a straight line, moving toward an asymptote, that is, a steep increase in a few generations and a large number of individuals, increasing every generation.

On the other hand, Malthus argued, the food base for this growing population over time is essentially fixed or, perhaps, amenable to slight alteration through "arithmetic" ("linear" in today's terms) expansion. Food supplies can grow by putting more land under the plow, for example, but not nearly at the rate that population expands. Over time "geometric" growth always outpaces "arithmetic" growth, with obvious implications.

These implications sit at the center of Malthus' key written work, *An Essay on the Principle of Population* (Malthus 1992), which he first published in 1798. Here, Malthus suggested, wars, famine, destitution, and disease are natural limits to growth and act to keep population in check. Second, he maintained that policies promoting the welfare of the poor are counterproductive, because they only encourage unnecessary reproduction and resource waste. Third, he argued that the key to averting periodic and inevitable resource crisis is a moral code of self-restraint.

In terms of natural limits Malthus suggested that famine, starvation, and death were predictable. He insisted, moreover, that the iron laws of scarcity meant that periodic

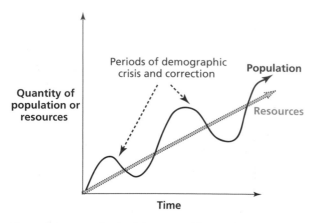

Figure 2.1 Hypothesized demographic trends in a Malthusian conception. Limits of the environment, though they are amenable to steady increases resulting from growths in resource production, control human population trends with periods of high growth followed by periodic calamities and corrections that bring population back in line with the environment.

crises and population collapses were practically inevitable, even in a world where some expansion in resources occurred over time. These hypothetical cyclical population-driven crises are sketched in Figure 2.1, which shows a model of the Malthusian dynamic of population versus natural resources.

Malthus freely admitted that the poorest people were the most vulnerable parts of the population. He insisted, however, that efforts to sustain, protect, or subsidize the conditions of the poor were largely pointless, insofar as they bolstered or supported population growth. Malthus, though, was even harsher in his assessment of the poor. He suggested that the poor are reliant on handouts, that they are bad managers of time and money, and that they are given to irrational procreation.

Rather than provide support for people, Malthus insisted that the best remedy to these crises is the expansion of moral restraint. Specifically he intended the moral restraint of women, whom he held responsible for the maintenance of virtue and, by implication, for population run amuck. He especially focused his criticism on "less civilized" peoples (seen as those from southern Europe at that time) whom he viewed as insufficiently capable of self-control, and so inevitably given to poverty.

> It can scarcely be doubted that, in modern Europe, a much larger proportion of women pass a considerable part of their lives in the exercise of virtue than in past times and among uncivilized nations. (Malthus 1992, Book II, Chapter XIII, 43–4)

> In some of the southern countries where every impulse may be almost immediately indulged, the passion sinks into mere animal desire, is soon weakened and extinguished by excess. (Malthus 1992, Book IV, Chapter I, 212)

The social and political biases of *Essay on the Principle of Population* and the context in which it was written are clear. Malthus developed an explanation for poverty that absolved economic systems, political structures, or the actions of the wealthy or elite from fault. His specific moral vision of women, perhaps even by the standards of his own time, reflects a profoundly biased view of the relationship between women and men.

Actual population growth

Examination of some recent trends also reveals that after two hundred years of demographic history, a few of Malthus' key claims are indeed sustained. To be sure, the exponential nature of human population growth in the past few centuries is quite clear.

That growth is roughly shown in Figure 2.2. Where the world at the time of the Roman Empire two thousand years ago contained only 300 million people, today it holds more than 7 billion, more than a 20-fold increase, most of which occurred in only the last century.

So even while there are numerous profound limits and problems in this formulation (and more as we will see below), the arguments of Malthus and his present-day followers certainly raise questions about the relationship between society and environment and the nature of resource scarcity, its possible inevitability, and our capacity to overcome it.

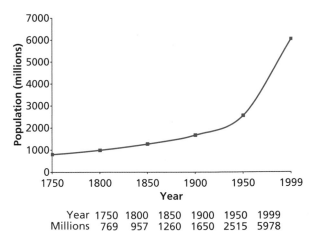

Year	1750	1800	1850	1900	1950	1999
Millions	769	957	1260	1650	2515	5978

Figure 2.2 World population since 1750. Rapid increases in recent decades reflect exponential growth. *Source*: After Demeny (1990).

Population, Development, and Environment Impact

The questions raised by Malthus have been taken up by other scholars interested in relationships between population, economic development, and environmental impacts. One approach, pioneered by Paul Ehrlich and John Holdren (1974), seeks to measure the impact of human beings on the environment, taking seriously not only raw numbers of people but also their overall rate and type of consumption. They proposed that every additional person added an impact on the Earth, though the exact rate of that impact was influenced by other factors including the average affluence of a population (a person in Bangladesh uses far less water and energy than one in the United States, for example) and the availability of technology that might lessen human impact (a population using solar power rather than coal power may have far lower carbon emissions, for example, depending on how solar panels are produced and how much energy their owners use). For this relationship they developed a shorthand equation (IPAT) to determine the level of environmental impact (I) as a product of population (P), affluence (A), and technology (T):

$$I = P*A*T$$

Here, environmental impacts are understood broadly as the deterioration of the resource base, the decline of ecosystems, the production of waste, and so on, while population is the number of people in a specific group (usually a country). Affluence, a measure that was not considered in any way by Malthus, is alternatively measured as either 1) the level of consumption of the population or 2) the per capita gross domestic product. In other words, one considers how many goods per capita (per person) are consumed in that country or area or the total production in the country, divided by the population. Technology, also not considered by Malthus, is the set of methods available to that population to produce the goods that are needed and consumed.

Table 2.1   Who is overpopulated? Some comparisons of population, per capita gross domestic product, energy use, and other resource demands. Different places have widely divergent levels of population, affluence, and technology, with unclear implications for environmental impact.

Country	Total population (millions)[1]	GDP ($ per capita)[2]	Energy use (kg of oil equivalent per capita)[3]	Annual % total forest cover change (including plantations)[4]	Annual % forest cover change (natural forest only)[4]	Greenhouse gas emissions (tons of CO_2 equivalent per capita)[5]
China	1,294	3,936	861	+1.2	+0.6	3.91
USA	288	33,939	8,095	+0.2	+0.1	23.92
Bangladesh	143	1,527	133	+1.3	−0.8	0.38
Turkey	68	6,830	1,071	+0.2	. . .	4.07
UK	60	23,637	3,886	+0.6	+1.5	11.19
Kenya	32	1,003	489	−0.5	−0.5	0.81

1: 2002
2: 2000 (figures controlled for Purchasing Power Parity: equivalence of buying power in local markets)
3: 1999
4: 1990–2000
5: 2005
Source: Data from World Resources Institute Data (2005).

Neo-Malthusians   Present-day adherents to a position – established by Malthus in the nineteenth century – that population growth outstrips limited natural resources and presents the single greatest driver of environmental degradation and crisis

Kuznets Curve (Environmental)   Based in the theory that income inequality will increase during economic development and decrease after reaching a state of overall affluence, this theory predicts that environmental impacts rise during development, only to fall after an economy matures

While this formulation certainly makes the relationship between population and environmental degradation more complicated than Malthus did, it has been used by "**neo-Malthusians**," those more recent adherents to a population-based way of thinking about environmental issues, to argue that population is the paramount factor in this equation. Paul Ehrlich (1974: 1216) explains that population requires the most immediate attention "precisely because population is the most difficult and slowest to yield among the components of environmental deterioration."

There are challenges to this assumption. Critics like Barry Commoner stress that technology has by far the greatest influence on environmental impact, far outweighing the total numbers of people, specifically citing the petrochemical-based economy, pesticides, fossil fuels, and a range of modern developments that increase individual impact enormously. As shown in Table 2.1, environmental impact varies enormously even in current economics. An alternative economy, by implication, would offset population growth (Commoner 1988).

Others have argued that development radically lowers human impact, at a rate far greater than the growth of population. In what some analysts call an **environmental Kuznets curve** (named for economist Simon Kuznets), it is predicted that as development initially occurs, environmental impact increases, with per capita use of resources rising, pollution increasing, and damage to ecosystems like forests rising, and doing so at a rising rate. After a threshold, however, regulation, affluence, and economic transition begin to increase and impacts of humans fall dramatically. Proponents of this argument point out that in many parts of the developing world that have historically experienced high levels of deforestation, urbanization and affluence have left many rural areas abandoned, allowing a **forest transition** back to thick forest cover (Perz 2007, and see Chapter 10).

> **Forest Transition Theory**   A model that predicts a period of deforestation in a region during development, when the forest is a resource or land is cleared for agriculture, followed by a return of forest when the economy changes and population outmigrates and/or becomes conservation-oriented
>
> **Carrying Capacity**   The theoretical limit of population (animal, human, or otherwise) that a system can sustain
>
> **Ecological Footprint**   The theoretical spatial extent of the earth's surface required to sustain an individual, group, system, organization; an index of environmental impact

Carrying capacity and the ecological footprint

On the other side of the equation, assuming agreement might be reached on how to measure impact per person, the degree to which each such impact is "too much" is also a matter of uncertainty. Just as IPAT and its variations predict future impacts of society on nature, the notion of **carrying capacity** is often invoked to signal the limits beyond which a local area can no longer absorb population. Carrying capacity is the number of people that could theoretically be sustained in one area (or the Earth) over an indeterminate amount of time, assuming a particular lifestyle (level of technology and consumption).

It has been estimated, for example, that if we calculate carrying capacity based on an assumption that all people *lived like people do in the United States*, the Earth could sustain only two billion people, or less than one-third of the world's current population (Chambers et al. 2002). If this is taken seriously, we might have to ask how we can possibly decide who should be allowed to live at what standard of living. In other words, is it reasonable to insist that China not develop any further, so that levels of consumption in the United States and Europe can remain the same? Should people in North America demand that India limit its growth so that North Americans (in the United States and Canada) can maintain their own standard of living? For many people, these extremely problematic ethical questions have led to a desire to decrease their own impact on the environment – their **ecological footprint**.

The idea of an ecological footprint analysis is not so much to define the potential of an area to support a particular number of people at a particular standard (although it can do that), but rather to estimate the total area of productive land and water required to produce the resources for and assimilate the waste from a given population. While this can be done at multiple scales – some people use it to analyze the environmental impacts of entire urban areas, or even countries – many people find it useful to estimate how their own daily practices of eating, showering, driving, using the bathroom, washing their clothes, etc. affect the environment. There are many websites available that allow users to enter their own data and receive a number representing their impact on the environment. Of course, you can always view this data with a degree of skepticism, but for many people it is a real eye-opener ("my restaurant dinners add 20 square kilometers to my footprint?!"). So even if human population will never truly "exhaust" the Earth, it is reasonable to ask what quality of life might be expected in specific places with large populations (e.g., Phoenix) and to ask what obligations the wealthy have to the Earth upon which they tread so heavily.

Box 2.1   Environmental Solution? The One-Child Policy

In 1979, the People's Republic of China instituted a radical family planning policy that upended reproductive decision-making across the country and changed the demographic face of the country. The change in family size was accomplished through a set of fines leveled against families having more than one child, coupled with incentives for single-child families to obtain education and other elite privileges. Though rural families and some ethnic minority groups are exempted, a significant proportion of the Chinese population lives under the constraints of this law, which strongly incentivizes small families. In 1979, the fertility rate in the country was a relatively high 2.9, and in rural areas it was perhaps double this figure. According to a World Bank report from 2012, the current fertility rate of the country is a remarkable 1.6. This wholesale transformation of family size has been greeted by many as a model and by others as unnecessary and regressive.

The advantages of a slowing growth rate are several. They include a potential lessening of demand for natural resources, though as a growing proportion of China's one billion citizens enter the middle class, the overall resource demands of the economy have expanded on the whole. The potential effect on the country's environmental impact from the generation of waste, air pollution, and greenhouse gases is also celebrated by observers, though here again the rapid industrialization of the country has meant an overall increase in all three problems.

The disadvantages of the policy are more indirect, but nonetheless widespread. First, a cultural preference for boys has caused widespread sex-selective abortion of females, resulting in a wildly skewed ratio of young men to young women in the current generation. Estimates put the ratio at roughly 120 males to 100 females in the population under 15 years. This trend is exaggerated over time, and the National Population and Family Planning Commission estimates that Chinese men will outnumber women by 30 million in 2020, with implications for social stability. Second, the traditional family structure, in which children collectively cared for aging parents, has been put under enormous stress. With an aging population and a smaller overall productive workforce, many elderly Chinese face serious problems.

Perhaps the most understated feature of the one-child policy is that the significant reduction in family size may only be partly attributable to the law. Falling birth rates have accompanied industrialization throughout Asia, as changing economic conditions have created their own incentives for smaller families. In countries like Japan and South Korea birth rates have plummeted in the past 40 years, without any state-sponsored population policies, and with fewer attendant social problems and shocks. Given that the Chinese resource and environmental impact footprints are still growing dramatically, critics suggest the policy was largely misconceived. In 2008, for example, China emitted 7 billion tonnes of carbon, 23.53 percent of the world's total. By 2011, that figure had risen to almost 10 billion tonnes. Supporters of the policy, needless to say, suggest that, as serious as these problems are, they would only have been worse without the one-child policy.

The Other Side of the Coin: Population and Innovation

Given the many scenarios of famine, scarcity, and ecological disaster typically laid at the feet of population growth, it might be hard to imagine that there are many thinkers, researchers, and historical observers who actually make the reverse argument: population growth is the root of innovation and civilization. Yet there is a great deal of evidence to support this claim.

In this way of thinking, a growth in human numbers, given a relative scarcity of available resources, induces the search for alternatives and new ways of making more from less.

Looking back at agricultural development over thousands of years, there is evidence to suggest that this happens all the time in the provision of food. This is because historically food was produced using extensive production techniques – meaning large areas of land were used for the production of limited amounts of food. Environmental systems (especially soil fertility) impose such limits on production because it is typically the case that the amount of food that can be grown on the same land after a season or two of cropping tends to decrease. The simplest remedy for such soil exhaustion is fallowing of land, meaning that the field is left to rest for a season or more. During the time that the field is at rest, land is cultivated elsewhere.

Such a system is perfectly straightforward and feasible for a limited population. But as human numbers grow and demand for food increases, either the number of fields must be increased (making the production system more extensive – that is, using more land) or the population will have to rotate through their fallow land more quickly, resting the land less often, if at all. If the latter decision is made, then some way of maintaining the fertility of the soil and therefore growing more food on the same amount of land must be devised. The history of agriculture is replete with such innovations, from soil fertilization using manure and more modern inputs to complex systems of intercropping where different crops are used together or in rotation to maintain soil fertility, rather than continuously cropping the same food plant. As explained in Ester Boserup's (1965) now-classic analysis, *Conditions of Agricultural Growth*, over long periods of history the amount of food produced on the same amount of land has increased exponentially, because demands for food rise with increases in population. More people means more food. This thesis is referred to as **induced intensification** and can be extended to all kinds of other problems and natural resources (see Chapter 3).

> **Induced Intensification** A thesis predicting that where agricultural populations grow, demands for food lead to technological innovations resulting in increased food production on the same amount of available land

> **Green Revolution** A suite of technological innovations, developed in universities and international research centers, which were applied to agriculture between the 1950s and 1980s and increased agricultural yields dramatically, but with a concomitant rise in chemical inputs (fertilizers and pesticides) as well as increased demands for water and machinery

Owing to new cultivation techniques and input-heavy systems of agricultural production, the so-called **Green Revolution**, food production has boomed worldwide. Wheat production in India tripled between 1965 and 1980, for example, far outpacing the rate of population growth. In Indonesia during the 1970s, rice production increased by 37 percent. In the Philippines it increased by more than 40 percent. The period from the middle 1960s to the present in fact has been a period in which more food has been produced than consumed, and in which more people have been moved above the level of starvation than in the century prior.

Nevertheless, a number of other environmental problems come with the Green Revolution and the expansion of food production, including the loss of unbroken soils across the prairies and rainforests of the Earth, and a concomitant loss in biodiversity. Where new land is not used to increase food supplies, increased intensity of production has also meant a massive input of fertilizers and pesticides. These chemicals take a toll on the land and are themselves made from petrochemicals, meaning that they depend upon petroleum extraction and manufacturing, with all of the environmental implications of that system. Energy is necessary, moreover, to produce farm equipment (like tractors, and harvesters), and to power that equipment. All of this energy comes from the ongoing exploitation of increasingly scarce petroleum resources, the production of which is costly and environmentally devastating. Each calorie of food in the years following the Green Revolution has become *far* more ecologically expensive. There appears to be no such thing as a free lunch.

These outcomes also raise questions about the problem of *scale* in assessing the impact of population. Agriculture might expand dramatically in a densely populated part of Brazil, for example, to produce soybeans for both consumption and industrial applications, with serious implications for the forest these crops replace. The "population" that drives this demand, however, lives thousands of miles away in Europe and the United States, and thrives in a high-impact lifestyle under conditions of low population density and growth. The circulation of agricultural products makes assessing the impact of local, regional, and global populations extremely difficult.

Nor is any of this to say that unlimited numbers of people lead to unlimited productive capacity and endless plenty, although the view has been described as "cornucopian" (literally "horn of plenty" from the Greek) by its critics. It does raise serious questions, however, about the problems of assuming natural limits. If population growth does not always lead to scarcity, or if it sometimes even results in increased resources, how useful is a Malthusian perspective?

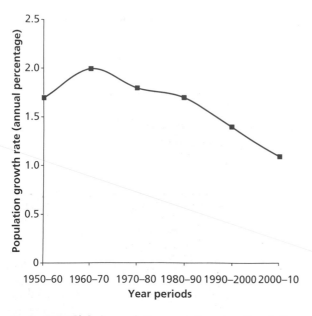

Figure 2.3 Global population growth rates. Population growth rates peaked in the 1960s and have steadily and continuously declined since then.

Zero Population Growth A condition in a population where the number of births matches the number of deaths and therefore there is no net increase; an idealized condition for those concerned about overpopulation

Limits to Population: An Effect Rather than a Cause?

Beyond this, recent trends in population have made some of the pronouncements and assumptions of population-centered thinking moot. Specifically, the rate of population growth around the world has fallen precipitously in the past few years. Some areas are indeed experiencing negative growth. This should be encouraging for Malthusians. But more profoundly, it raises a basic question about population: Is population a social *driver* of environmental change or is it actually the *product* or outcome of social and environmental circumstances and conditions?

Consider the following: Population growth rates, which measure (as a percentage) the rate of natural increase of the total number of people on the Earth, peaked in the period between 1960 and 1970 (Figure 2.3). In the period since, they have only declined, slowly approaching a rate below 1 percent, nearing a state of **zero population growth** (ZPG). Whatever one might think about the danger that population (versus affluence, for example) presents for the environment, one must wonder what causes such a change.

What makes population growth decline? What are the implications for human–environment relations in a world where population, while continuing to grow, is likely to reach stability in the next 50 years?

Development and demographic transition

The most obvious precedent for this global shift comes from the demographic history of Europe in the nineteenth and early twentieth centuries. There, population went from a relatively stable state before 1800 to very high levels of growth in the 1800s, followed by a leveling off, and indeed a current state of population decline in many countries. The drivers of this trend can be broken down more carefully. We can examine the specific rate of births and deaths in Europe (or anywhere else) to provide clues as to what happened.

In traditional agrarian societies, the **death rate** (typically measured in numbers of deaths per 1,000 people in a population in a year) and the **birth rate** (births per 1,000 people per year) vary somewhat, but are both relatively high (around 40 or 50 per thousand). They also typically offset each other so that annually no more people are born than die, leading to low or negligible population growth.

In the European case, the initial growth of population was caused by a decline in the overall death rate of the population. The death rate fell largely in response to better medicine and health care, which led to fewer deaths, especially of infants, women in childbirth, and other historically vulnerable populations. Going from a high of around 40 or 50 deaths per thousand to fewer than 15 deaths per thousand, more people lived, and lived longer, during the nineteenth and twentieth centuries in Europe than ever before. If the death rate falls and the birth rate remains unchanged, population growth occurs, and often at an exponential rate. As long as birth rates are higher than death rates, more people enter a population than leave it. Europe grew as a result.

In the years of the late nineteenth and early twentieth centuries, birth rates also began to fall. There are many reasons for this decline, and some remain a matter of debate. Nonetheless, as people moved into cities, the demand for family farm labor fell while the costs of raising and educating children increased. This led families to have fewer children and the birth rate fell, from a high between 40 or 50 births per thousand to a low closer to 10 or 15. Once the birth and death rates came to match, population growth halted. In many countries, like Russia, the death rate is currently higher than the birth rate, leading to a decrease in population. Current growth rates are mapped in Figure 2.4 and show great international variation in population growth.

The **demographic transition model** or DTM (sketched in Figure 2.5) is an abstract representation of this process that is often used to describe what happened in Europe during this period. Generally it assumes that some form of economic

Death Rate A measure of mortality in a population, typically expressed as the number of deaths per thousand population per year

Birth Rate A measure of natural growth in a population, typically expressed as the number of births per thousand population per year

Demographic Transition Model A model of population change that predicts a decline in population death rates associated with modernization, followed by a decline in birth rates resulting from industrialization and urbanization; this creates a sigmoidal curve where population growth increases rapidly for a period, then levels off

Figure 2.4 Population growth rates worldwide by country. *Source:* Data from Population Reference Bureau, http://www.prb.org/DataFinder/Topic/Rankings.aspx?ind=250.

0–negative

0.1–1.0

1.1–2.0

2.1+

development and change from agricultural to industrial society drive the population toward a period of high population growth, followed by a cessation of growth.

It is tempting to use the DTM to predict what might happen in other parts of the world and in other periods of history. After all, the processes that accompanied demographic transition in Europe are also ongoing in other parts of the globe. Urbanization, decreased proportion of the population in farming, changes in jobs, and the expenses and benefits related to having children are all facts of life in China, India, and much of Africa and Central and South America, although they happen at different times and under different conditions.

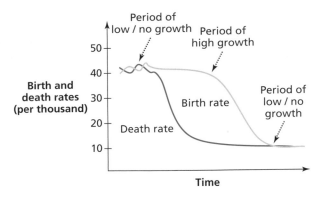

Figure 2.5 The demographic transition model. In theory, falling death rates lead to population growth, but as birth rates fall thereafter, the rate of growth slows, eventually ceasing when the two reach equilibrium.

For demographers, there is a parallel expectation of demographic transition (Newbold 2010). Human pressure on the environment, it might similarly be predicted, will also cease growing (assuming that affluence and consumption do not change for each person!).

Women's rights, education, autonomy, and fertility behavior

But mounting evidence from around the world demonstrates that population and resource transitions are far more diverse and have far more drivers and explanations than the DTM might suggest. In some countries or regions, population growth has fallen dramatically, for example, in the absence of significant economic growth and change. The state of Kerala in southern India is a paramount example of such an outcome. In the 1950s, this small rural state had the highest population growth rate in India but by the 1990s it was among the lowest, falling from 44 per thousand in 1951 to 18 per thousand in 1991 (Parayil 2000). How was this transition achieved, since – contrary to the DTM – the population remains largely rural and manages with a lower than average gross domestic product per capita, even lower than other states within India?

The secret may be outside of strictly economic factors. Kerala has a higher than average level of women's education and literacy and a higher than average availability of rural health care – especially for women. This is a universal phenomenon, moreover, and women's education and literacy correlate significantly with lower **fertility rates**, a measure of the number of children the average woman in a place has over her reproductive lifespan (Figure 2.6). Where women's rights are observed and protected, population growth ends.

Fertility Rate A measure describing the average number of children birthed by an average statistical woman during her reproductive lifetime

There are questions about whether correlation here is linked to causality. In countries with lower fertility rates, for example, women are freer to pursue education. Both women's education and lower fertility may themselves be caused by other factors in culture and society. Even so, reduced fertility rates are also associated with the availability of condoms, the availability of women's reproductive health care on demand, and the social/political

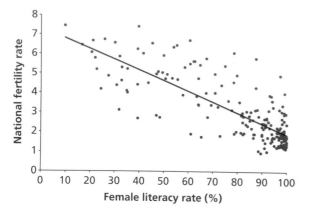

Figure 2.6 National fertility and female literacy rates around the world: 2006. As female literacy increases, and along with it women's autonomy and employment, fertility rates fall to replacement levels. *Source*: Analysis by authors; data: Population Reference Bureau (2008).

"autonomy" of women (meaning social ability to make independent decisions) within households and communities. Put simply, it is increasingly clear that the political and economic condition of women in society is the best and most reliable predictor of demographic conditions. To the degree that population is an influence on the environment, the solution to ecological problems therefore lies in women's rights around the world.

The potential violence and injustice of population-centered thinking

Given that population may be an effect of other economic and political processes, that affluence and consumption have a large hand in determining the environmental impacts of populations of any size, and that some growth in population may lead to increased rather than decreased resources, what are the implications of thinking about environmental problems in strictly demographic terms?

For critics of population control, the implications are serious indeed. For such critics, the history of population politics and efforts at control are fraught with violence and injustice. Consider, for example, the Indian emergency during the period of Indira Gandhi's rule in the 1970s. In 1975 Mrs Gandhi declared martial law and made the end of population growth, through dramatic measures, including mass sterilization camps, the rationing of food and services contingent on family size, and even forced sterilization of some villages and slums, a central part of state policy. Most of these draconian measures were enacted on groups with the least political power, moreover, including marginal caste communities and the urban poor. International neo-Malthusian observers heralded the effort, with some American and European observers calling for logistical support of all kinds in this war on overpopulation (Hartmann 1995).

Yet none of these measures slowed or halted India's population growth, which is only now slowing decades later as a result of complex political and economic factors, including women's rights and access to education. All that these efforts achieved was a horrible violence to those poor and unfortunate enough to be caught up in the panic and a general distrust among all Indians for any discussion of population at all. So, the persistence of Malthusian thinking in the international press, in coercive government population policies, and in environmental analyses of various kinds appears to many critical observers to be dangerous indeed, as it distracts attention away from other driving forces (in economy, society, or politics) of environmental degradation. It also tends to unjustly vilify places and people who may have little or nothing to do with ecological change or negative environmental impacts. While there may be a billion people in India, for example, the United States, with one-quarter that population, emits more than five times the amount of carbon dioxide gas – a key driver of global warming (see Chapter 9).

More pointedly, critics maintain that making the politics of the environment a politics of population directs policy action, blame, and social control specifically onto women and their bodies. As Elizabeth Hartmann argues in her critical book *Reproductive Rights and Wrongs*, by seeking to restrict population, neo-Malthusians effectively seek to restrict women, and yet:

> the solution to the population problems lies not in the diminution of rights, but in their expansion. This is because the population problem is not really about human numbers, but a lack of basic rights. Too many people have too little access to resources. Too many women have too little control over their own reproduction. Rapid population growth is not the cause of underdevelopment; it is a symptom of the slow pace of social reform. (Hartmann 1995: 39)

Thinking with Population

In this chapter we have learned that:

- Human population growth holds serious implications for sustainability of environmental systems, especially as growth tends historically to be "geometric" or exponential.
- Environmental impacts of individual people and groups can vary enormously, owing to variations in technology and affluence.
- Population growth has often led to increased carrying capacity, owing to induced intensification and innovation.
- Carrying capacity and ecological footprint analysis can be used as indices to think about impacts of human individuals and populations.
- Malthusian thinking has severe limits for predicting and understanding human–environment relations, since population is an effect of other processes, including development and the rights and education of women.

Even accepting important criticisms, of course, the question of population cannot be fully ignored. Given the lifestyle of the people of Phoenix, Arizona there may well be a limit to the number of people The Valley of the Sun can maintain, and every person over that limit certainly taxes the region's landscapes, with implications for native biodiversity, for open space, and for clean air. Still, as such resources become scarce and more valued, an incentive to provide them may emerge. Environmental groups (like The Nature Conservancy) are increasingly buying lands throughout Arizona, for example, simply to protect them from development, leave them open and unspoiled, and allow them to provide habitat for the flora and fauna of the desert. Advocates of such an approach suggest that the very scarcity of these environmental "services" is the ticket to their conservation. It is to this argument – that markets can provision and produce scarce environmental goods – that we turn next.

Questions for Review

1. What "crisis" did Malthus predict as inevitable? What was his proposed solution?
2. While Malthus blamed the poor for pending crises, contemporary thinkers like Paul Ehrlich place equal blame on the very wealthy. Why is this the case? (Hint: think I = P*A*T)
3. Who has a larger ecological footprint, you or a subsistence fisher in coastal Bangladesh? Explain.
4. How can population growth force a transition from extensive agriculture to intensive agriculture? How does this transition often lead to innovation?
5. What factors led to the dramatic decrease in population growth rates in Kerala, India? Compare the case of Kerala to India's national population control program put into place in the 1970s.

Exercise 2.1   What Is Your Ecological Footprint?

Go to http://myfootprint.org/en/ and read about ecological footprint analysis. Take the ecological footprint quiz, noting your responses and results. Now take the quiz again, three more times. Each time, change only ONE of your answers from your original answers, as if you had changed one of your own behaviors. Make note of: How does the changed behavior change the resulting final footprint? By how much does the footprint change? And, which particular changes appear to get the most ecological benefit?

What was your original footprint? How did it compare to the national and global averages? In what categories were you higher or lower than this average? How many Earths would be required to support a planet in which everyone lived as you do? Why do you think your overall impact is higher than/lower than/equal to the average? What factors in your life, background, or current situation account for your overall footprint? Will they change in the future? In what direction?

What three changes did you introduce in your proposed behaviors in the three further quizzes? Which of these changes had the greatest impact on your footprint? Which of these is actually the most feasible or likely change (i.e., which would be easiest)? Is the easiest change the one that would make the biggest difference in terms of ecological benefits? Why or why not? What makes some choices more difficult than others? In light of this, to what degree do you feel that global population is a factor in environmental change, relative to consumption, affluence, and lifestyle?

Exercise 2.2   Where are Fertility Rates High? Why?

Visit the Population Reference Bureau's data hub ("Datafinder") at http://www.prb.org/Datafinder.aspx. Using the tools you find there (which include tables, maps, and other resources), research the Total Fertility Rate of four or five countries, along with some other key indicators, like development, wealth, education for women. Where are large families (fertility rates >3.5) more normal and why? Where are fertility rates lower (<2.5) and why? What possible support, policies, or interventions might realistically accelerate a decrease in fertility in high-growth countries?

Exercise 2.3 Too *Few* People?

As of 2012, the Birth Rates in Japan and Germany were 9 per thousand and 8 per thousand respectively. These are very low rates and portend an overall "baby bust" as people have fewer children every year. Can you think of problems that might emerge in these places from having too *few* children? What challenges might such countries face in the next 20 years? How might they be solved?

References

Boserup, E. (1965). *Conditions of Agricultural Growth: The Economics of Agrarian Change under Population Pressure*. Chicago, IL: Aldine.

Chambers, N., C. Simmons, et al. (2002). *Sharing Nature's Interest*. London: Earthscan.

Commoner, B. (1988). "The environment." In P. Borelli (ed.) *Crossroads: Environmental Priorities for the Future*. Washington, DC: Island Press, pp. 121–69.

Demeny, P. (1990). "Population." In B. L. Turner, W. C. Clark, R. Kates, et al. (eds.) *The Earth as Transformed by Human Action*. Cambridge: Cambridge University Press.

Ehrlich, P. R., and J. Holdren (1974). "Impact of population growth." *Science* 171(3977): 1212–17.

Hartmann, B. (1995). *Reproductive Rights and Wrongs: The Global Politics of Population Control*. Boston, MA: South End Press.

Malthus, T. R. (1992). *An Essay on the Principle of Population (selected and introduced by D. Winch)*. Cambridge: Cambridge University Press.

Newbold, B. K. (2010). *Population Geography: Tools and Issues*. Oxford: Rowman & Littlefield.

Parayil, G. (ed.) (2000). *Kerala: The Development Experience*. London: Zed Books.

Perz, S. G. (2007). "Grand theory and context-specificity in the study of forest dynamics: Forest transition theory and other directions." *Professional Geographer* 59(1): 105–14.

Population Reference Bureau (2008). *World Population Data Sheet*. Retrieved October 7, 2009, from www.prb.org/Publications/Datasheets/2008/2008wpds.aspx.

World Bank (2012). World Development Indicators. Retrieved August 14, 2013, from http://data.worldbank.org/data-catalog/world-development-indicators.

World Resources Institute (2007). *Earth Trends Data*. Retrieved October 7, 2009, from http://earthtrends.wri.org/.

Suggested Reading

Ehrlich, P. R., and A. H. Ehrlich (1991). *The Population Explosion*. New York: Simon and Schuster.

Kates, C. A. (2004). "Reproductive liberty and overpopulation." *Environmental Values* 13(1): 51–79.

Lambin, E. F., B. L. Turner, et al. (2001). "The causes of land-use and land-cover change: Moving beyond the myths." *Global Environmental Change – Human and Policy Dimensions* 11(4): 261–9.

Mamdani, M. (1972). *The Myth of Population Control: Family, Caste, and Class in an Indian Village*. New York: Monthly Review Press.

Patel, T. (1994). *Fertility Behavior: Population and Society in a Rajasthani Village*. Bombay: Oxford University Press.

Sayre, N. F. (2008). "The genesis, history, and limits of carrying capacity." *Annals of the Association of American Geographers* 98(1): 120–34.

Warner, S. (2004). "Reproductive liberty and overpopulation: A response." *Environmental Values* 13(3): 393–9.

United Nations (2011). "As world passes 7 billion milestone, UN urges action to meet key challenges" [Online]. UN News Centre. Retrieved August 8, 2013, from http://www.un.org/apps/news/story.asp?NewsID=40257#.UNtVYndhnU.

3

Markets and Commodities

Source: sima/Shutterstock.

Keywords

- Cap and trade
- Coase theorem
- Externality
- Green certification
- Greenwashing
- Market failure
- Market response model
- Monopoly
- Monopsony
- Transaction costs

Chapter Menu

Environment and Society: A Critical Introduction, Second Edition. Paul Robbins, John Hintz, and Sarah A. Moore.
© 2014 John Wiley & Sons, Ltd. Published 2014 by John Wiley & Sons, Ltd.

The Bet

Can using more stuff lead to the availability of more stuff? Can human population growth be *good* for both nature and society? By the end of the 1970s, when population-centered thinking was dominant, such questions were counterintuitive and hard to even ask. At that time, Paul Ehrlich was the most prominent spokesperson for the population crisis and was typically identified as the paramount and persuasive neo-Malthusian of the time (Chapter 2). His book, *The Population Bomb* (1968), was a cornerstone of the thinking and rhetoric of many environmentalists.

It may have seemed surprising, then, for Ehrlich to be challenged to a very public bet in 1980 by a thinker largely unassociated with environmentalism, at least in the public mind. The wager came from economist Julian Simon, who had long maintained that human population growth improved living conditions and environmental quality, because a) more people means more good ideas, and b) more demand for things (including clean air and water) produces an incentive to find, make, and creatively maintain the world. His thinking culminated in a controversial article in the journal *Science* in 1980, entitled "Resources, population, environment: An oversupply of false bad news" (Simon 1980), which maintained that things get progressively better, not worse, with the advent of every birth.

As a journalist for the *New York Times* recorded a decade later (Tierney 1990), the wager consisted of the men betting $1,000 on whether the prices of five metals selected by Ehrlich and his associates – chrome, copper, nickel, tin, and tungsten – would rise or fall in value over the next decade. If Simon was right and the planet was one where the future was always better than the present, the scarcity of these goods would actually decline, owing to increasing human ingenuity and economic growth. If Ehrlich was right and the planet was a finite place bedeviled by rampant consumption, prices should rise considerably. After all, the 1980s was predicted to be a decade of unprecedented growth, with more people born, more quickly, than at any time in human history.

Ehrlich lost the bet. The prices of all five commodities fell dramatically as new sources for each were found and new substitutions for each were developed in laboratories and factories around the world. For Simon, it appeared to vindicate a view of the world wholly different from that of end-of-the-world Malthusian environmentalism.

Of course, questions might be asked about the real environmental value of such a bet, and certainly have been in the decades since. To what degree had these two men really "bet the planet"? Had they not really only wagered on the commodity prices of a handful of relatively trivial ecological assets? What if they had bet on whether global temperatures or atmospheric concentrations of greenhouse gases would rise or fall? What would the future hold for these commodities and others as population continued to grow at an expanding rate?

Nevertheless, Simon had, in a very public way, conveyed a view of the relationship between nature and society that was rather different than that of population-centered thinking. Simon's essential economic worldview was reflected in this bet. Beyond its essential optimism, this view held at its heart the *creative potential* of human beings, the importance of *incentives* in producing outcomes, and the utility of *price* for not only measuring but also creating brave new worlds (Field 2005).

Sustaining environmental goods: The market response model

Contrary to population-caused visions of scarcity (Malthusian or otherwise), thinking economically suggests that scarcity does not set the limits of the relations between society and environment, but instead operates as the engine of their interaction. Here, scarce resources are made available, or indeed abundant, through the working of supply and demand, which inspires the creative potential of human imagination to be unleashed by economic incentives.

In this way of thinking, available resources, because they are valuable, are exploited and used for social good. Oil is burned to propel cars that take people to work, landfills are made to dispose of waste far away from populations, and vegetables are consumed to maintain people's health. Exploitation of environmental goods, even renewable resources like forests or fisheries, does tend to decrease their supply (just as any good Malthusian would insist!). But when things become scarce, their price in a market tends to rise; consider: people pay more for gold than lead. This increase in prices, rather than spelling immediate or imminent ecological disaster, presents producers and consumers with new and interesting choices (Figure 3.1).

For producers, the increase in prices may open up innovative opportunities for finding new sources of resources or developing new technologies to extract, produce, or synthesize environmental goods, including those techniques previously too expensive, relative to the price of the resource, to consider.

Figure 3.1 Environmental scarcity drives markets. Shell gas station operator Steve Grossi's gasoline price board at his Shell station in Huntington Beach. *Source*: REUTERS/Robert Galbraith.

In the southwestern United States, for example, where it had dominated for a century, copper mining came to a sudden halt in the 1960s and 1970s. Mineral stocks had become too diffuse to merit the expensive effort of extracting them from the ground, where only traces remained. But when the price of copper rises, as it has in the last years of the first decade of the twenty-first century, applying more expensive extraction techniques to long-dormant surface mines begins to become profitable, leading to renewed mining and increased supplies.

Similarly, as the price of one good rises relative to the price of a less frequently used alternative, people might turn to this alternative as a cheaper substitute. History is full of such substitutions, from whale oil being replaced by carbon mineral oils to copper pipes giving way to polymer plastic ones. Innovations driven by such responses to scarcity create new economies in themselves, employing technicians, workers, and designers in new, previously unimagined production systems.

Producers and suppliers are not the only creative actors in such markets for environmental goods. Those who consume these goods, either firms that need them for production or individual people, also respond to prices. For consumers, an increase in the price of a good typically leads people to use that good less – decreasing demand. They may reuse or

Figure 3.2 The market response model. In theory, scarcity of environmental goods and services sets into motion a series of adaptations to rising prices, actually resulting in increasing resource availability. *Source*: Adapted from Rees (1990), p. 39.

recycle the goods they have already used, come up with new substitutes of their own, or increase their efficiency of use. If the price of water rises to a point where it is too expensive to water the garden, consumers might abandon outdoor plants, substitute less water-demanding species, or reuse the "graywater" from their washing machine and sink to care for their landscape. All of these efforts at conservation, it should be noted, are driven not by altruism or green sensibilities, but rather by a simple response to market forces.

Market Response Model A model that predicts economic responses to scarcity of a resource will lead to increases in prices that will result either in decreased demand for that resource or increased supply, or both

This process, where scarcity is relieved by laws of supply and demand, which together govern and sustain the relationship of people to nature, is what resource economists and geographers call the "**market response model**" (Figure 3.2). Here, price signals are translated into adaptations by rational and creative people in the market, providing abundance under conditions of scarcity. It is this logic that apparently allowed Simon to prevail over Ehrlich in their 1980 bet.

Managing Environmental Bads: The Coase Theorem

Environmental problems and issues are not always about the scarcity of discrete, individual things, like copper or oil. How can market thinking apply to all environmental objects and conditions (e.g., swimmable streams, diverse rainforests, clean beaches), not just traditional commodities (e.g., milk, tungsten, codfish)? In theory, if human activity makes clean air or water scarce, and I value clean air or water, I should be willing to pay for remediation of the situation. If *someone else* is polluting that air or water, however, and I am experiencing the effects of that deterioration downstream or further away, how could *my* willingness to pay be realized?

Many economists have addressed this problem, but the most prominent solution came from a Nobel laureate in economics, Ronald H. Coase. In 1960, Coase laid out one of the founding propositions of contemporary economics (often called the "**Coase theorem**"), which held that in cases of competing interests, the most efficient outcomes will occur through bargaining between property owners (Coase 1960).

> **Coase Theorem**   A thesis based in neoclassical economics, holding that externalities (e.g., pollution) can be most efficiently controlled through contracts and bargaining between parties, assuming the transaction costs of reaching a bargain are not excessive

What Coase proposes is that many environmental problems can be solved most effectively through contracts. Consider, for example, a family living in a beautiful valley spot in Montana next to a cattle ranch. As it turns out, the cattle ranch is both noisy and somewhat smelly. Such an effect, where one person's economic activity comes at the expense of another, is called an externality, and as we will see below and in Chapter 4, it is common to environmental problems. Such situations also cause lots of nasty arguments in Montana, moreover.

How can such a situation be regulated? One solution might be for the county government to ban ranching in the area, in order to protect homeowners, causing the ranch to shut down. Another would be to make it clear that cattle are more important than housing in rural areas, thus shutting down housing developments in the area. Alternatively, complex rules could be designed, telling developers how to build smell- and sound-proof housing and cattle ranchers how to move and keep their cattle more quietly. None of these solutions is necessarily socially fair or just to one side or the other. The last solution, while perhaps fairer, may be economically inefficient and far more expensive than the other alternatives. Who pays for these redesigning efforts and on what terms? What approach would produce an optimal outcome?

In Coase's way of thinking, it would be better to let the two parties sort the problem out themselves through contracts and, in the process, discover the *real* costs and values of ranching, mountain views, and cattle smells. By coming to terms with one another, *whatever they decide* is always the most efficient outcome, no matter what the initial rights are in the situation.

If the family moved in after the ranch had long been in business, for example, or if the family had no legal right to limit the rancher's actions, they would simply have to tolerate it, or absorb the cost of the smell by paying some higher price for property elsewhere, and moving far away from the ranch. The difference in the price of their current house and the new one reflects how much the people are willing to pay to not live around cattle. Perhaps, however, the cost of the new home is far higher than the cost they might be able to pay the rancher for simply moving her cattle shed to the other side of the property. By paying the rancher a lower sum, the family maintains its pretty view and reduces the smell while offsetting the rancher's costs for doing so. In that case, the price of the environmental nuisance is discovered through the negotiation between the two parties (rather than by relying on a regulator), and everyone experiences an optimal outcome.

If, on the other hand, the family came first or it held some kind of county-given right to a non-smelly environment, other options emerge. In that case, the cattle owner might cease ranching, at whatever cost, and sell to a housing developer. It may be even cheaper for the rancher to directly pay the homeowners, essentially bribing them to put up with it. On the other hand, if it turns out to be even less expensive to move the cattle shed than it is to pay off the neighbors, the rancher can always choose this option.

Notably, it does not matter what the configuration of legal rights is at the outset of the scenario – ranchers might hold the right to ranch, families might have the right to be free of cattle smells, or neither may pertain. In any case, if contracts can be worked out and enforced between the two parties, they always reach a decision that is economically most efficient. Such a determination is fully in line with the market response model, but extends its crystalline logics to the complex world of environmental **externalities**.

> **Externality**   The spillover of a cost or benefit, as where industrial activity at a plant leads to pollution off-site that must be paid for by someone else

Coase stipulated two key assumptions, however, that were required to be true for such smooth efficiencies to prevail: property rights have to be exclusive and the transfer and protection of contracted rights has to be free. This means, for the efficiencies of Coase to be realized in the above example, 1) both the rancher and the homeowner must have the full ability to control their land and the decisions made on it and, more importantly, 2) their negotiations and contracts must not cost time or money to negotiate, write, and enforce. Put in other terms, a free market system is efficient to the degree that actually sorting out agreements, coming to understandings, and designing fair rules and restrictions are socially and economically free or cheap. Similarly, it depends on enforcement (policing, monitoring, and punishing violations) of contracts and rights having no costs.

And in reality, of course, this is totally untrue. For our rancher and homeowner, the time it takes to negotiate the contract, the possible cost in lawyers, and the hidden cost of maintaining county court houses and civil servants to process and administer the contract are indeed quite high. Defining property rights for more intangible goods and services (e.g., biodiversity) is even more daunting. Enforcing contracts over incredibly complex systems (e.g., global climate) appears all the more impossible. The problem comes in the practical difficulty of assigning private rights to "fugitive," mobile, intangible things – like air – clearly contracting the relations between owners, and enforcing the results. For an "air market" to function, the air must be owned by someone who paid for it, who can get value from it, who has an individual interest in keeping it clean, and who can legally challenge someone else who dirties it or violates a contractual agreement over its condition.

While in some ways such a market seems inconceivable (because it is difficult to enclose, see Chapter 4), recent evidence suggests that it may be possible. Rather than assigning rights to clean air, recent efforts in the United States and elsewhere have worked to give *rights to pollute*. In a specific example, in the early 1990s, the United States Environmental Protection Agency (EPA) set limits on industries for the emission of sulfur dioxide, a primary cause of acid rain. But rather than setting a limit on each factory, the total allowable level of pollution was divided into units and distributed to producers, in the form of credits that could be sold. Should a company find a cheap way to reduce their sulfur dioxide production below the level for which they held credits, they could sell the spare credits for a profit. More radically, if environmental groups believe that the limit on total emissions provided in the credit system is too high, and they are *willing to pay* to reduce it, they have the right to buy credits on the market, like anyone else, and simply take them out of circulation. This also has the effect of raising the scarcity and cost of pollution credits, creating incentives for industry to become even more efficient. Such a market has been in operation for 15 years and is only one of many such efforts (see more on "cap and trade" below).

Whatever the flaws in such a system, it demonstrates that markets can function for all sorts of environmental goods and services, but that – as Coase suggests – to make them work, private property rights to nature must be clearly assigned to corporations or people. This is a logical and practical prerequisite to any market solution, but certainly one with serious social, environmental, and political implications, as we shall see.

Market Failure

There are several ways in which these market and contract-governed ways of living in nature might fail. Such **market failures** emerge from a mismatch between the assumptions of the market model and the real world. Chief challenges to market assumptions include the facts that 1) transactions are not by any means free (as per Coase's assumptions), 2) contracts and property rights have to be defined and enforced often at great legal and regulatory expense, and 3) not all parties to negotiations have perfect and equal information. This is especially the case for environmental goods and services that are spread across a large population of individuals.

Consider, for example, the problem of the ranch and residence provided above, but now imagine it with thousands of scattered homeowners and hundreds of ranches. Under such circumstances, the complexity of working out discrete contracted negotiations becomes enormous, as does the problem of monitoring and enforcing the rights of different ranchers each operating with different rules with differing property owners.

Market Failure   A situation or condition where the production or exchange of a good or service is *not* efficient; this refers to a range of perverse economic outcomes stemming from market problems like monopoly or uncontrolled externalities

Transaction Costs   In economics, the cost associated with making an exchange, including, for example, drawing a contract, traveling to market, or negotiating a price; while most economic models assume low transaction costs, in reality these costs can be quite high, especially for systems with high externalities

There is also always a temptation for some people to wait to accrue benefits from other people's negotiations without taking the time or energy to negotiate for themselves. Such a "free-rider" problem is typical of common property environmental problems (see Chapter 4). In such a case, the **transaction costs** of getting the problem sorted out contractually are simply much higher than the cost of the problem. Typically such cases lend themselves to regulatory and treaty-based, rather than market-based, solutions. For example, the system of tradable pollution credits that made acid rain reduction a success in the United States had to be created and enforced by the Environmental Protection Agency of that country, an entity with police powers paid for through federal taxation. Consider too, that reduction of sulfur emissions in Europe was managed through the creation of the "Helsinki Protocol," a treaty agreement to achieve 30 percent reductions by 21 nations signing the document. Efficient markets require public investments. Free markets are rarely free.

> **Monopoly**   A market condition where there is one seller for many buyers, leading to perverted and artificially inflated pricing of goods or services
>
> **Monopsony**   A market condition where there is one buyer for many sellers, leading to perverted and artificially deflated pricing of goods or services

Other asymmetries also plague markets. One of the most serious is that of **monopoly**, where many buyers face one service provider or owner, or **monopsony**, where many sellers face a single buyer. In either case, the individual or firm is in a position to set prices and buy and sell goods or services free from competition and with no incentive to be efficient. Neither are such cases rare; the histories of the American and European capitalist economies are filled with cases where monopolies and monopsonies emerged through the concentration of wealth (in railroads, meat packing, and communication, among many). For environmental goods and services, the record has been equally spotty. Most municipal water provision in the United States, for example, was developed by private companies in the 1800s. The failure of these utility monopolies to efficiently manage and price water, however, led to the transition of most such utilities to state control.

A further problem is raised if we consider that many of the potential parties in a contractual arrangement or in a market have not yet been born. People may negotiate with one another over the relative value of cutting down a forest or enjoying its timber for construction, but what about people a hundred years from now? Do they have a place in such a market? A strict adherent to market logics would make no provision for such people. Getting environmental economics right is difficult enough without considering future generations, after all! Alternatively, it could be argued that both economic development and conservation in the present, in whatever market-negotiated combination, are always in the interest of future generations, who benefit from better economic and environmental conditions.

Market-Based Solutions to Environmental Problems

We have seen that markets can fail and even vociferous supporters of market environmentalism admit the necessity of some form of regulatory guidance of the economy. Nevertheless, a range of market-based policy solutions have been introduced in recent years to solve countless environmental problems. These each, in some way, for better or for worse, use the concepts of incentives, ownership, pricing, and trading to address environmental problems (Table 3.1, p. 40).

Green taxes

One of the most direct ways to harness the market, and therefore to influence environmental decision-making by people and firms, is through artificially altering prices. According to the market response model, after all, it is increasing prices that drive providers to search for new sources, innovators to substitute, consumers to conserve, and alternatives to emerge. Taxing certain goods or services, and so increasing prices, should result in either

Box 3.1 Environmental Solution? Natural Gas as a Bridge Fuel

Consider a future where we get nearly all of the power needed for electricity, transportation, agriculture, and industry from renewable sources like wind, solar, geothermal, and tidal power. The fabled post-carbon economy represents (at least in theory) a great environmental win–win. Win #1: renewable fuels, by definition, cannot be depleted. A post-carbon economy would eliminate the need to endlessly pursue increasingly remote fossil fuels. Win #2: a post-carbon economy would reduce by orders of magnitude the total anthropogenic emissions of greenhouse gases that cause climate change.

But there is, of course, no free lunch. It will take decades to develop the technology and infrastructure necessary to power society primarily with renewable fuels and in the intervening years we cannot continue our current path. Three to six more coal- and oil-fueled decades would likely usher in a disastrous global temperature increase exceeding 4°C by the end of the century. The prudent course would be to transition to less carbon-intensive fuels that could serve as a "bridge" to a post-carbon future. Arguably, the most promising "bridge fuel" is natural gas.

Natural gas has several undeniable upsides over coal and oil. Converting coal-fired power plants to natural gas is feasible (and is indeed happening all over the world, in places where gas is available and inexpensive). Gas produces significantly lower carbon emissions than oil or coal (along with eliminating or greatly reducing airborne mercury, sulphur dioxide, and other pollutants). Moreover, natural gas is relatively abundant.

The problem, however, is that most of the remaining recoverable natural gas is so-called "tight gas," bound up within poorly connected pore spaces throughout a layer of sedimentary rock (usually shale). Recent advancements in an extraction technique known as hydraulic fracturing (or "fracking") enable the recovery of tight gas. This technology drills horizontal wells into gas-rich shale beds, and then injects water, sand, and chemicals under high pressure to fracture the rock and force the gas to the surface. Fracking has dramatically increased gas extraction in the past decade. In the United States, for example, gas production is up nearly 30 percent since the 1980s, and has unquestionably reduced the country's carbon footprint. Shale gas could meet energy demands in the United States for several decades, moreover.

Despite all the environmental upsides of gas, fracking produces undesirable environmental impacts where it is employed. The chemicals injected into the ground include several toxic compounds that might pollute local water. Liberated methane often finds its way into groundwater aquifers near fracking operations. Compressor stations emit noxious airborne contaminants. These (and other) environmentally problematic aspects make fracking enormously controversial.

Perhaps the largest environmental challenge to emerge from the fracking revolution, however, is the one it presents to renewable energy. As more gas is produced, and infrastructure is dedicated to its distribution, its price falls dramatically. Cheap gas under-prices not only "dirty" forms of energy production, like coal, but also critically important renewable energy sources, including wind and solar. The larger the gas supply, therefore, the less economically competitive important alternative and sustainable energy options become. This market outcome confounds the benefits of cheap gas and suggests that, rather than acting as a bridge to renewables, increased fracking may further "lock in" the energy economy to technologies that drive climate change.

decreased use of these resources or creative innovation of new sources or options. The money raised through the tax can be used directly by the government either to provision services or to search for alternatives.

Many examples of such "green taxes" exist. Facing landfill costs, labor expenses, and related costs in the provision of garbage disposal, for example, some municipalities have required households to dispose of all waste in special trash bags, purchased by consumers

Table 3.1 Market-based solutions. An overview of some dominant environmental regulatory mechanisms that involve market components and are based in part on market logics. Note that in all cases the state remains an important player in making markets work and achieving environmental goals.

Regulatory mechanism	Concept	Market component	Role of the state
Green taxes	Individuals or firms participate in "greener" behavior by avoiding more costly "brown" alternatives	Incentivized behavior	Sets and collects taxes
Cap and trade	Total amount of pollutant or other "bad" is limited and tradable rights to pollute are distributed to polluters	Rewarding efficiency	Sets limits and enforces contracts
Green consumption	Individual consumers choose goods or services based on their certified environmental impacts, typically paying more for more benign commodities	Willingness to pay	Oversees and authenticates claims of producers and sellers

themselves, and often costing a dollar or more each. The results have been greatly increased recycling and more careful attention by consumers to packaging and waste. By internalizing the costs of trash to consumers, there has been an observed decrease in the flow of garbage from households.

More radically, such taxes have been proposed for the control of greenhouse gases that drive global warming. Sweden enacted a carbon tax in 1991, followed by other countries, including the Netherlands, Finland, and Norway. This tax is leveled against oil, natural gas, coal, and a range of fuels. Such taxes have also been considered in the United States and the European Union, although they face significant political opposition.

Trading and banking environmental "bads"

Also prominent among these market approaches are policy efforts that draw upon Coase's insights to reduce environmental problems as efficiently as possible, using contractual exchange. Such mechanisms usually take the form of "**cap and trade**." Here, the state determines a regulatory maximum for emissions of an environmental hazard and allows firms to meet the goal themselves or to pay other firms, who are able to reduce outputs more efficiently, to do so for them. This achieves the same results as traditional regulation, but does so at lower overall cost (and so economists describe this outcome as "more efficient").

As shown in Figure 3.3, regulation can be used to reduce emissions in an industrial setting by demanding a 30 percent cut in

Cap and Trade A market-based system to manage environmental pollutants where a total limit is placed on all emissions in a jurisdiction (state, country, worldwide, etc.), and individual people or firms possess transferable shares of that total, theoretically leading to the most efficient overall system to maintain and reduce pollution levels overall

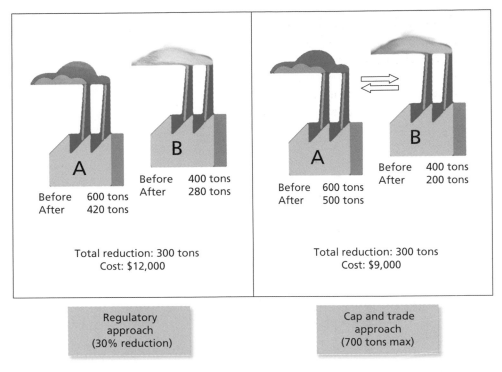

Figure 3.3 Regulation versus cap and trade. Both approaches result in net desired pollution reduction, but the cap-and-trade approach is theoretically cheaper overall.

tons of pollutants for both factories A and B, resulting in a total removal of 300 tons of pollution from the atmosphere, leaving 700 tons overall. Significantly, however, Factory B, owing to its technology and system of production, can eliminate pollution at a cost of $25 per ton, while the older Factory A requires $50 per ton invested to do the same. Rather than spending an overall total of $12,000 to reduce pollution, therefore, it would be more efficient to simply cap the total amount of pollution at 700 total tons and allow the two firms to trade permits if they desire. In that case, Factory A might make some reductions of its own, but purchase the remainder of pollution credits from the more efficient Factory B, whose aggressive reductions result in meeting the net target. Both systems then result in the same amount of pollution reduction, but cap and trade does so more efficiently.

The basic idea is that firms who are able to reduce emissions more cheaply (because of available technology, know-how, or experience) can do so *for* other firms who are less able, and then be paid for the trouble. The US SO_2 "Acid Rain" trading system began in 1995 and reports significant emissions reduction. Proponents claim that the trading system yielded 30 percent more reductions than non-flexible methods, where every factory had to meet the exact same requirements (see the bold claims of the global shipping industry, for example, at www.seaat.org/).

Such systems are not without problems and limitations, obviously. No allowance here has been made for geography, for example. If individual factories are allowed to pollute on site, offsetting their emissions with reductions at faraway locations, the environmental effects might be locally disastrous, even if the overall reduction meets a target. The problems of actually setting the cap, determining the limits, and monitoring and implementing the reduction all remain as well. The use of the market tool also does nothing to depoliticize pollution control, since determining *how much* pollution is allowable requires difficult tradeoffs and regulatory experience.

In a variation upon this approach, some regulations allow markets to be extended to "banking" and "withdrawing" environmental services through third-party providers. Most notably, wetland protection in the United States has moved to a banking system. Here, a cap is set on the total amount of wetlands, enforcing no *net* loss of wetlands overall, but allowing that any local loss of wetlands can be offset by the creation of a wetland elsewhere, so long as it is approved by the EPA in terms of its delivery of similar "services." A new big-box retail chain, for example, which destroys a wetland in the construction of a new store, is required under law to create a similar one somewhere else. Since building wetlands is a specialized practice, however, probably out of the technical and ecological capacity of the person or firm who destroyed the original ecosystem, a third party might be called upon to create and manage the new wetland. More radically, a savvy developer might build an enormous wetland or set of wetlands – a kind of bank – speculating that new constructions will need to purchase portions or shares in the future to meet their obligations.

Such a system presents any number of practical problems, which raise questions about the ecological efficacy of any such effort. In the case of wetlands, it is necessary, for example, to assure that newly built environments actually deliver the ecosystem services lost in the destruction of the original landscape. Such monitoring and oversight demand extensive regulatory efforts, many ecological experts on site examining the system, and careful scrutiny over time. Indeed, a market-based approach, often vaunted for its ability to cut out government intervention, may demand an *extension* of state regulations, with increasing numbers of state scientists and monitors, paid at the public expense, assuring the legitimacy of transactions in the market (Robertson 2006).

Green consumption

Market-based solutions to environmental problems also tend to stress the power of consumer demand for changing environmental conditions. Pointing to an overall social shift toward green values, market advocates suggest that the most powerful way to change production systems is to allow consumers to "vote with their money," and select and purchase green products, often at a premium. The success of organic foods, which are now very much in the mainstream of consumer culture, provides an example of consumers paying extra and creating incentives for more producers to change their methods and technologies.

Such approaches have drastic limitations. How does a consumer know, after all, the specific environmental impacts of products that carry handsome green labels? How do they know such products and companies have not been merely "**greenwashed**," presented and advertised heavily as environmentally sound or benign with little

Greenwashing The exaggerated or false marketing of a product, good, or service as environmentally friendly substantive change in actual production practices, packaging, or disposal? Indeed, for many firms far more time and money are invested in green advertising than green practices (TerraChoice Environmental Marketing Inc. 2007).

One way of confirming truth in green advertising is through the process of **green certification**, in which a third party monitors production of a range of products and provides a confirmatory "seal of approval" for products meeting specific standards. A number of governmental and nongovernmental green certification systems exist, including those for timber, organic foods, and energy-efficient appliances, among many others. As green certification systems continue to proliferate, however, their reliability and consistency become more questionable. Some certifications, for example, are established by companies themselves rather than third-party observers. Moreover, many countries have adopted their own standards. For example, the country of Malaysia has instituted its own independent certification for sustainable timber, which competes directly with international standards. This makes global trade in eco-friendly goods a confusing smorgasbord.

> **Green Certification** Programs to certify commodities for the purposes of assuring their ecological credentials, such as organically grown vegetables or sustainably harvested wood products

Beyond Market Failure: Gaps between Nature and Economy

Leaving aside problems in implementing market-based environmental policy, larger questions loom. Adopting an economic logic for nature presents more basic problems: it makes it difficult to maintain ecocentric values (see Chapter 5), because there is a mismatch in the behavior of money and ecosystems, and because basic economic inequity presents a barrier for reconciling markets and the environment in a socially just way.

Non-market values

At bottom, the market response model can only be deemed to be operating successfully if success is measured in strictly economic terms. When sperm whale oil became scarce and was replaced with fossil fuels, as actually happened in the nineteenth century, the outcome for people was negligible or beneficial. New resources, propelled by the scarcity of old sources, were made available through the magic of the marketplace. But what is the lesson of this story for the sperm whale itself? Long before market responses "kicked in" to send humans in search of new oil sources, the sperm whale was driven to the brink of extinction, a result that was only forestalled by the creation of international bans on whaling in the twentieth century. Indeed, global green markets have proven slow to adjust to the decline of rainforests, the plunge in biodiversity, and the potential catastrophic implications of global warming, raising questions about the capacity of trade to capture the value of these things, at least within the urgent time frame in which they will need to be addressed.

The problem is therefore not simply that the market may fail on its own terms (and indeed it does by the admission of many of its most enthusiastic supporters), but that its success can only be judged in economic and therefore anthropocentric terms. If there are values that cannot be captured in a market, like the evolutionary, aesthetic, or moral "value" of a species, what difference does it make that its depletion eventually allows its *substitution* by something else? While economic valuation allows us to identify what people might be willing to pay for abstract and intangible goods and services (i.e., the presence of sperm whales somewhere on the planet), it does not necessarily point a way for them to be valued, in monetary terms.

Money and nature

Beyond this, the valuing of ecological conditions through the market, and specifically in money terms, is fraught with other very basic problems. First, the history of capitalism has shown that markets are highly volatile, and given to bubbles and busts. This is not necessarily a bad thing for capital, which travels from crisis to crisis, moving from investments in forestry to plastics to biofuels. But these rapid fluctuations of money values of different natural objects, typically driven by speculation, may be out of step with both cycles of environmental systems and changes in social values. Without recourse to some other system of valuation, however, these eruptive metrics are the sole measure in a market. As geographer David Harvey describes, this becomes "a tautology in which achieved prices become the only indicators we have of the money value of assets whose independent values we are seeking to determine. Rapid shifts in market prices imply equally rapid shifts in asset values" (Harvey 1996: 152). But the crashes and crescendos of historical markets continuously show that market volatility may not reflect the social values they are understood to measure. Can we trust a turbulent commodity exchange market to reflect the slow and steady pace of changing environmental values?

A commodity approach to the environment also tends to stress the exchange of discrete and specific items or services. The complex ecosystem of a river is most effectively managed in a market through the discrete components that can be valued by differing parties. For example, the river in one condition or another may be able to provide wetlands or offer flood control, or to maximize trout habitat, or to facilitate transport or recreation. In theory, to the degree to which these services are mutually exclusive, a market can best adjudicate what is most desired and provide it from the river. In reality, however, these functions are connected and interdependent in many ways, precisely because the ecology of streams is complex. Discrete markets are "anti-ecological" in that many of the river's unvalued parts may be valuable to other components, mutually produced, and interdependent. By separating the system into marketable services, these interrelations are severed, displaced, and divided. Can the functioning of whole ecosystems be assured in markets that capture only the value of discrete goods and services?

The crisis of equity: Turning economic injustice into environmental injustice?

Applying the logics of the market to the environment raises basic questions about equity and rights. This is because, to the degree that the environment is "marketized," the ability of individuals and groups to participate in environmental action and remediation, or indeed even to have access to basic environmental services (e.g., clean air or wilderness), is limited by their available capital. This holds implications for democracy. By "democratic" here, and elsewhere in this book, we refer to people's ability within a society to have an equal voice in political decision-making and outcomes. Market environmentalism is democratic, therefore, only to the degree that the financial resources available are equally distributed throughout the population.

Nothing, of course, could be further from the truth. Turning decisions over nature into decisions within a market can be considered undemocratic because money is almost never evenly distributed within a polity. In the United States, an enormously wealthy country by global standards, the richest fifth of the population received 49 percent of the nation's income in 1999, while the poorest fifth received less than 4 percent. In terms of overall wealth, in 1998 the top 5 percent of the population owned 60 percent of the country's wealth. Globally, the statistics are more striking; the richest fifth of the world's population earn 83 percent of all income and the richest 10 percent of adults control 85 percent of the world's total assets. The specific concentration of wealth and income in the hands of corporate entities, rather than people, is also notable. So, too, is the unevenness over control of money and finances within households around the world, where women may be excluded from access to and control of money, even though their labor and effort provide household income. Given this reality, making politically charged environmental decisions dependent solely on economic willingness to pay may represent a profound subversion of democracy, in a world where ability to pay is so widely uneven.

As Sharon Beder has argued, moreover, the appearance of economic and scientific neutrality that market-based solutions possess may in part further disguise their fundamentally political characteristics:

> The portrayal of economic instruments as neutral tools removes them from public scrutiny and gives them into the hands of economists and regulators . . . A market system gives power to those most able to pay. (Beder 1996: 61)

Market advocates respond that individuals with even paltry means exercise significant power through market actions, especially when aggregated into large bodies of consumers. So, too, they argue that most environmental values are universally desired, and "we" lack only the means to efficiently achieve these global goals. Nevertheless, it is reasonable to ask whether current fundamental inequalities in income and capital should be the ground on which to construct environmental governance. Can markets produce not only efficient but also democratic relationships between people and the environment?

Finally, many observers insist that depending on markets to solve environmental problems is a problematic place to start considering the overall, and apparently unstoppable, growth of the global capitalist economy (see Chapter 6). As global trade continues to devour, mobilize, and dump resources, objects, and fuels at an accelerating pace, it becomes difficult to imagine how such energies could ever be harnessed and simultaneously controlled. And yet the language of "markets," "free trade," and "ecological economics" must be admitted to be the most dominant, widespread, and uncritically accepted ways of thinking about the environment in the early twenty-first century.

Thinking with Markets

In this chapter we have learned that:

- A dominant school of thought holds that, as long as environmental goods and services can be sold or traded, scarcity will be diminished by economic forces through the market response model.
- The market response model alleviates scarcity by creating incentives that either increase the supply of environmental goods and services or reduce demand for them.
- Environmental externalities can be mediated, in this theory, through private contracts more efficiently than through regulation.
- Many market-based mechanisms therefore may exist for solving environmental problems, including green taxes, markets for pollution, and green consumer choices.
- Markets, however, can fail, raising questions about holding faith in them for consistently solving environmental problems.
- Other problems face market-based environmentalism, including the fact that some environmental goods are difficult to value, that markets can be volatile and fickle, and that economic solutions are not necessarily democratic ones.

Questions for Review

1. Compare/contrast Julian Simon's and Paul Ehrlich's views on the general effects of human population growth on environmental conditions (include the term "scarcity" in your answer).
2. Provide an example of the "law" of supply and demand influencing the ways humans use or exploit a particular natural resource.
3. Which of the following environmental problems is better suited to solutions derived from the Coase theorem: a) land-use disputes on adjacent parcels of private property; or b) reducing water pollution across a region (explain)?
4. Review the market mechanisms available for environmental policy. Which require the most far-reaching levels of state enforcement?
5. How does the ecologically complex nature of a river (or any similar "piece" of nature, for that matter) make it difficult, if not impossible, to value in monetary terms?

Exercise 3.1   The Price of Green Consumption

Go to a grocery store or supermarket near you. Select four or five different types of products (for example: fruits, vegetables, packaged goods, meats, paper products, cleaners, etc.). Find a conventional version of this product as well as a "green" alternative. This may include an "organically" grown fruit or vegetable, a "free range" meat, "locally grown" produce, "green" or "eco-friendly" products, or products made from "recycled" or "recovered" materials, for example. What is the price difference (per unit where appropriate) between the "green" and conventional versions of each product?

What is the average percentage increase in cost of the groceries if your "green" products are selected instead of conventional ones? The average American family of four spends $8,500 per year on groceries (the average British family spends approximately $6,300). Assuming your percentage increase is typical and that all conventional groceries have "green" alternatives, how much more would the average family have to pay for only "green" groceries? Who can afford to pay such extra costs for groceries?

What is the benefit from this extra cost? Why are "green" alternatives more expensive to produce? Where does the extra money spent on each product go? How would you know? Where would you go to find out?

Exercise 3.2   Marketing Green Technology

In this exercise, you will identify a "green" innovation or new technology and consider ways to market it. First, name and describe an environmentally desirable technology or process that might be used on campus or by your friends or classmates. These might include devices like reduced-flow showerheads or efficient light bulbs, or it might entail a product that changes how people do things, like freely available shared bicycles. Next, consider how much this alternative might cost relative to current technologies or available alternatives. Is it a great deal more expensive or inconvenient? Why is this? Finally, develop a convincing marketing strategy for this product, which might include short text, photos, slogans, catchphrases, or even a jingle. This will necessarily include some information to prove that your innovation is actually an environmental improvement over the status quo. What would actually make such an alternative compelling, especially if it is more expensive?

Exercise 3.3   Thinking Economically

Imagine a scenic canyon, visited by many local people as well as tourists from beyond the local area. Consider a scenario in which a mining company has proposed to the local authority that it be closed to the public and put into the production of coal. Thinking in terms of *economics* as a way of adjudicating the relative value of one use of the canyon over the other, what would you need to know in order to make a comparison or assessment? What kinds of quantitative data would inform your decision, and where might they come from? What kinds of things might you need to know that are hard to measure? Once you have listed the kinds of information and data that might be available to inform this decision, do you think it would be sufficient to making this decision, why or why not?

References

Beder, S. (1996). "Charging the earth: The promotion of price-based measures for pollution control." *Ecological Economics* 16(1): 51–63.

Coase, R. H. (1960). "The problem of social cost." *Journal of Law and Economics* 3 (October): 1–44.

Ehrlich, P. R. (1968). *The Population Bomb*. New York: Ballantine Books.

Field, B. C. (2005). *Natural Resource Economics: An Introduction*. Long Grove, IL: Waveland Press.

Harvey, D. (1996). *Justice, Nature, and the Geography of Difference*. Cambridge, MA: Blackwell.

Rees, J. (1990). *Natural Resources: Allocation, Economics, and Policy*. New York: Routledge.

Robertson, M. M. (2006). "The nature that capital can see: Science, state, and market in the commodification of ecosystem services." *Environment and Planning D: Society and Space* 24(3): 367–87.

Simon, J. L. (1980). "Resources, population, environment: An oversupply of false bad news." *Science* 208(4451): 1431–7.

TerraChoice Environmental Marketing Inc. (2007). *The Six Sins of Greenwashing: A Study of Environmental Claims in North American Consumer Markets*. Reading, PA: Author.

Tierney, J. (1990). "Betting on the planet." *The New York Times*, December 2, pp. 52–3, 76–81.

Suggested Reading

Crook, C., and R. A. Clapp (1998). "Is market-oriented forest conservation a contradiction in terms?" *Environmental Conservation* 25(2): 131–45.

Field, B. C. (2001). *Natural Resource Economics: An Introduction*. Long Grove, IL: Waveland Press.

Godal, O., Y. Ermoliev, et al. (2003). "Carbon trading with imperfectly observable emissions." *Environmental and Resource Economics* 25(2): 151–69.

Johnson, E., and R. Heinen (2004). "Carbon trading: Time for industry involvement." *Environment International* 30(2): 279–88.

Randall, A. (1983). "The problem of market failure." *Natural Resources Journal* 23: 131–48.

Rees, J. (1990). *Natural Resources: Allocation, Economics, and Policy*. New York: Routledge.

Robertson, M. M. (2006). "Emerging ecosystem service markets: Trends in a decade of entrepreneurial wetland banking." *Frontiers in Ecology and the Environment* 4(6): 297–302.

Sen, A. K. (2001). *Development as Freedom*. Oxford: Oxford University Press.

Taylor, P. L., D. L. Murray, et al. (2005). "Keeping trade fair: Governance challenges in the fair trade coffee initiative." *Sustainable Development* 13(3): 199–208.

4

Institutions and "The Commons"

Source: iko/Shutterstock.

Keywords

- Common property
- Game theory
- Institutions
- Prisoner's Dilemma

Chapter Menu

Environment and Society: A Critical Introduction, Second Edition. Paul Robbins, John Hintz, and Sarah A. Moore.
© 2014 John Wiley & Sons, Ltd. Published 2014 by John Wiley & Sons, Ltd.

Controlling Carbon?

There is a growing consensus on the science of climate change and the urgency of the problem. According to the Intergovernmental Panel on Climate Change, whose job it is to vet the science surrounding global warming, global temperatures are rising, sea-level rise is expected, water availability may be impeded, and extreme weather events are likely to become more common and more severe. These changes will be felt unevenly but no country will be immune to such effects.

Given the widespread and severe nature of the problem, why are global carbon emissions so hard to control? One might think of many good reasons for this to be true. People tend to ignore problems they cannot see, governments are under the influence of oil companies, and so on.

One compelling argument holds that the root of the problem is that carbon quite simply *does not stay put*. With every combustion event (driving a car, burning a log, firing a coal plant for electricity, etc.) the carbon that is released quickly finds its way into the atmosphere. Carbon released in one country is – *instantly* – a burden shared by all countries. From the point of view of any individual country, moreover, carbon reductions are not "free," since they require creating new rules, potentially reducing or redirecting economic production. A "carbon-reduced" product – whether a car, computer, or vegetable – may be more difficult to produce than its "status quo" counterpart. If such a product is more expensive as a result, it may not be competitive on a global market, especially if it must compete against products produced where carbon reductions have not been imposed. Many governments, including that of the United States, therefore express fear that if they make sacrifices in this direction while others do not, they will no longer be competitive. The benefits of carbon reduction, in a parallel way, would be experienced by all countries, but must be paid for by individual countries.

For many environmental problems, costs are often borne collectively, while benefits accrue to individuals; on the other hand, individual costs may lead to collective benefits. Nations must cooperate where there is no "super-government" to impose environmental laws and where there are few or no punitive measures for not cooperating. Such mismatches mean that hoping for spontaneous global action on climate change might be unrealistic. Arguably, some kind of rules and trust must be established to cooperate when incentives constantly lure people and states to follow their own self-interest . . . toward collective planetary ruin. In this chapter, we address this persistent and vexing problem: *How, if at all, can rules and norms of global behavior be fashioned to encourage shared costs and collective benefits? At what scale is cooperation possible?*

The Prisoner's Dilemma

Such questions are of universal concern since problems of this sort are ubiquitous. There are countless examples from our own daily ecologies as well as those around the globe.

Neighbors, for example, need to pull weeds from their lawns to keep them from spreading across property lines. By failing to do so, any one non-cooperating neighbor enjoys some benefits from their neighbors' sweaty work (fewer dandelions in their yard), but simultaneously provides an ongoing seed source for dandelions that might spread to the lawns of others.

It is tempting for someone to spill the small quantity of paint left over from renovating a bathroom into a storm drain rather than take the time to dispose of it legally at an approved dump site. Should a single household be the only one to behave in this way, it enjoys a lower labor burden *and* benefits from the healthy environment resulting from the majority of hard-working cooperative neighbors who do not dump paint into public waterways. But since such temptation exists to all, the incidence of paint dumping is far higher than anyone individually desires.

Nor is the situation of a homeowner in urban America or Europe entirely different from that of a villager in rural India. There, the benefits from a community forest include the ability to graze livestock in the shade of trees and the availability of seeds and pods that fall from trees, among other resources. These collectively enjoyed benefits are only available if the trees of the forest are not cut down for fuel or construction timber. It is inviting for any individual household to cut down a tree or two for their own purposes, making only an incremental change in the density and health of the village forest. As long as others refrain from doing the same, these minimal costs are spread across the village and the benefits to the household, which may need to go great distances to collect fuelwood otherwise, are obvious. But again, since the incentive to break the rules is shared by all, and in anticipation of the fact that others may well "cheat" and cut trees, householders might well be tempted to cut trees as soon and as quickly as they can, in an effort to gain resources before their neighbors do.

In all of these cases, cooperation is necessary for the best outcome, but an incentive exists to take a "free ride" and let others invest time or money or restrain their behavior while we do not. Since the incentive exists for everyone, the possibility of total failure always looms.

A popular metaphor for situations such as these is the story of the **Prisoner's Dilemma**. In this tale, so often replayed on contemporary television crime dramas like *Law and Order* or *The Closer*, you are asked to imagine two people charged with a crime, perhaps something like burglary, in which the best evidence that the police have (though not the only evidence) would be the testimony of one of the burglars against the other. Both suspects

> **Prisoner's Dilemma** An allegorical description of a game-theoretical situation in which multiple individuals making decisions in pursuit of their own interests tend to create collective outcomes that are non-optimal for everyone

are taken into custody by the police and interrogated individually. Each is separately told that if they testify against the other person, they will go free or have a greatly reduced sentence. The logical decision in a perfect world is for both of the suspects to keep their mouths shut. With no one talking, they might each serve a short jail term, if any term at all. The problem stems from the fact that each knows that the other might well "rat" him out. If one chooses not to talk while the other "rats," the reticent one will do hard time while the other one goes free. Since no one wants to be a "sucker" and suffer at the hands of the other, the predictable outcome is that both testify against the other, leading to the worst possible mutual outcome, one in which both do hard time. Trying to anticipate and avoid the punitive "defection" of the other person, the two partners act in service of the police. Such a situation not only invites each person to "rat" out the other, it actually makes it *rational* to do so, even though the outcome is inevitably bad for everyone, something no rational person would choose if they could control the behaviors of *both* parties.

> **Game Theory** A form of applied mathematics used to model and predict people's behavior in strategic situations where people's choices are predicated on predicting the behavior of others

These sorts of fascinating dilemmas are the province of **game theory**, adopted by thinkers who employ a form of mathematical analysis of decision-making, examining those sorts of situations that might be expressed in game terms. For game theorists, certain games provide models for how people think and behave. Of most interest are games where the crux of the problem is anticipating what the other player might choose to do, where bluffing and second-guessing are paramount. Such is the case of our two prisoners, who individually reach what is ultimately a bad mutual decision because they are trying to *anticipate* what the other prisoner might decide to do. Along these lines, and as established by the refugee scientist John von Neumann after World War II, game theory understands a "game" to be "a conflict situation where one must make a choice knowing that others are making choices too, and the outcome of the conflict will be determined in a prescribed way by all the choices made" (Poundstone 1992: 6).

In game theory, as in the Prisoner's Dilemma, the best outcomes are typically achieved by cooperating, while individual incentives tend to lead to a reason not to cooperate. The problem of our two suspects might be expressed in abstract terms by game theorists as in Figure 4.1. These games can be made ever more complicated by introducing quantitative cash rewards and punishments and making the decisions more complex, involving, for example, investment in a public good versus a private bank, and so on. Complex mathematics can be used to predict behaviors, including retaliations, mutual learning, and system collapse.

	Prisoner B "clams up"	Prisoner B "rats"
Prisoner A "clams up"	Both prisoners do light sentences	Prisoner B walks free, Prisoner A goes to jail
Prisoner A "rats"	Prisoner A walks free, Prisoner B goes to jail	Both prisoners do hard time

Figure 4.1 The Prisoner's Dilemma in game-theoretical terms. The best outcome, in the upper left, is also the least likely, since each player prefers to avoid the worst individual outcomes, in the upper right and lower left corners, leading to the worst collective outcome, in the lower right.

The Tragedy of the Commons

The first applications of game theory mathematics were directed to the Cold War logic of mutual nuclear annihilation. Funded by the RAND Corporation and the US Pentagon in the 1950s, game theorists asked the unthinkable: Is it rational to strike first with nuclear weapons, not knowing whether and when the enemy might do so? Is it rational to drop the bomb?!

But what might any of this have to do with environment and society? Applying this kind of thinking to our interactions with the natural world leads to some potentially grim and tragic conclusions. For while there is a possibility of cooperation around environmental conservation, there is a potentially overriding incentive to "defect," in the language of game theory, leading to a general inability to manage or control our consumption and use of the environment, and so to environmental destruction.

Thinking along these lines, Garrett Hardin presented one of the most compelling, persistent, and in some ways problematic arguments linking environment to society through the commons. In his article "The Tragedy of the Commons," published in *Science* in 1968 (where von Neumann is prominently cited), he directed this logic to the problem of overpopulation. He argued that while the advantages for any individual or family of reproducing freely are immediate, their costs are diffused across the planet, increasing incrementally the burden of humanity upon the Earth. This is a Prisoner's Dilemma, insofar as some people may choose to forgo more children in the interests of the planet, but others will inevitably "defect" or cop a "free ride." The worst outcome is much more likely (now sometimes called the "Nash Equilibrium" for its mathematical discoverer John Forbes Nash, made famous in the film *A Beautiful Mind*), at least without some form of coercive restraint on people's behavior. Overpopulation, as this logic goes, is inevitable without some form of enforcement mechanism (Chapter 2).

The article was made more compelling by its use of an agricultural metaphor for the problem. Rather than think directly about people's reproduction, Hardin asked us to "picture a pasture open to all . . ." in which numerous herdsmen managed their individual herds. Following precisely the logic of the Prisoner's Dilemma, it is in the interest of each herder to increase the size of their own herd, Hardin argued, since each new animal costs him nothing but gains him much. But since all herdsmen enjoy the same incentive, the inevitable result is a destroyed pasture. Because it belongs to everyone, the resource belongs to no one, and will inevitably be grazed into destruction. In language typical of the article he explains:

> Ruin is the destination toward which all men rush, each pursuing his own best interest in a society that believes in the freedom of the commons. Freedom in a commons brings ruin to all. (Hardin 1968: 1243)

Conscience and goodwill, Hardin further asserted, were useless in the face of compelling, internal, adaptive, evolutionary logics. Real solutions, however distasteful, must inevitably take some other form. People of the Earth must choose either coercion ("mutual coercion mutually agreed upon," p. 1247), to tyrannize ourselves into control, or turn to strict forms of private property and inheritance so that all impacts of poor decision-making will be visited only upon the owner of that property. The former approach was rejected by Hardin, as he concluded that the problem with tyranny is that there is always a possibility that a system of governance will come under the undue sway of one of the users of the commons and cannot itself be controlled: "*Quis custodiet ipsos custodes* – 'Who shall watch the watchers themselves?'" (pp. 1245–6). The latter approach – privatization – was preferred and defended by Hardin since, no matter how unjust it might be (not all rich people are smart people, he pointed out: "an idiot can inherent millions," p. 1247), such a solution was the best one available. In either case, whether state or private control, some form of *enclosure* was deemed as essential, where an "open access" resource is bounded and given over to control either by individual owners or by a strong state management body.

The power and influence of this argument were enormous, and remain so to this day. It continues to be perhaps the most cited academic article in the social sciences, it provided foundational arguments for fields as widespread as evolutionary biology and economics, and it is typically invoked in debates over environmental scarcity. Because Hardin convincingly used an environmental crisis as his metaphoric example, his essay on population quickly became the key defining metaphor for many people (managers and scholars) in guiding their thinking about *all* environmental problems more generally. Nature in all its forms (fisheries, oil fields, climate systems) might be seen as commons, those difficult-to-enclose systems that invite free-riding and defection.

Viewed this way, the solutions to environmental problems do appear to take the form Hardin suggests: either some form of environmental super-police state, or private property rights over all environmental systems or objects. Environmental commons in this way of thinking lead inevitably to tragedy and so must be made into non-commons through the power of law and property. There is close match of this way of thinking with the market logics (i.e., internalizing externalities) reviewed in Chapter 3.

The Evidence and Logic of Collective Action

Exactly at the same time that the logic of the Prisoner's Dilemma and the Tragedy of the Commons was becoming widely accepted, confusing and incongruent evidence was beginning to mount. As anthropologists, sociologists, historians, and geographers observed resource management around the world, they continued to report behaviors that in no way fit Hardin's predictions. Specifically, they found countless examples of complex systems for management of difficult-to-enclose resources – ranging from fish, trees, and pasture to computer processing time – that relied neither upon some form of tyrannical enforcement authority nor upon the assignment of exclusive private property rights to the resources in question. Some other form of management appeared not only possible but actually predominant in natural commons around the world.

Lobster fisheries in Maine, for example, were observed to be supported and maintained less through centralized state law than through the behavior of lobster fishers themselves, who self-limited the number of boats allowed in the fishery and their distribution of traps. Village irrigation systems in southern India were shown to be carefully self-managed systems where irrigators followed careful rules concerning the opening and closing of flood gates to water their fields while keeping the array functioning for the flow of water to downstream users. Tree tenure traditions in East Africa were organized to allow the use of forest products by households who did not hold title to the land on which the trees stood, while limiting their access to sustain the harvest. Across the world, countless, highly variable systems of institutions appeared to violate the iron laws of the Prisoner's Dilemma through some form of local organization.

What all of these cases appear to have in common is the presence of some form of **institutions**, understood here as systems of recognized constraints on individual behavior, including formal laws, but also unofficial rules or even strong social norms that guide people's expectations of one another's behaviors, leading to orderly and constrained use of natural resources. Such institutions, even in their most informal manifestations, can be quickly recognized all around us. People typically queue at the box office of a movie theater rather than shove one another in a pack at the ticket window, for example. For more complex problems, sustaining a fishery, for example, the rules may be quite complex, and the mechanisms of self-governance and enforcement may be deeply rooted in traditional social systems. Nevertheless, the root principle applies; collective good and environmentally sustainable outcomes were achieved through cooperation.

> **Institutions** Rules and norms governing collective action, especially referring to rules governing common property environmental resources, like rivers, oceans, or the atmosphere
>
> **Common Property** A good or resource (e.g., bandwidth, pasture, oceans) whose characteristics make it difficult to fully enclose and partition, making it possible for non-owners to enjoy resource benefits and owners to sustain costs from the actions of others, typically necessitating some form of creative institutional management

Observers of these successfully cooperative systems needed to assemble new stories, metaphors, and theories, however, to better explain what they saw. All of these revisions of "Tragedy" thinking shared one thing: a need to explain how rules and norms were able to constrain behavior and achieve cooperative outcomes.

Chief among these reconsiderations is an effort to try to define the difference between these observed systems and the property imagined in the "Tragedy of the Commons." Acknowledging that the total absence of rules would lead to tragic outcomes, it remains necessary to also acknowledge the existence of forms of property that function through customs, rules, and/or regulations, but not in the form of exclusive private ownership rights. "**Common property**" is a descriptor that includes all of these diverse forms. Different from wholly unowned resources (Latin: *res nullius*), common property (Latin: *res communes*) includes some form of group ownership, so that it is neither open to everyone in the world nor necessarily held exclusively by an individual (Ciriacy-Wantrup and Bishop 1975). Such a group or community of owners may take many forms, of course, to include people who know one another face-to-face in a village fishery or those more far-flung across a city, who together hold cooperative rights to urban garden plots.

But even where a right can be held by a community, this does not explain how and why members of that group might be able to achieve mutual understandings, agreements, and most importantly constraints. Rather, there must be an underlying logic that allows people to overcome, through collective action, the worst environmental case outcomes of the "Tragedy of the Commons." Returning to the game-theoretical logic of the Prisoner's Dilemma, a generation of "neo-institutionalist" scholars, led by Nobel Prize-winning political scientist Elinor Ostrom, began to critically analyze the assumptions of game theory. Specifically, they asked: What if our two hypothetical prisoners had been allowed to speak with one another prior to their interrogation and "get their stories straight"? Would that have changed the outcome? Logic holds that it might. Subsequent economic experiments – in which people played complex cooperation games for money incentives – bore this out as well. When the players of a game can collude together or negotiate, they are far

Box 4.1   Environmental Solution? The Montreal Protocol

Chlorofluorocarbons (or CFCs) are artificial chemical compounds that have a range of industrial uses, including applications in refrigeration and fire fighting and uses ranging from solvents to propellants in spray cans. Part of the chemical revolution of the 1920s and 1930s, CFCs were viewed as a flexible, cheap, and efficient set of chemicals and they were widely used throughout the twentieth century. The most exciting thing about these chemicals, from an economic point of view, was that they are highly non-reactive; they break down only very, very slowly.

This blessing proved to be a curse, as soon as it was discovered that the chlorine in CFCs, when exposed to the atmosphere, broke down ozone, leaving behind more trace chlorine for hundreds more such reactions. Such ongoing reactions can lead to whole gaps in the ozone layer shrouding the Earth: an ozone hole. That hole in the stratosphere was observed by scientists in the 1970s and became a source of grave concern. Because atmospheric ozone keeps deadly radiation from reaching Earth, and because trace amounts of CFCs can destroy lots of ozone, and since CFCs are otherwise so non-reactive that they can survive in the atmosphere for more than a century before becoming inert, it was determined by the late 1980s that the world had an extremely serious problem on its hands. Worse still, by that time, CFCs were employed in an unimagi-

nable range of economic activities, with many industries depending heavily on the chemicals; chemical companies in particular defended their product.

If this was not bad enough, the ozone crisis represented a classic common property problem and a Prisoner's Dilemma. The cost for any firm or country to switch to alternatives was extremely high, so unless everyone stopped using CFCs at once, the opportunities and incentives to "free-ride" – by continuing to use CFCs and underselling other countries and companies with cheaper goods and services – were extremely high. While some individual countries and states (Oregon, for example) did create their own bans on CFC use, the problem could not be solved without collective action.

Remarkably, the world community overcame the cost and difficulty of coordinating their actions and sat down for an international meeting in Montreal in 1987. They signed a treaty in that year that resulted in a global reduction (indeed a near-total worldwide ban) on most CFCs. This Montreal Protocol was strengthened over the years with follow-up meetings and decisions, and the treaty represents perhaps the single most effective global environmental agreement in history. Many look to the successes of the Montreal Protocol as a model for future global agreements, especially surrounding the very different problem of climate change and greenhouse gas emissions.

more likely to cooperate (Ostrom 1990). Certain conditions seem to make communal management of natural resources quite possible, and indeed likely. In this way, the "neo-institutionalists" (adherents to a school of economics that stresses rules and social organization) do not deny the logical incentives that underpin Hardin's tragedy, but do point to conditions where commons are not "free" but instead governed by rules that encourage cooperation.

Crafting Sustainable Environmental Institutions

To understand how "the commons" actually works, institutional thinkers have stressed certain rules or principles that tend to lead to sustainable outcomes. In any real-world commons, the central challenge of managing the resource sustainably focuses on a number of discrete grounded problems, each of which poses difficult questions. Consider, for example, the problems of managing a fishery. Here is a resource that is largely invisible, highly mobile, depletable (if overfished), and impossible to enclose. For institutionalists, the central challenge becomes: *How do fishers avoid a "free-for-all" where each mounts increasing efforts to compete for dwindling resources, removing fish faster than the rate at which the fish population can reproduce?* The broad challenge now defined, we are immediately confronted with a slew of other questions:

- How do fishers keep the number of fishing boats to a reasonable level?
- How do fishers compensate individuals for time or effort expended in managing the fishery?
- How does the group reach decisions about what rules are fair?
- How do they know if rules are being followed, given that fish populations are hard to track and count?
- What do they do to rule breakers who over-harvest fish at times the group have decided to be restricted?
- How do they solve conflicts over rights?
- What keeps any locally crafted system from being nullified by a higher authority from the central state or "federal" level?

As most commons management challenges share similar sets of issues, general design principles for management of such resources have been developed. Following Ostrom (1992), successful commons management must include the following.

Boundaries

The resource and the user group should have clearly defined boundaries. That means that the fishery in our example should be a specific territory or population of fish rather than a nebulous area. Equally important, the fishers who have rights to use the fishery by necessity must be specified; it cannot be open to anyone with a boat that simply sails into the area from elsewhere.

Proportionality

Costs accrued in managing should be in line with benefits. People who bear the costs of organizing or monitoring our hypothetical fishery should enjoy equal or higher access rights than those who do not. There should be some form of compensation for any investments in equipment or labor that members of the commons commit to the group.

Collective choice

Arrangements need to be in place so that the specific rules for managing the resource are made by the resource users themselves and/or can be modified through some kind of deliberative group forum. Fishers, in our example, should be able to set the limits for fishing together.

Monitoring

Some system of monitoring needs to exist so that people's behaviors and uses are known to the group and so that the status of the resource itself is checked in order to allow for adjustments. This means that some resources must be dedicated to keeping an eye on what vessels are coming and going from the fishery and to taking a reliable sampled census of fish stocks. In line with previously noted principles, the costs of such activities need to be borne fairly throughout the group, and the system for implementation should be decided collectively.

Sanctions

Sanctions must be imposed on violators, but these should be graduated, meaning that the system should encourage voluntary compliance with rules, have low punishments for first offenders, and only turn to coercion as a last resort. For our fishery, this means that fishers should expect to monitor one another and comply with rules voluntarily. Should a fisher be found in violation of a limit on the amount of fish they take or some other provision (through the monitoring system established above), they can be encouraged to return to compliance without undue or disproportionate duress or expulsion.

Conflict resolution

Social mechanisms must be developed to resolve conflicts between users. There are many possibilities for mutual complaints in a common property system, and in the case of our fishery, a robust management system would allow a low-cost way to work out mutual grievances without turning toward expensive litigation or calling in higher-order authorities. These mechanisms might be a small council of respected citizens, a mediation system using an outside third party, or any number of other socially appropriate systems.

Autonomy

For a common property management system to work, it is essential that it is allowed at least some measure of autonomy from higher or non-local authorities. Imagine dedicating several years of careful work in developing a community management system of fishers described above, only to have a government official from a distant municipality arrive, review the rules, and begin meddling with their specifics. Where this can be expected to happen, it is unlikely fishers would take the time and effort to craft such a system in the first place.

Given the apparent complexity of making common property systems work, it would seem they would be very rare indeed! Nothing could be further from the truth. The world is brimming with "commons," once a neo-institutional eye is brought to bear on the question. Indeed, it is a sad commentary on our prevailing collective wisdom that cooperation is treated as an oddity or an exception, when indeed it is quite often the rule.

Ingenious flowing commons: Irrigation

Most of the world's crops, including almost all of the vegetables and many of the grains you probably consume, come from irrigated fields. Getting water to food plants might be the oldest problem in civilization. Indeed, the difficulties in maintaining and managing irrigation have occupied environmental managers for thousands of years. One of the greatest challenges in managing irrigation is that, typically, many water users are connected through the same complex system of ditches and walls, through which water flows from the highest point (the system "head") to its lowest fields (its "tail"). Fields may be held privately, but the irrigation water must be managed collectively. Such systems are labyrinths of sluices, canals, and gates, requiring that each user follows a careful set of rules that allow them their share of the water for a time, but also maintenance of the supply so other users, especially downstream, get their fair share as well (Figure 4.2). The opportunities for system failure are obvious. If one person at the head of the system fails to open or close a gate after

(a)   (b)

Figure 4.2 Irrigation systems are labyrinths of sluices, canals, and gates, which test the limits of people's ability to cooperate in managing environmental goods. This example, from the village of Musha in the Nile Valley, shows the interrelationships of one private field to the next, tied together by the mutual need for water held communally. *Source*: Reproduced from Turner and Brush (1987).

they use their supply of water, the downstream user will receive none. If all parties do not work together to flush the system as a whole, the water can become salty, leading to the loss of the crops of all farmers. These difficulties notwithstanding, the world is filled with local irrigation systems where multiple users cooperate in the actions, make decisions together, monitor the infrastructure, and achieve equitable outcomes with little waste or loss of precious water.

Wildlife commons: Collective management through hunting

Even the world's wildlife can be considered a kind of commons. In the United States, where herds of elk and other important species were in serious decline a century ago, management has worked to develop common property solutions to problems of over-hunting. Historically, since such animals were wide-ranging and the property of no single land owner, they could be hunted with impunity, leading to population declines in the late 1800s. Current systems of management in states like Montana utilize many of the principles of common property design. Limits are placed by the government on the number of hunters and the number of hunting licenses in any given year based on extensive monitoring of game populations. Preferences for licenses are given to residents of the state. While the overall limits are set by officials, all the rules are overseen through a collective review process that includes Montana hunters themselves. The result is a system where a potential "open access" resource (free-ranging elk) is made into "common property" by 1) excluding some potential outside users, 2) establishing rules and limits, and 3) reviewing and overseeing these rules through consultation with resource users themselves. Versions of this system are in place across the United States.

The biggest commons: Global climate

But not all commons are local, like irrigation, or regional, like elk herds. This brings us full circle to the problem of governing the climate. The global climate has all the qualities of a common property system headed for failure: exclusion is difficult and costs to defer depletion of the collective good can be high to individuals, firms, or states. By treating the global climate as common property, it is possible to think about it in a new way, however. As a commons, we can imagine climate as a shared good, and that people polluting it might constrain their behavior through some kind of collective agreement.

Clearly the possibilities for collective action exist, and many new systems to manage the problem have emerged in the last decade, including the Kyoto Protocol (see Chapter 9). That agreement essentially imposes a mutual set of restrictions that countries must follow on their emissions, with mechanisms for crafting rules and making decisions even in the absence of any kind of higher authority; there is no real "world government" to enforce global agreements, after all.

The problems facing the common property of a fishery are largely similar to global climate, of course. It is hard to monitor who is doing what. Sanctions are difficult to impose on free-riders who do not comply with the rules or on users of the resource (polluters) who are not part of the agreement (e.g., the United States). The presence of collective choice systems for setting and revising the rules is also unclear, beyond the fact that signatories participate in negotiation rounds to work out provisions. For these reasons, an institutional analysis of the climate problem sheds light on the prospects for success in controlling climate change by identifying areas where creativity will be necessary to solve it as a common property problem.

Are All Commoners Equal? Does Scale Matter?

As attractive and effective as an institutional perspective appears to be, it is not without detractors. At their core, these criticisms revolve around some of the assumptions that common property theory inherits from game theory. Specifically, these theories, as embodied in the Prisoner's Dilemma and the Tragedy of the Commons, assume individual free agents of relatively similar power in both determining the outcome of the game and making choices to cooperate. In a world of complex political power and inequality, such assumptions are unrealistic and potentially dangerous.

Consider the ways that access to resources and the rules that govern them have been heavily influenced by social and political conditions surrounding, for example, gender. In many places ownership or inheritance of property is traditionally patriarchal and patrilineal, meaning women cannot own, or at least not inherit, property. At the same time, women's labor may be essential for the maintenance or use of commons, including the drawing of water, the management of irrigation infrastructure, the tending of community gardens or forests, among many others. What this means for common property management is important, since matching rules with users and developing systems of collective choice becomes extremely difficult in places where not all users have equal access or responsibilities.

For these reasons, developing common property management regimes in village India, for example, can be difficult. Here, traditional decision-making bodies (called *panchayats*) tend to be dominated by men, and usually men from elite families or castes. If these decision-making bodies are the ones that make the rules about access to village pastures for grazing, they may be viewed as totally illegitimate by the people who use the resource, including women and more marginal groups who tend cattle. If, on the other hand, new collective decision groups are formed to make new rules, and these groups include women and more marginal groups, they might still be dominated by historically powerful communities, again leading to a lack of legitimacy. In either case, a weak authority may lead to indiscriminate use of the grazing lands by people who feel excluded or, worse, view the establishment of rules as effectively representing a taking-away of their traditional rights. Forming clear common property systems may be desirable in complex power-laden contexts, but it may not be easy by any means (Figure 4.3).

This insight (from the field of feminist political economy: see Chapter 7) can be extended to all commons, whether users are differentially empowered because of income, race, or a host of other discriminatory factors. Under such conditions, the dynamics of the commons become dramatically more complex and sometimes untenable. Social difference and social

Figure 4.3 A woman tending her herd in India. In many parts of the world the responsibility for using common property and the control over the rules of the commons are often split along lines of gender, class, or race, portending problems for management.

power make collective decision-making far more difficult, since parties may not trust one another and because the self-imposed group rules determined from common property management may suit the interests of only a small proportion of commons users. Bear in mind that the first and foremost rule of common property resource management is the bounding and exclusion of some potential user populations (Ostrom 2002). Where such exclusions are founded on basic inequalities, many people will be less inclined to cooperate and failure becomes inevitable. So while "getting the rules right" is the favored approach for an institutional solution to environmental crises, some problems, especially problems of power, come far prior.

A final problem of institutional analysis emerges from disagreement over the degree to which the lessons of the countless local common property regimes around the world can easily transfer to larger problems, spread over more diverse populations, at scales beyond the daily experience of people. Some have argued that collective action can only occur in small groups, where face-to-face interaction builds trust, as in an irrigator community. Other evidence suggests, however, that distant people can come together in cooperative regimes, because they are united by the common property they share, as in the case of the atmosphere and climate system.

Can we "scale up" from the local commons to the global commons? It is possible that the future of the planet rests on the resolution of this very question.

Thinking with Institutions

In this chapter, we have learned that:

- Many environmental problems appear intractable because they are prone to problems of collective action.
- Coordination around such problems fails owing to the "Prisoner's Dilemma," a metaphor describing the tendency of individuals to rationally seek their immediate gain at the expense of greater gains that might have been made through cooperation.
- Such failure to cooperate around environmental problems typically leads to a "Tragedy of the Commons" where collective goods (e.g., air, water, biodiversity) are degraded.

- Evidence exists from around the world, however, that people succeed at cooperating to preserve common property.
- Theories of common property have therefore emerged, which stress that Hardin's tragedy might occur where there are absolutely no owners or responsible parties, but most commons are owned and controlled by groups as common property.
- By crafting and evolving social institutions that direct cooperative behavior on common property, communities can overcome commons tragedies.
- Barriers to institutional formation and collective action emerge from social, political, and economic inequities, which make cooperation difficult or impossible.

Questions for Review

1. Review the "Prisoner's Dilemma." What assumptions does the scenario make? What conditions must prevail so that the outcome is bad for both hypothetical prisoners? How might the assumptions be changed so that the outcome is better for both?
2. What is the inevitable and "tragic" behavior exhibited by the herdsmen in Hardin's hypothetical grazing commons?
3. For Hardin, what are the only two options for averting "tragedies of the commons"? Which option does Hardin prefer, and why?
4. In a valuable ocean fishery, how can well-crafted boundaries help create a manageable *res communes* (while keeping it from degenerating into an unmanageable *res nullius*)?
5. Why might the atmosphere stand as the most difficult to manage of all imaginable common property resources?

Exercise 4.1   Enclosure and Technology

Proponents of the Tragedy of the Commons suggest attempting to "enclose," privatize, or make exclusive the rights to access and use what had been freely or openly available resources. Sometimes this is difficult owing to the physical character of the resource, like a large shared open pasture or a cache of electronic information available to anyone on the web. Technology can sometimes be used to help limit access to commons and make it easier to distribute property rights, as barbed wire fences did by cheaply dividing up the vast cattle pastures of the US West in the nineteenth century. Describe three resources that have been made more divisible by use of new inventions and technologies. What resources continue to elude technological solutions to enforcing property rights?

Exercise 4.2   Are Commons Overexploited Everywhere?

List ten real-world common property resources with which you are familiar. Describe an example of one of these common property resources that is not (tragically) overexploited (use the term "institution/s" in your discussion).

Exercise 4.3   Institutions Nearby

Name a common property resource to which you have access. This might be an environmental resource (a local park) or a shared good (a computer network). With whom is access to this resource shared? What risks are there to depletion, overuse, problems, or degradation from failures of cooperation or collective action? Is there a tacit set of norms or rules governing the use of the resource? Could these rules or systems of management be improved by application of the principles of institutional analysis? What barriers are there to improving the way the resource is used or shared?

References

Ciriacy-Wantrup, S. V., and R. C. Bishop (1975). "Common property as a concept in natural resources policy." *Natural Resources Journal* 15: 713–27.

Ostrom, E. (1992). *Crafting Institutions for Self-Governing Irrigation Systems*. San Francisco, CA: Institute for Contemporary Studies.

Ostrom, E. (ed.) (2002). *The Drama of the Commons*. Washington, DC: National Academy Press.

Poundstone, W. (1992). *Prisoner's Dilemma*. New York: Anchor Books.

Turner, B. L. II, and S. B. Brush (eds.) (1987). *Comparative Farming Systems*. New York: Guildford Press.

Suggested Reading

Benjaminsen, T. A., and E. Sjaastad (2008). "Where to draw the line: Mapping of land rights in a South African commons." *Political Geography* 27(3): 263–79.

Commons, J. R. (1934). *Institutional Economics*. New York: Macmillan.

Community Economies Project (2005). "Community economies." Retrieved May 30, 2005, from www.communityeconomies.org/.

Hardin, G. (1968). "The Tragedy of the Commons." *Science* 162: 1243–8.

Kropotkin, P. (1888). *Mutual Aid: A Factor in Evolution*. Boston, MA: Porter Sargent.

Mansfield, B. (2004). "Neoliberalism in the oceans: 'Rationalization,' property rights, and the commons question." *Geoforum* 35: 313–26.

Ostrom, E. (1990). *Governing the Commons: The Evolution of Institutions for Collective Action*. Cambridge: Cambridge University Press.

Ostrom, E. (2005). *Understanding Institutional Diversity*. Princeton, NJ: Princeton University Press.

St. Martin, K. (2001). "Making space for community resource management in fisheries." *Annals of the Association of American Geographers* 91(1): 122–42.

Tucker, C. M., J. C. Randolph, et al. (2007). "Institutions, biophysical factors and history: An integrative analysis of private and common property forests in Guatemala and Honduras." *Human Ecology* 35: 259–74.

5

Environmental Ethics

Source: © OnTheRoad/Alamy.

Chapter Menu

Keywords

- Animal liberation
- Anthropocentrism
- Conservation
- Deep ecology
- Dominion thesis
- Ecocentrism
- Ecology
- Environmental justice
- Ethics
- Factory farms
- Holism
- Intrinsic value
- Moral extensionism
- Naturalistic fallacy
- Preservation
- Scientism
- Social ecology
- Stewardship
- Utilitarian
- Wilderness

Environment and Society: A Critical Introduction, Second Edition. Paul Robbins, John Hintz, and Sarah A. Moore.
© 2014 John Wiley & Sons, Ltd. Published 2014 by John Wiley & Sons, Ltd.

The Price of Cheap Meat

Factory Farms Intensive animal-raising agricultural operations; factory farms attempt to maximize production by raising as many animals in as little space as possible, often resulting in significant air and water pollution

Being a pig just isn't what it used to be. Gone are the days when hogs had the run of the barnyard, served as garbage disposals for kitchen scraps, and, of course, wallowed in that delectable mud on steamy hot days. Gone, at least, for the roughly 95 percent of all hogs in the United States that are being raised on industrial-scale "**factory farms**."

Take a "breeder sow," for example (a female pig raised solely for the purpose of birthing and nursing future pork). At about 8 months old, a sow is (artificially) impregnated for the first time. Immediately after being impregnated, the sow is moved into a "gestation crate." The crate is usually about two by seven feet and not even large enough for the sow to turn around, nor can she stand up or lie down without rubbing up against the metal bars that form the walls. Just before giving birth, she is moved to a "farrowing crate," which is basically a modified gestation crate (Figure 5.1), with pockets for the piglets to nurse without being crushed (though many still wiggle out of the pockets and are soon crushed to death). Almost as soon as the piglets are weaned, the sow is impregnated again, denied the normal period of five to six months "off" between pregnancies (Marcus 2005).

Figure 5.1 A sow's "farrowing crate," where she will remain for the 35 (or so) days her young are nursing. Crating is an economically efficient method of raising hogs, but is it *wrong*? *Source*: © Jonathan Hallett.

So why are these animals penned in such cramped conditions? Why are they not allowed to rest and recover after each period of pregnancy and nursing? For the sake of industrial efficiency. These factory farms are, after all, run more like factories than farms. Smaller crates mean more sows in the same amount of space. Confining the sows allows their gestation periods and projected birthing dates to be tracked with incredible precision. A non-pregnant, non-nursing breeding sow is, by the logic of business, wasted capital. This industrial model is by no means limited to hog farming. The vast majority of layer hens (chickens raised for egg production), broilers (chickens raised for meat), and turkeys spend their entire (short) lives in similar indoor, confined quarters. Similarly, cattle increasingly see little or no time grazing pastures and spend the majority of their days in a cramped feedlot eating an unnatural corn-based diet.

Many people have strong opinions – some for and some against – on the increasingly industrialized nature of animal farming. One proponent might like the fact that more animals can be raised on less land, freeing up space for other economic development activities. Another might cite the fact that – courtesy of factory farming (and government subsidies and other often-overlooked variables) – the price of meat in the United States has dropped considerably over the past 30 years. Families living near the officially designated poverty line can, for perhaps the first time in history, afford to eat meat every day. Granted, these arguments are most vociferously espoused by representatives of the industry itself, but they do represent a set of grounded claims – reasons to justify this action. Utility, most notably, is at the root of this set of arguments, with the case for more economic growth and more available consumer goods taken to be the "good" reasons for factory farming.

Simultaneously, opponents of factory farms also have varied arguments. Some speak out against the de-peopling of rural communities, a process concomitant with industrial intensification, as small farms go belly-up in the face of competition across the Corn Belt and the Southeast. Others speak out against the significant air and water pollution produced by these mammoth-scale operations – some holding tens or even hundreds of thousands of hogs on a single production unit, with problems for other residents and for the costs related to cleaning periodic disastrous spills. These are compelling arguments, located in a (mostly) human-centered view of the problem, and the "bad" reasons against factory farming.

Many of the most vocal opponents of factory farming, however, oppose it for what appears on the surface to be the simplest and most straightforward argument of all: Animals are not "capital." They are living, sentient, beings. For them, it is just plain *wrong* to treat animals in this manner. Factory farming, for those critics, is an *ethically indefensible* practice. This is again an ethical argument, like the ones above, but it is one grounded in a somewhat different place: the experience of the animals themselves.

In each case, **ethics** is at work: the study of right and wrong. What *ought* people do in certain situations and why? Throughout history, codes of ethics have provided guiding principles for civilizations, including a number of key philosophies and religions. There are countless such ethical traditions in the world, from the precepts of Buddhism to the ethical laws of scientific humanism. As you can see from our opening argument, however, for the purposes of this chapter we are especially interested in the ethical considerations and ways of viewing environmental problems that question human-centered logics and propose an environmentally-centered alternative.

Unlike in Buddhism and many other traditional ethical systems, in the specific ethical traditions of "Western" civilization, such reconsiderations (from human-centered to environmentally-centered views of right and wrong) are remarkably recent. Throughout much of "Western" philosophical tradition, questions of right and wrong action have largely centered on actions *of people toward other people*. Indeed, many important environmental movements, regulations, and ideas are themselves founded on such ethical concerns of humans for other humans. Consider, for example, the concerns of **environmental justice** (see Chapter 7 for more detailed discussion), where environmental risks are criticized because of higher exposures of poor and minority

Ethics/Ethical   The branch of philosophy dealing with morality, or, questions of right and wrong human action in the world

Environmental Justice   A principle, as well as a body of thought and research, stressing the need for equitable distribution of environmental goods (parks, clean air, healthful working conditions) and environmental bads (pollution, hazards, waste) between people, no matter their race, ethnicity, or gender. Conversely, environmental injustice describes a condition where unhealthful or dangerous conditions are disproportionately proximate to minority communities populations. Only recently, however, have ethicists expanded inquiry and consideration to include *environmental ethics*. That is, what are right – and wrong – ways of acting in nature and toward the *non-human* world? For example, one might ask, after reading the story that opens this chapter, does a sow need to be able to turn around to live a full life? Is the full life of a sow important? *Is it wrong to treat sows this way?* Before we can address this and other contemporary questions from an environmental ethics perspective, let us backtrack to some influential documents that helped lay the foundations of right action toward the non-human world.

Improving Nature: From Biblical Tradition to John Locke

Many environmental thinkers cite two common beliefs that have governed the relationship of Western civilization to the natural world, in one way or another, until the last century. The first of these is the idea that humans are separate from, and superior to, nature. The second is that nature is only as valuable as it is useful to humans. Where do these ideas come from? In "The Historical Roots of Our Ecologic Crisis," Lynn White (1968) argued that the **dominion thesis** from the Old Testament established humans as the sole earthly creatures made in God's image (therefore, logically separate from and superior to the rest):

> Be fruitful and multiply, and replenish the Earth, and subdue it; have dominion over the fish of the Sea, and over the fowl of the air, and over every living thing that moves upon the Earth. (Genesis, 1:28)

This mandate is no small order. There are neither places nor creatures – *anywhere on Earth* – that should not be "subdued" by humans. If people have indeed been commanded by an all-powerful deity to do this, then quite clearly, not only is subduing and dominating all of Earth permitted, it is, moreover, an ethical imperative. It is the *right* thing to do. As such, according to White (and many others), biblical tradition provided humans with an environmental ethic, albeit one that is at best silent about, or at worst hostile toward, those animals, plants, and places not useful to humans, or under their direct control. Is it any wonder, then, that the puritans of colonial New England so feared and despised the wilderness? Is it surprising that the first governmental environmental action in North America was not the creation of a park, or regulatory limits on cutting trees, but rather a publicly subsidized wolf eradication program for the Massachusetts colony (in the sixteenth century, no less!)?

On the other hand, the inherent hostility or indifference of the Bible to the non-human world can be strongly debated. For example, many find throughout the Bible a strong call for human **stewardship** of nature, the moral responsibility to care for and protect the natural world. As stewards of nature, the mandate to subdue is subsumed under an ethic to care and maintain. Such a

Dominion Thesis   Arising from the Book of Genesis, the dominion thesis states that humans are the pinnacle of creation; as such, humans are granted ethical free rein to use nature in any way deemed beneficial

Stewardship   Taking responsibility for the property or fate of others; stewardship of land and natural resources is often used in a religious context, such as "caring for creation"

religious ethic of stewardship can be seen in human activities and movements around the world; witness the Kibbutz movement in Israel, the anti-corporate French "peasant" farmers' movement, and the recent energetic movement of evangelical churches in the United States to halt global warming. But from whichever angle – dominion, stewardship, or somewhere in between – Western civilizations, especially those of the modern era, do appear to demonstrate an **anthropocentric** (literally, human-centered) ethic that, for many environmental advocates, leaves much to be desired.

Anthropocentrism An ethical standpoint that views humans as the central factor in considerations of right and wrong action in and toward nature (compare to ecocentrism)

These ethics, however, may be less rooted in the Bible than they are in political philosophy. Fast-forwarding from the Old Testament to seventeenth-century Britain, we find the philosopher John Locke penning a key document that further articulated a Western, human-centered environmental ethic.

With his *Second Treatise on Government*, written in 1690, Locke wrote what would become the definitive statement of libertarian philosophy. In this unabashedly political work, Locke's "chief concern . . . was to establish the legitimacy of a popularly elected democratic government, and thereby to oppose the prevalent view of the divine right of the monarchy" (Katz 1997: 225).

Utilitarian An ethical theory that posits that the value of a good should be judged solely (or at least primarily) by its usefulness to society; following the eighteenth–nineteenth-century philosopher Jeremy Bentham, usefulness is equated with maximizing pleasure or happiness and minimizing pain and suffering

Not surprisingly, Locke's anti-monarchist views were popular in eighteenth-century America. In the newly independent United States, Locke's theory of *property* from the *Second Treatise* helped lay the foundation for a new Enlightenment-era rationale for the human domination of nature.

Political libertarians believe in government, but always and only in a very limited role. For Locke, and most libertarians who have followed, government should function only as is necessary to protect the "natural" freedoms of individual citizens. Freedom, in this context, is the right and ability to acquire, possess, and maintain property. Without property, government would be unnecessary, because with no possessions, there is nothing to defend.

What, then, is property? In Locke's view, an individual's property begins with his physical body. Beyond the body, an individual's physical labor is also part of his property. A free individual, therefore, has the sole right to the use of his body and labor. (The gendering here is intentional: It is worth noting that Locke was referring to *free men* of the time, which, for the eighteenth-century reader, would have excluded the bodies of many, especially women and non-whites, from their own control. In any case, acquiring (or "appropriating," for Locke) property from nature merely requires that an individual mixes labor with some or another "chunk" of nature. By shooting a deer, picking an apple, cutting down a tree to make sawlogs, or clearing a patch of forest to plant a field, an individual has turned external nature into personal property. They have, moreover, done the *right* thing.

Using nature, for Locke, meant very specifically the transformation of external nature (which has little or no value), through individual human labor, into *property* (improved nature, now *valuable*). So not only is the environmental ethic established by Locke clearly anthropocentric, it is also purely **utilitarian**. This means that the *value* of any part of nature is determined solely by its *usefulness* to humans. The implications, for the newly independent United States and beyond, cannot be overstated. A domesticated animal (*property*, the product of human labor) is, by fiat, more valuable than any wild animal. An agricultural field or a forest cut for timber is more valuable than any native prairie or wild forest. The US Western frontier was, for Locke, a literal wasteland. Even as it may have been a storehouse of *potential* value, the "Wild West" (its indigenous human communities included) was valueless insofar as it was unused.

Locke's theory of the ethics of appropriating nature did come with two (arguably rather minor) constraints on what qualifies as just uses of nature. An individual should not, first of all, take more than they can use before it would spoil or go to waste. Further, no individual should appropriate more land than he can work. As such, Locke's theory was a perfect match for early American ideals, justifying Westward imperial expansion, but at the same time advancing an ideal that honors the sanctity of the individual citizen and egalitarian opportunity. Nearing the end of the nineteenth century, this anthropocentric, utilitarian environmental ethic would find an articulate and powerful proponent in Gifford Pinchot, good friend of Theodore Roosevelt and first chief of the US Forest Service. Pinchot's strong advocacy for the efficient use of natural resources would not, however, go unchallenged.

Gifford Pinchot vs. John Muir in Yosemite, California

Gifford Pinchot is an iconic figure in the history of environmental conservation. After graduating with a bachelor's degree from Yale, Pinchot received postgraduate training in scientific forestry in France (there was, at the time, no college of forestry in North America). Just a few years later, President Grover Cleveland appointed Pinchot to the federal Division of Forestry, and during the subsequent administration of Theodore Roosevelt, Pinchot became the first chief of the US Forest Service. Pinchot was a lifelong advocate of what he called "**conservation**" – the efficient and sustainable use of natural resources, always for "the greatest good for the greatest number." This phrase, Pinchot's most famous aphorism, epitomizes his staunchly utilitarian environmental ethic.

> **Conservation**   The management of a resource or system to sustain its productivity over time, typically associated with scientific management of collective goods like fisheries or forests (compare to preservation)

At the time, it should be noted, a vast proportion of the United States was held by the federal government, especially in the western part of the country (indeed, almost 30 percent of land in the United States remains under federal control today). These lands comprised forests, deserts, mountains, rivers, wetlands, and gorges, which were rich with resources, including timber, minerals, and hydropower. While a lot of land had been given over to private interests, including agriculture and the railroads, enormous areas remained. How these public lands should be managed put Pinchot at the center of an ethical debate that remains at the heart of environmental politics today.

Pinchot viewed himself as a centrist. Opponents on one side of him were lumbermen, mining interests, and other large corporations who wanted (legal and ethical) free rein to chop and dig over the privately and publicly owned lands of the country as quickly and profitably as they could. These "timber barons" and their allies had unsustainably pillaged vast natural resources throughout the nineteenth century. But with the arrival of President Roosevelt and other trust-busting political populists at the turn of the twentieth century, Pinchot and his vision of government intervention to rationalize resource use could take center stage.

On Pinchot's other side, however, were proponents of **preservation** – an environmental ethic that would rival conservation. Preservationists argued against the human exploitation of nature, efficient or otherwise. Nature, particularly unspoiled or scenic tracts of "**wilderness**," should be left alone, preserved *from* human use and abuse. This tradition of preservation itself developed over the nineteenth century, with its national roots in philosophical American Transcendentalism, advocated by Henry David Thoreau and his contemporaries, which held that human potential lay in intuition and a close relationship to the natural world. This philosophy, embodied in the National Parks movement, stressed protection of nature for its own sake.

> **Preservation**   The management of a resource or environment for protection and preservation, typically for its own sake, as in wilderness preservation (compare to conservation)
>
> **Wilderness**   A natural parcel of land, more or less unaffected by human forces; increasingly, wilderness is viewed as a social construction

At the turn of the twentieth century, the most articulate and famous spokesperson for preservation was the wiry Scottish immigrant John Muir. After years of traveling from the Midwest to Florida to Central America to Alaska, Muir finally settled in the Sierra Nevada Mountains of California. In 1892 he founded the Sierra Club, and it was largely through the lobbying of Muir and the Sierra Club that Yosemite National Park was expanded to its current boundaries.

It was in his beloved Yosemite that, a couple of decades later, Muir would face off with his former environmental ally Pinchot in what would become one of the defining environmental debates in American history. The debate was over the fate of Hetch Hetchy Valley. Hetch Hetchy was a deep, scenic glaciated valley in the remote northwest corner of Yosemite, similar to but smaller and less famous than Yosemite Valley. The city of San Francisco wanted to dam Hetch Hetchy Valley to create a large reservoir and permanent municipal water source for the growing municipality (Figure 5.2).

For Pinchot, the decision was easy. Which choice, reservoir or wilderness, was the *right* one? It was simple. As Pinchot testified before Congress, he explained that the reservoir provided a greater benefit for more people than preserving the valley in its natural state. Through this simple calculus, damming the valley was argued to be the right thing to do. Muir, on the other hand, saw things differently. As he had argued years before, when he successfully lobbied to get permanent protection for Yosemite Valley and the Mariposa Grove of giant sequoias, this park was a unique natural treasure. It was a storehouse of scenic wonder, a place for weary, modern humans to witness the spiritual grandeur of the natural world, a place *not* dedicated to human progress.

He was arguing for preservation for its own sake and the protection of scenic landscapes with little to no human imprint: *wilderness*. For nearly a century, the preservation movement argued for wilderness along these intangible, non-utilitarian lines. The right thing to do, according to these advocates, was to leave alone what little pristine nature was left. As Yosemite, Yellowstone, Glacier, and other national parks had already been established, lands were in the process of being set aside from direct, obvious human exploitation.

Figure 5.2 (a + b) Hetch Hetchy Valley, undammed before 1914 (left), and today (right), now dammed to provide the city of San Francisco with a clean and reliable source of fresh water. The fate of this valley was debated between leaving it "wild" versus appropriating it for its direct human usefulness. *Source*: a) F. E. Matthes/United States Geological Survey Photographic Archive; b) © Anthony Dunn/Alamy.

A large part of the reason these lands were "set aside" in the first place, however, was because they were viewed as having no "better" use than being more or less left alone, as parks. What marked Hetch Hetchy as such a watershed in the history of environmental politics was that it was the first highly publicized debate over the fate of a particular place directly drawn along utilitarian versus non-utilitarian lines. Previous allies in the fight against the unchecked abuse of nature, conservationists and preservationists parted ways over Hetch Hetchy. This divide – conservation vs. preservation or wise resource use vs. wilderness preservation – would persist within North American environmentalism through the twentieth and into the twenty-first centuries. By mid-twentieth century, however, the burgeoning science of ecology would provide an impetus for a new environmental ethic, a "third way," broader in scope than the narrow confines of either anthropocentric conservation or wilderness preservation.

Aldo Leopold and "The Land Ethic"

Ecology The scientific study of interactions among organisms and between organisms and the habitat or ecosystem in which they live

Ecology – the scientific study of the interconnections between organisms and their (living and non-living) environment – is a relatively young field of inquiry. Indeed, the term "ecosystem," central to ecology and now commonplace, was not coined until the 1930s. One of the leading early ecologists in North America, and one who, more than any other, would weave the insights of ecology into an environmental ethic, was Aldo Leopold. Trained as a forester at the Yale School of Forestry (founded by Pinchot, and the first school of scientific natural resource management in North America), Leopold was an influential and prolific environmental writer.

Box 5.1   Environmental Solution? Endangered Species Act

In 1973, both houses of the US Congress passed the Endangered Species Act (ESA) with overwhelming bipartisan support (votes were 90–0 in the Senate and 390–12 in the House; US Senate 2012). The ESA provides regulatory protection for imperiled animal and plant species and the ecosystems on which they depend. "Species" is broadly defined to include any species or subspecies of plant or animal. For vertebrate animals, "distinct population segments" can also be listed. The ESA provides two classifications of protected status, endangered and threatened. An endangered species is "any species which is in danger of extinction throughout all or a significant portion of its range" while a threatened species is "any species which is likely to become an endangered species."

Once a species is listed, the US Fish and Wildlife Service (the agency in charge of listing and managing endangered species) must design and implement a recovery plan for the species. The stated (and logical) goal of listing is timely recovery of the species and removal from the ESA. If a species is designated as recovered, it is "delisted" and the management of the species reverts to the states.

There are two regulatory provisions that give the ESA its teeth. First, the ESA prohibits the federal government from taking any action that would further jeopardize listed species. This requirement has been rigorously upheld by federal courts since the *snail darter* controversy in 1978 that temporarily halted construction of a large dam on the Tellico River for protection of that relatively small fish. Second, the ESA prohibits the killing or harming of listed species on all lands, whether publicly or privately owned. This clause is perhaps the single most controversial component of the ESA, as it severely limits what private landowners can do with their property, if endangered species are present. Perhaps not surprisingly, an anti-ESA countermovement known as the "property rights movement" argues that federal regulations should not dictate what landowners do on their own land, as long as it does not directly harm others.

Currently there are over 1,200 animals and 700 plants listed. Most listed species are not well known, like the Ozark big-eared bat or the San Joaquin kit fox. A few, however, are high-profile conservation icons, like the grizzly bear and the California condor. Some critics of the ESA note that it has a low "success rate," meaning that few species recover to the point of delisting. While that may be true, it could also be noted that only a very few species have actually gone extinct after listing (the Eskimo curlew, a medium-sized shorebird now thought to be extinct, would be one of only a few examples). The ESA does have its share of notable successes as well. The bald eagle and brown pelican, for example, once decimated due to the effects of the insecticide DDT, are now quite common and have been delisted throughout most of their range. In addition to the snail darter mentioned above, there have been several endangered species whose protection invoked firestorms of controversy. Perhaps the most notable recent example would be the northern spotted owl, whose listing resulted in a great reduction of logging in the old-growth Douglas fir forests of the Pacific Northwest.

Leopold's most famous essay, written late in his life is "The Land Ethic," from his 1949 book *A Sand County Almanac* (Leopold 1987). "The Land Ethic" stands as an important essay for several reasons. First, it was groundbreaking in integrating the new insights of ecology into an ethical framework. It was also notable for the clarity and simplicity of its argument. Additionally, perhaps the most extraordinary thing about this essay has been its persistence. It remains one of the most widely read and influential statements of environmental ethics ever written.

Leopold's system of ethics is clear and easy to appreciate. There are two existing forms of ethics and a missing but needed third form. According to Leopold, the earliest formal ethics were statements of right and wrong action between human individuals, as with, for example, the Ten Commandments. Not long after, ethical relations between individuals and society (for example, the Golden Rule) and between society and individual (for example, democratic governance) were established. Missing, according to Leopold, was an "ethic dealing with man's relation to land and to the animals and plants which grow upon it. Land . . . is still property. The land-relation is still strictly economic, entailing privileges but not obligations." Now more enlightened by scientific ecology, and with our knowledge of biological evolution, humans should realize that not only are they, as a species, part of the natural order, but that they are also wholly dependent on their environment – the lands, the plants, the animals, and the healthy functioning of our ecosystems.

The notion of dependence is apparent in the institutions of human *community*. People typically realize that they must cooperate, giving up some of their liberties and freedoms, to be an "interdependent part" of a human community, so they do so willingly. Now that we understand *ecological* connections as well – our *interdependence* with our environment – it is only logical and reasonable to extend outward the boundaries of the community to "include soils, waters, plants, and animals, or collectively: the land." Since one cannot at once be a conqueror and member of a community, we must change our relationship with nature from "conqueror . . . to plain member and citizen" (Leopold 1949: 204).

So how to judge right versus wrong action? The most famous and pithy maxim from "The Land Ethic" proposes a litmus test: "A thing is right when it tends to preserve the integrity, stability, and beauty of the biotic community. It is wrong when it tends otherwise" (Leopold 1949: 224–5). The land ethic, as such, parts ways with the simpler ethics of conservation and preservation, where *human use* is more or less right (à la Pinchot) or wrong (à la Muir). Use of the land will – *must* – continue (indeed, Leopold wrote considerably on agricultural land use and conservation; he was not just an advocate for wild nature). Land use must now, however, be guided by our knowledge of ecological connections and ecosystem health. Indeed, the land ethic stands as the key **ecocentric** (ecology-centered) environmental ethic, though the term "ecocentric" itself would not be coined until decades later. Not surprisingly, many contemporary environmentalists – from biodiversity conservationists to proponents of "ecological sustainability" – claim Leopold as their own.

Beyond the recognition of ecosystem health as fundamental to any sufficient environmental ethic, a fundamental contribution to be sure, this essay marked another key idea in environmental ethics. "The Land Ethic" was one of the first widely read pieces to argue for **moral extensionism**, that is, extending our sphere of moral consideration beyond the human realm (now, to "include soils, waters, plants, and animals, or collectively: the land"). A couple of decades later, the specific idea of granting animals

Ecocentrism   An environmental ethical stance that argues that ecological concerns should, over and above human priorities, be central to decisions about right and wrong action (compare to anthropocentrism)

Moral Extensionism   An ethical principle stating that humans should extend their sphere of moral concern beyond the human realm; most commonly, it is argued that intelligent or sentient animals are worthy ethical subjects (including domestic animals) moral consideration would rise to prominence, spark considerable debate, and inspire a popular social activist movement.

Liberation for Animals!

When Aldo Leopold argued that animals, plants, and soil should receive ethical consideration, he was thinking as a scientific ecologist. The animals Leopold had in mind, therefore, were not the individual critters themselves but rather species, like the gray wolf, the Iberian lynx, Stellar's sea eagle, or even a less "charismatic" species like the now-extinct dusky seaside sparrow. In the 1970s, new social movements dedicated to extending our range of moral consideration arose. The "**animal liberation**" and "animal rights" movements argued that individual animals – wild or domestic – were worthy of our moral consideration.

> **Animal Liberation**   Named after Peter Singer's groundbreaking 1975 book, a radical social movement that aims to free all animals from use by humans, whether those uses are for food, medical testing, industry, personal adornment, entertainment or anything else

Peter Singer's book *Animal Liberation* (1975) is notable in environmental ethics writing because it is perhaps the only such book to become a popular bestseller. Not surprisingly, as such, it also inspired the rise of a vocal – and often quite effective – social movement, the animal liberation movement.

Singer's argument is straightforward enough, and for many people, resonates strongly as a reasonable call to *right action*. He asks: How is it that we have (quite *rightly*) broadened our moral horizon to those populations who have historically had few or no rights (including women, minorities, the infirm, and the handicapped) without similarly extending beyond the human species to include animals as well? Distinctions drawn, Singer argues – whether drawn along lines of race, class, or gender, or along the human/nonhuman species divide – are arbitrary. How did people once rationalize denying moral standing to members of other races? Only through now discredited *racist* theories. In extending our sphere of moral standing, our *motivation* – that others have interests that deserve equal consideration – was correct. Moreover, our *direction* – increasingly inclusive, outward from an unjustifiably narrow conception of who counts – was correct and laudable as well.

The shortcoming of these previous successes, for an animal rights advocate, is simply that they did not go far enough. The reason? According to Singer, it is because they failed to use a sufficient measuring-stick to test the notion of who (or what) deserves moral standing. Following the nineteenth-century philosopher Jeremy Bentham, Singer argued that ethics should strive for maximizing the "good" that society can produce. A prerequisite for maximizing good (as pleasure and happiness) is to eliminate, as much as possible, suffering. As such, all beings who can suffer (Singer calls them "sentient beings") have interests, and warrant equal consideration in matters of ethics.

Contrary to what some detractors might claim, Singer does not advocate exactly *equal treatment* of all animals. He does not, for example, claim that the life of a rat and the life of a human are equal, and should be treated with equal weight in questions of ethics. (Critics of Singer have remarked that he would oppose any action that might be taken to eradicate an urban population of rats that are vectors for transmission of bubonic plague on account of their sentience, a stance he has never espoused.) Rather, Singer claims that all sentient beings deserve *equal consideration*, that minimizing or even eliminating their suffering should be part of any ethical decision. Through this calculus, Singer concludes that almost any use of animals for human purposes is unethical. He staunchly opposes the use of animal-based products in cosmetics and fashion. He also opposes almost all use of animals in medical research. Not surprisingly, he also advocates the elimination of animals from agriculture. Through vivid and often-harrowing accounts of these practices, Singer has convinced thousands of activists worldwide to fight for the elimination of animal suffering at the hands of humans. Not all animal rights advocates are as absolutist (e.g., *no* animals in agriculture, *no* animals in research, etc.) as Singer, but even the most moderate supporter of this view would be an advocate for major changes to many aspects of modern life. Stated another way, to put into action what Singer advocates – *animal liberation* – would indeed require a radical restructuring of our current culture. Another self-styled radical environmental ethic that inspires activism, if of a different type, is deep ecology.

From shallow to deep ecology

Norwegian philosopher Arne Naess (Naess 1973) coined the term "**deep ecology**" in the short essay "The Shallow and the Deep, Long-Range Ecology Movement: A Summary." As the title of the paper suggests, this was at once a positive formulation of a new, "deep ecology" and a critique of what he termed "shallow ecology." These divergent "ecologies" were not divisions within scientific ecology but rather branches of the environmental movement. Consumed with the search for piecemeal solutions to particular *issues* (e.g., pollution or resource depletion), shallow ecology failed to ask "deeper questions" about the *causes* of ecological problems and therefore could never hope to solve the ecological crisis itself. Deep ecology, on the other hand, offered a wholesale critique of human society and particularly the human relationship with non-human nature.

The bookends of Naess's philosophy of deep ecology are "self-realization" and ecocentrism. "*Self-realization*," for Naess, is the logical conclusion of any truly deep ecological questioning. When "we" (individuals) realize the interconnectedness of all things, it becomes evident that any concept of the self must expand beyond the individual to include all things. *Ecocentrism*, the second key component of Naess's deep ecology, is a logical derivation of self-realization. Once an individual realizes that he or she is not a narrow enclosed self and properly identifies with all of nature, anthropocentric (human-centered) thought or action becomes – simply – *illogical*.

Deep ecology was relatively unheard of in North America until 1985 with the publication of Devall's and Sessions' *Deep Ecology: Living as if Nature Mattered*, which presents a "platform" for a "deep ecology movement." The platform was based on the fundamental tenet that nature has "***intrinsic value*** . . . independent of the usefulness of the nonhuman world for

Deep Ecology A philosophy of environmental ethics that distances itself from "shallow" or mainstream environmentalism by arguing for a "deeper" and supposedly more truly ecologically-informed view of the world

Intrinsic Value The value of a natural object (e.g., an owl or a stream) in and for itself, as an end rather than a means human purposes." The platform also called for a reduction in human population, a decrease in human interference in the natural world, a change in environmental policies, and a personal commitment to environmental activism. Simple, direct, and resonating with familiar themes (e.g., Malthusian overpopulation, see Chapter 2), deep ecology has made its mark on environmental activism, perhaps most indelibly on the radical wing of the North American wilderness preservation movement. Like all of the strands of environmental ethics reviewed in this chapter, deep ecology is certainly not without its critics, and in the following concluding section of the chapter, we review some criticisms of deep ecology and other strands of environmental ethics.

Holism, Scientism, and Other Pitfalls

Is protecting the environment *right*? Is overexploiting nature – forests, animals, ecosystem processes – *wrong*? Posing environmental dilemmas in this manner can, at least for some, make reworking our environmental ethics seem like a logical first step toward reorienting society in a needed direction. There are critics, though, who fear that some popular environmental ethics would, if taken to a logical end, lead to a reactionary, authoritarian politics.

Leopold's land ethic and (some of) the environmental activism it has inspired are perhaps the most common targets of the "*eco-authoritarian*" critique. This critique rests on misgivings about the land ethic's **holism**, that is, its insistence that protection of *wholes* (e.g., ecosystems, species, natural processes) takes precedence over the protection – or rights – of *parts* (e.g., individual animals, humans included). It is hard not to read Leopold's famous "a thing is right when it tends to preserve the . . . integrity of the biotic community" maxim as advocating such a preference. This could mean that, if an action bolstered the good of the whole (for example, sacrificing individuals to decrease population pressures), it might well be deemed not just permissible, but *right*. Critics fear that ecocentric ethics could, more generally, justify the subversion of basic individual liberties. Defenders of the land ethic disagree, arguing that the authoritarian charge relies on a comically inflexible reading of the theory. The land ethic argues for integrating a missing, needed criterion into our moral consideration, not using ecology to override all existing criteria.

Another charge against the land ethic, deep ecology, and their offshoots is that they are guilty of what philosophers call the "**naturalistic fallacy.**" By using the findings of ecological science to figure out what is good and therefore what is right, an "ought" has been derived from an "is," or a value from a fact, a practice now almost universally viewed as philosophically indefensible (all kinds of things exist that are not right, after all). Recently, critics have ramped up this charge even more, accusing some deep ecologists of "**scientism,**" meaning raising (supposedly objective and value-free) science up to the level of *ultimate authority*. Authority of this form of knowledge over all other sources of value and judgment, for example, religion, philosophy,

Holism Any theory that holds that a whole system (e.g., an "ecosystem" or the Earth) is more than the sum of its parts

Naturalistic Fallacy A philosophically invalid derivation of an ethical "ought" from a natural "is"

Scientism Usually deployed as a term of derision; refers to an uncritical reliance on the natural sciences as the basis for social decision-making and ethical judgments and humanistic notions of justice, in this sense, means unchecked expert power flying in the face of democratic ideals. Advocates of ecocentric ethics might, therefore, be wary of the philosophical and political pitfalls of staking too much of their claim on ecology.

The most sustained and challenging critique along these lines has come from proponents of **social ecology**, particularly through four decades of writing by the late Murray Bookchin. Informed by a form of radical political economy (see Chapter 7), rather than natural science or philosophical ethics, social ecologists argue that deep ecologists and land ethics proponents are aiming for the wrong target. Society's root problems are not matters of misguided ethics, bogus ideas, or ecological naiveté. Rather, our ecological ills are social in nature. This tradition of thought, related to social anarchism and rooted in the research and thinking of nineteenth-century researchers like Peter Kropotkin, suggests that domination and exploitation of nature is inevitable in a society rooted in social hierarchies, domination and exploitation of other humans. Until an egalitarian, *just* society is established, people have no hope of ceasing environmental destruction, no matter what ethical lens people use to view nature.

> **Social Ecology**   A school of thought and set of social movements, associated with the thinker Murray Bookchin, asserting that environmental problems and crises are rooted in typical social structures and relationships, since these tend to be hierarchical, state-controlled, and predicated on domination of both people and nature

Animal rights advocates, as well, are far from immune to political critique. Practically speaking, what does it mean to say that an animal has interests equal to a human? How do we differentiate between human and non-human animal interests? If, from an ethical standpoint, the line between the species is arbitrary, then is it right and reasonable (or even possible) to make decisions along the human/animal line when, in specific instances, the welfares of humans and animals are at odds? All but the most radical (or misanthropic) animal rights activists would likely respond that questions such as these are straw-men (overstated and unfair caricatures of positions that make easy targets for critics, like the bubonic plague example above) thrown up to intentionally make the ideas presented sound inhumane and unworkable. Fair enough, but that does not solve the problem for activists who ultimately must (or at least should) be able to address difficult, actual conflicts with defensible solutions.

So far we have reviewed *external critiques* of environmental ethics, meaning that these are criticisms drawn mostly from outside the circle of self-identified environmentalists. Environmental ethics, a field comprising both academic scholars and environmental advocates (and many scholar-advocates), also includes considerable internal debates as well. Perhaps the most well developed of these intramural debates is between (some) animal rights advocates and (some) land ethics advocates. To put it simply, the former care about individual organisms while the latter care about protecting species, ecosystems, evolutionary processes, and the like. These two priorities can and often do clash, for example, along the issue of hunting. Many, if not most, animal rights advocates disdain hunting in almost all its forms (it does, after all, cause sentient beings to suffer). But just as many environmentalists see hunting as an ecologically useful – even *necessary* – activity. Which can lead one to ask: Must people really choose between extending ethics outward (to non-human animals) or upward (to ecology and evolution)? Many on both sides of the debate answer this with an unapologetic "yes," seeing the other "side" as an obstacle in their path to right action. Others argue that this is an unnecessary impasse, a false wall erected by people more interested in maintaining ideological purity than achieving workable solutions.

Does anthropocentric thinking necessarily lead to an anti-ecological ethics? Are there fundamental problems with the human relationship to non-human animals? Environmental ethics poses these and other fundamentally challenging questions to society. If, as many environmental ethicists argue, the answer to these questions is "yes," then fundamental, ideological changes are truly needed if people are to cure their planetary ills. Even so, holding to a personal or group ideal, ideology, or vision of right behavior may be only a small part of a complex puzzle, where economic drivers, political forces, and institutional impasses all provide barriers to individual action. While the theoretical and practical challenges to environmental ethics are daunting on their own, the deeply entrenched political and economic conditions of the current world deserve scrutiny in and of themselves.

Thinking with Ethics

In this chapter we have learned that:

- Competing ethical systems have influenced human treatment of non-human nature for thousands of years, including especially systems that are anthropocentric versus those that are ecocentric.
- In the contemporary era, priorities of conservation have competed with those favoring preservation.
- More recently, the land ethic has been forwarded as a way to value nature from an ecological standpoint without eliminating a role for humanity.
- More radically, deep ecology represents an ethic that staunchly asserts the value of nature in, of, and for itself.
- Other critical traditions view environmental problems as fundamentally rooted in contemporary social structures.

Questions for Review

1. Summarize the "dominion thesis." Is it an "ethical theory"? Explain.
2. How does John Locke's theory of property put forward a particular environmental ethic? What, for example, would it suggest is the proper use for a tract of uncut "old-growth" forest?
3. The famous debate between Pinchot and Muir over Hetch Hetchy Valley marked a split between "conservationists" and "preservationists." Summarize the debate around an explanation of these two terms.
4. Peter Singer makes a case for "animal liberation." From what does he argue animals should be liberated, and how should we go about making this happen?
5. Explain the "deep" in "deep ecology." What does it mean to say that deep ecology espouses an *ecocentric* ethics?

Exercise 5.1   Pass the Bacon (or don't)

Considering the theories (as well as their critics) surveyed here, let us reexamine our opening story and ask the question: *Is factory farming a defensible practice?* Environmental ethics can be helpful in answering this question, but the answers that arise are far from simple or self-evident. Using books, magazines or the internet, find at least three arguments each from opponents and proponents of factory hog farming. Read the material and then answer the following questions: *How much of their arguments are based in ethics? Of the ethical arguments, are they based on ecological or animal rights grounds (or both)? What other factors enter into their support or opposition? Having read from both sides, what is your opinion?* Complete the exercise by writing a two-paragraph statement of opposition to or support of this practice.

Exercise 5.2   Animals in Medical and Commercial Research and Testing

One of the longstanding, high-profile overtly ethical debates about nature and society is whether or to what degree animals should be used in medical and commercial research and testing. Locate a recent (published in the last two years) news piece covering some aspect of this debate (possible web search terms and phrases could include "animal subject testing," "animal testing cosmetics," "animal rights medical testing," etc.). Once you have located a current specific debate on the subject, find two (or more) more credible, written pieces on the subject. Read up on the subject and then write an opinion piece. Think of it as a mock letter to the editor of your local paper. Cite your sources.

Exercise 5.3   The Land Ethic

Read Aldo Leopold's 1948 essay "The Land Ethic" (available on the web: home.btconnect.com/tipiglen/landethic.html). How does Leopold see the concept of "community" as central to the needed development of a land ethic? Do you think that we (everyday citizens) see ourselves as members of the "land community"? Why or why not? Think of one or more ways in which contemporary society displays a "land ethic." Think of one or more ways in which it fails to. Discuss.

References

Devall, W., and G. Sessions (1985). *Deep Ecology: Living as if Nature Mattered*. Salt Lake City: Gibbs M. Smith, Inc.

Katz, E. (1997). *Nature as Subject: Human Obligation and Natural Community*. Lanham, MD: Rowman & Littlefield.

Leopold, A. (1949). *A Sand County Almanac*. New York: Oxford University Press.

Leopold, A. (1987). *A Sand County Almanac and Sketches Here and There*. New York: Oxford University Press.

Locke, J. (1690). *The Second Treatise on Government*. Publicly available in several locations on the World Wide Web.

Marcus, E. (2005). *Meat Market: Animals, Ethics, and Money*. Boston, MA: Brio Press.

Naess, A. (1973). "The shallow and the deep, long-range ecology movement: A summary." *Inquiry* 16: 95–100.

Singer, P. (1975). *Animal Liberation: A New Ethics for our Treatment of Animals*. New York: New York Review (distributed by Random House).

Turner, B. L. II, and S. B. Brush (eds.) (1987). *Comparative Farming Systems*. New York: Guilford Press.

US Senate (2012). *Endangered Species Act of 1973*. Retrieved October 10, 2012, from http://epw.senate.gov/esa73.pdf.

White, Jr., L. (1968). "The historical roots of our ecologic crisis." In L. T. White, *Machina Ex Deo: Essays in the Dynamism of Western Culture*. Cambridge, MA: MIT, pp. 57–74.

Suggested Reading

Abbey, E. (2000). *The Monkey Wrench Gang*. New York: Harper Perennial Modern Classics.

Bookchin, M. (2005). *The Ecology of Freedom*. Oakland, CA: AK Press.

Des Jardins, J. R. (2006). *Environmental Ethics: An Introduction to Environmental Philosophy*, 6th edn. Belmont, CA: Thomson Wadsworth.

Light, A., and H. Rolston (eds.) (2003). *Environmental Ethics: An Anthology*. Malden, MA: Blackwell.

Norton, B. G. (2003). *Searching for Sustainability: Interdisciplinary Essays in the Philosophy of Conservation Biology*. New York: Cambridge University Press.

6

Risks and Hazards

Source: © James Dawson/Image Farm Inc/Alamy.

Keywords

- Affect
- Cultural theory
- Externality
- Hazard
- Risk
- Risk perception
- Uncertainty

Chapter Menu

Environment and Society: A Critical Introduction, Second Edition. Paul Robbins, John Hintz, and Sarah A. Moore.
© 2014 John Wiley & Sons, Ltd. Published 2014 by John Wiley & Sons, Ltd.

Great Floods

In late July of 2010, the monsoon rains came in torrents in Pakistan and did not let up for weeks. As the rain continued to fall steadily, the water behind thousands of dams and embankments in the Indus River Basin rose and tens of millions of people in small towns and big cities across the region all nervously watched the water inch toward a point of crisis. At last, the water spilled over levees (earthen embankments) on the river, which hold the water back from populated areas, and water poured across cities and farms. At the height of the water, almost 800,000 square kilometers, or one-fifth of Pakistan's land area, was underwater. The Great Pakistani floods of 2010 killed thousands of people, displaced hundreds of thousands, left 6 million people without access to clean water, and did more than $40 billion of damage to infrastructure and crops.

The event was certainly unusual. The record rainfall of that summer was many times higher than average and achieved flood levels seen only every 100 years in some parts of the region.

On the other hand, flooding of the Indus River is by no means unprecedented. Starting in the late nineteenth century, engineers have gone to great lengths to manage and control the river, with complex systems of diversion and engineering. That system was designed, however, to maximize the productivity of the system for farming, decreasing the risk of year-to-year flooding so that cash crop agriculture might thrive. As geographer Majed Akhter points out, the labyrinth of dikes and canals constructed in the Indus system slowly raised the elevation of its canal-beds, making the system as a whole more vulnerable to large-scale flooding (Akhter, 2012). The effort to reduce short-term risk for crops actually increased the long-term risk of catastrophic flooding.

Nor is this unique to Pakistan. In the United States, the Mississippi River Commission was charged with controlling that vast and unpredictable river, and chose a "levees only" policy rather than maintaining wetland floodplains or encouraging river outlets to absorb catastrophic flows. Seeing the folly of such an approach, Mark Twain wrote in his 1896 book *Life on the Mississippi*: "ten thousand River Commissions . . . cannot tame that lawless stream, cannot curb it or confine it, cannot say to it, Go here, or Go there, and make it obey; cannot save a shore which it has sentenced; cannot bar its path with an obstruction which it will not tear down, dance over, and laugh at" (Twain 1981: 138). His words were prophetic; in 1927 the Mississippi overflowed its banks, broke its levees, and flooded 27,000 square miles, only a year after the Commission and the US Army Corps of engineers predicted that the levees would hold forever. It happened again in 1993.

Given what we know about the Indus and Mississippi Rivers, were these Great Floods unpredictable? Were they caused by underinvestment in levees and other infrastructure? Or did over-engineering the rivers exacerbate the crisis? Or were these events turned from relatively benign weather episodes into national disasters by poor floodplain decisions that put settlers and property into the inevitable path of periodic high water, letting people build and live in dangerous places? How do you plan for disasters that you cannot predict? Who should pay for the restoration of the land? Those who live there and took "irrational" risks? City dwellers who ate cheap food off that land for a century, enjoying the benefits of floodplain development without exposing themselves to a hazard? The governments that subsidized growth in these places while investing little into mitigating possible disaster? How does society adjust to a chaotic, more-than-human world in a way that is socially just and environmentally sustainable? These are the questions that come to our attention when we choose to think about the environment as a hazard and to consider social relationships to nature as management of the constant risks that the non-human world inevitably presents.

Environments as Hazard

Hazard   An object, condition, or process that threatens individuals and society in terms of production or reproduction

Risk   The known (or estimated) probability that a hazard-related decision will have a negative consequence

For those who examine the environment in this way, a set of three clarifying concepts help us sort out problems in the world: hazard, risk, and uncertainty. A **hazard** is a thing (e.g., ultraviolet (UV) radiation in sunlight), a condition (e.g., periodic flooding of a river), or a process (e.g., nitrification of water) that threatens individuals and society in terms of production (making a living) or reproduction (being alive). Hazards are real, essentially inevitable, and intricately linked with the boons and benefits that people and societies accrue from nature and technology. The South Asian monsoon supports the entire summer food crop of the region but its periodic failure leads to catastrophic drought while heavy rainfall leads to flooding and loss of life. Nuclear power supplies roughly 20 percent of electrical power in the United States but its production facilities are vulnerable to dangerous failures and its waste by-products are hazardous for thousands of years. Thus, hazards are merely the negative potentials of all things; they can be described, quantified, and discovered over time.

Of course, not all hazards are "natural," insofar as many hazardous things are entirely anthropogenic (human caused), including chemicals like DDT or processes like nuclear power. Most hazards fall in between natural and anthropogenic, since the influence of human practices on environmental systems and the impact that these systems have on human behaviors often make such distinctions irrelevant. In either case, an understanding of the character of the environment as a hazard allows people, governments, and firms to make informed decisions about how to deal with these socio-natures.

The fact that many of these problems are intermittent or not entirely predictable makes coping with them more difficult, however. Droughts (periods with sub-average rainfall) can pose a risk for crops, for example, but do not occur every year. Do we plan pessimistically, assume a state of perpetual drought, and dampen our overall production? Do we ignore the hazard altogether and proceed ahead with our fingers crossed? Or can we develop some middle path, where we hope for the best, but create contingency plans for the worst?

Decisions as risk

Deciding between such alternatives is to make decisions based on **risk**, which is understood as the known (or estimated) probability that a hazard-related decision will have a negative consequence. All decisions have some risk, but some risks are miniscule and others enormous. The chance of rolling snake-eyes (a pair of ones) on two dice is 1 in 36, meaning that on average, you will fail to roll it 35 out of 36 times you throw the dice. This is not a problem if you have no stake in the outcome. Betting your life savings on such a roll is a considerable risk, however. Wagering your savings on the roll of a seven, which occurs 1 in 6 times, is a better bet (though the authors recommend against it). Dealing with the environment in this light, decisions can be calculated in terms of the probability of success or failure and of good or bad outcomes.

There is always risk, for example, in planting a rain-fed crop, because droughts are always possible. In some areas, however, droughts are so infrequent as to present a minimal risk. In other areas, they are common enough for farmers to make creative adaptations to lower their exposure to the risk of crop failure by planting drought-resistant varieties mixed in with their regular crops. These adaptations may be more expensive than business-as-usual and so yield less profit from year to year, but they minimize the probability of total disaster. Such ingenious risk-averse farming adaptations to drought are common in most arid and semi-arid parts of the world.

The geographer Gilbert F. White pioneered the effort to manage risk in floodplain management. White was a public servant in a number of Depression-era federal agencies asked by Franklin Roosevelt to assess the management of the Mississippi, still reeling from the events of 1927. Studying the problem, White concluded that it was the single-minded focus on engineered solutions (levees and river constraints) that was at the root of the problem, and that "multiple adjustments" to flood problems needed to be devised for local conditions. These multiple adjustments would take into account the specific risks posed by different parts of the problem. This included social aspects, including insurance subsidies for people living in floodplains, poor information on periodicity and location of flood hazards, bad evacuation planning, sloppy zoning, and badly managed relief systems. The river, he essentially concluded, is prone to flooding. So the question becomes: How can people working and living in and around this river accept this fact more rationally? These conclusions were discussed in his later dissertation, *Human Adjustment to Floods: A Geographical Approach to the Flood Problem in the United States* (White 1945), which is now a classic work of environment–society research.

Given the more recent flood disasters in places where resources are abundantly available, including Hurricane Katrina in the United States in 2005 and the disastrous flooding in the United Kingdom in winter 2003, for example, and leaving aside the horrific flooding catastrophes in the developing world in recent years, it is not clear that White's recommendations have ever been heeded fully. What sort of risk assessment was performed for determining federal and state investments in levees in New Orleans? Were the levels of commitment concomitant with the levels of risk? How might "multiple adjustments" yet be brought to bear for decision-making on the Mississippi?

By understanding environment as hazard and decision as risk, creative and improved decisions might yet be made, assuming you can calculate and consider exposure to risk by knowing with some certainty the probability, frequency, and/or severity of hazards.

Environmental conditions as uncertain

> **Uncertainty** The degree to which the outcomes of a decision or situation are unknown
>
> **Risk Perception** A phenomenon, and related field of study, describing the tendency of people to evaluate the hazardousness of a situation or decision in not-always-rational terms, depending on individual biases, culture, or human tendencies

Risk must be distinguished from **uncertainty**, however, which is a condition describing the degree to which the outcomes of a decision or situation are *unknown*. Uncertainty plagues most risk calculations and its sources are numerous.

The first source of uncertainty comes from the highly uneven or unstable behavior of many environmental systems over time. People may base their decisions about water supplies, for example, on the fact that a serious drought has occurred once every 20 years in the past century. But this time frame may not be typical. What if droughts are far more common (perhaps twice a decade) over the past thousand years, and the period of the past century, upon which people are making decisions, is anomalous? Such was the case with the Colorado River Compact, the formal legal charter by which states in the western United States divided up their shares of Colorado River water in 1922. That document was written and signed during a period of unusually high rainfall and high water flow, and so it underestimated the risk of "severe drought," a condition now known to be more common to the region than ever assumed. As a result, the river is constantly *over-allocated*: the states together have legal rights to more water than physically exists in most years!

Uncertainty can also come from encounters with new hazards, for which no meaningful experience exists to help assess risks. This is especially true of technological hazards. The dawn of petrochemical pesticides in the 1930s, for example, led to decisions like the widespread use of DDT, a chemical whose accumulation in the tissues of wildlife led to the decline of many species, especially of birds. Bans and controls were imposed far later, long after their effects were felt. Thus, uncertainty affects risk calculation and draws a veil over human knowledge of complex natural systems. New information can improve risk decisions by increasing what people know, but some degree of uncertainty is inevitable.

The Problem of Risk Perception

Risk decisions are not only hindered by objective uncertainty, according to students of hazards. They are further complicated by structured biases in the way human beings subjectively tend to see and calculate risk. Examining the behavior, opinions, and psychological characteristics of real people, researchers in the field of **risk perception** have demonstrated that the real or measurable risks of some decisions are sometimes far overestimated or underestimated in daily life. This has important implications for more rational management of hazards.

While the level of physical risk to individuals, for example, is far higher for every mile traveled by car than by aircraft, people overwhelmingly fear aircraft travel more. Fears of vaccination and of fluoridation of water are commonplace, though their statistical impact on health and role in annual injury rates may be lower than that of power lawnmowers, about which people express little or no concern. *Why?*

Box 6.1   Environmental Solution? Insuring for Climate Change

Most global industries have been slow to respond to, or even acknowledge, global climate change. There are good reasons for this. Changing production systems to mitigate climate change by greening the workplace, using alternative energy sources, and creating products with lower climate footprint can be expensive. Acknowledging climate change can cut into the corporate bottom line.

There are some industries, however, where addressing climate change represents an immediate opportunity to avoid lost revenue, or even to make money. The most notable example is insurance, the world's largest industry, with $4.6 trillion in revenues annually. Insurance is different from other industries since it sells financial products to mitigate risk. Essentially, insurers make the greatest profit when buyers feel a need to protect themselves from risks (like flooding, drought or bad weather), but where these unfortunate events are unlikely to happen. Insurance companies, in other words, need to be able to predict how risky situations are, quantify that risk, and reduce that risk for their buyers wherever possible, so that the insurer collects the most premiums, but pays expensive claims as infrequently as possible.

As such, the insurance industry has a deep interest in understanding, measuring, planning for, and reducing the rate of climate change. This is first because insurers set their rates and calculations based on records from the past, records of decreasing utility in a changing world. If insurers know that a catastrophic flood happens every century, for example, they can calculate how to set rates or whether to insure a high-risk property. But with climate change, the future frequency of these kinds of floods is harder to predict or determine. Insurers need to support good climate science to plan for a changing risk profile. Insurers are also interested in helping their buyers to change their exposure to risk, doing things like protecting their property or using alternative or diverse energy sources, to make them more resilient to changing conditions.

So what is the insurance industry actually doing? First, it is providing new kinds of products to buyers, which favor things like green building practices and decreased energy usage. Insurers worldwide, for example, have introduced 65 different insurance products in the past few years, specifically favoring renewable energy systems. Second, it is paying claims out favorably to buyers who experienced losses (in a major storm, flooding, or drought event) where the buyer rebuilds in a way that is more resilient to future risks, and less likely to suffer losses.

There are, of course, some things that insurance cannot do. Some risks may become so great that insurers will simply no longer cover them. Crop losses in the Midwestern United States, for example, may become so frequent and devastating that insurers may leave that market altogether. So too, insurers have a limited influence on large-scale transformation of national energy systems and transportation networks, which are major drivers of greenhouse gas emissions. Nevertheless, it is clear that thinking about the environment through the lens of financial risk and uncertainty shows that climate change is a major industrial challenge and an opportunity.

Researchers have sought for many decades to scientifically explore these biases in order to explain why poor environmental management and human health decisions persist in the face of better information (and by implication decreasing uncertainty) (Slovic 2000). It is increasingly apparent that many risk-related biases are shared by a large number of people, which suggests deep tendencies in human risk perception.

Hazards that are seen by human beings as involuntary, uncontrollable, and having slow or delayed long-term effects are disproportionately feared by people, relative to those hazards that involve individual and voluntary choices and whose effects are immediate.

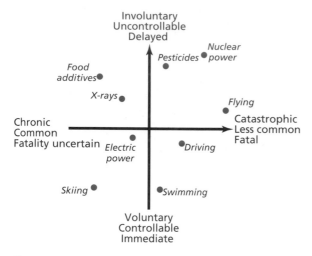

Figure 6.1 Voluntary/Involuntary–Common/Catastrophic: A matrix for explaining what people think is risky and why. Each axis describes the characteristic of a hazard that tends to lead people, however erroneously, to assume it is or is not risky. *Source*: Adapted from Fischhoff et al. (1978).

The automobile, for example, is far more dangerous than the aircraft in terms of chances of accidents and injury per mile traveled, but people tend to minimize their perceived risk of driving, typically because they *feel* artificially safer knowing *they* are behind the wheel rather than someone else. Similarly, those risks viewed as catastrophic, fatal, and high impact, no matter how infrequent or rare, tend to be perceived as disproportionately risky relative to those hazards that are common and chronic. Lawnmowers may claim more victims than nuclear power, but a nuclear meltdown seizes the human imagination far more immediately than any power tool. These tendencies are summarized in Figure 6.1, which shows the results of survey research stressing the way some risks are assessed based on characteristics not linked to actual probabilities of harm or injury.

Such biases in perception, if not offset by informational checks and balances, might lead to poor decision-making in dealing with the environment. Low-probability spectacular events may capture the attention of planners or activists for regulatory action, but the environmental and public health impacts of persistent, chronic, hazards may be equally or more widespread and damaging. Regulation of household pesticides, for example, has been a low priority for citizens and regulators both, in part because it is a "voluntary" behavior, disaggregated in small doses across vast areas. The aggregate effect of these chemicals, however, is increasingly acknowledged to be hazardous to both human health and the health of aquatic ecosystems (Robbins 2007).

Making informed decisions: Risk communication

With this in mind, those who study environmental decision-making from the point of view of risk, instead of stubbornly opposing people's emotional, commonsense ways of seeing the world, have worked in recent years to find ways to take advantage of them. Working in the field of risk communication, they explore different ways of conveying information so that people can draw on their commonsense and emotional ability to decide, while decreasing their uncertainty.

This work has shown that detailed scientific data supplied in copious quantities to citizen decision-makers (lengthy technical reports, for example) does improve people's knowledge somewhat. It has also shown, however, that "values-oriented" information, conveyed in terms of local and personal priorities rather than simply scientific facts, allows people to make tradeoffs and decisions in a way that is more deliberative and that leads to outcomes people tend to be more satisfied with afterwards. Such decisions are, in a sense, more rational than those based only on cold hard facts, because people make them with a more careful view of tradeoffs and competing priorities. In other words, ironically, information that includes emotional and values-oriented components (**affect**) leads to less "affective" or more rationally concluded decisions. The way risk is communicated, it seems, may help counter human tendencies in the perception of environmental hazards, leading to better and more socially and environmentally sustainable decisions (Arvai 2003).

> **Affect**   Emotions and unconscious responses to the world that influence decision-making
>
> **Cultural Theory**   A theoretical framework associated with anthropologist Mary Douglas that stresses the way individual perceptions (of risk, for example) are reinforced by group social dynamics, leading to a few paradigmatic, typical, and discrete ways of seeing and addressing problems

Risk as Culture

There are significant assumptions built into this perspective, of course, worth considering before adopting a "risk perception" approach to dealing with nature. Specifically, in the same way that market approaches to the environment are rooted in the science of economics and its assumptions and methods, risk approaches to the environment are predominantly fixed in the science of psychology, and its associated presuppositions and techniques. The most important of these assumptions is that the objects of scrutiny are individual people and that the tendencies of people are universal: in human psychology, they reflect the effects of cognition and of the deep workings of the human brain.

But to some degree our sense of environmental hazards, risk, and uncertainty is learned. It comes out of school and work environments, from family, and from whether people are rural or urban dwellers, among a range of other influences. A century of research in disciplines like anthropology has demonstrated that many biases, perceptions, and systems of interpreting the natural world are rooted in culture, that is, the system of meanings, concepts, and behaviors that people learn from their peers and surroundings. This raises the question of whether there are universal patterns to our learned biases or whether there are distinct cultures of risk.

In response, one of the most well-known descriptions of these cultural tendencies in risk – referred to as **cultural theory** – explains that human ways of thinking about nature and risk are neither universal (which would mean we all think the same way) nor idiosyncratic (meaning everyone thinks differently). As explained by anthropologist Mary Douglas in her book *Risk and Culture* (Douglas and Wildavsky 1983), the way people think about environmental risk is closely tied to how they think about the place of individuals within society.

Specifically, some cultures tend to stress the degree of free will and latitude of individuals in society, and the universe more generally, than others. Conversely, some cultures acknowledge or emphasize the limits and constraints that are inevitably part of living in nature and society. People in certain cultures hold that individuals tend to be constrained by social and environmental context and circumstance (for better or for worse), while others reject this and stress free agency.

Some cultures also tend to stress the desirability of solidarity and obligation between their members in order to achieve social and environmental stability, stressing the collective in the universe. Conversely, some cultures assemble the world through a notion of individuals as largely isolated and independent in a universe that is relatively robust and indifferent.

People in certain cultures hold strongly that collectives or groups are important or necessary to social stability and success, while others reject this and stress autonomy.

For the purposes of understanding both risk perception and preferred risk management, Douglas argues that each culture also has a specific and extremely distinct way of seeing the behavior and qualities of the non-human world. For some, nature is a resilient system, in which disturbances cause only temporary harm. This encourages an approach to risk that is somewhat open and "trial and error" oriented, with little concern for consequences that may not be far-reaching or permanent. Conversely, others view nature as extremely fragile and vulnerable to perturbation with little chance of recovery. Any disturbance may bring ruin to a balanced system, encouraging a risk management strategy using the "precautionary principle" – to not act without full and comprehensive information.

What does this tell us about dealing with hazards? Contrary to a universal view of risk perception, there is no single structure to human bias. The same information about hazards communicated to members of different communities may be interpreted and used very differently.

Similarly, conflicts over risk management priorities, rather than being explained by a difference between those with a perception bias versus those without one, can be effectively explained by differences between representatives of different risk cultures. In this way, cultural theory offers important insight to differences in the regulation of risk. This holds implications for comparing the regulatory environment in which genetically modified organisms are received, for example. Genetically modified (GM) crops, notably, are species based on existing plants that have been genetically altered to result in higher levels of productivity, resistance to certain diseases, or tolerance to cold and drought. These have not been embraced similarly throughout the world. Compare, for example, the emerging policies in the United Kingdom, where a strong regulation insists on a "precautionary principle" and where no such organisms have yet been allowed to be planted publicly or on a large scale. In the United States, on the other hand, GM crops have been treated largely like other existing varieties, with no particular increase in scrutiny toward their potential, albeit largely unknown, environmental effects. *Neither* of these might necessarily be described as irrational. Rather, these decisions could be understood as the divergence of differing cultures of risk. Critically, these two cultures may not directly reflect those of the national populations at large, but instead only those with the power to control regulation.

At its best, then, this approach provides an interesting contribution. Risk perception is not a universal brain function, but is instead located in culture, can be embedded in institutions (like environmental organizations or government agencies), and is tied to competing priorities of environmental management. Risk perception therefore is, by implication, profoundly *political*.

Beyond Risk: The Political Economy of Hazards

Once we begin to consider the politics of hazards, however, the lens of risk, risk perception, and risk communication becomes somewhat inadequate. This is because:

1   risk is something that is sometimes imposed on others because the risk decision-maker is not the individual or group in control of decisions;
2   even where individuals make risky decisions on their own, their practical range of alternatives already has been severely diminished by political and economic context; and
3   the ability to make informed risk decisions is hampered by the political control, manipulation, and interpretation of crucial information.

Each of these facts suggests that risk analysis is a necessary but insufficient view of society–environment interactions.

Control of decisions – the political economy of environmental justice

A key limit of risk assessment as a technique for better decision-making is that people, groups, and firms often make decisions about risk *for other people*. Consider the problem of toxic hazards and waste. More than 1,300 "superfund" sites (federally identified cleanup locations representing hazards in violation of environmental law) are scheduled for cleanup in the United States (Figure 6.2). Roughly 11 million people (4 million of whom are children) live within a mile of these, with significant related health risks. Those living in and around hazardous sites are far more likely to come from poor and minority communities (Bullard 1990). Certainly some people "choose" to live near such sites, since they are typically lower in rent and have more easily available housing. Nevertheless, most of these sites were created by former businesses, military installations, or municipal services that are long gone, whose owners have benefited from their actions, and who never consulted local communities or people concerning their activities. This represents a situation of environmental injustice, therefore; hazards are distributed unequally over space and throughout society, with a structured bias toward vulnerable populations (see Chapter 7).

We can certainly improve situations like these by providing more and better risk information to people living in and around such sites. But the problems run far deeper. To the degree that the costs of risky decisions are borne by others (and so become **externalities**; see Chapters 3 and 4), there is mismatch between the site of decision and the location of the hazard. This mismatch is deeply ingrained in the political and economic structures of communities, cities, and regions. Reconnecting the risk decision-maker to the hazard, therefore, requires

> **Externality**   The spillover of a cost or benefit, as where industrial activity at a plant leads to pollution off-site that must be paid for by someone else

more than careful or rational analysis of the hazard itself; it demands scrutiny and restructuring of the system of power relations surrounding decision-making.

Constraints on decisions – political economy of the range of choice

Even where people find themselves in control of their risk decision-making, they are by no means in control of the social and ecological constraints that affect their decisions. Consider the case of farmers in drought-stricken West African environments. Observed in a

Figure 6.2   Map of tribal lands and superfund sites. *Source*: Reproduced from http://regionalworkbench.org/renewal_niehs_files/May20_2004/community_outreach.php.

state of crisis in the 1970s and 1980s, when many starved and out-migrated from the region, it might be possible for a naïve observer to argue that the specific weather conditions of the period were entirely unprecedented, that the society was poorly adapted to drought, that its constituent members made poor risk assessments, or – when seeing them pray for rain – that they came from a culture group of Douglas's "fatalists."

Careful examination of the longer history of their situation, however, as geographer Michael Watts (1983) asserted in his essay "On the Poverty of Theory," shows that the rules governing the economy and society of people in the region had been so fully transformed in recent decades as to make "adjustment" to the drought of the period essentially impossible. Specifically, he demonstrates that coping with severe water shortages is an historical trademark of the people of the region, and that only with the onset of colonial rule, and later regional and international commodity trading, did taxation and complex demands for cash in the economy make it hard for farmers to maintain and exchange resources in the face of crisis. In other words, changes in social and economic structures meant that the choices and assets available to farmers were severely reduced in a period of climatic stress. The result was widespread starvation in a region with hundreds of years of successful adaptation to drought.

Can a risk approach improve our understanding of such situations? Certainly, but it must be first acknowledged that the suite of resources available to people and societies facing hazards changes through political and economic processes. Addressing risks means understanding not only the characteristics of the environmental hazard in question, but also the way households, communities, and states are constrained by larger systems. These systems that govern exchange (e.g., commodity prices), access to resources (e.g., credit or social services), obligations (e.g., debt), and power (e.g., autonomy of decision-makers) are themselves part of the socio-environmental risk equation and a simple optimization or calculation of probability is inadequate to address them together (Chapter 7).

Such transformations are also by no means unique to traditional African societies. It could be argued that modern urban culture in places like the United States and the United Kingdom has itself undergone a radical reshaping of its risk landscape. Within the past few decades the traditional economic and political tools available to address risk (like state social services, for example) have decreased, exactly at a time when new risks and hazards (e.g., SARS) stemming from new technologies and interactions are on the horizon. Whole global systems of environmental risk have emerged that are closely linked to financial markets and global social systems. A typhoon in China presents a complex set of problems for financial markets in the United Kingdom, for example, which impinge on available capital for home buyers in the United States, with implications for state resources that set the conditions for levee construction in New Orleans, and so on. Living within such conditions means moving past various simple risk calculations for individual hazards and rethinking the management and distribution of hazards in a political and economic global "risk society" (Beck 1999).

Control of information – the political economy of information

Finally, risk assessment and communication approaches to society–environment interactions have demonstrated the inevitability of uncertainty but cannot resolve how much certainty is required to act. Any decision is inevitably social and political and divergent interests are unlikely to agree. But where elite institutions (large firms, well-organized social classes, governments, or bureaucratic bodies) control the process of deriving and communicating information about risk, there is an inherent tendency to overstate the certainty of current knowledge or to understate how much information is necessary to make an informed decision. Risk decisions are often made, therefore, amidst competing accounts (or constructions – see Chapter 8) of the hazards related to the decision.

Such situations are by no means unusual! They include decision-making around many technological hazards, including nuclear power and nuclear waste. For such cases, uncertainty is inevitable and some kind of risk assessments must be made: to produce nuclear energy, for example, or not; or to bury the waste either in deep permanent storage facilities or in more easily retrievable sites. But many things control and inhibit the interpretation of information in such cases. Commonly, risks are simply miscommunicated or explained in partial terms. Perhaps the most dramatic case was that of risks associated with cigarette smoking, which were long known and proven within the industry, but withheld by tobacco companies only until whistle-blowing former employees risked life and reputation to challenge them, only then leading to the release of the facts (a dramatic conflict made famous by the film *The Insider*).

In a more directly environmental case, tetra-ethyl lead in gasoline was also long known by the gasoline industry in the United States to be terrifically toxic and widespread through fumes. The delay in communicating these risks to the public slowed regulatory response, and only in 1986, after decades of exposure, were alternative additives used to replace the toxin, leading to a 75 percent reduction of lead in the blood levels of people in the United States (Kitman 2000). History has shown that the manufacturers and producers of products that pose these kinds of risks are unlikely to provide full information about these without some consumer or government coercion; after all, it is simply against their commercial interest to do so.

Beyond this, even when a full set of facts are communicated to citizens and consumers, exactly analogous to the information that government experts or private firms possess, there may be disagreements over the degree to which the current level of certainty is sufficient to act (Shrader-Frechette 1993). The incentives and benefits for decision-makers and firms to resolve debate quickly and to act are high, and therefore they have an interest in diminishing (or underplaying) uncertainty. The difference between state regulators/power companies who may seek to develop nuclear waste and related waste storage, for example, and average citizens who may invoke precaution, may not be simply "cultural" in the sense Douglas suggests, therefore. It may instead reflect fundamental differences in where each group sits in a complex political economy. Both can make rational risk decisions and still not agree. Risk assessment can no more resolve such differences than it can change the nature of bureaucratic government or the capitalist economy. Though a powerful tool, the limits of a risk perspective are essential to acknowledge.

Thinking with Hazards and Risk

In this chapter we learned that:

- By thinking about environmental problems as hazards, it is possible to more rationally consider and weigh risks.
- Risk is understood as the known (or estimated) probability that a decision will have a negative consequence.
- This is different than uncertainty, which surrounds all of the possible unknown characteristics of a hazard.
- One of the problems with assessing risk is that people's perception and estimation of risk is not fully rational and is influenced by emotion or affect.

- Indeed, differing communities or groups of people may have cultural predispositions for thinking about risks in different ways, and assigning responsibility for risk to different parties (like individuals or the government).
- Because individuals and groups are differentially exposed to risk owing to conditions beyond their control (like poverty and low political or social status), risk and hazard approaches to the environment are best considered within political and economic frameworks.

Questions for Review

1. Using the example of hurricanes, support the statement (from page 84) that "most hazards fall in between natural and anthropogenic."
2. To what degree are your perceptions of risk similar to, or different from, those of the culture around you? Support your answer with some specific examples.
3. Residents and governments of Europe have been much more critical of genetically modified crops and foods than have residents and governments of the United States. To what degree is this a cultural difference? (Bonus: Supplement your answer using political economy.)
4. Why do toxic-waste dumps usually represent examples of environmental injustice? (Think: Who chooses to live near a toxic-waste dump?)

Exercise 6.1   Evaluating Risk

You have a choice of three different possible residences in the same town. The characteristics of the three possibilities are as follows:

	Choice 1	Choice 2	Choice 3
Risk	No flood	250-year floodplain	50-year floodplain
Benefits	No river view/access	River view	River view and access
Time to pay off	8 years	15 years	30 years

Property #3 is subject to a devastating flood every 50 years, an event that can destroy your house and all of your property. Property #2 can be subject to similar flooding, but only once every 250 years. On the other hand, there is no risk of flooding to property #1.

Property #3 has a beautiful view of the river and private access to swimming and boating. Property #2 has a good river view, but no direct access to the water. Property #1 has neither a river view nor access to the river.

Property #3 will take you 30 years to pay off, while property #2 will take you 15 years. Property #1 can be paid off in 8 years.

Which property would you choose and why? Compare your decision with your classmates' choices. Are they the same or different? Do you think that the differences in decisions are based on your personal backgrounds, cultures, or other factors? How would you mitigate some of the negative possibilities of your decision (either lack of amenities or high risk)?

If you chose *x*, what might make you choose *y* instead?

Exercise 6.2   Labeling Risk

Examine the list of precautions and risks on the label of an over-the-counter insecticide or herbicide (check one out at your local home and garden shop if you do not have any at home). How would this list differ in the absence of governmental regulations? To what degree do you believe this information impacts consumer and user decisions? Why?

Exercise 6.3   Mapping Risk

Visit the World Resources Institute "Aqueduct" page, where risks of water stress are mapped in an interactive digital atlas (http://insights.wri.org/aqueduct/atlas). Explore the global maps they provide there. Spcifically compare two different global maps: 1) the map of "Baseline Water Stress" (a map of the degree to which freshwater availability is an ongoing concern) and 2) the map of "Three Year Socioeconomic Drought" (a map of areas where available freshwater supplies are insufficient to support normal water withdrawals over a three-year period). To what degree is the risk of socioeconomic drought a close match to basic underlying water stress and scarcity? Where is the risk of drought less than underlying stress and where is it equal to or greater than basic stress? What might account for the differences you see here? What might cause drought risks to be higher or lower than basic scarcity of water? What might this tell you about environmental risks more generally? To what degree are they determined by basic environmental conditions and to what degree are they influenced by human factors?

References

Akhter, M. (2012). "Floods are not (just) natural." *Tanqueed*, December 9.

Arvai, J. (2003). "Testing alternative decision approaches for identifying cleanup priorities at contaminated sites." *Environmental Science and Technology* 37(8): 1469–76.

Beck, U. (1999). *World Risk Society*. Oxford: Blackwell.

Bullard, R. D. (1990). *Dumping in Dixie: Race, Class, and Environmental Quality*. Boulder, CO: Westview Press.

Douglas, M., and A. Wildavsky (1983). *Risk and Culture: An Essay on the Selection of Technological and Environmental Dangers*. Berkeley, CA: University of California Press.

Fischhoff, B., P. Slovic, et al. (1978). "How safe is safe enough? A psychometric study of attitudes towards technological risks and benefits." *Policy Sciences* 9(2): 127–52.

Kitman, J. L. (2000). "The secret history of lead." *The Nation* March 20: 11–30.

Robbins, P. (2007). *Lawn People: How Grasses, Weeds, and Chemicals Make Us Who We Are*. Philadelphia, PA: Temple University Press.

Shrader-Frechette, K. S. (1993). *Burying Uncertainty: Risk and the Case Against Geological Disposal of Nuclear Waste*. Berkeley, CA: University of California Press.

Slovic, P. (2000). *The Perception of Risk*. London: Earthscan.

Twain, M. (1981). *Life on the Mississippi*. New York: Bantam Books.

Watts, M. J. (1983). "On the poverty of theory: Natural hazards research in context." In K. Hewitt (ed.) *Interpretations of Calamity*. Boston, MA: Allen & Unwin, pp. 231–62.

White, G. F. (1945). *Human Adjustments to Floods: A Geographical Approach to the Flood Problem in the United States*. Chicago, IL: University of Chicago, Dept. of Geography, Research paper no. 29.

Suggested Reading

Beck, U. (1992). *Risk Society: Towards a New Modernity*. London: Sage.

Bostrom, A. (2003). "Future risk communication." *Futures* 35: 553–73.

Jasanoff, S. (1999). "The songlines of risk." *Environmental Values* 8(2): 135–52.

Johnson, B. B., and C. Chess (2006). "From the inside out: Environmental agency views about communications with the public." *Risk Analysis* 26(5): 1395–407.

Kasperson, R. E., D. Golding, et al. (1992). "Social distrust as a factor in siting hazardous facilities and communicating risks." *Journal of Social Issues* 48(4): 161–87.

Rissler, J., and M. Mellon (1996). *The Ecological Risks of Engineered Crops*. Cambridge, MA: The MIT Press.

7

Political Economy

Source: Sergey Nivens/Shutterstock.

Chapter Menu

Keywords

- Anthropocentrism
- Commodification
- Commodity
- Conditions of production
- Eco-feminism
- Environmental justice
- First contradiction of capitalism
- Globalization
- Means of production
- Overaccumulation
- Primitive accumulation
- Production of nature
- Relations of production
- Second contradiction of capitalism
- Social reproduction
- Spatial fix
- Superfund
- Surplus value

Environment and Society: A Critical Introduction, Second Edition. Paul Robbins, John Hintz, and Sarah A. Moore.
© 2014 John Wiley & Sons, Ltd. Published 2014 by John Wiley & Sons, Ltd.

The Strange Logic of "Under-pollution"

"'Dirty' Industries: Just between you and me, shouldn't the World Bank be encouraging MORE migration of the dirty industries to the LDC [Lesser Developed Countries]?"

In December 1991 World Bank Chief Economist Lawrence Summers (now economic advisor to US President Barack Obama) sent a memo with the quote above as the subject line. In the body of the memo, he laid out his argument for why it would be more efficient and cost-effective to export polluting industries to poorer countries. First, because wage structures are lowest in less developed countries, pollution would mean fewer losses in earnings due to morbidity and mortality. That is to say, because workers in poor countries are generally paid less, if they became ill or died because of pollution, the economy would suffer fewer losses to potential earnings than if the equivalent happened in more developed areas. Second, he argued that to his mind, "under-populated countries in Africa are vastly UNDER-polluted." In other words, some countries were not absorbing their fair share of global pollution. The real problem here was that, because the effects of "dirty industries" occur in specific places, there was an over-concentration of pollution in more developed countries. This fact, combined with the high cost of moving solid waste from one place to another, Summers argued, "prevented world welfare enhancing trade in air pollution and waste." Finally, he argued that the level of demand for a clean environment for either aesthetic or public health reasons depended on income. Poor people would rather have economic development than a clean environment.

The memo was leaked to a number of environmental groups and outrage ensued. Mr Summers explained that the memo was a sarcastic response to the proposal of a colleague at the Bank. Whether he was being sincere or sarcastic, though, the market logic Summers used is manifest in many of today's green development policies. Take, for example, carbon trading. This form of regulation allows for the production of waste in one place to be absorbed in another using a global exchange of pollution (see Chapters 3 and 9). In such a scheme, industries in the United States, for example, can purchase carbon credits from other firms that are not using their full allotment, so that the pollution created by one company can be "offset" by another. Effectively, we are creating a global trade in air pollution, something that Summers argued for.

Consider, also, the case of international trade in solid waste. While Summers argued that the high cost of solid waste transport would prevent it from occurring on a wide scale, he implies that this would be a more efficient way of managing pollution. Today, we have largely overcome the barriers to a worldwide market in importing and exporting waste. The international waste trade is a multi-billion-dollar business. Millions of tons of hazardous waste are transported across international boundaries every year. Many of these flows are from more developed countries to less developed countries where disposal costs are lower and environmental regulations are more lax or are more likely to go unenforced. In many ways, even if Summers' proposals were not serious, they have come to pass.

In addition to its eerie prescience, the memo raises basic questions about society's relationship to nature. How is it possible to imagine that part of the world is under-polluted?

What kind of economic logic does this require and what drives such reasoning and action?

This chapter presents a perspective on environment and society that helps us to understand how the logic of the memo is an artifact of the modern capitalist world in which we live, with disturbing implications. A political economy approach to understanding environment and society argues that, at base, it is the structure of the economy and the set of power-laden relationships (worker–owner, industrialist–politician) that produce both the environment in which we live and our perceptions of it.

This chapter, therefore, seeks to introduce four basic sets of ideas. First, it aims to summarize the insights of Karl Marx for ecological problems, pointing to the way the capitalist economy is prone to *crisis*, especially ecological crisis. Second, it works to show how the natural world around us might be viewed as *produced*, explaining the strange ways we have come to live in, and consume, nature. Third, it explains how the economy attempts to resolve the problems and crises it has created by increasingly globalizing and exporting both production and waste, showing how *uneven development* and unevenly distributed environmental problems are symptoms of the contemporary economy. Finally, it shows how movements to protect the environment, as in **environmental justice** or antitoxins activism, are often rooted in issues surrounding *social reproduction*, with implications for gender and environmental action.

> **Environmental Justice**   A principle, as well as a body of thought and research, stressing the need for equitable distribution of environmental goods (parks, clean air, healthful working conditions) and environmental bads (pollution, hazards, waste) between people, no matter their race, ethnicity, or gender. Conversely, environmental injustice describes a condition where unhealthful or dangerous conditions are disproportionately proximate to minority communities

Labor, Accumulation, and Crisis

Karl Marx, an economic philosopher of the nineteenth century, was one of the most influential scholars to study the relationship between political, economic, and social systems. While he said relatively little about nature directly, many have extended his analysis to explore the role that natural systems play in society. This section will describe some of the most salient tenets of this analysis and then discuss how these can be extended to understand contemporary relationships between environment and society. While much of the terminology of this theory may seem specialized and abstract, the basic concepts are universal and familiar. The most relevant concepts that we can draw from Marx for understanding nature–society relations are labor, accumulation, contradiction, and crisis. These elements, Marx explains, are all part of different economies throughout history (medieval feudalism, for example, or modern capitalism born during the industrial revolution), but they relate to one another differently in differing eras. In today's "modern capitalism" these elements are basically arranged so that:

- people's *labor* is sold on a market;
- which allows for the *accumulation* of capital by a small number of individuals;
- this creates *contradictions* since capital becomes over-concentrated;
- which leads to disruptive financial and ecological *crises*.

In other words, in political economy, environmental problems are already built into the economy.

Labor

The key component of Marx's thought is the role of labor in integrating nature and society. For Marx, when people mix their labor with the resources of the natural world to make a living, nature and society become bound together inextricably. In everything we use and consume, therefore, in every **commodity** (running shoes, laptop computers, golf lessons, pizzas, carpets, handguns) are both the human labor that made the object (or that made the machine that made the object) and the diverse elements of the natural world of which it is comprised. The table you are sitting at while reading this book is obviously made of wood (from trees) or plastic (from petroleum), screws (from steel and therefore iron), and shellac (derived from insect resin). But it also contains all of the human labor necessary to bring those elements together and combine them into a single object. Anyone who has ever tried to make their own furniture recognizes that there is both lumber and sweat in every such object. Labor is the act of altering nature and bringing it into the process of making the human world.

In a modern economy very few people own their own business and equipment, and very few have access to raw materials like oil or iron. Most people work for someone else, someone who owns the machinery, computers, equipment or factories (called the **means of production**) and who secures the natural raw materials (called the **conditions of production**). Put another way, in the capitalist system of today, some people (workers) *sell their "labor power"* to other people (capitalists) who put it to use however they please. They then combine the labor of these workers with raw materials and machinery to produce commodities. These objects are then sold to consumers. Usually, these consumers are also workers themselves, which means they are actually buying back the products of their own hard work.

Capitalists take a share of this sale, the **surplus value**, and keep it for themselves (otherwise what's the point of owning a factory?) and pay the worker what is left over, perhaps setting aside some of the surplus to maintain or invest in the conditions of production: planting new trees to replace those cut down, for example. Crucially, if workers are paid the full value of their labor or natural systems are reinvigorated at the same rate they are drawn down, there is little or nothing left for the capitalist. Capitalists have to "underpay" labor and/or nature or there cannot be capitalism. This presents a fundamental challenge to the social or ecological sustainability of capitalism (Figure 7.1).

Commodity An object of economic value that is valued generically, rather than as a specific object (example: pork is a commodity, rather than a particular pig). In political economy (and Marxist) thought, an object made for exchange

Means of Production In political economic (and Marxist) thought, the infrastructure, equipment, machinery, etc. required to make things, goods, and commodities

Conditions of Production In political economic (and Marxist) thought, the material or environmental conditions required for a specific economy to function, which may include things as varied as water for use in an industrial process to the health of workers to do the labor

Surplus Value In political economic (and Marxist) thought, the value produced by underpaying labor or over-extracting from the environment, which is accumulated by owners and investors

Figure 7.1 The secret of surplus value, in a nutshell. By the same principle, the environment must be worked harder and underinvested in order to sustain surpluses. The artist, Fred Wright (1907–1984), made panel-cartoons and animated shorts for the United Electrical Workers Union throughout his career. *Source*: Fred Wright Papers, 1953–1986, UE 13, Archives Service Center, University of Pittsburgh.

Accumulation

Marx viewed capitalism as a relatively new kind of economy, a recent product of the industrial revolution. Previously, people combined their own labor with the natural materials of the world around them and either made all of the goods they needed themselves, or traded with their neighbors to meet their needs. In other words, goods were exchanged for their value as useful things, measured as the value of these objects to the person making and trading the products of their own work. This was possible, at least in part, because people controlled their own means of production (a cobbler owned the basic tools required to make shoes, for example), and the raw materials were largely available in the world around them.

In such a view, there is nothing inevitable about organizing an economy in a way where workers and their products are separated from each other by a market and a bunch of capitalists. It has been organized in other ways in the past and could be organized differently in the future. How, then, did the economy get this way? Why are people forced to sell their labor instead of employing it themselves? How did capitalists come to control the means and the conditions of production?

Looking back at economic history, there are clear periods where it was made more difficult for people to utilize their own labor and to gain access to natural resources. Marx specifically refers to the example of the Enclosure Laws in England. These laws, mostly enacted between 1780 and the 1820s, privatized communal areas and forests and therefore pushed many independent smallholders off of the land. This was an essential building block of modern capitalism, because it not only allowed for a select group of people to own and control the means and conditions of production (in this case, land), but it also took away the ability for people to feed themselves independently. With no land on which to grow food or gather materials to produce goods for trade, many people were left with nothing except their own labor power. They had to sell this labor power in order to survive and were thus forced into wage work. This process of enclosure and appropriating previously communal or free land is sometimes referred to as **primitive accumulation**.

Primitive Accumulation In Marxist thought, the direct appropriation by capitalists of natural resources or goods from communities that historically tend to hold them collectively, as, for example, where the common lands of Britain were enclosed by wealthy elites and the state in the 1700s

Relations of Production In political economic (and Marxist) thought, the social relationships associated with, and necessary for, a specific economy, as serfs/knights are to feudalism and workers/owners are to modern capitalism

From this historical point forward, accumulation would be the central driving imperative of the economy, with serious implications for the environment. Once a set of social relationships like these (described as the **relations of production**) is established between a few people in the world who are capitalists and many people who are wage-earning workers (whether they cut meat, write code for computers, wash cars, sell household products, or perform financial services), a set of imperatives is introduced into the economy. To produce a surplus (and so make a living without applying their own labor to the manufacture of goods), capitalists must keep capital (money that is invested in the system to make more money) in circulation, constantly investing in labor power, in the means of production, and in the conditions of production. Also, since competition between capitalists continues to drive down surpluses over time, capitalists must frantically

1) keep innovating production techniques to squeeze more surplus out of the same amount of labor, 2) keep accelerating the process of buying and selling to maximize the number of profitable transactions, and 3) keep cutting some of the value put back into workers and the environment. These ongoing pressures demand the constant circulation of capital and the continuing expansion of the system, which are both critical for the survival of capitalism and capitalists. This account of the economy as an accelerating treadmill (Foster 2005), constantly racing to keep itself in place and devouring labor and materials to survive, raises further questions about the sustainability of capitalism.

Contradiction and crisis

One can well imagine that such a system might crash if it were faced with a slowdown in buying and selling of goods or a scarcity of resources, or some combination of these. Consider the socioeconomic events of 2008 in the United States and the United Kingdom, a time when resource scarcity (fuel and housing) squeezed the capacity of workers to buy goods (houses, cars, and even food), leading to downturns in the rate of turnover and surplus, leading to further pressure on wages (and massive layoffs) and on nature (aggressive exploration for energy resources in environmentally sensitive areas), resulting in . . . further crisis.

In contrast to a free market theory of the economy (Chapter 3), a political economic approach posits that such crises happen *all the time*, that they are endemic to the modern economy, that they define the history of social and political adjustments of the past two centuries, and that they inevitably lead to perverse and undesirable social and environmental conditions. Though we like to think of such situations as aberrations, as cases where the system has failed to work, in political economy such crises are viewed as an expression of the internal contradictions of the capitalist system itself. Crisis – with layoffs, homelessness, environmental destruction, and firms scrambling to stay in business – is actually the system working.

> **Overaccumulation**   In political economy (and Marxism), a condition in the economy where capital becomes concentrated in very few hands (e.g., wealthy individuals) or firms (e.g., banks), causing economic slowdown and potential socioeconomic crisis

A contradiction is understood to lie at the heart of these crises: **overaccumulation**, the over-concentration of wealth in the hands of a few. On the one hand, accumulation is necessary to the continued expansion of the capitalist system. The more owners earn, the more they can put back into production and the more surplus value they can appropriate. This tends to lead to a concentration of wealth in fewer and fewer hands. On the other hand, accumulation is bad for the system as a whole because it limits the capital available to circulate, especially when a few wealthy people and large firms control most of the capital. Such a condition is certainly evident in the global economy. Exxon Mobil Corporation's 2011 revenues were $486 billion and its net income was $41 billion, making it bigger than most of the economies measured by the World Bank.

This situation of overaccumulation leads to strange symptoms in the economy, crises caused by either overproduction or underconsumption. In the first case, there is simply too much stuff being made to be bought in a reasonable amount of time. This can be due, for example, to improvements in technology that allow for extremely high levels of production, resulting in gluts. Underconsumption, on the other hand, means that consumers are not buying products at a sufficient rate to clear the market. This is generally the result of workers earning insufficient wages to buy all of the goods available to them. This is also unsurprising, especially considering the simultaneous effort on the part of capitalists to keep workers' pay as low as possible when workers are the main body of consumers. Of course, overproduction and underconsumption are two sides of the same coin. The problem is that each product that is not sold or bought represents a value that is no longer circulating through the system.

As crises accelerate, the need to increase production while cutting costs leads to "heroic" efforts on the part of capitalists, companies, and boards of directors, all of which lead down a path of diminishing returns. Massive wage cuts can be introduced or companies can move production and jobs to places where lower wage rates and benefits are normal. But, if you put all of your potential buyers out of work, or pay them lower wages, who will buy your goods? If this happens on a significant scale, the system is in danger of collapsing, bringing about a transition to some other form of economy. This drive to accumulate and its accompanying transformative results are sometimes referred to as the **first contradiction of capitalism**.

Consider, though, that another, related, way to maintain accumulation, aside from placing further stress on workers, is to draw heavily on natural resources, which are often free "common" goods (Chapter 4). What are the implications of trying to forestall a social crisis by igniting an environmental one?

> **First Contradiction of Capitalism**
> In Marxist thought, this describes the tendency for capitalism to eventually undermine the economic conditions for its own perpetuation, through overproduction of commodities, reduction of wages for would-be consumers, etc., predicted to eventually lead to responses by workers to resist capitalism leading to a new form of economy. Compare to the second contradiction of capitalism

The second contradiction

According to the theorist James O'Connor, Marx said only a few things about nature directly, but they have significant implications for environmental sustainability. First, Marx argued that periodic bad environmental conditions can result in an economic crisis. This means that scarcity of raw materials due to drought, hurricane, or other natural disasters might cause a crisis in the production system. If raw materials are unavailable, or simply too expensive to mine or harvest, this means that the costs of producing goods will go up. In turn, production of certain commodities could be reduced, leading to slowdowns in circulation as described above.

More disturbingly, Marx argued that capitalist forms of production/extraction, especially in the areas of agriculture and forestry, were bad for nature in a way that parallels the exploitation of human labor. To maintain surplus, value must be overdrawn from either labor or nature:

> the increase in the productivity and the mobility of labour is purchased at the cost of laying waste and debilitating labour itself. Moreover, all progress in capitalist agriculture is a progress in the art, not only of robbing the worker, but of robbing the soil. (Marx 1990: 638)

The more severely you exploit the land (or workforce), the less able the land (or workforce) will be to sustain production over the long run, again leading to crisis. Rather than thinking of scarcity as a problem caused by rising demand (Malthusian overpopulation – Chapter 2), or as a technical issue to be managed within the system (risk analysis – Chapter 6), or as an inevitable result of the separation between humans and nature (deep ecology – Chapter 5), in this view, scarcity is produced by capitalism, which extracts resources necessary to make commodities. Scarcity, then, is not a natural condition, but one that is created by marketing of nature (as we will discuss in the case of bottled water, Chapter 13). So, capitalism creates its own limits, not only because it changes humans into cogs in a machine, but because it also extends into, and uses up, nature.

If this is true, the environment may present a limit to economic growth. As capitalism relies on the exploitation of nature as a resource, the propensity to destroy nature could be another path toward the disintegration of the economic system and the rise of alternatives. This ecological theory of crisis and social transformation is often referred to as the **second contradiction of capitalism**.

Second Contradiction of Capitalism   In Marxist thought, this describes the tendency for capitalism to eventually undermine the environmental conditions for its own perpetuation, through degradation of natural resources or damage to the health of workers, etc., predicted to eventually lead to environmentalist and workers' movements to resist capitalism, leading to a new form of economy. Compare to the first contradiction of capitalism

Social Reproduction   That part of the economy, especially including household work, that depends on unremunerated labor, but without which the more formal cash economy would suffer and collapse

Summarizing this argument, O'Connor explains that environmental conditions are not just a limit to economic production, but that the pollution of nature by capitalist enterprises also threatens the health and wellbeing of the Earth and the workers who live on it. This leads to a struggle over **social reproduction** (see also below), understood as the process of procuring the basic needs required to keep people healthy and productive. If laborers cannot reproduce themselves effectively, labor power is decreased. Since capitalism is constantly undermining its own conditions to save costs – producing waste, unclean air, bad water, and other conditions that can threaten workers – this is a predictable outcome (recall the incredible 75 percent reduction in blood lead levels after imposing limits on the gas industry, explained in Chapter 6!).

Paychecks, then, are not the only reason for groups to organize against capitalism. Some of the most important contemporary agents of social change are not labor unions, after all, but rather "new social movements." These movements focus on workplace safety, toxic-waste disposal and production, etc. (see the section on environmental justice below). Here, instead of seeking better wages or work conditions, people assert the basic right to a clean environment. These new social movements also differ from more traditional worker movements in that they are often wary of industrial technology, since many new technologies endanger the environment and human health. Rather than look to increased economic and technological development as the answer, then, some new social movements view development as part of the problem (Figure 7.2).

Part of what these new social movements demand, therefore, is a more environmentally friendly way of producing necessary commodities. As new demands are made on the capitalist system to be less polluting, capitalists are no longer allowed to treat nature however they want, and are subject to scrutiny on the part of the public and regulatory bodies. In

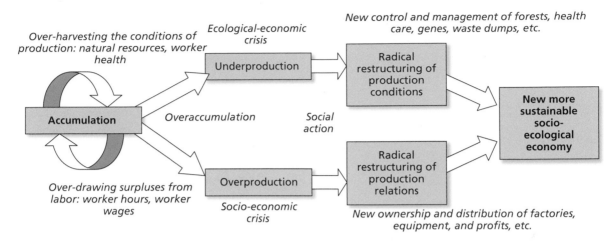

Figure 7.2 Schematic representation of the possible contradictions that capitalism produces and the social and environmental responses they engender, possibly leading the way to a more sustainable and transparent society. *Source*: Adapted from O'Connor (1988).

theory, this new level of public accountability and scrutiny would set us on the path to some other, better, more sustainable and transparent society and economy (O'Connor 1988: 32).

Production of Nature

Given the state of environmental and working conditions, from a political economy perspective it is reasonable to ask why such a rebellion and reformation of the economy has not occurred. While O'Connor sees a high potential for nature to set limits to capitalist production and to incite social action and undermine the system itself, there are other, more pessimistic interpretations of the relationship between the environment and society. Most prominently, the **production of nature** thesis suggests that *nature itself* is often made and remade through economic processes and that people have come to consume it as a commodity.

Geographer Neil Smith (1996) points out a paramount example of this problem. In the 1990s, The Nature Company (most recently acquired and renamed by the Discovery Channel) made significant profits selling petrified wood, butterfly nets, and books on penguins to consumers hungry for green products. Simultaneously, however, the store's parent company was cited as a party responsible for pollution at a **Superfund** site and further violations related to hazardous waste treatment and storage. This appears at first to be simply an unpleasant irony. Smith suggests, however, that it is exactly because nature can be treated as an object of

> **Production of Nature** In political economic thought, the idea that the environment, if it ever did exist separate from people, is now a product of human industry or activity
>
> **Superfund** The environmental program established to address abandoned hazardous waste sites in the United States

consumption – as a commodity – by consumers that social and ecological issues in *production* are disguised, hidden, or forgotten.

Specifically, scholars concerned with the production of nature explore our ideologies of nature. They argue that modern worker/consumers hold two contradictory notions of nature at the same time, which together serve continued exploitation. The first of these ideas is that nature is something *external* to ourselves and society. By seeing human society as separate from nature, we have allowed humanity the apparent right to use it in whatever manner we see fit. In the case of capitalist society, this generally means the exploitation of nature as raw materials for commodity production, or the **commodification** of nature itself. If we want to buy or sell something on the market, after all, we must be able to see it as an object, external to us.

> **Commodification**   The transformation of an object or resource from something valued in and for itself, to something valued generically for exchange. In Marxist thought, the rise of the exchange value of a thing, over its use value

At the same time, however, we hold an *internal* conception of nature that suggests that all humans and non-humans are subject to natural processes. Here, we are internal to nature and therefore at the mercy of its laws. Because of this notion of nature, we view human society and the capitalist system as natural entities guided by the rules of nature. This means that the current state of society is simply an outcome of natural and inevitable rules. By universalizing the economy and society, economic competition and other concepts that are quite specific and recent seem to be timeless and inevitable. This latter view has made it difficult to question the current socio-ecological system or imagine alternatives (see Chapter 8).

These contradictory viewpoints (nature is separate from people/people are part of nature) are the key to understanding capitalist ecology. On one level, as Smith argues, this is realized in the way that "green" companies sell people products aimed at making us feel closer to nature. Nature has been made an object (a bird feeder, a microscope, a remote controlled shark . . .) in order to market it for consumption. At the same time, though, we view this consumption as a way of immersing ourselves in, or taking ourselves back to, nature.

The process of commodification, however, takes other forms. Firms and investors are always trying to commodify nature, in order to maintain accumulation as described before. If natural goods remain free to everyone, there is no potential for profit. But, if someone can claim ownership of a resource, then he or she can charge others for the use of it. The move toward privatization of natural resources like water is a prime example. In Bolivia over the past decade, attempts were made by a multinational corporation, Bechtel, to commodify water delivery. The state would sell the rights to the water supply of the city of Cochabamba to the company, who would, in turn, sell the water to residents through unit pricing. Here, a previously free good, water, having been commodified, becomes a source of accumulation for Bechtel. A political economy approach stresses the degree to which many forms of nature we all share and experience have increasingly come to be commodities we exchange.

Taking the production of nature seriously leads to two conclusions about contemporary environmentalism. First, we should be suspicious of any attempt to use market principles to solve environmental problems, especially those that seek to turn natural materials into tradable goods. Second, we must be critical of any environmental activity or activism that treats nature as external to politics and the economy. Though such activities may be able to save a few key areas of wildlife habitat or impose sanctions on individual companies for polluting, they cannot address head-on the contradictions at the core of the environmental crises that created habitat loss and pollution in the first place: the perverse relationship between nature and society which is inherent to contemporary capitalism.

Instead, according to the production of nature argument, a viable approach to the environment must follow a very different route. First, it must assume the inevitability and creativity of the social relationship with nature. This means that we should surrender to the fact that the nature that we know has been altered through its inevitable entanglement with human labor, and vice versa. We must acknowledge the implausibility of an autonomous nature, something that we might find in an essential and pristine condition, including romantic ideas about maintaining or going back to "wilderness" (see Chapter 8). Only by eschewing this nostalgia is it possible to have meaningful debates over what kinds of produced natures are most desirable.

Second, a production of nature approach means that environmentalism must keep in mind the global system of domination inevitably embodied in the economy. While capital can never fully control nature or people, it will always try. Given the accumulation of power and wealth inherent in capitalism, we must pay attention to the ways human relationships with nature vary among people differently situated in the economy, whether they work in a sweatshop in Indonesia, a rural ranch in Montana, or a grocery store in London. These people differ in their knowledge and experience of nature precisely because they work in different parts of the economy, in different relationships to capital. To create a meaningful environmental movement, these many economic and ecological positions will have to be united, bringing together people from very different places and backgrounds. No small task!

Global Capitalism and the Ecology of Uneven Development

This is made all the more difficult by the spatial strategies employed in capitalist production. Specifically, as Summers' memo suggested, we now have the ability to export hazardous and solid waste internationally, meaning that many of the by-products of the high-consumption lifestyle of the United States are absorbed by poor people half the world away. From the point of view of capitalism, Africa *is* under-polluted, but perhaps, not for long.

To this point, we have largely discussed the growth of capitalism and the contradictions that emerge from it in the developed world. Political economy approaches to the environment–society relationship, though, also help to explain the increasingly global reach of capitalism and its worldwide impacts on people and nature.

The capitalist economic system, as discussed above, requires sustained accumulation of capital and its continued circulation through the system. The ability to create economic growth can be endangered by contradictions inherent in the system itself which lead to periodic crises. Crises usually stem from overproduction and/or underconsumption, as we saw earlier. In either case, goods are not moving quickly enough through the system to sustain accumulation and produce profits. One way to resolve these periodic crises is to use the increasingly global reach of trade to subdivide the world of production and consumption. If workers in your own country are too expensive because of regulation, or if environmental regulations prevent you from getting cheap raw materials, why not move production somewhere else? Alternately, if your workers have already bought all of the goods that they can, why not find new markets abroad?

Spatial Fix   The tendency of capitalism to temporarily solve its inevitable periodic crises by establishing new markets, new resources, and new sites of production in other places

Globalization   An ongoing process by which regional economies, societies, and cultures have become integrated through a globe-spanning network of exchange

Both of these are examples of what geographer David Harvey has called the **spatial fix** (Harvey 1999). The crises caused by the treadmill of accumulation can be avoided, in theory, as long as capitalist production and consumption can be extended to new places around the world. This is the logic that leads to offshoring (the practice of transnational companies (TNCs) who move production facilities abroad) in an attempt to lower production costs and to create new consumers. Often production is moved to countries with fewer labor and environmental regulations. Since the 1970s many North American and European companies have moved production to Latin America and Asia. This has had profound impacts on environmental quality in these regions.

Some have argued, though, that such processes might be good for the host countries. Production means jobs. Jobs mean money. Money equals economic growth. Economic growth means development. Development is good for everyone. This resembles some of the logic behind free market accounts of the relationship between environment and society (Chapter 3). A political economy perspective, however, would raise questions. In addition to questions about the specific quality of life for workers in these new factories and the important environmental issues that arise, critics might take issue with the characterization of development as always and everywhere being a good thing. Development, particularly when measured in terms of economic variables like gross national product (GNP), often means further exploitation of workers and nature. Further, in a capitalist system, development is always uneven. While workers in the system might earn money, it is very little in comparison to the surplus that is flowing back to factory owners. While capitalists from Europe and North America are earning money, hand over fist, the environments of Latin America, Asia, and Africa are being destroyed, privatized, and commodified to further increase profits. Moreover, because international companies are removed from these effects by distance, they have little incentive to protect resources or even to provide for the continued health of their workers. They can always move. Workers and nature become disposable. This pattern is referred to as uneven development (Smith 1984).

It might also be viewed as the foundation of **globalization**, the tendency for economic production and consumption practices to spread to the global scale. This process is a logical extension and result of the spatial fix, since transnational companies often have lower production costs and can drive out more local smaller producers (see Chapter 12). Converging global consumption patterns also follow from this geographic strategy, as for example in the worldwide spread of fast food (see Chapter 14), which has meant increasing demands for industrial-scale food production, usually in the form of single crops that require intensive inputs of pesticides, fertilizers, water, and energy to grow and process, and which leave behind clear-cut forests (Chapter 10) and heavy loads of carbon in the atmosphere (Chapter 9).

Social Reproduction and Nature

All of these externalized environmental damages, whether in the United Kingdom or Mexico, the United States or India, have real impacts on people's daily lives. In this regard, political economy approaches, even as they often focus on the problem of production (how, where, and under what conditions stuff is made), also have an interest in how people live, and are sustained (what is sometimes called social reproduction). To maintain an economy, any economy, its lifeblood must be preserved, after all. This includes natural resources, like air, water, and raw materials, but also, as we saw above, people themselves. The daily lives of people and their families, what Cindi Katz calls the "fleshy, messy, and indeterminate stuff of everyday life" (Katz 2001: 711), are a key part of the political economy of nature. Given that many of society's interactions with the environment are precisely in this sphere (consider: you encounter more wild species in the forms of microbes and bacteria in kitchens and bathrooms than anywhere else in your daily life), the notion of social reproduction is clearly important for a political economy of nature.

For Katz, we can only understand society's relationship to the environment if we come to terms with how people live, how they interact to survive, and how they might work to improve or change the conditions of their lives. The environmental aspects of this sphere of the economy are the conditions in which people live, which can indeed be degraded in pursuit of surpluses. If a company, for example, dumps its toxic wastes in the ground, they have not only harmed the environment, but they have also endangered their workers' abilities to do their jobs (sick workers are less productive). Alternatively, as in the Bolivian case, if water is privatized and commodified, this also limits workers' access to the essential resource. In either case, there are possibilities for environmental change, if people demand that the company clean up pollution or if citizens organize to stop the privatization of water.

Environmental justice

That this kind of collective action does not happen more often, as suggested by the production of nature thesis, may be because people have come to think of the environment as a commodity that can be bought and sold, rather than an intrinsic part of people's daily lives. It may also be a question of the differential spatial impacts of pollution. That is, some people may enjoy the consumption of a commodity produced far away, where the nasty effects of its production are more directly felt.

Environmental justice activists point directly at this problem, and highlight the persistent tendency for environmental hazards, waste, and noxious facilities to be sited in and around minority and low-income communities. The observation that poor, black, and immigrant communities are disproportionately put at risk from exposure to things like lead, silica dust, and pesticides is in fact an old one, with activists in the early twentieth century working in vulnerable communities among people who were most socially and politically disempowered (Gottlieb 1995). Some of the earliest environmental activists in the United States were urban social workers, primarily women, agitating for regulation of dumping and sewage and pressing for reform of public health and safety.

In the past hundred years, evidence has mounted of a simple, reliable, and direct correlation between proximity to dangerous things, like lead smelters and toxic-waste dumps, and race and class. Low-income, black communities are consistently more likely to be close to hazards than whiter, wealthier ones. This spatial correlation between toxic facilities and minority populations was brought to broader public attention in the 1980s by Robert Bullard, who studied the distribution of waste facilities in the American South. In his book *Dumping in Dixie: Race, Class, and Environmental Quality* (1990), he famously concluded that:

> Growing empirical evidence shows that toxic-waste dumps, municipal landfills, garbage incinerators, and similar noxious facilities are not randomly scattered across the American landscape. The siting process has resulted in minority neighborhoods (regardless of class) carrying a greater burden of localized costs than either affluent or poor white neighborhoods. Differential access to power and decision making found among black and white communities also institutionalizes siting disparities.

Though many activist groups and scholars agreed with Bullard's assessment, a debate emerged about whether the phenomenon was based on race or class. That is, are certain people living with toxic waste and other hazards because they are minorities or because they are poor? There is still disagreement on this point today, although it is clear that both are factors. Another debate in the field hinged on the question of whether vulnerable populations lived in certain areas where hazardous facilities were then sited, or if they moved into these areas after the establishment of such facilities, owing to lower housing costs. The answer to that question is, of course, both.

Both of these debates are arguably "red herrings." Rather than arguing about the timing of waste disposal and residential growth, or whether discrimination was based on race or class, it would be more useful to think about how these are related to larger processes of economic growth and disenfranchisement. Whether or not people lived in an area before dumping of hazardous materials occurred, the current structure of land development and ownership means that poor people and minorities were bound to be located in the same, marginal areas. This is partly due to land rents and partly due to the relative power of white wealthy neighborhoods to resist any proposed disposal sites or other toxic facilities near them. This differential ability of some people to resist having hazards dumped in their neighborhoods is sometimes referred to as NIMBYism (Not In My Back Yard-ism). A political economic approach to environmental justice goes beyond this parochial thinking to suggest how differential exposure to hazards is inextricably linked to the economy and the power structures within it.

Gender and the political economy of environmental activism

In addition to questions about class and race, many people interested in environmental justice study the role of gender in environmental politics, reform, and crisis, an approach often referred to as **eco-feminist**. Consider that, in a startling number of cases, protests against hazardous materials have been spearheaded by women. Women make up 60–80 percent of the membership of mainstream environmental organizations, but they figure even more prominently in grassroots organizations addressing environmental health and related issues (Seager 1996). The antitoxins movements of the past half century, by and large, have been dominated by women, including high-profile scientists like Rachel Carson as well as citizen activists like Lois Gibbs and Erin Brockovich.

Eco-feminism   Any of a number of theories critical of the role of patriarchal society for degrading both the natural environment and the social condition of women

Why would this be? Many argue that since responsibility for the health and maintenance of the household traditionally falls to women in many cultures, they are the first to notice, and act to oppose, environmental dangers that are products of capitalist production (water, air, and soil pollution that affect human health, for example). This position in the household is not, however, based on any inherent characteristics of women. Rather, it is a social circumstance with roots in the modern economic system. Historically, capitalism exploited people's labor in the workplace but also their labor at home. Someone had to work to produce the workers, after all. While historically men were taken out of the domestic sphere to perform wage work, women were left in the home and given the responsibility to provide food, clothing, and other basic (reproductive) necessities for the entire household.

At the same time, however, and as a painful irony, the opinions, observations, and concerns of women in this capacity have been at times woefully overlooked by experts. Women often launch initial complaints about what are only later acknowledged to be major environmental crises.

The watershed case of Love Canal is exemplary. Between 1942 and 1952, the Hooker Chemical Company of New York dumped more than 20,000 tons of hazardous materials, including highly toxic chlorinated hydrocarbons, in a clay-lined canal in this Niagara Falls neighborhood. When Hooker was done, they covered the site with dirt. Years later, the local school board obtained the property and built on the site. By the late 1970s, health problems were rife throughout the community, including epilepsy, asthma, and urinary tract infections, as well as miscarriages and a range of birth defects.

Seeking a thorough investigation of this crisis, Lois Gibbs, a local woman with no previous political experience, brought national attention to the problem through direct activism, protest, and wrangling with state authorities. Women activists were dismissed as "hysterical housewives." This characterization, by the media and by the companies involved in dumping, was used to argue that the women activists lacked sufficient knowledge, expertise, or rational judgment (Seager 1996). Nevertheless, their efforts resulted in a full disclosure of problems at the site, an evacuation of residents, and a federal cleanup.

Love Canal established several critical precedents and made a symbolic international breakthrough as a result: 1) average middle-class citizens might be exposed to extremely hazardous materials in and around their homes, 2) companies free to operate outside of serious scrutiny have the capacity to put enormous numbers of people at risk with little legal recourse or transparency, 3) citizen activism can galvanize national attention and support on environmental problems through direct action, and 4) women often represent the central leadership on issues of environmental justice. More radically, the case paved the way for a comprehensive revision of how one might think about risk and responsibility in environmental law.

As a result, these become struggles not just about pollution, but also about expert knowledge. Traditional scientific understandings of nature pride themselves on objectivity and an external relationship to nature. This scientism is challenged by activists, often women, who hold more experiential views of what types of environmental problems society faces. This kind of relationship to the environment means that women often notice subtle changes in the environment (often ones that affect the health of loved ones and community members) that may be missed by big environmental groups more concerned with issues like wilderness or biodiversity preservation. Environmentalism, in this sense, needs to be a political economic movement.

Box 7.1   Environmental Solution? Joint and Several Liability

In the years after Love Canal (see above), defenders of the responsible chemical company insisted that they gave warning concerning the presence of the chemicals to the local officials and so the company should not be held liable. Nonetheless, it is clear that many local people are not well versed in issues surrounding hazardous waste and that the chemical company might well still be accountable for producing the hazard in the first place. A central problem, therefore, lies beyond the horrors of exposure to toxic chemicals; it lies in determining which actors are responsible for a complex history of environmental destruction.

Who is legally liable for damages and human health problems and who is responsible for cleaning up messes? The question is often whether or not liability ceases when a contaminated property changes hands, or when materials are handed off to transporters or buyers, whether or not there has been disclosure of risks. At the time of the Love Canal case, and to this day in many places around the world, these matters are not clear in law. Since hazardous materials can change hands many times, passing from the producer, to a transporter, to the owner of a dumpsite, and then on to the buyer of that site at a later time, the liability for waste can be widely distributed. The complex circula-

tion of hazards in complex national and international economy makes it very easy for responsible parties to claim ignorance or "point fingers" at other players in the complex chain.

This messy labyrinth was navigated in the United States by the landmark passage in 1980 of the Comprehensive Environmental Response, Compensation, and Liability Act (CERCLA – sometimes known as Superfund). That law insists on "joint, strict, and several" liability, which means all of the parties involved are responsible, creating a serious disincentive for any such dumping in the future, since once a mess is in the ground, its creator is in part responsible for it, no matter who buys the land, under whatever circumstances.

The importance of this legal innovation (and hundreds of similar laws around the world) is that it acknowledges and directs legal power at the economic exchanges that sit at the heart of many environmental problems. In most cases, environmental damage is an externality of production and exchange and, as the economy accelerates and expands, hazardous activities expand over time and space, enrolling more and more players. Joint and several liability is a legal tool that casts a political economic net around runaway hazardous activities.

Environments and Economism

Such an analysis of environmentalism is compelling, because it causes us to think rather differently about environment and society. By exploring the relationship between nature and capitalist production, such approaches open up new areas for regulation, possibilities for environmental organization, and grounds upon which to be skeptical of the claims of neo-Malthusians (Chapter 2), free market evangelists (Chapter 3), and institutionalists (Chapter 4). While this certainly opens new paths to understanding environment and society, there are potential pitfalls.

Specifically, political economy approaches risk the extremely **anthropocentric** view of nature solely as a resource for production and social reproduction (with its attendant limits, as per Chapter 5). By tying together the society and environment through the analysis of economic processes, this approach makes other ways

> **Anthropocentrism**   An ethical standpoint that views humans as the central factor in considerations of right and wrong action in and toward nature (compare to ecocentrism)

of thinking about non-humans (in terms of animal rights, for example) difficult. By declaring the environmental movement ineffectively "bourgeois" in its unwillingness to confront the economy, for example, this perspective abandons some avenues of politically organizing around the interest of non-humans. This closes down an enormous number of potential allies and regulatory approaches for managing nature.

Additionally, there is potential for these approaches to reify the economy, meaning that this way of thinking often treats "capitalism," which is merely an abstract conceptualization of complex relationships, as if it were a solid thing with a concrete existence. This provides less room for seeing or imagining other existing productive social and ecological relationships in the world around us. By pinning all explanations for environmental problems and issues on capitalism, moreover, a range of other causes, relationships, and issues might be left off the table in an effort to solve problems.

In many of its iterations, the political economy approach also defers progress on environmental issues to a point *after* economic ones are solved. We may not be able to afford such a luxury in a time when society faces an enormous range of ecological problems and capitalism shows no immediate sign of vanishing.

Thinking with Political Economy

In this chapter we have learned that:

- An influential school of thought stresses the way politics and economics are merged throughout history and the way human interactions with nature are mostly mediated through work, labor, and the economy.
- By observing the history of economies since the industrial era, the political economy approach concludes that the global economy tends toward accumulation of capital in very few hands, but that it is also highly prone to periodic and spectacular crises.

- The implications of this for the natural environment include the contradictory tendency for the economy to overexploit natural resources, leading to further economic problems but also to the rise of environmental movements.
- A political economy approach also focuses on the way nature becomes commodified and the way it is unevenly developed and degraded.
- It further points toward the way that many of these environmental and economic problems are worked out and experienced in everyday life (or social reproduction), leading to environmental justice movements, often led by women.
- While they are extremely powerful tools for understanding the relationship between nature and society, critics have suggested that these approaches tend to be anthropocentric and economistic.

Questions for Review

1. Using political economy, describe a contemporary common private sector job (say, a nurse at a private hospital or a retail clerk). Include the term "surplus value" in your description.
2. What is primitive accumulation? Why was/is it necessary for the development of capitalism?
3. Why (according to a political economy perspective) do capitalist economies inevitably tend toward crises caused by overaccumulation?
4. Discuss the first and second contradictions of capitalism. Be explicit as to why (again, according to political economy) these are unavoidable contradictions inherent to capitalism.
5. Women's environmental experience and knowledge is sometimes different from that of men, owing to the political economic structures. Describe why this might be so and provide an example.

Exercise 7.1   Is Waste Accidental?

The contemporary economy produces increasing masses of "e-waste" – computer monitors, processors, cell phones, televisions, and other goods that, while still functional, are thrown away or occasionally recycled. These typically become hazards, as they contain mercury and other heavy metals that enter waterways and the ecosystem. A political economy approach to this issue would insist that such planned obsolescence of "e-waste" is not an incidental or accidental product of the system, but instead an essential one. Explain why this might be so. What are the tendencies of capital that make such waste necessary? How is surplus produced so that waste is inevitable? What environmental justice issues might arise in the disposal and recycling of these goods?

Exercise 7.2   Commodity Analysis

Choose something that belongs to you: an article of clothing, a simple device, or a food product. Of what is it assembled? Use internet resources, phone calls, or other detective work to try to trace the origins of at least some of its component elements (the fiber, glue, metals). Where was the object assembled (note that it is very possible that it was assembled in several locations)? Now consider what you paid for the object. How is there a profit in the manufacture and sale of the product? What hidden or externalized environmental costs might allow the object to be made?

Exercise 7.3   Mapping Environmental Justice

Visit EJView, a mapping website of the United States Environmental Protection Agency (http://epamap14.epa.gov/ejmap/entry.html). Experiment with the tool, by entering locations you might find interesting (your home town, your school). At these locations, you can toggle to display sites reporting to the EPA (like monitored Superfund sites), air quality and other emissions. You can also overlay demographics, including percentage of minority population, by census block group or tract. Experiment with these maps, especially examining percentage minority areas and hazardous Superfund sites. Do any patterns emerge that suggest environmental justice issues? If so, how do you think these patterns emerged? What other forms of evidence and analysis might you need to determine the presence or extent of environmental justice problems?

References

Bullard, R. D. (1990). *Dumping in Dixie: Race, Class, and Environmental Quality*. Boulder, CO: Westview Press.

Foster, J. B. (2005). "The treadmill of accumulation: Schnaiberg's environment and Marxian political economy." *Organization and Environment* 18: 7–18.

Harvey, D. (1999). *The Limits to Capital*. London: Verso.

Gottlieb, R. (1995). *Forcing the Spring: The Transformation of the American Environmental Movement*. Washington, DC: Island Press.

Katz, C. (2001). "Vagabond capitalism and the necessity of social reproduction." *Antipode* 33(4): 709–28.

Marx, K. (1990). *Capital: A Critique of Political Economy, Volume I*. New York: Penguin.

O'Connor, J. (1988). "Capitalism, nature, socialism: A theoretical introduction." *Capitalism, Nature, Socialism* 1: 11–38.

Seager, J. (1996). "'Hysterical housewives' and other mad women: Grassroots environmental organizing in the United States." In D. Rocheleau, B. Thomas-Slayter, and E. Wangari (eds.) *Feminist Political Ecology: Global Issues and Local Experiences*. New York: Routledge, pp. 271–83.

Smith, N. (1984). *Uneven Development: Nature, Capital, and the Production of Space*. New York: Blackwell.

Smith, N. (1996). "The production of nature." In G. Robertson, M. Mash, L. Tickner, et al. (eds.) *FutureNatural: Nature/Science/Culture*. New York: Routledge, pp. 35–54.

Suggested Reading

Blum, E. D. (2008). *Love Canal Revisited*. Lawrence: University Press of Kansas.

Harvey, D. (2010). *The Enigma of Capital: And the Crises of Capitalism*. Oxford: Oxford University Press.

Marx, K., and F. Engels (ed. H. L. Parsons) (1994). "Marx and Engels on Ecology." In C. Merchant (ed.) *Ecology: Key Concepts in Critical Theory*. Atlantic Highlands, NJ: Humanities Press.

Perrault, T. (2008). "Popular protest and unpopular policies: State restructuring, resource conflict and social justice in Bolivia." In D. Carruthers (ed.) *Environmental Justice in Latin America*. Cambridge, MA: MIT Press, pp. 239–62.

Robbins, P. (2012). *Political Ecology: A Critical Introduction*. Oxford: Wiley Blackwell.

Wheen, F. (2007). *Marx's Das Kapital: A Biography*. Boston, MA: The Atlantic Monthly Press.

8

Social Construction of Nature

Source: Lane V. Erickson/Shutterstock.

Keywords

- Concept
- Constructivist
- Co-production
- Discourse
- Ideologies
- Narratives
- Nature
- Race
- Relativism
- Signifying practices
- Social construction
- Social context
- Wilderness

Chapter Menu

Environment and Society: A Critical Introduction, Second Edition. Paul Robbins, John Hintz, and Sarah A. Moore.
© 2014 John Wiley & Sons, Ltd. Published 2014 by John Wiley & Sons, Ltd.

Welcome to the Jungle

Imagine the following scenario: You have embarked on the journey of a lifetime!

Perhaps you have a great interest in wild places. Maybe you have canoed the Boundary Waters in Canada, or hiked Scafell Pike in the Lake District of the United Kingdom, or walked part of the Appalachian Trail, Yellowstone, or the Grand Canyon in the United States. Even summers and winters at home may have natural phenomena of interest to you: ice forming on lakes, migrating birds, blooming trees. You may be an avid viewer of nature films, like *March of the Penguins*, or television programs on *Animal Planet*, or maybe you read magazines like *National Geographic*.

For you and people who share an interest in nature, few places captivate the imagination as much as the jungles of Borneo. Borneo is an enormous island in the South Pacific, split between the nations of Malaysia, Indonesia, and tiny Brunei. Many *National Geographic* essays featured Borneo's justifiably famous wildlife – Sumatran rhinoceroses, clouded leopards, pygmy elephants, gaudy birds like hornbills and barbets, and of course the critically endangered orangutan.

And now imagine you get to experience this nature first hand. Arriving in Borneo you fly into Kota Kinabalu, Malaysia, a bustling city of some 700,000 people. From there you take a one and a half hour bus ride, followed by a jeep taxi to your first destination, a remote and rustic inn. You appreciate the authentic feel of the inn. Not only can you sleep under mosquito netting in an open-walled room, but the thatch-roofed inn seems to melt into the surrounding forest. You may also be happy that the people working the inn (cooking, cleaning rooms, serving tea) are all native Borneans – at least, they appear to be.

On your first full day on Borneo, you hire a local guide for a hike deep into the jungle of a nearby national park, hoping to glimpse some of the island's famous wildlife. After a disappointingly long line at the entrance gate to the national park (so many tourists!), your guide zips past the larger bus groups in his jeep and heads all the way up the road into the cloud forest, stopping at a small, nearly unmarked turnout. "This is where we will first hike. You have your binoculars, right?" he reminds you. So you head out onto the trail. After about 15 minutes the sounds of birds, insects, and running water have overtaken the noise of buses on the main park road. People have disappeared from view. At the same time, the trail is surprisingly well maintained, and between your guide, your guidebook, and the interpretive signs (in English, no less!) all along the trail, you feel safe, well informed, and *finally*, your dream come true, deep in the wild jungle of Borneo.

You might recognize that this story relates to some of the themes already presented in this book. There is, for example, a political economy at work here. The bustling ecotourism gives a select few locals an opportunity to make a decent wage working, but at the same time, as more land is set aside in nature reserves, constraints are put on where indigenous people can hunt in the forest. Your choice of vacation destinations – a rustic inn and a national park, rather than a beach resort or cruise ship – is influenced by your personal environmental ethics and belief in the "sustainability" of low-impact ecotourism.

But something more may be at work here too. Many parts of this forest have been inhabited and used by people for many thousands of years. Where did they go? Your experience benefits from the carefully maintained paths and the signs that point out important species or views. Who put them there? While the place you are observing is of course profoundly *natural* – it is extremely remote, has insects, wild animals, and jungle plants – it is also undeniably *social*. Your social priorities determined where you would go and what you might expect. A conscious decision has been made to remove people from the landscape to preserve the jungle's condition for your experience. The helpful signs are scientifically accurate but they also inevitably reflect human and social choices about what (of the literally billions of things you might observe in the forest) is most important.

In this sense, what you see in the forest and what you *think you see* are both influenced by other people. Your ideas about Borneo come from other sources (movies, television, family), just as the Borneo presented to you on your trip combines indigenous and scientific representations of the forest. These ideas, images, and assumptions are all **socially constructed** – made up piece by piece – elsewhere and by other people.

What would it mean, then, to say that the nature that you have long imagined and that you are now experiencing is socially constructed? At first glance, this claim might seem patently absurd. Isn't this as *authentic* as nature gets? A tropical rain forest, a *protected* treasure trove of biodiversity: This is **wilderness**, right? And, as wilderness, must it not be fully separate from its opposite – society?

While the answers to these questions seem self-evident, a **constructivist** perspective starts by looking behind these answers, asking, for example: What unspoken assumptions are buried within the ideas of authenticity, protection, and wilderness? Once we begin to scrutinize our experience of the environment in this way, we begin to see how your nature, and everyone else's, is a product of social processes, beliefs, ideologies, and history.

The "**nature**" in this story – a tropical cloud forest – is socially constructed in at least two ways. First, our *ideas* of "pristine" and "authentic" tropical nature are not simply raw mental images that come into our minds from the air. Rather, our ideas of the tropics as Edenic paradise, our personal valuation of biodiversity, even the idea of wilderness itself: these are all the products of culture, media, education, and the like. But it is more than just our ideas about nature that are social constructs (again: *products of social processes*). The national park itself is a construct, rather than a fragment of raw, asocial nature, captured and protected, frozen in time. The entrance fees, maintained roads, hiking trails, limits on indigenous uses, interpretive exhibits, and forest management practices – all of these together *construct* the very nature that we expect to see when we visit such parks. Even before the park itself was established, the indigenous residents actively managed this area for millennia, selecting plant and animal species, planting and setting fires. Like the pine forests of colonial New England and the rainforests of the Amazon, the cloud forests of Borneo are not simply the end result of the physical processes of brute nature at work. They are, rather, the products

Social Construction Any category, condition, or thing that exists or is understood to have certain characteristics because people socially agree that it does

Wilderness A natural parcel of land, more or less unaffected by human forces; increasingly, wilderness is viewed as a social construction

Constructivist Emphasizing the significance of concepts, ideologies, and social practices to our understanding and making of (literally, *constructing*) the world

Nature The natural world, everything that exists that is not a product of human activity; often put in quotes to designate that it is difficult if not impossible to divvy up the entire world into discrete natural and human components of biophysical processes, a specific physical environment, *and* a long history of human occupation and management.

In this chapter, we will examine what it means to scrutinize our ideas about nature and environmental knowledge, as products of history and social processes, as *social constructs*. A logical place to begin this overview is with an examination of the word "nature" itself.

So You Say It's "Natural"?

As Raymond Williams famously wrote nearly 40 years ago, "nature is perhaps the most complex word in the English language" (Williams 1976: 184). As Williams points out, the word nature has at least three common usages:

(i)   the essential quality and character of something;
(ii)   the inherent force which directs either the world or human beings or both;
(iii)   the material world itself, taken as including or not including human beings.

Since these three definitions are closely related, and tend to overlap in our thinking, discussions of "nature" do not always adequately specify the way in which the term is being used. If we stated, for example, that peasant societies live "closer to nature" than urban ones, are we saying that they are more in touch with some "true human nature" (perhaps that urban dwellers have become removed from)? Or are we saying that they are more moved by natural laws? Or perhaps they have a better sense of these natural laws? Or are they simply closer to material nature itself: soil, rain, and wind? This lack of precision in the use of the word "nature" can lead to confusion and misunderstanding.

Nature presents a further problem. In all of the definitions presented above, and in most common speech and thinking, nature is understood as that state, condition, or quality that is before, separate from, or outside of society, human history, and volition. For example, the first definition provided above describes the assumed timeless, universal, and basic quality of something. Bears eat berries, for example, it's in their nature. Nothing people might say or do is likely to change this underlying and immutable characteristic.

Or so it would seem, anyway. Difficulties ensue when we begin to examine how we arrived at our knowledge of these properties. If we examine our knowledge of these characteristics, hints of society and human history frequently intrude. Even when natural properties of things are derived from authoritative methods (such as the scientific method) or sources (such as texts), for example, these methods and sources themselves rely upon social concepts, constructs, and a **social context**. For scientific facts to exist, for example, scientists must *agree* on the characteristics of the natural world. These characteristics must be described in socially developed languages and words. And these concepts all have histories, moments of invention, and political contexts that make them seem normal and taken for granted, at least for a time. They also have places and periods when they become less stable and convincing.

Social Context   The ensemble of social relations in a particular place at a particular time; includes belief systems, economic relations of production, and institutions of governance

Take the troubled concept of **race**, for example. For well longer than two centuries, it was believed by many educated Westerners to be scientific fact that there were different biological races of humans. By the turn of the twentieth century, many people believed, moreover, that the different races represented different levels of biological evolution. Many people (scientists, clergy, and

> **Race** A set of imaginary categories distinguishing types of people, typically based on skin color or body morphology, which varies significantly between cultures, locations, and periods of history

lay people alike) placed some groups (such as Africans and Australian aborigines) on a "lower level" of evolutionary hierarchy and believed them to be more closely related to apes, that is, *less human*, than others. Such an understanding justified a huge range of ugly historical practices (the slave trade among them) and arbitrary forms of discrimination and oppression. This concept, however appalling to us, was quite convenient for many people for a long time.

Needless to say (or so one would hope), the notion of different biological races of humans has been comprehensively debunked in the past century. Actual evidence of essential racial differences is nonexistent. Genetic analysis has advanced in recent decades, moreover, to demonstrate that similarities between all people, despite superficial outward appearances, are overwhelming. In genetic and physiological terms, there simply are no essential or definitive races of people.

Yet racial categories indeed remain very "real" for many people and places. The racial categories we know, even while they have no natural physical basis, are rooted in a power-laden historical social consensus. Stated another way, supposedly factual information (about the "*nature* of humanity") has been shown to be a thoroughly social construct, one supported by non-innocent concepts and practices, and rooted in a very particular historical context (Western European imperial expansion). More than this, the power of racism as a way to order society has been, at least in part, bolstered by the apparent "naturalness" of racial differences. People did not *appear* to have invented these racial categories (though it turns out they had!); instead the categories seemed to preexist any social decision. The apparent "naturalness" of such social constructions makes the pernicious categories on which they are based harder to challenge.

This raises some important and disturbing questions about what we know to be true about the world and how we come to know it. More than this, it suggests that understanding something as natural, pre-given, and non-social may be problematic in itself and indeed undesirable.

To say that some claim or concept that we think of as "natural" actually might be "socially constructed," therefore, is to ask at least one of the following questions:

1   Is this claim or concept natural, inevitable, timeless, and universal?
2   If not, at what point was it invented? Under what conditions?
3   What are the social, political, or environmental effects of believing that this claim or concept is true, natural, or inevitable?
4   Would we be better off doing away with the concept altogether, or rethinking it in a fundamental way?

Such a set of questions can be applied to a great many things (Hacking 1999), with implications for how we think about problems of the relationships of nature and society.

The social construction of New World natures

Consider the case of "pristine" pre-Columbian America. For hundreds of years, explorers, writers, teachers, politicians, and average people have operated under the assumption that the landscapes of North and South America in the time preceding 1492 were largely unaffected by human activity. They were, in a word: pristine. It was assumed that, while native people certainly used the resources of the land, their relatively small population size and crude tools and technology meant that they had little impact on their environment. Some forms of the argument further suggest that native peoples maintained a land ethic that made their ecological footprint especially light; being closer to nature and more in touch with environmental systems and flows, the impact of the many peoples of the Amazon, the Mississippi, the California coast, and the Yucatan was assumed to be relatively minimal and benign. When Europeans arrived, and from that time forward, they believed themselves to be visitors in, or tamers or invaders of, a wild natural landscape.

Even at the time of initial contact between Europeans and native people, however, there was plenty of evidence to the contrary, including complex land-use patterns, large cleared regions, and effective forest thinning through use of fire. Centuries of historical research and archaeology, moreover, have consistently demonstrated that native impacts were quite heavy in many places as species were aggressively selected, forests were felled, and large areas were planted and burned (Figure 8.1). In Chapter 16, for example, we see that the Incas had long since domesticated potatoes by the time Columbus set foot on the shores of the Americas, and they had fully transformed the mountainous terrain of the Andes in the process, to grow and harvest this food.

If this is true, what made it so hard for Europeans to see, and eventually acknowledge, the facts in front of them? In part, European perceptions were deeply influenced by their biblical notions of the Earth. They placed their Eden, as a real geographic place, on the far side of the Atlantic. The forests, rivers, and plains of the New World appeared to them as unchanged since the time of creation. The facts that many of the forests were carefully cleared by natives for hunting, that the plains were heavily worked cornfields, and that the rivers were rich with silt from the construction of native cities, markets, and monuments could not penetrate the preexisting social construction of nature that settlers carried with them in their Bibles.

As much or more than religion, however, political imagination played a crucial role. European belief in a non-transformed New World nature was perfectly congruent with territorial ambitions. For colonial Spanish, French, and English settlers, a central guiding assumption about the relationship between labor and natural rights was that land and resources are possessed only insofar as they are put to use (see discussion of John Locke in Chapter 5). Unused land was, for Europeans, unowned land, available for improvement under colonial rule. Productive land was expected to look a certain way, like typical farms or managed forests in the Old World. Because of these preconceived notions, lands that had been systematically used and improved by native peoples, before the conquistadores arrived in Vera Cruz, Mexico, came to be defined and designated as "baldios" or "yermas": wastelands. Wasted land was available for improvement, indeed by implication it *demanded* improvement (Sluyter 1999) and therefore appropriation by the colonizers.

Figure 8.1 Though Pacific Northwest forest is "Old Growth," since many of its trees are more than 150 years old, many of these forests are quite young, have been highly disturbed, swept by fire, and impacted by human uses. In this sense, not all Old Growth Forest is "pristine." *Source:* © Ian Grant/Design Pics/Corbis.

This construction of a pristine nature in the Americas made not only systematic land uses, but also complex and productive New World cultures, completely invisible. This was a belief that matched European assumptions about the backwardness of native peoples (and indeed the characteristics of their race, as per above). Contemporary stories that insist Mayan temples or Nazca desert lines had to have been made by space aliens rather than sophisticated native architects do much the same. Either way, the natural conditions of the New World as they were understood by later generations of people were prefigured by a social construction of native landscapes. This social construction helped to establish and justify European rule and rendered the native peoples of the Americas invisible and mute.

The point of examining the social construction of nature in this case is not simply to deny the truth of an incorrect claim (that people had not impacted the land prior to Europeans), although this is, of course, important. It is to ask a further set of questions: If this claim about the Americas is not true, what were the effects of assuming it to be true? How did this claim remain "true" and widely believed even in the face of evidence to the contrary? Whose interests are served by its remaining "true"? Who becomes more powerful and who less powerful in the establishment of a certain set of environmental facts as the "true" ones?

The answers to these questions shed light not only on the history of the Americas but also on how we think about environment–society relations more generally. They suggest that there is a relationship between environmental *knowledge* – which claims and ideas about the state of the environment are known to be true – and environmental *power* – what groups and interests control the environment and its resources. To approach environmental issues from the point of view of the social construction of nature, then, is to question what we know about nature and how we came to know it.

Environmental Discourse

So far we have shown how both a) nature itself (the material world we live in, study, and explain) and b) our knowledge of nature and the world can be understood as socially constructed. Employing the notion of "**discourse**," we can take this understanding further to explain how and why specific ideas of nature come to be normal, taken for granted, or inevitable, when they are not.

> **Discourse** At root, written and spoken communication; thicker deployments of the term acknowledge that statements and texts are not mere representations of a material world, but rather power-embedded constructions that (partially) make the world we live in
>
> **Narrative** A story with a beginning and end; environmental narratives such as "biological evolution" and "the tragedy of the commons" aid our comprehension and construction of the world
>
> **Concept** A single idea, usually captured in a word or a phrase
>
> **Ideologies** Normative, value-laden, worldviews that spell out how the world is and how it ought to be
>
> **Signifying Practices** Modes and methods of representation; the techniques used to tell stories, introduce and define concepts, and communicate ideologies

Geographers Barnes and Duncan (1992: 8) define discourses as "frameworks that embrace particular combinations of narratives, concepts, ideologies, and signifying practices." This definition is a little dense, but its pieces can be made plain. A **narrative** is a story. Examples of environmental narratives include "the tragedy of the commons" (Chapter 4), for example, though there are countless others. In a narrative, there is a story line with a beginning and end. A **concept** is a single idea, usually captured in a word or a phrase. "Carrying capacity" (Chapter 2) is a concept, as is "market" (Chapter 3), or even apparently natural things, like "risk" (Chapter 6) or "forest" (Chapter 10). **Ideologies** are normative, value-laden, worldviews that spell out how the world is and how it ought to be. That all living things have natural rights (Chapter 5) is ideological, as is the notion that people are naturally free and that the role of government is to realize and enable that freedom. **Signifying practices** are modes and methods of representation, the actual techniques used to tell the stories, introduce and define the concepts, and communicate the ideologies: geographic information systems, newspapers, television advertising, scientific papers, are all signifying practices, but there are many more.

Discourses put these elements together into powerful, coherent, mutually supporting frameworks, which are persuasive and tend to stand the test of time. Consider the "tragedy of the commons" from Chapter 4. This discourse has a powerful and ironic story at its core: two herders compete for a common pasture and destroy it in the process. It is bolstered by a set of interlocking concepts, like the "Prisoner's Dilemma" and "free-riding." Ideologically, it is powerfully connected to the notion that people make free and rational choices but that they may not always act in their own enlightened self-interest. The story is conveyed in an enormous range of media, from scientific papers on the topic to environmental magazine articles to textbooks (like this one!). Many of these elements are borrowed from elsewhere and cobbled together from earlier persuasive concepts and systems of ideas. Once these pieces are in place, they set the terms of discussion, suggest imagery and outcomes, and direct our ways of thinking. In the process, the assumptions on which the ideas are based, the places from which the concepts are borrowed, and the history of the ideas are often lost or obscured. This transition makes it more and more difficult to remember that discourses are stories; the social context of their invention disappears, and they become true.

Environmental discourse analysis is a method for examining these constructions of nature that attempts to reverse this trend toward the stability of discourses by placing them under scrutiny, and attempting to foreground the ways in which *social context* influences their production and maintenance. This represents a critical departure from traditional approaches because it often focuses on the concepts (e.g., health, sustainability, hunger) and sources of knowledge (e.g., government experts, scientific laboratories) that other accounts take for granted and assume to be independent and authoritative. A social constructionist approach to the environment is not simply interested in discourses only, therefore, but the social institutions to which they are tied.

Historically, discourses, including discourses about nature, have been propagated and reinforced by important social institutions, like community patriarchs, the church, or the monarchy. In modern society, environmental discourses are increasingly tied to institutions such as governments, schools, hospitals, and laboratories. These institutions are sites of power that are in the business of managing the relationship between environment and society, not so much by telling people what can and cannot be done, but instead by cementing specific understandings of what is and is not true.

The discourse of North African desertification

Consider the case of desertification in North Africa. As recently as 1997, a UN report concluded that the Sahara Desert is on the advance northwards and that the region, once the Roman Empire's "breadbasket," had become a desert. Radical measures would be required, by implication, on the part of governments, the international community, and nongovernmental organizations, to restore the region's lost potential. It is increasingly clear, however, that this conclusion is one based on old ideas, texts, and claims originally made by colonial officers. As geographer Diana Davis demonstrates in an exhaustive and detailed historical analysis of the "desertification discourse," there has been a longstanding and well-established assumption that the region was once heavily forested and that its degradation came from overgrazing, especially in the period following what was called the "Arab Invasion" in the past thousand years. As part of this assertion, maps of the region were drawn up over the eighteenth and nineteenth centuries laying out what kind of land cover ought to occur in the region, based on assumptions about what the "climax" communities

Figure 8.2 Pollen evidence from Morocco over 14,000 years. Despite the ongoing dominant discourse that post-Roman North Africa experienced "desertification" and loss of tree cover following "Arab Invasions," pollen data show no significant decrease in tree pollen in the past thousand years. *Source*: Reproduced from Davis (2007).

should be: how the landscape should look, if properly managed. In this case, climax communities were assumed to look like the forests of Europe. In contrast then, photos of the open desert were used to capture a sense of forlorn emptiness. These kinds of claims and documents can be dated back to the earliest surveys of French colonizers in Morocco, forming the basis of an important environmental story (Davis 2007).

Pollen core data from the region positively refutes any such story, however. These data, which show the relative abundance and diversity of flowering plant species across the area for thousands of years (including trees, grasses, herbs, and shrubs), suggest a significant increase in tree cover around 8,000 years ago, and then a long period of shifts, up and down, but without any evidence of loss of trees, tree species, or vegetation more generally. Put simply, accounts of post-Roman desertification and an expansion of the Sahara following an "Arab Invasion" have no basis in anything like contemporary scientific knowledge (Figure 8.2).

There are a few ways to think about this apparent misunderstanding. One can certainly argue that pollen data and other paleoecological information simply were not available to French colonizers. Their misunderstanding was based on scattered information and ancient texts with little scientific validity. Basically, we might conclude that this was an "honest mistake."

A constructivist research effort goes further, however. It asks who benefited from a discourse of desertification? How does such a discourse take form and gain momentum? How is it tied to institutional, political, and even ethnic power relationships? As a discourse, the structure of these elements can be viewed as internally powerful and coherent, accounting for some of its longevity. It contains a compelling narrative ("paradise lost"), key concepts ("climax vegetation"), an ideology of progress and restoration, and signifying practices in the form of government documents, landscape photography, and scientific papers. As far as power goes, the discourse of desertification clearly suited the needs of colonial officers. It has long been a crucial justification for land-use controls and investment in land improvement mechanisms, especially the settlement of nomads and other native peoples. Assuming that a vast forest had been destroyed by irrational indigenes provides a powerful justification for land control and improvement.

None of this is to say that land degradation has not occurred in places in North Africa, or that massive overgrazing might not lead to a depletion of grass cover, or that people do not impact the environment in arid regions. All of these things may be true and yet the evidence for a massive anthropogenic creation of the desert in this region is minimal. What exists in its place is a strong, coherent, and compelling discourse of desertification, linked to colonial and state authorities. Nor is any of this unique to North Africa.

Wilderness: A troublesome discourse

In his landmark essay "The Trouble with Wilderness," environmental historian William Cronon argues that "the time has come to rethink wilderness" (Cronon 1995: 69). The dominant view of wilderness, he suggests, as a land untouched by humans, a pre-historical and pure nature, is troublesome for a number of reasons. First, the feelings and experiences we have about, within, and around wilderness areas are learned, inherited, and at bottom, "quite profoundly a human invention" (p. 69), or what we have been calling in this chapter a social construction. So what does it mean, exactly, to say that wilderness is a social construct? For one, it forces us to recognize that the word itself has a culturally and historically specific meaning. Wilderness – as pure nature, landscapes untouched by humans – is a construct most specific to Western European-based, modern cultures. Indeed, most indigenous and non-Western cultures do not even have a word for lands untouched by humans and do not distinguish between "wild" and "non-wild" landscapes. Wilderness is a *culturally specific* construct. But even within this culture of wilderness, the meaning of the term itself has changed enormously within its brief history, even within the past 250 years.

Wilderness today is prized. It is mapped, sought out, hiked through, and protected in reserves. But you do not have to go back far in history to find quite different meanings:

> As late as the eighteenth century . . . to be in a wilderness was to be 'deserted,' 'savage,' 'desolate,' 'barren' – in short, a 'waste,' the word's nearest synonym. Its connotations were anything but positive, and the emotion one was most likely to feel in its presence was 'bewilderment' – or terror. (Cronon 1995: 70)

Much of this comes from the Bible itself. Adam and Eve, after all, were banished from a garden (a cultural landscape, paradise) to the wilderness. It was nothing less than the God-given project of human history to reclaim the wilderness for humanity. Even into the nineteenth century, the project of American Western expansion was often viewed (and explicitly portrayed) as bringing civilization to the wilderness (Figure 8.3).

By the turn of the twentieth century, however, this meaning had been turned on its head. Wilderness had become scarce and with expansion now coast to coast, Americans sensed that the vast untrammeled (and supposedly unpeopled) landscapes of the "American frontier" were gone, forever. The debate over the damming of Hetch Hetchy Valley in Yosemite National Park (as outlined in Chapter 5) serves as the classic example of this new, highly valued conception of wilderness. As Cronon puts it: "For [John] Muir and the growing number of Americans who shared his views, Satan's home had become God's own temple" (p. 72). In this way, wilderness as a concept is troubling because it disguises human priorities and values as "natural" conditions.

More problematically, as noted previously in this chapter, the very lands of the New World that were perceived to be wilderness by arriving European settlers were not empty of people in any way. Some 4–12 million indigenous Americans at the time of Columbus's arrival had radically modified the land for cultivation, hunting, and other uses. They are lands with a history. Even Yosemite Valley and the High Sierra mountains – paragons of wilderness and wildness – were inhabited, managed landscapes long before the arrival

Figure 8.3   John Gast, "American Progress," 1872. Lady Liberty brings light (and farmers, plowed fields, telegraph lines, trains, etc.) as she drives the darkness (and the "Indians" and wild animals) out of the *wilderness*. *Source*: Library of Congress, engraving after 1872 painting.

of European Americans in the early nineteenth century. Most of the very "wildest" landscapes that conservationists have fought to protect for the past 150 years are very much the *products of human labor*.

To make them into wilderness, therefore, requires a form of violence. The very natives that managed the vegetation of Yosemite Valley with controlled, seasonal fires had to be forcefully removed before a wilderness could be created. This is not, mind you, just a matter of history. To this day, members of the Blackfeet Nation in Montana are cited for "poaching" in Glacier National Park, on lands to which they were guaranteed hunting and fishing rights *in perpetuity* through their treaty with the US government. In this way, wilderness is troubling because it has enabled and even necessitated violent social and political relationships.

Additionally, Cronon argues that the idea of wilderness has a more subtle yet equally problematic effect on the American environmental movement as a whole. The US environmental movement has long relied on the idea of wilderness as one of its foundational constructs. A century ago, when protection of large tracts of (only apparently) untouched land was the central priority, the emotional value of wilderness was undoubtedly useful for the creation of national parks and other reserves.

But what does it mean to valorize wilderness today in the same way? The implication of wilderness environmentalism, according to Cronon, is that the natures most deserving of preservation "must also be pristine – remote from humanity and untouched by our common past" (p. 83). Yet environmental history teaches us that few of those places exist now, if they ever did. Placing wilderness at the center of environmentalism serves to disguise and minimize the range of important natures all around us, in cities, vacant lots, and old farm fields. An environmental movement aimed only at preserving wilderness, therefore, will largely ignore places we live, work, and play (see "environmental justice" in Chapter 7).

Like all other discourses, wilderness merges stories, concepts, and ideologies that make it possible to see and do certain things, while at the same time disguising and hiding other things. To argue that wilderness and nature more generally are social constructions is not to argue against preserving this or that tract of land. It is, rather, to demand a more honest and reflective examination of our beliefs and actions, and the role of social power in creating the nature we think we know.

The Limits of Constructivism: Science, Relativism, and the Very Material World

That said, not everyone has embraced the turn toward constructivist accounts. Among the problems identified by critics is the challenge of science, the threat of relativism, and the need to take seriously the more-than-constructed nature of the world.

What about science?

A fundamental part of our understanding of environmental problems comes from scientific investigation. Ever since the Enlightenment, it was assumed (at least by scientists) that scientific knowledge offered a transparent perspective on nature, "a uniquely privileged vehicle to true knowledge about the world" (Demeritt 2001: 26). Science, as such, is a method for finding truths already "out there," "natural laws" or the "natural properties of things."

A constructivist perspective turns this fundamental assumption of science on its head, arguing that "scientific knowledges are made in historically specific, socially situated practices, rather than 'found'" (Castree and Braun 1998: 27). Moreover, many constructivists argue that the very "things" we take to be the natural objects of scientific inquiry (e.g., quarks, DNA, soil samples) are not found (or discovered) either, but rather socially constructed through the process and practices of science, reflecting more about the social world of science than the natural world. Researcher Donna Haraway has demonstrated, for example, that successive ideas and paradigms in primate research (on topics like parenting behavior, sex, resource use, and warfare) have tended to reflect the historical social concerns and anxieties of the period of their investigation, and were often imbued with sexist, racist, and colonial discourses (Haraway 1989). Even and especially scientific knowledge, in this way of thinking, is social and political.

Box 8.1   Environmental Solution? Preserving "Alien" Species in Wild Horse Conservation

What's in the power of a name? Consider this: Which of the following would you consider worthy of conserving, a population of wild horses or one of feral horses? On one hand, the question presents a false dilemma, because in several places across North America (as well as in many others worldwide), both names refer to the same animal, *Equus ferus caballus*, the domestic horse. On the other hand, the fates of local populations of these animals often rest in which *construction*, wild or feral, wins out in the end. To better flesh out the (literal) power of contested social constructions of nature, we will briefly examine a case study of one controversial band of wild/feral horses.

The Ozark National Scenic Riverways (ONSR), a unit of the US National Park Service located in the southern Missouri Ozarks region, contains a small population (usually between 20 and 35 individuals) of free-roaming horses. The presence of the "wild" horses, which are believed to be primarily descendants of Depression-era draft horses abandoned by poor farmers, predates the park, which was established in 1964. Beginning in 1970, federal legislation mandated that national parks manage designated "natural areas" primarily for ecological integrity over cultural or recreational considerations. In the official park management plans, ONSR managers began referring to the horses as "feral horses," alien denizens of an otherwise "natural" ecosystem. Park documents made no reference to the cultural significance of the horses. Rather, they repeatedly cited the dangers that "alien" species pose to "natural" ecological processes. Indeed, by the 1990s managers were considering removing the herd under the guise of ecosystem management.

The proposal to remove the horses from the park appalled many locals. In 1992, the Missouri Wild Horse League formed to fight for permanent protection of the band of horses. For many area residents, the horses were a pleasing and noteworthy part of the landscape (they remain, after all, the only free-roaming horses in the US Midwest). But they were also much more than this. The horses represented a symbolic and material link to their communal, agrarian history. Indeed, Ozark local history (as it is in many places) is infused with narratives of loss of control to outside forces: loss of farms to the Depression, loss of forests to timber barons, even loss of common lands to the strictures of a federally managed park. The horses were survivors of all this. They *belonged* there.

So which side was "right"? Well, both, really. From the Park Service perspective, *yes*, the horses do alter the local ecology. Even acknowledging that equids are native to North America, *these* equids are not. Moreover, "native" North American equids lived in a very different ecosystem, which included (among other differences) equid predators like cougars and wolves. On the other hand, the wild horse advocates are "right," too. The horses are a beloved feature of the local culture and landscape. And they *are* "wild," right? They are a self-sustaining population of animals, after all. In the end, the wild horse advocates won out, courtesy of a piece of federal legislation granting permanent protection to the horses.

So who's to say, anyway, what is "natural" and what isn't, what belongs and what doesn't? Please note: this is not a rhetorical question. Someone *will* define these boundaries. And others *will* disagree. What (or *who*) is allowed to stick around is often decided by clashes of contested social constructions.

And yet the practice of science is largely congruent with many of the environmental goals and values that constructivists espouse, including scientific investigation of the hazards of modern industry and its demonstration of the threat of global warming, among countless examples. Indeed, constructivist research, with its amassing of evidence and logical forms of argument, is often itself a form of scientific inquiry. How can treating science as discourse square with seeing science as a unique way of getting at important truths?

The threat of relativism

For some, by retreating from the universal power of science to adjudicate debates about nature, social construction leads to the problem of **relativism**. In theory, if knowledge of the "natural" world is rooted in "social" constructs, stories, and ideologies, it becomes difficult or impossible to establish reliable information and knowledge upon which to act. When disputes occur, what and who are we to believe? On what basis can we argue for or against various human behaviors: dumping in rivers, using nuclear power, cutting trees? In its stronger forms, relativism argues that all statements and knowledge are *only* relative to their

> **Relativism** Questioning the veracity of universal truth statements, relativism holds that all beliefs, truths, and facts are at root products of the particular set of social relations from which they arise
>
> **Co-production** The inevitable and ongoing process whereby humans and non-humans produce and change one another through their interaction and interrelation

social context. This strong form of relativism can, in theory at least, devolve into *nihilism*, the "view that nothing is knowable" (Proctor 1998: 359).

In response to this, constructivists argue that not all forms of relativism are as debilitating as others. In its weaker forms, relativism simply reminds us that all statements about reality are conditioned and recognized (written and read; said and heard) in a social and political context. No statement can present a "mirror of nature" (Rorty 1979). Even so, most constructivists take a path of moderation, adhering to the idea that while environmental science is never free of social and contextual influences, these alone do not determine scientific findings in any simple way. Certainly, acknowledging the validity of constructivism makes it more challenging to make bold statements about reality and about truth.

Constructivism in a material world

This still leaves a difficult point. There is plenty of reason to believe that the environment and the objects of the world around us influence our social and political context as much as the social and political context influences our knowledge of these objects. Global climate change is a scientific construct *and* a globally observed temperature phenomenon (Chapter 9). Wolves are a politically constructed site for ideological rancor *and* a species of wild animals that operates with its own rules (Chapter 11). At what point do the material qualities of nature become important to explaining social and environmental outcomes? Can we admit to a constructed nature and still take seriously the sticks and stones of a complex material world? Many critics insist not.

We would suggest, however, that the concept of **co-production** offers a route out of the perceived constructivist impasse. By co-production we mean the inevitable and ongoing process whereby humans and non-humans produce and change one another through their interaction and interrelation. Humans and non-humans are discrete, but always entangled. As Donna Haraway observes: "beings do not pre-exist their relatings" (Haraway 2003: 6). Humans constantly remake the world but are remade in the process. Social discourses and narratives are fundamentally "material" since they are crucial in directing human under-standings, impacts, and behaviors, which in turn act to change landscapes, exterminate or generate new species, emit gases, and change the flow of water on the surface of the Earth. At the same time, however, these landscapes, species, and gases are "social" in that they act on and confront the taken-for-granted in dramatic ways, reworking social systems, dis-courses, and ways of understanding the world.

Consider the case of Hurricane Katrina, which made landfall in 2005 in the largely unprepared city of New Orleans, with an enormous death toll, especially among poor and minority populations. The disaster is widely recognized to be the result of engineering failures in regional infrastructure of dams and levees, and it brought to light deeply social-ized differences in resources and opportunities among the city's black and white residents, which had been heavily erased by representations of the city in the past. News sources during the event cast the storm in a range of perverse lights (consider online images of black people with salvaged goods described as "looters" and white people described as "finders" – see http://politicalhumor.about.com/library/images/blkatrinalooting.htm).

Here was a disaster exacerbated by risk decisions, filtered through racially tainted cover-age, interpreted through complex discursive lenses and perhaps even increased in severity by anthropogenic global warming. In all these ways there are social and constructed ele-ments to the horrible events of that storm. But it would be analytically useless and definitely bizarre to claim that the cyclonic phenomenon itself, its high winds, and its deluge of water were a discourse. Rather we might observe that politics and wind, language and water, ideology and levees, discourses and storm surges together produced an outcome that remade the world.

In every interaction, with every object on Earth, such outcomes are produced on a tiny scale every day. The lesson of constructivism is to take seriously the complexity of the conditions under which we understand those interactions and make sense of the world around us.

Thinking with Construction

In this chapter, we have learned that:

- Many things or conditions we have thought of as normal or "natural" have later been shown to be social inventions or merely ideas (for example: race).
- "Social constructions" typically take the form of taken-for-granted concepts or ideas that direct our thinking or action, often unbeknownst to us without critical examination.
- This holds implications for many key concepts we use to think about society and envi-ronment, including ideas like "wilderness" or "desertification."
- Environmental stories or narratives formed from constructions of this kind can hold enormous political and social implications by placing blame, directing policy, or developing solutions that may be inappropriate, undemocratic, or environmentally unsustainable.

- By analyzing environmental discourses, stories, and narratives, we can learn where our taken-for-granted ideas come from and how they might be resisted or changed.
- Critics suggest that taking this approach too far may lead to relativism or dismissal of science.
- Reconciling the material reality of the environment with the powerful social constructions that influence our thinking is therefore a major challenge.

Questions for Review

1. Is a national park a more "natural" place than a region dominated by farms? Try to answer this question using a constructivist perspective (in which the correct answer is not a simple "yes").
2. Describe how history and science expose the concept of "race" as a social construction.
3. When Europeans explored the New World, how did they perceive the "nature" they came into contact with? How did these perceptions legitimate their taking of the land?
4. Discuss the profound difference between viewing North African desertification as an objective phenomenon and as a *discourse*. (Bonus or alternate: Do the same thing for "wilderness.")
5. Does thinking with social constructionism make it impossible to take science seriously? Why or why not?

Exercise 8.1   Analysis of Energy Discourses

Consulting magazines, newspapers, television and the internet, identify several advertisements from energy-producing companies (e.g., Exxon, BP, etc.) and several publicity ads for major environmental groups (e.g., Sierra Club, Wilderness Society, etc.). What discourses (narratives, concepts, and ideologies) are embodied in the pictures and words in these advertisements? What stories do they tell or imply about nature and society? How are the two sets of discourses similar? What work do they do for each of the interest groups involved?

Exercise 8.2   What is Obesity?

In many developed-world countries there are grave concerns about serious health problems stemming from increases in overall body mass of the population over the past few decades. These concerns come with a problem, however: defining who is overweight and what that means. Review at least five prominent websites, magazines, or other media and answer the following: What is obesity and how is it defined? Are all definitions uniform? Which are more credible and why? What assumptions are these definitions based on? To what degree is "obesity" a social construction and to what degree is it a simple and apparent fact? On what basis do you make your own distinction?

Exercise 8.3   What is Organic about Organic Food?

Consider the United States Department of Agriculture's official regulatory definition of organic food (http://www.nal.usda.gov/afsic/pubs/ofp/ofp.shtml). Notice in particular the insistence that "Organic food is produced without using most conventional pesticides; fertilizers made with synthetic ingredients or sewage sludge; bioengineering; or ionizing radiation." Some have criticized this definition since it does not mean that the food was not raised on industrial farms by large agribusinesses, nor does it say anything about the health or safety of the people who work on organic farms. Writer Michael Pollan has called organics "The Organic-Industrial Complex" (http://www.commondreams.org/views01/0603-03.htm). Is "organic food" a discourse? If it is, what are its narratives, concepts, ideologies, and signifying practices? What makes up the discourse of organics? What work does it do?

References

Barnes, T. J., and J. S. Duncan (1992). "Introduction: Writing worlds." In T. J. Barnes and J. S. Duncan (eds.) *Writing Worlds: Discourse, Text, and Metaphor in the Representation of Landscape*. New York: Routledge, pp. 1–17.

Castree, N., and B. Braun (1998). "The construction of nature and the nature of construction: Analytical and political tools for building survivable futures." In N. Castree and B. Braun (eds.) *Remaking Reality: Nature at the Millennium*. London: Routledge, pp. 3–42.

Cronon, W. (1995). "The trouble with wilderness; or, getting back to the wrong nature." In *Uncommon Ground: Rethinking the Human Place in Nature*. New York: W. W. Norton, pp. 69–90.

Davis, D. K. (2007). *Resurrecting the Granary of Rome: Environmental History and French Colonial Expansion in North Africa*. Athens, OH: Ohio University Press.

Demeritt, D. (2001). "Being constructive about nature." In N. Castree and B. Braun (eds.) *Social Nature: Theory, Practice, and Politics*. Oxford: Blackwell.

Hacking, I. (1999). *The Social Construction of What?* Cambridge, MA: Harvard University Press.

Haraway, D. (1989). *Primate Visions: Gender, Race, and Nature in the World of Modern Science*. New York: Routledge.

Haraway, D. (2003). *The Companion Species Manifesto: Dogs, People, and Significant Otherness*. Chicago, IL: Prickly Paradigm Press.

Proctor, J. (1998). "The social construction of nature: Relativist accusations, pragmatic and realist responses." *Annals of the Association of American Geographers* 88(3): 353–76.

Rorty, R. (1979). *Philosophy and the Mirror of Nature.* Princeton, NJ: Princeton University Press.

Sluyter, A. (1999). "The making of the myth in postcolonial development: Material-conceptual landscape transformation in sixteenth century Veracruz." *Annals of the Association of American Geographers* 89(3): 377–401.

Williams, R. (1976). *Keywords: A Vocabulary of Culture and Society.* New York: Oxford University Press.

Suggested Reading

Braun, B. (2002). *The Intemperate Rainforest: Nature, Culture, and Power on Canada's West Coast.* Minneapolis, MN: University of Minnesota Press.

Castree, N. (2005). *Nature.* New York: Routledge.Demeritt, D. (1998). "Science, social constructivism and nature." In B. Braun and N. Castree (eds.) *Remaking Reality: Nature at the Millennium.* New York: Routledge, pp. 173–93.

Rikoon, S., and R. Albee (1998). "'Wild-and-free,-leave-'em-be': Wild horses and the struggle over nature in the Missouri Ozarks." *Journal of Folklore Research* 35(3): 203–22.

Robbins, P. (1998). "Paper forests: Imagining and deploying exogenous ecologies in arid India." *Geoforum* 29(1): 69–86.

Wainwright, J. (2008). *Decolonizing Development.* Oxford: Wiley Blackwell.

Part 2

Objects of Concern

9

Carbon Dioxide

Source: Vladimir Salman/Shutterstock.

Keywords

- Cap and trade
- Capital accumulation
- Carbon cycle
- Carbon sequestration
- Coase theorem
- Collective action
- Command-and-control
- Greenhouse effect
- Greenwashing
- Photosynthesis
- Surplus value
- Uneven development

Chapter Menu

Environment and Society: A Critical Introduction, Second Edition. Paul Robbins, John Hintz,
and Sarah A. Moore.
© 2014 John Wiley & Sons, Ltd. Published 2014 by John Wiley & Sons, Ltd.

Stuck in Pittsburgh Traffic

At 4:45 on a hot summer afternoon, commuter traffic approaching the Liberty Tunnels outside of Pittsburgh, Pennsylvania comes to a halt, as it does in cities all over the world during rush hour. Perhaps 100,000 cars will pass through these tunnels in a single day, a reliable daily reflection of the commuter culture of cities. The average American worker commutes approximately 45 minutes every day, with many commuters traveling twice as long or more. Bumper to bumper for 20 minutes, this traffic jam is an expected part of the workday for everyone involved. It is a normal part of life and the economy, if an unpleasant one.

As cars crawl through the "tubes" (as they're known locally), with air conditioning making the temperatures bearable for drivers, a complex set of exchanges is occurring. Fluids and gases are flowing through the vehicles, maintaining the pace of traffic, however slow. These cars are propelled by a process of combustion, which combines oxygen from the air with gasoline in the tank to make tiny explosions that break apart the bonds of the fuel (which is basically a tangle of carbon and hydrogen atoms) and release energy that makes it possible to drive. What's left over after the reaction? Some H_2O (water) and a bunch of CO_2 (carbon dioxide). Raw fuel and oxygen go in one end and water and carbon dioxide come out the other. Notably, for every two molecules of fuel that go into the process, at least 16 molecules of waste CO_2 come out.

The CO_2 that escapes from these tailpipes is entirely invisible. It rises into the atmosphere, mixes with other gases and apparently disappears. Regrettably, what is out of sight and out of mind is by no means out of action. The carbon dioxide emitted by these cars today may reside in the atmosphere for a century or far longer, being only slowly reabsorbed into the world's oceans and vegetation over long time periods. In the meantime, those molecules will float through the air, trapping heat energy coming from the Earth and raising the overall temperature of the planet, with potentially disastrous consequences.

Surely though, what harm could come from 16 tiny molecules of CO_2? A typical car, regrettably, produces considerably more than that. The average vehicle emits ~150 grams of carbon dioxide per kilometer traveled. Since the average American driver covers ~19,000 km per year, the average car is actually producing around 2,800 kilograms of CO_2 every year, significantly *more than its own weight*.

This calculation, moreover, excludes the carbon required to produce the energy to make the car in the first place as well as the energy to make and maintain the roads and to extract the fuel and raw materials that go into the car's tank, tires, and body. This is also beyond the carbon required to transport and power the rest of a commuter's life, from the food on their breakfast table to the heating and cooling of their home and work, indeed even the energy that built their house and workplace in the first place. All of these things required the emission of carbon dioxide (along with a great many other gases and waste products, of course). How did a tasteless, odorless, invisible gas become so fundamentally tied to our lives, and to the foundations of our society?

A Short History of CO_2

The element carbon actually makes up only a tiny fraction of the Earth. Most of that (perhaps 99 percent) is buried in the Earth's crust and locked up in sedimentary rocks. The rest of the world's carbon is in a state of continuous motion. Moving between the oceans (where most of it resides), the atmosphere, plants, and soils, carbon circulates, occurring most notably as solids (graphite and diamond) and gases (carbon is in methane and carbon dioxide). It moves beyond these states into a huge range of organic molecules, however, including fats and sugars. In this way, it moves in and out of plants and animals and forms the fundamental building block of life on Earth.

CO_2 – the most common gaseous form of the element – is constantly circulated into life forms and also recaptured in oceans and the atmosphere. The process of **photosynthesis**, which is the basis of all life on Earth, essentially combines the sun's energy with CO_2 and water to make sugars that form the tissue of plants, with oxygen left over. In this way plants draw carbon from the soil and atmosphere as they grow but emit carbon back into the air and put carbon back into the soil when they decay. The same is true of animals (including you and me), which further participate in the **carbon cycle** (Figure 9.1).

A small proportion of carbon escapes this cycle, as it drops from the ocean floor and from deep soils back into the Earth's crust. Sedimentary rocks, which contain lots of carbon, are formed from this slow deposition of layers of silt and organic material on the ocean floor, hardening over millions of years to become part of the Earth's crust. On the other hand, by removing sediments from the earth, including coal (carbonized wood) and petroleum (a transformed fossil of marine life), and setting them on fire, people release large quantities of carbon into the atmosphere very quickly, and (quite significantly) *at a rate far faster than they are naturally returned to geological storage.*

> **Photosynthesis** The process through which plants use the sun's energy to convert carbon dioxide into organic compounds, especially sugars that are used to build tissues
>
> **Carbon Cycle** The system through which carbon circulates through the Earth's geosphere, atmosphere, and biosphere, specifically including exchanges between carbon in the earth (e.g., as petroleum) and the atmosphere (as CO_2) through combustion and back again through sequestration

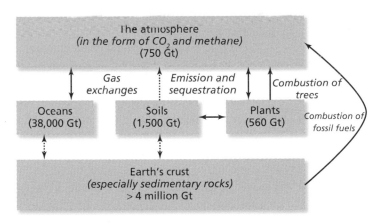

Figure 9.1 Carbon on Earth. A Gt is a gigaton, or a billion tons. Ninety-nine percent of carbon is contained in the Earth's crust. Most of the flow of carbon is between the oceans, the atmosphere, and soils and plants. Modern industry has removed large quantities of carbon from the Earth's crust and, through combustion, has released them into the atmosphere as CO_2.

The changing CO_2 content of the atmosphere

The amount of CO_2 in the atmosphere is by no means fixed. Indeed, it has changed dramatically over the past several hundred million years. At the beginning of life on Earth, some two billion years ago, microbiota teemed across the planet. Tiny prokaryotes thrived thanks to an atmosphere consisting of very little oxygen, one that instead contained a great deal of carbon dioxide. These tiny, simple life forms all lived by breaking down the inorganic compounds around them to build their bodies. They were especially good at using abundant water, breaking it apart to use hydrogen atoms, and turning sunlight and CO_2 (both of which were plentiful) into energy. The incidental by-product – the *waste* – of all these processes was oxygen, released into the atmosphere as O_2. As these "cyanobacteria" continued to thrive, the atmosphere slowly changed from one with high proportions of CO_2 to one with a more significant proportion of oxygen. Today the Earth's atmosphere (though still dominated by nitrogen) now contains around 20 percent oxygen and less than a tenth of a percent CO_2 (about 381 parts per million (ppm) of CO_2, to be more exact). New life forms came to take advantage of the now available oxygen (as we ourselves do) as these older ones began to vanish. For these older bacteria, an atmospheric cataclysm occurred: they were *poisoned by the very atmosphere they had produced*. Anaerobic bacteria, the descendants of Earth's first life, still persist but they live in different environments and smaller areas than they used to, including mud flats and your own intestines (Margulis and Dolan 2002).

There is a lesson here. Living things have the ability to influence the biochemical characteristics of the Earth, often in ways that change the conditions to which they must adapt in order to survive.

Certainly, what is true of ancient prokaryotes is still true for human societies. We are as intimately tied to carbon dioxide as those tiny bacteria were.

Ever since the advent of fire, however, our relationship to carbon has intensified profoundly. *Homo erectus* likely mastered the use of fire more than 400,000 years ago. Ever since, human civilization has been characterized by ever-increasing demands for energy. Cooking food, for example, requires a considerable amount of energy, as does staying warm under cold conditions (or cold under hot ones!), but so does building structures or moving objects, everything from automobiles to water.

In simpler societies, much of this energy is provided by manual labor. As societies have become larger, more complex, and more productive, however, they have come to depend on supplemental energy, which in the modern world comes primarily from burning fossil fuels: coal, oil, and natural gas most notably. The process of burning these liquids and rocks results in the release of enormous amounts of energy, but also in the emission of carbon, which flows into the atmosphere in the form of CO_2. As contemporary economies have learned to build larger buildings and cities, move freight around the globe, and grow more food by inputting fertilizers and pesticides (themselves made from petroleum), more energy is required, and so the combustion of fossil fuels increases apace. Modern civilization, put simply, is carbon civilization.

The results of this growing carbon-based economic activity are now quite apparent from measures of the atmosphere over time. Since the 1950s, scientist Charles Keeling and his colleagues have been measuring concentrations of carbon dioxide in the atmosphere from an observatory atop Mauna Loa in Hawaii. Graphed over time, the data show CO_2 (in ppm) content as a steep curve, steadily increasing (Figure 9.2).

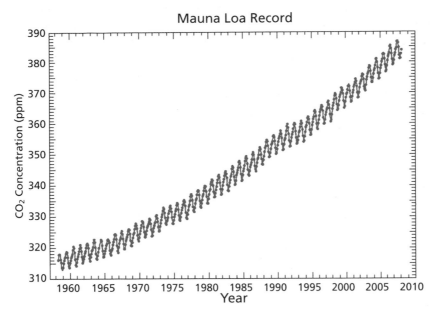

Figure 9.2   The Keeling curve: Atmospheric concentrations of CO_2 since 1958. The overall trend is a steady upwards curve. Annual variability (smaller up and down oscillations) is a result of the seasons in the northern hemisphere; plants green up in the spring, taking CO_2 out of the atmosphere, and die-off in the fall, re-releasing that carbon. *Source*: Reproduced with permission from the Scripps CO_2 program. http://scrippsco2.ucsd.edu/program_history/keeling_curve_lessons.html.

This clear recent trend is only the tail end, moreover, of a longer-term change toward a carbon-centered civilization. As the economy shifted from labor and animal power in the nineteenth century to mechanized conveyance and power generation, it came to produce more CO_2. Other modern economic activities alter the carbon content of the atmosphere as well. By clearing large areas of forest for development or agriculture, for example, people perform a double impact. Destroying forests whose photosynthesis captures (or **sequesters**) carbon reduces the power of the trees to capture that carbon. Burning them then releases the carbon stored in each tree back into the atmosphere. It also leaves fewer plants on Earth to recapture that carbon.

> **Carbon Sequestration**   The capture and storage of carbon from the atmosphere into the biosphere or the geosphere through either biological means, as in plant photosynthesis, or engineered means

Although our direct measurement of CO_2 in the atmosphere begins only in the 1950s, we have records at our disposal from far earlier that show the unmistakable fingerprint of this machine-age transition. Tree rings and sediment can be used to reconstruct climate conditions in the past thousand years or more, and the gases locked up in deep and ancient ice cores from the Antarctic and Greenland can be analyzed to tell us about the atmosphere when the ice was first laid down (Figure 9.3).

Evidence from the past millennium is compelling. There is certainly some slight variability from decade to decade over the period spanning the Middle Ages, a time of feudalism,

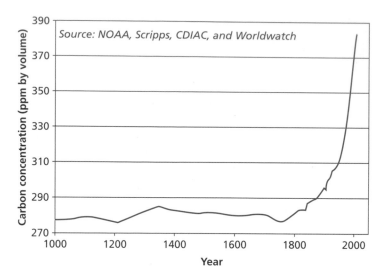

Figure 9.3 Atmospheric concentration of carbon. Over the past thousand years carbon in the atmosphere has hovered at around 280 parts per million. With the explosion of industrial activity starting in 1800, more parts of human activity depend on combustion of fossil fuels and atmospheric carbon has increased exponentially as a result. *Source*: reproduced with permission from http://www.earthpolicy.org/indicators/C52.

peasant production, and religious hierarchy, to the 1700s, a period of global contact, scientific expansion, and colonialism. But these minimal variations are dwarfed by the massive influx of carbon dioxide into the atmosphere accompanying the industrial revolution after 1800 (Intergovernmental Panel on Climate Change 2007).

From carbon loading to climate change

This ongoing transformation of the atmosphere would receive little comment or attention if it did not have profound implications for the environmental and social systems of our planet. The central problem is that carbon dioxide, along with a number of other gases that are part of the atmosphere, plays a major role in regulating the temperature of the Earth.

This is because much of the incoming short-wave radiation of the sun that strikes the Earth is absorbed into earth surfaces and is transformed into long-wave radiation, which we experience as heat, and which is re-radiated back into space. Some portion of that re-radiated energy does not escape the Earth, however, and instead is absorbed in the atmosphere that cloaks the planet. This atmospheric energy is trapped by a set of specific gases, including carbon dioxide. And make no mistake, this is good news! The result of this naturally trapped heat is a temperature on Earth that can support life; without this effect – the **greenhouse effect** – the planet would be very cold indeed. But if a buildup of gases

Greenhouse Effect   The characteristic of the Earth's atmosphere, based on the presence of important gases including water vapor and carbon dioxide, to trap and retain heat, leading to temperatures that can sustain life increases the level of heat-trapping over time, it can be reasonably predicted that global temperatures will rise.

This process, linking gases in the atmosphere with global temperatures, has occurred since long before human beings arrived on the scene. It has also proven extremely sensitive to changes in the gas content of the atmosphere. We know, for example, that the decline of carbon dioxide in the atmosphere, hundreds and millions of years ago (discussed above), had the effect of cooling global temperatures dramatically. So the buildup of these gases in the atmosphere over such a short period of recent history raises the prospect of serious environmental change. The short-term global climate record reflects an overall pattern of warming. This warming has led to indirect effects as well, including the rise of sea levels resulting from the melting of ice, as well as overall decline in global snow cover (Figure 9.4). On average, the world is indeed getting warmer.

Carbon dioxide is only one of a number of greenhouse gases that act in this way. The others include naturally occurring gases like water vapor, methane, and nitrous oxide, along with entirely artificial industrial compounds, including chlorofluorocarbons (CFCs). All of these gases are currently building up in the atmosphere and temperatures are indeed rising.

In this sense, "global warming" is an accurate description, but it is an incomplete one. In terms of *warming*, we do know that, because these gases reside for long periods in the atmosphere, there will be ongoing warming and that the average global temperature will likely rise between 1 and 4°C in the next century. But this also sets into motion a large range of possible regional changes in climate and weather patterns. The myriad effects of this change in the global energy balance may include drying of some areas and increased rainfall in others, increased drought in some places and increased floods in others, decreasing sea ice, rising sea levels, and even the collapse of circulating currents that regulate the warm and moist conditions of some areas, possibly leading to isolated regional cooling.

The effects of this change will be *global* in the sense that everyone in the

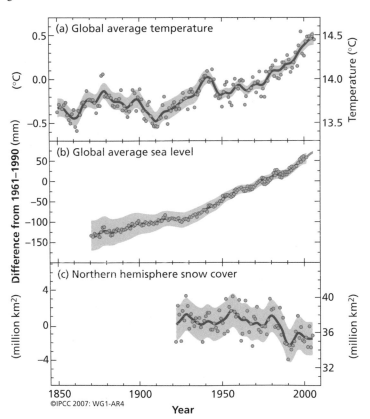

Figure 9.4 Global average temperatures, sea level, and snow cover. Over precisely the period when there has been a radical increase in the emission by people of gases that are understood to trap heat in the atmosphere, global temperatures have risen steadily, sea levels have increased, and snow cover has declined. *Source*: Reproduced with permission from Climate Change 2007: The Physical Science Basis. Working Group I Contribution to the Fourth Assessment Report of the Intergovernmental Panel on Climate Change, Figure SPM.3. Cambridge University Press.

world will be affected. But here too the variability of impact will be enormous. Given a rise in sea level of a meter or more, countries in the island Pacific (actually home to 14 million people) are likely to disappear altogether. Drought in sub-Saharan Africa, where a large proportion of the population survives on rain-fed agriculture, means massive starvation and migration. Wealthy people all over the world may be able to direct a larger proportion of their budgets to air conditioning and food provisioning, but the poor will not. Without some change in the trend of atmospheric concentration of CO_2 and related gases, therefore, the ironic effect of massive carbon-fed economic development during the past century may be an environmental situation that challenges and dismantles the very possibility of further economic growth and that punishes those who have contributed least to the problem.

Beyond people, the effects of such an environmental shift are just as profound. With rapidly changing temperature and precipitation, an enormous number of plant and animal species are likely to become suddenly endangered; many will be quickly lost. While high-profile cases like the polar bear are already receiving attention, the problems are much more serious if species more critical to the global food and energy web are eliminated. Such species (especially insects, plants, and marine plankton) are crucial to the survival of a range of others, meaning the potential collapse of whole ecosystems.

The puzzle of carbon dioxide

This brief review of the natural history of carbon dioxide reveals many things about the relationship of environment to society. First, it suggests that the history of civilization is necessarily also a history of gases, that molecules (CO_2) and elements (carbon) are as much a part of society as people, and that humans and non-humans influence each other in complex ways. It further suggests that the state of the environment is given to dramatic changes over the long term and that there is not necessarily a balanced, eternal, or inevitable state of nature. Greenhouse gas content in the atmosphere has changed over the eons, as have global temperatures. On the other hand, it also points to the profound influence and difficult-to-reverse effects that a specific form of society (industrial society) can have on complex Earth systems, with implications not only for sustaining that form of society, but also for sustaining the current diversity of life on the planet.

More specifically, this review stresses two things about carbon dioxide that make it a specific kind of object:

- First, it is ubiquitous; carbon is everywhere, in all of us, and in a state of constant flow, making it hard to capture, pin down, and isolate and making its impacts often distant in time and place from its sources.
- Second, it is extremely sensitive to economic activity: the history of modern economic growth is completely intertwined with carbon dioxide, making a simple delinking of human social formations and the content of the atmosphere difficult, like an operation on conjoined twins rather than a mere amputation.

Carbon dioxide therefore provides lessons for understanding where humans are positioned in the world, but it also presents a *puzzle*: given its ubiquity and economic sensitivity, how might atmospheric carbon loading be stemmed or reversed? Differing perspectives provide differing insights into this question, with regrettably somewhat contradictory answers.

Institutions: Climate Free-Riders and Carbon Cooperation

In Chapter 4 we established that problems associated with the environment were commonly problems of **collective action**, where there is a necessity for joint action by many people but where there is an incentive for each of them to not cooperate.

Collective Action Cooperation and coordination between individuals to achieve common goals and outcomes

Controlling and diminishing the flow of carbon dioxide into the atmosphere, as mentioned previously, is exactly this sort of problem. Using an institutional perspective that stresses these features of socio-environmental problems provides some insight into the question, therefore.

The carbon Prisoner's Dilemma

Consider, in a simplified case, that two countries emit carbon. Both would benefit from halting global warming by "biting the bullet" and bearing the costs of reducing their own emissions. There are myriad reasons, however, why each would not act.

First, of course, is the inevitable disadvantage each country would suffer if they were to act while the other country did not. While both countries would benefit from a lower carbon load in the atmosphere, only one country would have suffered the sacrifice of making it so. To complicate matters, there are inevitable uncertainties surrounding global climate change and its possible effects. Without knowing the precise costs of inaction, it is difficult for either country to gauge their own commitment to potentially expensive decisions, especially if the effects will be uneven, with some countries bearing greater costs of inaction than others. Similarly, it is difficult to monitor whether another country is fully meeting any commitments to decreasing greenhouse gas emissions. While burning forests might be seen from space, the CO_2 coming out of every power plant in a country is difficult to measure. Each of these is a classic element of the *Prisoner's Dilemma*, that metaphoric explanation that stresses why cooperation and collective action so often fail. But there is even more than this!

Carbon's common role in a fully globalized economy also makes it a difficult problem to solve. One country might impose limits on carbon, forcing entrepreneurs to develop ingenious but expensive methods to make products that emit less carbon. But these products compete on a global market where the firms of the inactive nation market their cheaper carbon-dependent products for far less. One country acts aggressively, while the other "free-rides," enjoying both the benefits of the first country's reduced emissions and the better market position from having not imposed carbon limits.

At the same time, not all countries start their bargaining from the same point. The industrial revolution that occurred in Europe and the United States turned these regions into major carbon emitters for hundreds of years. Over that time, Europeans and

Americans enjoyed greatly increased standards of living but at tremendous costs in terms of atmospheric change. Poorer countries may have large and/or more rapidly growing populations but their per capita carbon emissions are a tiny fraction of those of their counterparts in wealthy nations (Chapter 2). Why should a poorer nation, with its low per capita carbon emissions, agree to stringent controls when they have not yet enjoyed the fruits of a carbon economy? Why should a richer nation sacrifice its economy to reduce emissions while poorer nations, with their larger populations, stand to become the largest emitters over the medium or long term? Carbon's mobility exacerbates this conflict since it disconnects its places of emission from its locations of impacts: one person in the United States enjoys the benefits of emitting carbon through daily car commuting, while the costs are borne in a failed crop harvest among farmers and countries in West Africa, a half-world away. One country has an incentive to act, the other does not (Figure 9.5).

Finally, add to this the fact that there is no effective higher authority than the individual nations themselves to enforce any agreement: a de facto "state of anarchy" (Thompson 2006). While the United Nations is a powerful deliberative body, it does not represent a central power that can easily force international compliance with a regulatory statute. Instead, the model of international law must be followed, and the negotiators themselves must enforce the rules. Taking all of this into account, it would be hard to believe that international agreement of any kind might be reached. And yet one has been reached.

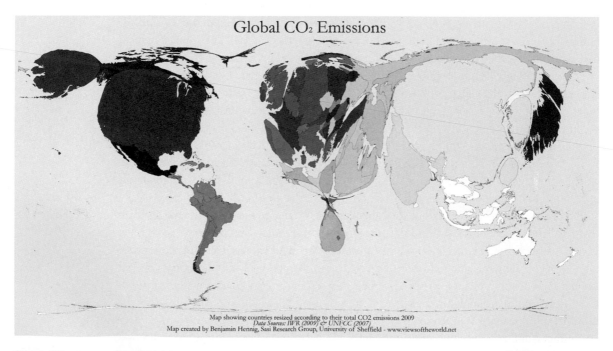

Figure 9.5 Cartogram of carbon emissions. In this map, countries are shown with their apparent size proportional to their total annual emissions in 2009. *Source*: http://www.viewsoftheworld.net/?p=1976. CC BY-NC-ND 3.0.

Overcoming barriers through flexibility: Climate treaties

When the international community sat down in the late 1980s to work out a strategy to address climate change, the United Nations Framework Convention on Climate Change, they were faced with all of the hypothetical barriers to cooperation described above and several more. Eventually they established an international agreement in 1997, the Kyoto Protocol, a binding document of international law, which addresses and seeks to overcome these barriers and imposes emission reductions (of all greenhouse gases including carbon) on signatory countries. The solution to these problems was to include elements of flexibility in the treaty that made it easier for signing countries to agree to join the effort.

First, the treaty contained specific provisions for alteration, update, and expansion over time. It also establishes graduated goals, giving countries time to develop technologies and enforcement strategies to deal with emissions. The protocol imposed national limits on carbon emissions and increasingly stringent reductions demanded for signatories over time, with the intermediate goal of forcing countries to eventually reach emission levels equal to 5.2 percent below their 1990 levels. The protocol also contained a wealth of provisions to increase national flexibility in reaching those goals. Most obviously, Kyoto does not tell countries how they must reduce emissions. Countries can impose draconian restrictions, flexible carbon taxes, cap-and-trade systems (see below), or any other policy instrument they choose to meet their goals. Finally, the protocol effectively exempted a number of large developing countries, most notably China and India, from many of the obligations of the treaty, further making them beneficiaries of technology transfer through a "Clean Development Mechanism," where developed countries could meet their reduction goals in part by developing carbon emission reduction schemes and technologies in poorer nations.

For all the flexibility that was written into the agreement, it might largely be viewed as a failure. The United States, one of the largest carbon emitters in the world, withdrew from the treaty before it ever began. Thirty-seven developed-world countries remained in the treaty and though they can defensibly claim a reduction in greenhouse gas emissions close to or in excess of their commitments, most of that was due to the massive economic downturn of the past five years, which only inadvertently curtailed those emissions. Loopholes in the treaty allowed nations that moved polluting industries abroad (China, for example) to claim reductions. The most recent follow-up rounds of negotiation after Kyoto, including meetings (or "convening of the parties" – CoPs) in Copenhagen (2009), Durban (2011), and Doha (2012), were even less productive than those that came before, leaving the institutional landscape possibly weaker than at the outset.

An institutional perspective (as summarized in Chapter 4) reinforces an expectation that these outcomes might have occurred. Where some nations believe others are "free-riding" and where enforcement is minimal and soft, compliance in common property arrangements are often ineffective.

On the other hand, institutional theory stresses that if collective decision-making is encouraged and rules can be established, however tentatively, agreements are reached that build trust. With trust and experience between parties (what institutional theorists call social capital), it becomes possible to make more aggressive, more far-reaching sets of rules over time, to continue to tackle commons dilemmas. Did the Kyoto experience pave the foundations for something better in the future?

Beyond Kyoto: Toward new institutions?

The nations of the world are now considering what a future climate agreement might look like, beginning in 2015 and beyond. Several things have been learned from Kyoto, which will be instructive in any such effort. There is discussion of a treaty that cleverly works to lower not what carbon countries emit, but instead what they consume, in an effort to get at the real drivers of climate change in an equitable way. Carbon cap-and-trade systems (see below) that suggest market instruments for addressing the problems have emerged in Europe and elsewhere. Plans to include large developing nations are also under consideration. There may be room for a new global treaty that builds on the Kyoto experience, therefore.

Having said this, a great deal of activity on climate change appears to be occurring that poorly resembles the kinds of things predicted and advocated in institutional thinking. In the United States, for example, the "Mayor's Climate Protection Agreement" (Box 9.1) has initiated activities across the country, specifically without many of the necessary elements outlined by institutional theory, including any form of enforcement. Here, highly local and somewhat uncoordinated activities appear to have led to real reductions in emissions in cities, each with its own potential climate problems and strategies. This suggests that while a "post-Kyoto" period in managing CO_2 and other greenhouse gases may contain strong, negotiated, international efforts at dealing with the atmosphere as "common property," as predicted by institutional theory, other kinds of more ad hoc, local, and regional efforts, based on entirely different logics, may be more important than anyone has previously predicted.

Markets: Trading More Gases, Buying Less Carbon

Many critics of the Kyoto approach to managing emissions suggest that treaties are inefficient and rely too heavily on state mandates and too little on trade mechanisms to determine priorities and techniques for carbon reduction. One way of thinking about this problem that takes these concerns seriously, market-based thinking, invites us to consider the carbon flowing into the atmosphere, along with its potential negative effects, as externalities of market transactions and economic activity (Chapter 3). Viewed this way, we understand the potential effects of warming merely as the hidden costs of production that have not been appropriately borne and paid for by emitters of greenhouse gases reaping the benefits. After all, the potential costs of global warming are predictably economic as well as social and ecological. New costs of cooling homes can be predicted from warming, for example, as can failed crop harvests resulting from undesirable and disastrous weather events. Even a massive loss of biodiversity resulting from global climate change represents a kind of hidden cost, insofar as new and unknown species may be economically valuable now or in the future.

Box 9.1   Environmental Solution? The Mayor's Climate Protection Agreement

Climate change is almost universally assumed to be a "global" problem. This is because carbon doesn't stay put and circulates through the atmosphere, having effects (e.g., global warming) far from its source. This view also leads to an understanding of the problem as largely one of international treaty-making to solve an international common property problem.

It might at first seem unclear, therefore, why the smaller political jurisdictions in the world – cities – would be leading actors in initiating a coordinated response to climate change. And yet, by May of 2007, over 500 US mayors had signed an agreement to meet or exceed Kyoto Protocol targets within their jurisdictions (a 7 percent reduction from 1990 levels by 2012). The Mayor's Climate Protection Agreement stresses that municipalities use the tools at their disposal, including planning, transportation, forest plantation, and public education, to decrease greenhouse gas outputs, especially carbon. Originally launched by Seattle Mayor Greg Nickels, the agreement now spans the country, and includes cities in every state. While for some municipalities the agreement may be symbolic, for most it has led to radical action and real reductions. The city government of Seattle, for example, has cut its own greenhouse gas output by more than 60 percent of 1990 levels and is moving quickly to bring the city as a whole into compliance. Taking advantage of obvious capacities in urban governance, like new density zoning and the provision of public transportation, cities are far more effective than individual people in changing regional climate footprints (Mayor's Climate Protection Center 2009).

But why did cities act? In some cases, it is clear that the potential effects of global change on specific municipal resources (water, for example) prodded cities into action. Some coastal cities face sea-level rise, others depend on ski tourism that depends on snow pack. There is some instrumental logic, therefore, for city action to precede that of US federal government, which, at the time of writing, had not yet signed and ratified the Kyoto Protocol. So too, many of the efforts of cities to meet these targets – reducing the energy demands of municipal buildings for example – represent win–win cases, where the city benefits in cost savings by meeting emission goals.

This case also suggests some of the limits of strictly instrumental logic for explaining environmental governance behaviors, however. These cities all have clear disincentives to participate. Transition to a climate-friendly city can be expensive. Institutional common property theory does not necessarily predict rapid cooperative action from disconnected parties like cities, especially when they are under no coercive obligation to act. And yet they did act. Cities are not the only such actors, moreover. US states have set themselves binding targets, as have interstate compacts. Clearly the political will to address climate change is broader and more universally distributed than might have been guessed. The Mayor's Climate Protection Agreement represents a very real and also happily surprising effort to stop the runaway train of climate change.

From a market-centered way of thinking, the problem here is that the economy is working inefficiently if those emitting the carbon (including commuting drivers, factory owners, or forest-clearing loggers) are not paying the "true" costs of their activities, which are instead visited upon other people or society as a whole. This hidden subsidy (of sorts) needs to be remedied one way or another.

Regulating emission reductions, as in Kyoto, is one way of managing the problem. It is possible to argue, however, that this approach may be terribly inefficient and therefore may lead to unnecessary sacrifices because the benefits of reduction are far lower than the costs.

How do we know when the benefits from carbon reduction are worth the costs required to achieve them? How do we know what techniques are most effective in managing the problem? Who should pay for managing the problem and how should the responsibility be shared? Kyoto answers these questions, as we have seen above, by negotiating a set of rules between diverse parties and imposing the resulting framework on the negotiators. It is democratic, in that sense, but is it efficient?

In contrast, the way of thinking summarized in Chapter 3 suggests that the most efficient way of dealing with such a problem is to discover the true costs and benefits and determine the best actors to shoulder them in a market. Using a market approach might 1) let those experiencing costs of climate change *contract* with those causing the nuisance and pay them to cease, 2) insist that those who demand carbon reductions alter their own *consumption* behaviors to create new supplies of carbon-neutral goods and services, and/or 3) cause emitters to *internalize* these externalities so that the costs are borne by the producers, providing them with an incentive to lessen or halt the impacts. The first approaches are largely consumer-driven, while the latter is producer-driven. All should achieve the same result, an efficient diminution of undesirable environmental harms, but only insofar as people are willing to pay for that outcome.

Consumer choice: Green carbon consumption

Coase Theorem   A thesis based in neoclassical economics, holding that externalities (e.g., pollution) can be most efficiently controlled through contracts and bargaining between parties, assuming the transaction costs of reaching a bargain are not excessive

If people are worried about temperatures rising, they can pay the owner of a factory some fee in exchange for the reduction of their emissions. This contractual approach to the problem follows from the logic of the **Coase theorem**: no matter who the polluters or the aggrieved parties are, the most efficient solutions come from market transactions. If maintaining the climate is truly important and failing to do so visits serious costs on some people, then people should be willing to pay to forgo negative outcomes.

As Coase also pointed out, however, the efficiency of a contractually negotiated outcome requires minimal transaction costs, those expenses associated with actually negotiating the deal. On that front, turning this idea into a reality faces serious obstacles. If someone in Guam is threatened by sea-level rise owing to my driving a half-ton truck in California, how can we come to reach a negotiated settlement? How can a contract be applied that requires five billion people to negotiate with hundreds of thousands of factories and hundreds of millions of automobile drivers?

Barring this, how can the real cost of carbon be determined? Approached through the market, a more attractive solution emerges through consumer choice. If people do not want carbon to be emitted in industrial production, they are free to vote with their wallet, and buy only those products that are "climate-safe." Products might be labeled with per-unit carbon emissions to allow consumers to comparison-shop for the most climate-friendly products. Those products that do not provide such options would lose revenue and be forced out of the market, or their manufacturers compelled to invest in technology that makes them competitive in a new consumer culture. Green labeling on an enormous range of products already follows this logic.

A second solution is more direct. Consumers have the option of directly purchasing back their carbon emissions through offsetting. Carbon offsetting typically involves a consumer sending money to support some form of activity that "retires" carbon from the carbon cycle, by sequestering it in growing trees or otherwise facilitating an activity that reduces carbon (replacing a coal power plant with a solar-powered one that produces an equivalent amount of energy using a lower amount of carbon).

According to the organization "Carbonfund," for example (www.carbonfund.org/), an individual seat on a 7,792-mile flight from Chicago, Illinois to London, England contributes 3.82 tons of carbon to the atmosphere. Carbonfund will accept a check for $38.53, which they will transfer into projects including some combination of renewable energy ("supports clean energy development, such as wind, solar, and biomass"), energy efficiency ("reduces existing energy use, much of which comes from coal, oil, and natural gas"), or reforestation ("absorbs existing CO_2 emissions, which helps to reduce the excess greenhouse gases that humans have added to the atmosphere"). The results of these activities, they assure, will sequester almost four tons of carbon from atmospheric circulation. And for your trouble, you also receive a certificate, a bumper sticker, a window decal, and a pen.

In theory as well as practice therefore, people's willingness to pay has been harnessed into new markets in this way, and directed toward effectively reducing individual carbon footprints, consuming our way to a greener world.

Producer-driven climate control: Carbon markets and cap and trade

At the other end of the commodity chain, companies controlling the production of goods and services (from airlines to pulp and paper mills) can be considered equally culpable in carbon emissions as consumers. As pointed out in Chapter 3, one approach to carbon emissions is to impose rules on companies, telling them how much carbon they can emit and even the technologies they need to use to lower their rate of emissions.

A market approach eschews such **command-and-control** thinking under the assumption that firms will innovate solutions better on their own, albeit only if some financial incentive is attached to doing so. Here the solution lies in creating an incentive for the emitters of carbon dioxide to invest in new technology on their own, and find the least costly way of doing so. This requires an imposed collective limit of emissions on a group of participant members. Such a limit may be designed to decrease over years or decades, moreover, leading to reduced emissions over time. Each individual firm within the market owns a specific number of units of emissions, which represent the amount of pollution they can produce. Those who release fewer emissions than their allotted units may sell their surpluses to firms who cannot meet their limits (Figure 9.6).

Command-and-Control Forms of regulation that depend on government laws and agencies to enforce rules, including such things as regulated limits on pollution or fuel efficiency standards; contrasts with market-based or incentive-based approaches

Such a carbon market is by no means hypothetical. The European Climate Exchange (or ECX) opened for business in 2005. In this market, participants face annual greenhouse gas emissions targets. Firms able to reduce their emissions below these thresholds

Figure 9.6   The strange logic of carbon offsets. *Source*: Joy of Tech comic courtesy of geekculture
.com.

through innovation or change in production levels can bank their "surpluses" or sell them
to other firms.

Cap and trade has also become a potentially more important
part of whatever international regime follows Kyoto (as described
above). A program called "Reducing Emissions from Deforestation and Forest Degradation" (or REDD) is now proposed that
will stress purchasable offsets of forest, targeted especially at
marginal communities, indigenous groups, and other, typically
poorer communities, in forested and deforested areas. The mechanisms of this instrument are still under debate and discussion,
but the basic elements are increasingly clear, and would include
credits purchased by emitters to maintain and enhance carbon sequestration, with capital

> **Cap and Trade**   A market-based system
> to manage environmental pollutants
> where a total limit is placed on all
> emissions in a jurisdiction (state, country,
> worldwide, etc.), and individual people
> or firms possess transferable shares of
> that total, theoretically leading to the
> most efficient overall system to maintain
> and reduce pollution levels overall

benefits of the program ostensibly directed at communities who protect and develop forest cover. As we will see below, the history of various forms of offsetting, especially among marginal communities, is filled with failures. Nevertheless, the appealing logic of the approach – offsetting carbon emissions in wealthy industrial countries by paying people to protect their own environments elsewhere – matches the theoretical leanings of market proponents: discovering and paying the real price of the environment.

In sum, market mechanisms for rethinking and reworking human relationships to greenhouse gases are more than theoretical. Between carbon-sensitive products, carbon offset services, and carbon markets, it would seem that the most active area of addressing the problem of climate change is happening through capitalist systems of exchange. But there are reasons to treat these approaches with profound skepticism. As adherents to political economic approaches to the environment ask: If capital accumulation got us into this mess, why should we have such confidence that it can get us out?

Political Economy: Who Killed the Atmosphere?

As we explained in Chapter 7, a political economy approach to nature–society relationships stresses that the roots of social and environmental crises are in the economy. For political economists, reliance on markets, or even on rationalized management institutions, represents a distraction (or worse a deception) from the underlying drivers of the problem. For these theorists, most of the benefits of carbon emissions accrue to a tiny minority of people and corporate entities, who have little or no interest in allowing institutions to control their behaviors. Instead these interests actually seek to propel *further consumption* as a route out of the "carbon trap."

Green consumption is still consumption

From an economic point of view, the voluntary nature of the green transaction is the advantage of market mechanisms. People will only participate in an environmental effort, after all, if they get value from their investment, even if this is merely a sense of satisfaction. In this case, aggregated consumer willingness to pay effectively reveals both social preferences and the value of carbon.

From a *political* economy point of view, however, volunteerism is the great drawback of market mechanisms as a long-term solution. As pointed out earlier, those with the greatest ability to pay for offsets are typically those *least* directly affected by the actual climate impacts of carbon dioxide emissions and vice versa. Some green consumers in France, the United Kingdom, and the United States may be emotionally driven to pay for offsetting. Because of **uneven development**, however, it is the farmers in Côte d'Ivoire (whose income may be falling as a result of climate change) who are most poorly positioned to economically drive a change in the system. These poor, indebted, and nearly

> **Uneven Development** The geographic tendency within capitalism to produce highly disparate economic conditions (wealth/poverty) and economic activity (production/consumption) in different places

politically powerless farmers do not have the luxury of communicating their preference (for survival!) in a carbon market transaction. Money-valuation of a global problem in this way is both inherently undemocratic and ecologically ineffectual, since most "votes" and power rest with very few people, most of whom are distant from the impact of their own behaviors.

And the mismatch between sites of emissions and sites of impacts may be considerable. Small island nations throughout the South Pacific, most notably, face total inundation from sea-level rise associated with melting ice caps. Agriculturally dependent tropical countries, including India and other South and Southeast Asian nations that depend on monsoonal rain, are likely to experience more frequent, lengthy, and potentially more severe droughts (Cruz et al. 2007). These kinds of effects will have far more severe consequences in states with little money available for relief and emergency provisioning.

> **Capital Accumulation**   The tendency in capitalism for profits, capital goods, savings, and value to flow toward, pool in, and/or accrue in specific places, leading to the centralization and concentration of both money and power
>
> **Surplus Value**   In political economic (and Marxist) thought, the value produced by underpaying labor or over-extracting from the environment, which is accumulated by owners and investors

More fundamentally, a political economy perspective on carbon dioxide stresses the fact that **capital accumulation** demands sustained consumption and the production of **surplus value** by shedding of labor and environmental costs. Recall that, for *every* seller, there is a strong and ever-present incentive to make sure that people buy, utilize, dispose of, and repurchase as much as possible, as often as possible. Green consumption is still consumption, after all, and economic growth and sustained return for investment require growth of consumption (or continued cutting of costs by externalizing more waste). So too, political economy suggests that the demands of competition make it impossible for profit-driven firms to unilaterally reduce their subsidies from the environment (for example, by increasing costs to contain emissions) and still survive in a global market. This is especially true as economic growth means competition between firms and factories all around the world, including places like China and India, where environmental regulations are historically more modest. In sum, given 1) disconnections between sources and impacts that characterize *both* the carbon cycle and uneven economic development itself, 2) the gap between the power of those affected and that of those causing the effect, and 3) the importance of sustained consumption to keep production costs low, market-based approaches based on consumption have serious limitations.

To summarize, we can isolate at least five general and persistent factors that limit the overall effective potential of consumer-based solutions to carbon emissions:

- Companies/firms *must* strive for continuously increasing consumption levels.
- Companies/firms *must* strive to keep production costs low.
- The carbon cycle is marked by extreme disconnections between sources and impacts.
- Uneven economic development (as its name suggests) is also marked by disconnections between sources and impacts.
- Those who have the most power to change the market (the affluent, generally) are far removed from those who are going to bear the brunt of the negative effects of climate change (the poor, particularly poor residents of the "Global South").

Critique of carbon trading and other markets

Critic Larry Lohmann (2006) has extended the political economy perspective to include problems with the institutional mechanisms designed to capture and trade carbon outlined previously. Institutionalized solutions (offsetting, cap and trade, etc.), however attractive, have profound limits and pitfalls. First, there are basic problems in information, confirmation, and transparency. How do I know that this transaction *actually* results in a carbon reduction? Assuming the money goes to planting trees, nothing has actually been offset if those trees were to be planted anyway or if $15 worth of trees fails to grow in such a way as to sequester 1.5 tons of carbon. Who confirms and counts this carbon trail? What assumptions are made in the math and how is the accounting overseen? How much carbon is required in the process of confirming the transaction of managing and marketing the firm that oversees it? Given the prevalence of **greenwashing** throughout all consumer goods and the blatant exaggerations, misinformation, and downright lies that typify marketing more generally, this obscure procedure must be treated with skepticism.

Greenwashing The exaggerated or false marketing of a product, good, or service as environmentally friendly

Tracing dozens of failed experiments in offsetting, for example – where wealthy northern countries and firms pay poorer southern countries to plant trees – Lohmann and a large number of other on-the-ground observers show that local communities get little value from the investment. Time and time again, the commitment of land for such projects has resulted in loss of resources for the world's poor, and very little carbon is actually sequestered in these projects. Take the case of carbon forestry in Uganda, where a Norwegian energy company (that burns coal) paid the government to plant trees, rather than reduce their own power plant emissions. The results were typical (Bender 2006; Lohmann 2006). The company (and its forestry partners):

- bought up a massive 20,000 hectares of land but planted merely 600 hectares in trees, mostly fast-growing, ecologically less desirable, and exotic species;
- provided far lower real carbon sequestration results than anticipated on paper, although the value of those assets, since they allow firms to not expend on industrial equipment for carbon reductions, is on the order of US$10 million;
- paid a fee to the government that declined rapidly as inflation increased in Uganda, totaling less than $110,000 for use of the land for 50 years;
- evicted hundreds of families of farmers and herders from the land and provided 43 jobs in the process.

The clearly colonial implications of such an outcome are evident. Costs are visited on poorer countries, benefits accrued in wealthier ones, and limitations in real environmental improvements are hidden behind well-intentioned rhetoric. Since most of these transactions are obscure, under-regulated, and built into already existing economic relations, a political economy approach would predict such underperformance. Political economy highlights how, rather than being a step in the right ("green") direction, this project was actually a very savvy *investment* for the producers, with the end result being a typically uneven landscape of development (in Norway) and underdevelopment (in Uganda).

In sum, political economy thinking tends to privilege "structural" drivers behind the emission problem, favoring public investment in green infrastructure (solar and wind energy production), changes in subsidy structures (favoring tax breaks for the installation of home solar panels rather than subsidies for ethanol production), strong regulatory systems (setting direct limits on industrial CO_2 emissions), along with green taxes and other non-market economic incentives and global agreements that favor fixed and inflexible regional limits on greenhouse gases. These approaches are the same ones, it should be pointed out, that market-oriented thinking finds to be most inefficient. From a political economy point of view, however, they direct attention back to its source: *contradictions* in the economy that favor sustained growth over sustaining the conditions that make the economy possible (the atmosphere). As the effects of CO_2 emissions become increasingly evident, the debate over which of these approaches can produce the most tangible and immediate results is far from academic!

The Carbon Puzzle

In this chapter we have learned that:

- Carbon dioxide in the atmosphere has changed over millennia and that the conditions for global life can be altered by living things and people on the Earth.
- The rise of industrial production meant a parallel rise in an entirely carbon-dependent economy and society.
- Carbon dioxide concentrations in the atmosphere (along with other greenhouse gases) contribute to serious but unpredictable global climate change.
- Institutional approaches to the problem stress achieving international cooperation through careful compromise and effective rule-design.
- Market approaches to the problem stress the efficiency of green consumption and transferable rights to the atmosphere.
- Political economy perspectives stress the inherent limits and undemocratic implications of economic carbon reduction solutions to carbon production problems ultimately rooted in the economy itself.

Which brings us back to the slow-moving traffic crawling through "the tubes" in western Pennsylvania. Can international rules be designed to encourage governments to reduce the emissions of these cars in time to forestall serious problems, or are global climate treaties inherently too "shallow" to propel needed local action in places like Pittsburgh? Can consumer demand for a smaller carbon footprint alone lead to replacing those 100,000 cars with ones that run on electricity and that are fueled by solar and wind power? Can wholesale public infrastructural change eliminate the Pittsburgh commute altogether or is such an approach too expensive or draconian?

The puzzle of carbon dioxide clearly demonstrates the way contemporary society is deeply intertwined with environmental systems; the global climate system can no longer be understood separately from the global economic system.

Questions for Review

1. How has modern society dramatically altered the carbon cycle?
2. Without the greenhouse effect, life on Earth would not exist. But too much of a good thing can spell trouble. Explain.
3. How is the "free-rider" problem so potentially vexing to the challenge of mitigating climate change?
4. How does a cap-and-trade system for carbon emissions differ from the traditional regulatory approach?
5. Describe the example given of the market-based "solution" to climate change that exacerbated global uneven development. Did this program at least achieve its stated environmental goals?

Exercise 9.1   The Ethics of CO_2

In this chapter, we have reviewed how the puzzle of CO_2 might be addressed by markets, institutions, and political economy. Explain how you might understand this problem using an ethics framework (as described in Chapter 5). How might an anthropocentric approach differ from an ecocentric one? Do polar bears have intrinsic value? How might pragmatism and utilitarianism be employed to consider options for the control of carbon? What are the limits of an ethical approach to CO_2?

Exercise 9.2   Can You Do Better than the United Nations Framework Convention on Climate Change?

Outline an international climate treaty that would reduce emissions around the world to their 1990 levels. Things you will want to consider include whether stipulations will be the same for all countries, whether emissions or consumption of carbon is targeted, whether there will be trading or other kinds of flexibility, whether there will be monitoring or enforcement? How? Will offsets be allowed from forests or other efforts at sequestration? Once you have a sketch of what your treaty might look like, consider the following: What are the weaknesses in the treaty? What nations are more or less likely to sign on to your treaty? Why? What kinds of further compromises might be necessary to achieve a treaty that maximizes participation?

Exercise 9.3   Should Cities Think about Climate Change?

Visit and read the Climate Action Plan for the City of Seattle (http://www.seattle.gov/environment/climate_plan.htm). What kinds of steps does that city envision for itself? To what degree are their efforts directed toward reducing greenhouse emissions and to what degree are they about adapting to change? Given this is a "global problem," what motivates the city to address these issues at all? Do you think cities can make a difference in climate change, or is this something that requires a coordinated global action? Why or why not? What is the role of cities in governing climate change?

References

Bender, K. (2006). "Men chained to tree to protest UC." Oakland, CA: *Oakland Tribune.*

Cruz, R. V., H. Harasawa, et al. (2007). "Asia." In M. L. Parry, O. F. Canziani, J. P. Palutikof, et al. (eds.) *Climate Change 2007: Impacts, Adaptation and Vulnerability. Contribution of Working Group II to the Fourth Assessment Report of the Intergovernmental Panel on Climate Change.* Cambridge: Cambridge University Press, pp. 469–506.

Intergovernmental Panel on Climate Change (2007). *Climate Change 2007: The Physical Basis. Contribution of Working Group I to the Fourth Assessment Report of the Intergovernmental Panel on Climate Change.* S. Solomon, D. Qin, M. Manning et al. Cambridge: Cambridge University Press.

Lohmann, L. (2006). "Carbon trading: A critical conversation on climate change, privatization, and power." *Development Dialogue* 48.

Margulis, L., and M. F. Dolan (2002). *Early Life: Evolution on the PreCambrian Earth*, 2nd edn. Boston, MA: Jones and Bartlett.

Mayor's Climate Protection Center (2009). Retrieved March 19, 2009, from www.usmayors.org/climateprotection/.

Thompson, A. (2006). "Management under anarchy: The international politics of climate change." *Climatic Change* 78(1): 7–29.

Suggested Reading

Pearce, F. (2007). *With Speed and Violence: Why Scientists Fear Tipping Points in Climate Change.* Boston, MA: Beacon Press.

Sandor, R., M. Walsh, et al. (2002). "Greenhouse-gas-trading markets." *Philosophical Transactions of the Royal Society of London Series A – Mathematical Physical and Engineering Sciences* 360(1797): 1889–900.

10

Trees

Source: Wang Song/Shutterstock.

Chapter Menu

Keywords

- Acid rain
- Anthropocentrism
- Biodiversity
- Climax vegetation
- Disturbance
- Ecocentrism
- Ecosystem services
- Forest transition theory
- Induced intensification
- Market response model
- Preservation
- Primitive accumulation
- Reconciliation ecology
- Secondary succession
- Succession

Environment and Society: A Critical Introduction, Second Edition. Paul Robbins, John Hintz, and Sarah A. Moore.
© 2014 John Wiley & Sons, Ltd. Published 2014 by John Wiley & Sons, Ltd.

Chained to a Tree in Berkeley, California

On September 8, 2008, municipal authorities, riding in the basket of an enormous cherry picker, removed four men from the upper bough of a redwood tree on the University of California campus in Berkeley, and put them under arrest. This ended a long stand-off, in which the trees of the surrounding grove had been inhabited by protesters continuously for almost two years. Zachary Running Wolf had kicked off the protest when he climbed into the boughs of a tree 21 months before, in an effort to block the university's plan to build an athletic facility on the site. An organization of protesters, local activists, and environmental groups rallied around the cause and engaged in three lawsuits against the university. Calling themselves "Save the Oaks at the Stadium," they named themselves for the 200-year-old Heritage Oak and the more than 30 mature live oaks (among many other trees) that would have to be removed to make way for construction. One of the protesters explained: "There are no other oak groves like this. Some of [the trees] have been here longer than the school has. There's no reason to cut them down when they could just as easily adjust their development plans to avoid destruction of the grove" (McKinley 2008).

In the end, the protest was a failure and the ancient grove was removed to make way for the university's construction. In the intervening period, however, the protest was conveyed through national and international media, and gained the attention and vocal support of an enormous range of people around the country and the world. Doug Buckwald, a spokesman for Save the Oaks, suggested that the protest was one with global resonance: "When people see people standing up and taking a stand, it gives them the courage to envision possibilities in their own places. And I saw that in the oak grove."

Why did this protest so fully capture the public imagination and enjoin such dramatic conflict? Besides the spectacular nature of the feat – people living aloft in a redwood tree for two years – similar protests have occurred in places around the world, from Canada to India, where the fate of people and trees are entwined through economic development, political opposition, and ethical wrangling. Trees are fundamentally *symbolic* for people, after all. Consider the Christmas tree or the tree in the Garden of Eden, George Washington's cherry tree, or the story of Newton beneath the apple tree. And yet trees are also a very *material* part of human history (Delcourt 2002). Trees fueled civilization for the millennia prior to petroleum and their disappearance from the Earth's surface has paralleled the extension of agriculture and cities. In many ways, the tree is the core marker of the complex relationship of environment and society. As Buckwald observes above, the trees of Berkeley's oak grove do seem to stand in for something larger than themselves.

A Short History of Trees

In this chapter, we will introduce the puzzles that trees present society, stressing that the emotional role of trees for people is as significant as civilization's deep historical need for land clearance and forest destruction. We will stress that the reproductive capacity of trees makes forests (like many ecosystems) capable of recovery and creation, even while they are liable to ongoing destruction. We will also review three radically different approaches to thinking about tree-cover decline and recovery: population/markets, political economy, and ethics.

Notably in this chapter, like the others, we attempt to stress the difference between the objects in question (in this case trees) and the systems and problems to which they are intimately tied (in this case forests and deforestation). We do this to encourage readers to think about the specific characteristics of trees, and the importance of these for considering trees for contexts and problems beyond those few we review here. For example, how do trees fit in urban environments, in arguments between people over property boundaries, or in the development of new kinds of agriculture? So while forest cover is a central concern around the world, there are more to trees than forests. In this sense, we think it useful to start from the tree itself.

We define a tree here as a perennial plant with a woody structure. This broad definition includes more than 100,000 species worldwide (though it is impossible to know for certain), encompassing a quarter of all living plant species. The number, extent, and diversity of trees across the surface of the globe between the first appearance of trees and the present day have been highly dynamic, with eras during which leafy forests likely covered much of the Earth's land mass to others in which all but a very few conifers retreated before glaciers and other global climatic shifts (Cohen 2004).

More dramatically, there was a time on Earth entirely without trees. The first trees appeared a little more than 300 million years ago (MYA), an arguably recent event on a six-billion-year-old planet. These giant ferns only later gave way to non-flowering conifers (like our contemporary pine tree), and deciduous flowering trees appeared most recently, approximately 140 MYA.

Trees and civilization: A complex relationship

Nevertheless, for human beings, who themselves only made a recent appearance on the scene, trees and forests have typically appeared ancient and timeless, owing to their size and longevity. In a time before buildings or other large human-made monuments, some of the largest things around would have been trees. Given their enormity and their crucial role in providing food for humans, construction materials for shelter, and habitat for other species of importance to people, it is unsurprising that trees have long been a central symbol and site for worship and notions of the divine. And the history of human religious culture is filled with trees, including among countless examples the tree cult of Diana Nemorensis in Rome, the Bodhi tree beneath which Buddha found enlightenment, the Tree of Knowledge from the Bible, or Yggdrasil, the tree upon which the world sits in Norse mythology. Linked to these religious associations, trees and forests have often stood in for nature, the environment, and the non-human more generally, both as dangerous alien places and as sites for nurturing primeval truth (Figure 10.1).

Earliest uses of the word "forest" (or Old French: *forêt*), for example, specifically refer to wooded areas *outside* of the walls or fences of a park; an exterior space, associated with "wilderness" and "waste" (see Chapter 8 on the social construction of wilderness). Forest, in such an understanding, is a place away from culture. This ideology certainly made it all

Figure 10.1 *Sequoia sempervirens*, the genus in the cypress family Cupressaceae. Sequoia National Park, California. Trees are some of the largest and longest-lived organisms around which human beings live. Their influence on human culture has been enormous. *Source*: urosr archive/Shutterstock.

Climax Vegetation The theoretical assemblage of plants arising from succession over time, determined by climatic and soil conditions

Disturbance An event or shock that disrupts an ecological system, thereafter leading either to recovery of that system (e.g., through succession) or movement of the system into a new state

Succession Ecologically, the idealized tendency for disturbed forest areas to recover through stages of species invasion and growth, progressing from grassland, to shrubs, and eventually back to tree cover

the easier to cut trees and clear forests for cultivation and urban expansion over the past thousand years.

When forests and trees are venerated or romanticized, on the other hand, tree-centered thinking can emerge, for better and for worse. When forest destruction was noted in Europe and America in the early 1800s, romantic poets and philosophers began to associate trees and forests with virtue and freedom separate from the vices of civilization. Such feelings were later cultivated intentionally by government and industry to offer tree-planting as a panacea for social and environmental problems. These ideas, both fearful and romantic, remind us that the often ideological associations between trees and people need to be kept in mind as we sort out social and ecological explanations for actual forest-cover change.

Climax, disturbance, and secondary succession

Chief among the tools available to ecologists in explaining and exploring tree-cover change are the concepts of **climax vegetation**, **disturbance**, and **succession**. These three linked concepts, and their continued evolution in the field of forest ecology, have guided thinking about forest dynamics for a century.

The concept of climax vegetation was developed by Frederic Edward Clements, who worked at field stations around North America during his career as an ecologist in the early twentieth century. The concept suggests that broad physiographic and climatological conditions account for a "normal" or average vegetation type, "best suited" to local conditions, if things are left to themselves. For example, throughout the arid plains of Central Asia, it is to be expected that the typical land cover will be hardy perennial grasses. On the other hand, in Eastern North America we would expect various forms of deciduous forests, including oak–pine forest for example, or beech–maple.

When a periodic event occurs in such a region, like a massive rock fall, a fire, a hurricane, or a human-induced clearance, large areas of this land cover might be eliminated or dramatically altered. Hurricanes knock down trees. Fires or forest fires clear whole areas, and so on. Such an event is typically referred to as a disturbance. Disturbances are viewed as natural but also as unusual or atypical deviations that lead to only temporary changes. Over time, areas cleared of climax vegetation experience the colonization of new plants, which slowly give way to others, and eventually lead to the restoration of the climax community.

After a fire, for example, grasses invade burned patches, followed by various shrubs, which are slowly shaded out by trees. This is referred to as succession.

The implications for conservation and management of trees and forests from this understanding are clear: Minimize disturbances whenever possible and allow areas to recover through stages of succession after such events by preventing human intervention or pressure.

More recent ecological science has raised questions about the simplicity of this model, especially in terms of the role of disturbance. Specifically, contemporary ecological science has demonstrated that some important species (and often typical or dominant ones) often actually *require* disturbance to reproduce and function. Many pine trees of North America, for example, have evolved with fire and so require fire events to open their cones and clear the land for their successful germination. Some perennial grasses co-evolved with animal grazing and so require some animal disturbance activity to thrive.

The implications of this for trees and forests cannot be overstated. Rather than assuming that an *absence* of disturbance is necessary for a successful or diverse ecosystem, it may sometimes be the case that keeping such events from occurring (by suppressing fire, for example) may do more harm than letting them occur. Preventing disturbance in forests may actually alter their trajectory away from the "climax" community desired by people.

A related criticism of traditional climax theory emphasizes, on the other hand, that certain scales and types of disturbances may be dramatic enough to make it impossible for ecosystems to return to their original state. Allowing some forms of disturbance, therefore, may lead to permanent changes to existing ecosystems.

These scientific debates over the role of human beings in maintaining forest cover echo the larger cultural and historical debates about trees. Are forests things apart from society that should be left alone to thrive? To what degree is human intervention necessary for creating and fostering certain kinds of tree cover? Where should we expect forests and where might we create them? Ecological questions about the role of humans and the environment mirror far older questions about culture and nature.

How much forest is there now?

Of course, these debates occur in a context where total global forest cover has long been in dramatic decline. The total area of forests and woodlands around the world is estimated to have declined from 6,215 million hectares in the year 1700 to 5,053 million hectares by 1980, a loss of almost a fifth of the world's forest over a relatively short period (Grainger 2008). Where did all of these trees go?

Most available evidence points to deforestation being closely associated with the expansion of human industry, urbanization, and agricultural expansion. Forest is cleared to produce food and cash crops and to make way for urban development. Many secondary effects of human activity also hamper forests, including climate change and atmospheric pollution effects, like **acid rain**, which has damaged and destroyed forests throughout North America and Europe.

Acid Rain Deposition of rain or snowfall with unusually high acidity, resulting from the emission of sulfur dioxide and nitrogen oxides into the air, typically from industrial emissions. This form of precipitation is harmful for plant life and aquatic ecosystems

Yet, there is not necessarily a linear relationship between population growth and loss of tree cover. Consider, for example, that in many places where population has grown greatly (for example, Europe), forests are in a state of recovery. At the same time, urbanization actually leads to an increasing density of people in smaller spatial areas, which in theory makes room for more forests. Agricultural intensification, finally (see Chapter 2), enables the use of less land for the same amount of food production. There are reasons to believe, therefore, that forests have the possibility of recovery in a world full of people.

To better determine what causes forest-cover decline and recovery, more detailed analysis is therefore essential. The United Nations Food and Agriculture Organization's 2005 Global Forest Resources Assessment, a commonly cited source, estimates that current global forest cover is 3,952 million hectares, or about a third of total land area. Figure 10.2 shows the change in forest cover in the period between 1995 and 2005. Some caution should be used in examining these figures. Clustering world regions is always arbitrary and this skews statistics somewhat. For example, the large forest-cover figure for Europe (a region with a long and sustained history of forest loss) is increased enormously by the inclusion

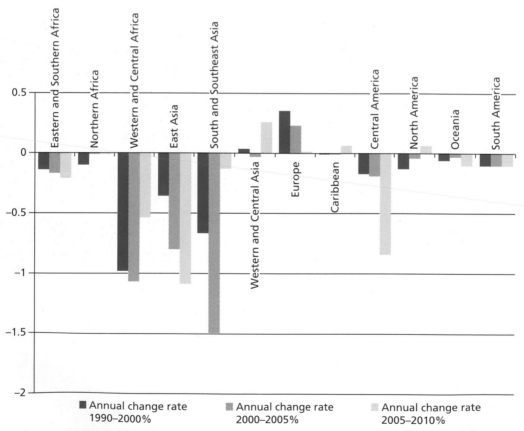

Figure 10.2   Global deforestation rates. *Source*: Data from Food and Agriculture Organization of the United Nations, Global Forest Assessment 2010, http://www.fao.org/forestry/fra/fra2010/en/.

of the Russian Federation, with its vast Siberian forests (in continental Asia) that account for four-fifths of that number.

The future of trees

Keeping this in mind, three things are still critically evident. First, forest cover continues to decline globally, with significant losses in Africa and South America especially. Second, however, and more subtly, declines in forest cover between 1995 and 2000 were greater than those between 2000 and 2005, suggesting that the net rate of deforestation (total deforestation offset by any regrowth or planting of trees) is declining, with possibly a cessation in the near future. Finally, some regions are actually experiencing reforestation, especially in the most recent period in Asia and Europe.

The return of trees to some areas is a complex matter (discussed at greater length below), but it can be accounted for by a number of processes. First, tree plantation often occurs on a massive scale. In the United States, for example, there are more than 17 million hectares of plantation forest, created and maintained by the government in conjunction with timber companies. That is a figure larger than the total forest cover of most countries in the world. Plantation forests are rarely ecologically similar to the original or older growth forests they come to replace. They are typically lower in diversity of tree species and are mostly even-aged, meaning the tree canopy lacks mixed structure and complexity. Plantations tend to support a lower range of native biodiversity and provide far fewer of the **ecosystem services** of native forests. In particular, this holds implications for **biodiversity**, since tree and forest protection and plantation is often not an end in itself, but rather a goal reflecting **preservation** values (see Chapter 5), which see the conservation of forests as a vehicle for the protection of myriad other species for which trees, forest soils, and complex forest growth form critical habitat. For many such species, plantations are a poor substitute for previously existing forests.

Second, forests regrow on their own, though at rates that are difficult to measure and generalize. As noted above, secondary succession quickly brings pioneer species into cleared regions, which leads in time to a mixed tree canopy and increasingly dense forest, though possibly one that may differ significantly from the forests that came before. Even so, forest recovery dynamics demand acknowledgment as much as tree-cover losses.

All of this suggests that a long history of deforestation is quite real but that current trends are hard to generalize. Some areas of forest cover are definitely returning, however. This short history of trees may give us reason for cautious optimism.

> **Ecosystem Services** Benefits that an organic system creates through its function, including food resources, clean air or water, pollination, carbon sequestration, energy, and nutrient cycling, among many others
>
> **Biodiversity** The total variability and variety of life forms in a region, ecosystem, or around the world; typically used as a measure of the health of an environmental system
>
> **Preservation** The management of a resource or environment for protection and preservation, typically for its own sake, as in wilderness preservation (compare to conservation)

Trees, people, and biodiversity

A final critical point is in order, however, one that again stresses the difference between trees – a diverse set of species and individuals – and forests, a systemic collection of many

Table 10.1 Comparison of the number of important insect species measured to be present in differing systems of coffee production in Costa Rica.

	Traditional production	Modern agrochemical production
Beetles in shade trees	128	0
Ants in shade trees	30	0
Wasps in shade trees	103	0
Ants on ground	25	8
Beetles on coffee bushes	39	29
Ants on coffee bushes	14	8
Wasps on coffee bushes	34	30

Source: Adapted from Vandermeer and Perfecto (2005).

plants, animals, and soils. A significant proportion of the world's trees are not in forests. People's interaction with trees, especially in agriculture, has meant that trees are commonly a part of complex land-use mosaics maintained by people. Trees are typically mixed into crop fields throughout Africa, Asia, and Latin America, and tree crops themselves represent a significant agricultural product. These trees interact with their surroundings to produce valuable and complex ecosystems that differ both from forests and from those agricultural spaces free from tree cover.

Consider the example of coffee plantations. Though modern coffee production removes all of the trees from the landscape in order to maximize production, traditional methods of coffee production integrate coffee plants into forest canopy, leaving many trees present. So-called "shade grown" coffee, with its mix of agriculture and tree cover, provides a range of ecosystem services and can actually sustain a great deal of native biodiversity, even while being used for commodity production. The data from Costa Rica shown in Table 10.1 demonstrate the dramatic difference between production systems that incorporate trees and those that do not.

Similarly, in the countryside of India, where intensive cultivation of cash crops is typical, the maintenance of productive tree-covered areas can actually contribute as much to conservation as native forest. In the growing of valuable arecanut (a nut used and consumed by 10 percent of the world's population in some form or another), for example, dozens of native bird species (including critically threatened hornbills; Ranganathan et al. 2008) are provided tree habitat. The diversity of important bird species is as high in densely populated agricultural areas as it is in protected conservation areas nearby. This emphasizes again the notion of **reconciliation ecology**, where even amidst productive human economic activities a range of ecosystem services are maintained and so biodiversity thrives. Trees have long been incorporated into the life worlds and production systems of human beings, even outside of "forests." This points the way forward to new ways of thinking about environment and society.

Reconciliation Ecology   A science of imagining, creating, and sustaining habitats, productive environments, and biodiversity in places used, traveled, and inhabited by human beings

Box 10.1   Environmental Solution? Shade Grown Coffee

Coffee is a crop for which there is a seemingly endless demand. Since the time of colonialism, when the plant was brought from its native Africa and Asia to Central and South America, it has been grown more and more intensively, meaning more coffee is produced on the same amount of land, year after year. To achieve these high levels of production, coffee is typically grown on vast plantations, where the land is cleared of forest, weeds and insects are vigorously controlled, and the full energy of the sun is used for growth.

The environmental costs of conventional coffee production are extremely high. Most notably, native forest is permanently destroyed in the creation of the plantation. In tropical and semi-tropical areas, this typically represents forest areas containing high floral, faunal, and insect diversity. It is hard to know exactly how much tropical forest and attendant biodiversity has been lost to coffee plantations over the past two hundred years, but the massive declines in forest cover in countries like Mexico in recent decades are closely associated with commodity production, especially coffee. Moreover, by managing this conventional "sun grown" coffee with intensive chemical inputs, non-target insect and plant species are typically killed and soils tend to degrade, losing nutrients and structure over time. This dependence on monocultural (single crop) coffee plantation also results in social and economic vulnerability. When prices for coffee collapsed in the late 1990s, many producers around the world became immediately destitute, with no resources at hand for recovery.

For all these reasons, there is growing interest in returning coffee production to its more traditional ecological and social roots. Originally, coffee was not grown in vast open areas. Instead, coffee bushes were seeded throughout existing forest with other crops, resulting in lower levels of production, but much higher diversity of crops, as well as wild flora or fauna. Such "shade grown" coffee could thrive amidst native vegetation, removing the either/or choice of forest versus coffee, or more generally: environment versus society. Shade grown coffee systems can vary enormously, from plantations that resemble intensive production but where coffee is simply intercropped with various trees, to systems so resembling native forest that it is difficult for visitors to tell by looking that farming is going on at all.

The problem with such a system is straightforward, however. Shade grown coffee, by definition, has lower yields than conventional plantation production. And during periods of low prices, as in the coffee price collapse of recent years, this leaves farmers even more economically vulnerable and indeed encourages them to clear forests for more intensive cultivation of different crops. To be sustained, shade grown coffee must, therefore, be supported somehow, either by consumers who are willing to pay a premium for more green or sustainable production, by governments interested in maintaining forest cover, or through cooperatives that can lower production and transportation costs for farmers. This makes shade grown coffee one of the more promising examples of reconciliation ecology, but raises questions about our willingness to collectively support sustainable enterprise.

The puzzle of trees

This brief review of the history of trees reveals many things about the relationship of nature to society. First, it emphasizes that the history of human activity on the land, including the agricultural revolution, urbanization, and industrialization, is deeply entwined with trees, for better and for worse. Overall tree cover and the composition of forested and wooded areas have been transformed dramatically by human activity, although the complexity of disturbance and recovery dynamics is still not fully understood. More specifically, this review stresses several things about trees that make them a specific kind of puzzle:

- First, because of their universal symbolic value, trees have come to stand in for all environmental change, in a way that makes them a useful conservation target for people, but sometimes also sidetracks or obscures other environmental trends.
- Second, human influences have caused precipitous transformation in dominant tree compositions and overall decline of forest cover over many centuries. Trees are therefore excellent (albeit disturbing) indicators of human economic growth and expansion.
- At the same time, however, trees show an ability to recover from disturbances and shocks and forest regrowth is as important a part of environmental history as forest decline.
- Finally, trees have oftentimes been a basic part of human life systems and productive activities, leaving open the possibility that continued human economic activity need not lead to a zero-sum choice of people versus trees, despite the real threat of global climate change.

Trees therefore provide lessons for understanding where humans are positioned in the world, but they also present a *puzzle*: given the capacity for humanity to destroy forest cover and alter species compositions of forests, and the simultaneous ability of tree cover to recover over time, what explains areas where deforestation does or does not occur? What explains patterns of forest decline and recovery? And to the degree that protecting forests is an important part of sustaining the global environment, how might we best consider and include the fate of forests in our planning, actions, and environmental ethics? Differing perspectives provide differing insight into these questions, with a wide range of answers.

Population and Markets: The Forest Transition Theory

Explaining why tree-cover changes is no easy matter. People cut and plant trees for a range of reasons, and the health and survival of forests and woodlands are often tied to air quality, climate, and a host of other factors. Overall patterns hint at some interesting global trends.

Consider the fate of forests in Europe. Figure 10.3 shows the estimated coverage of forests in the region (here excluding forests in interior Russia and Siberia) over the long term (Richards 1990). Forest losses in Europe certainly predate the 1700s and major tree-cover declines likely occurred as early as the Bronze Age (ca. 1200 BCE). Nevertheless, dramatic deforestation is immediately evident during the early industrial period, in which urbanization and the rise of manufacturing led to rapid use of forest resources. This is also a period in which agriculture spread into many areas previously left out of the reach of the plow. There is a clear connection here between increased economic activity and decreased forest cover. This makes the recovery of forests, evident in the most recent historical period, somewhat confusing. After all, economic activity has not decreased in the past hundred years. To the contrary, cities, roads, and farms have continued to thrive and expand. Is it some combination of population trends and economic activity that has led to this outcome?

In Chapters 2 and 3, we learned that applying demographic and market-oriented thinking to environmental problems often produces counterintuitive insights. An approach that begins from combining demographic transitions and market logics, therefore, may suggest a hidden pattern beneath this apparently contradictory trend. According to this way of thinking, there is nothing inconsistent in this reversal. Consistent with the idea of **induced intensification** and the **market response model**, early socioeconomic activity might account for the initial decline of forest, while the later pace and intensity of ongoing growth might begin to provide opportunities for forest recovery. Initially, expanding populations and economic activity put pressure on forest resources and the destruction of trees frees up land for agriculture and raw materials for fuel and construction. Later, however, that ongoing pressure is manifested in new land uses. This is because intensification of agriculture, coming from increased population pressure but also from increasingly commercial farm production, allows more crops to be grown on less land (see Chapter 2), opening the possibility of unneeded or marginal land to transition back into forest. At the same time, the rise in urban employment takes more people out of rural areas, leaving lands fallow, eventually allowing **secondary succession**, and reforestation. In theory, as productivity increases through intensification, and as demographic transition results from later industrialization, the value of potential agricultural land underneath forests declines, and tree cover can rebound.

Extending this insight to form a more universal rule, a combined population and market-based approach to forest-cover change predicts that, following a period of forest decline correlated with population and economic expansion, later economic activity and growth leads to forest return and recovery. This prediction is usually referred to as the **forest transition theory**, which holds that:

> over time, forest cover declines, but at some point a transition occurs, such that the decline halts and reverses and forest cover thereafter expands. This transition yields a U-shaped (or at least reverse J-shaped) curve for forest cover plotted against time ... (Owusu 1998: 105–6)

The very economic growth that destroys forests is necessary for their restoration and return. From this way of thinking, it

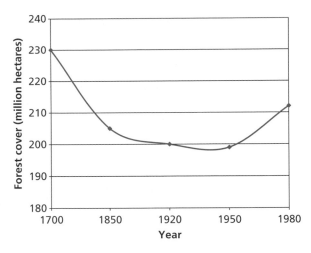

Figure 10.3 European forest cover from 1700 to 1980. The pattern of decline and regrowth follows a notably "U-shaped" curve, which has been a key argument in favor of the so-called forest transition theory. *Source*: Adapted from data from Richards (1990).

Induced Intensification A thesis predicting that where agricultural populations grow, demands for food lead to technological innovations resulting in increased food production on the same amount of available land

Market Response Model A model that predicts economic responses to scarcity of a resource will lead to increases in prices that will result either in decreased demand for that resource or increased supply, or both

Secondary Succession The regrowth of vegetation and return of species to an area cleared or reduced by disturbance, as where a forest recovers its "climax vegetation" cover after a fire

Forest Transition Theory A model that predicts a period of deforestation in a region during development, when the forest is a resource or land is cleared for agriculture, followed by a return of forest when the economy changes and population outmigrates and/or becomes conservation-oriented should be pointed out, high levels of expensive conservation efforts to protect forests must be seen as counterproductive. By delaying use and exploitation of forests, especially in economically poor but forest-rich nations, conservation is seen as retarding the use of crucial resources, which are essential to an economic transition that will yield less destructive economic forms and better environmental conditions down the road.

Certainly this is consistent with the positions of key international development lending institutions around the world. The World Bank Group and the International Monetary Fund (IMF) were both highly supportive of large-scale forest use in the developing world in the 1980s and 1990s. The country of Ghana, for example, as part of its IMF-sponsored structural adjustment program, increased its revenue from forestry by a hundred million dollars by the early 1990s, generating large-scale economic activity and using the revenue to pay down a significant portion of its massive external debt (Owusu 1998). Assuming a more stable future economy in Ghana following the crisis (no small assumption), trees would be predicted to return in a country that is more urban, less agrarian, and decreasingly dependent on forestry and agriculture. And some evidence is indeed available that forest recovery has occurred in developing countries around the world. Countries like Algeria (with a growing oil-revenue-based economy), India, Egypt, China (with entirely plantation-based forest expansions), and Chile (with an increasingly diversified economy) now all report forest cover increases after long periods of loss or decline.

Limits of the U-curve model

Though attractive and convincing on the merits of the data available from the European historical case, the prediction of a U-curve recovery of trees is by no means without problems. First, as noted previously, the ecology and composition of secondary forests are by no means similar to the primary forests they come to replace. These later forests tend to be lower in biomass, less diverse in the range of tree species they contain, and often less useful for local human populations, to say nothing of the fauna that depended on the original forest cover for habitat. Plantation forests are even further ecologically removed from native tree cover, and are sometimes typified by a small range of fast-growing species. So even to the extent that forest recovery may be a product of economic transition, there is no guarantee that recovery does not still represent a significant and highly undesirable loss of original forests.

More troubling, a vast majority of nations around the world are experiencing deforestation and show little or no sign of immediate forest recovery. In the Ghanaian case described above, the country lost 1,300,000 hectares of old-growth hardwood forest between 1980 and 1990, with a mere 11 percent of its original closed-canopy moist forest remaining at the end of the millennium. Despite a massive revenue stream from forest exploitation in that country and a significant reduction of debt in the process, moreover, deforestation continues unabated, with very high 2 percent deforestation rates in both the periods 1995–2000 and 2000–5. From the point of view of both protecting native biodiversity and sustaining the still heavily forestry-dependent economy, if a U-curve recovery of trees is on the way in Ghana, it had probably better happen soon.

This latter problem, the unevenness of forest transition outcomes between countries, might be considered from a few different angles. In part, it may be necessary to conclude that forest transition is inevitably uneven and that the peculiar geographies and histories of some nations and forests make it more likely in some places than in others. We might conclude that some countries are simply easier places for forests to recover than others.

It might also be argued, on the other hand, that this very unevenness is a symptom of a larger problem reflected by tree-cover decline. Specifically, it might be argued that the decline of forests in one region is *linked* to their recovery in another. In this view, the expansion of the global economy actually facilitates the extraction of forests from poorer regions (sites of deforestation) to serve as raw materials and commodities for wealthier economies (sites of reforestation). Such an argument is rooted in political economy.

Political Economy: Accumulation and Deforestation

You will recall from Chapter 7 that the history of the expansion of economic growth is frequently viewed as inherently problematic for the environment. From a political economy point of view, decline in tree cover is foremost a problem of the expansion of development, here understood specifically as capitalist agriculture.

For example, small farm producers in a tropical country may traditionally operate by keeping their land in a range of crops, including some for the market and others for subsistence, leaving some proportion of the land in fallow, and some portion of the area under trees and tree crops. Some local forests might also be held as community land or resources. This is a typical situation around the world.

Deforestation may begin when a large company, working either legitimately or illegally, claims large areas of this communally held land, which is cleared for the most efficient mode of cash crop production: plantation agriculture. Those who have lost land or supplemental resources in this seizure (**primitive accumulation**) face some difficult choices. First, they may remain on the land and attempt to compete with larger producers, who are selling products at lower prices. This will necessarily entail putting more land under cultivation (and so cutting trees on cropland). It may also require that the producers increase their available cash on hand in order to pay for increased inputs into their land, in the form of fertilizers or pesticides. That new income will either demand an increase in cultivated land (again leading to tree clearing) or the sale of labor on nearby plantation farms, turning producers into workers.

> **Primitive Accumulation**   In Marxist thought, the direct appropriation by capitalists of natural resources or goods from communities that historically tend to hold them collectively as, for example, where the common lands of Britain were enclosed by wealthy elites and the state in the 1700s

For both the large plantation operator and the small producers left on the land, moreover, the extensification of production (expanding the area under crops) and the intensification of production (putting more capital inputs like pesticides into the land to gain higher yields) have ecological impacts, both in the form of immediate forest cover loss, as well as declines in soil conditions favoring historical tree species coverage. Both retard the return or recovery of trees and both result in the increased availability of these cash crops (say, bananas) on the market, leading to a decline in prices. As prices fall further

Table 10.2 Some key tropical exports and their leading export countries. Most major tropical commodities are grown in forest frontiers of countries experiencing tropical deforestation.

Tropical commodity	Leading exporters	Deforestation rates 2005–2010 (% annual)*
Robusta Coffee	Vietnam	+1.08
	Brazil	−0.42
	Indonesia	−0.71
Cacoa	Côte d'Ivoire	NA
	Indonesia	−0.71
	Ghana	−2.19
Bananas	Ecuador	−1.89
	Costa Rica	+0.90
	Colombia	−0.17

*Source: Data from FAO Global forest Resource Assessment (http://www.fao.org/forestry/fra/fra2010/en/).

in a commodity crisis, the need to continue to extend farming into more forest land and to intensify production using modern, forest-averse techniques becomes greater. Producers continue to expand and intensify production to make up for losses accrued in falling markets, leading to poorer prices, more forest clearance, and more intensive mining of soils. From a political economy perspective, therefore, deforestation is a symptom of inevitable crises in capitalist agriculture.

Such bouts of sustained deforestation and their association with the booms and busts of commodity prices are a basic and repeated part of the ecological history of the poorer parts of the world, especially the forested tropics. As shown in Table 10.2, exports like coffee, bananas, and cacao are grown in forested tropical countries, typically at the forest edge, where deforestation advances.

Deforestation as uneven development

From a political economy point of view, the second feature of this development history is that there is a tendency for the value from agricultural development in these forested areas to accumulate in faraway places. Specifically, the companies that own the coffee and banana plantations that displace forest cover, as well as the companies that buy, process, and resell these commodities, are typically headquartered in distant countries and financed by banks and firms far from the site of forest-cover decline. They are also highly concentrated and extremely few in number. In banana production and export, for example, five companies control the entire global trade in the commodity and are typically headquartered and financed in the United States and Europe (Table 10.3).

The examples of tropical commodities like bananas and coffee are ones that most immediately come to mind when considering tropical deforestation, but they are by no means

Table 10.3 The predominant banana export companies operating globally, their share of the market, and their headquartered locations.

Banana company	Est. % of global market	Headquarters and financing
Dole Food Co. (formerly Standard Fruit)	25	USA
Chiquita Brands International (formerly United Fruit Company)	25	USA
Fresh Del Monte Produce	15	USA (Chilean-based IAT Group w/capital held in the United Arab Emirates)
Exportadora Bananera Noboa (Bonita brand)	9	Ecuador (Grupo Noboa)
Fyffes	7	Republic of Ireland

Source: Data from Bananalink (http://www.bananalink.org.uk/content/companies).

the only ones. Soybeans present a perhaps even more spectacular example. This crop can be grown in a range of climates and is a dominant cash crop in North America and China among other locations. Yet the increasing amount of land cover given over to this crop in South America is astounding, with more than 20 million hectares of land under soybeans today in Brazil, for example, a country that grew no soybeans in 1960. The expansion of these cash crops commonly comes at the continued expense of tree cover.

The luxury to allow and subsidize the regrowth of forests in places like Europe and North America, therefore, depends on economic growth and affluence, created from investments and profits made in deforesting tropical countries. In this sense, the forest transition in developed countries *depends upon* forest-cover loss somewhere else. The rise of forests in Europe is predicated on their continued decline elsewhere in the world. The political economy approach therefore may acknowledge a forest transition, but views it as one where forest cover moves from locations of exploitation to those of accumulation. The crisis of deforestation is not solved by economic growth in such an account; instead it is *simply moved around*.

Ethics, Justice, and Equity: Should Trees Have Standing?

As noted in Chapter 7, the insistence of a political economy approach on interpreting society's relationship to the environment as solely rooted in human economic interests has some shortcomings. How might we explain the expanding environmental consciousness of the global public, including not only marginal communities but global elites? And to the degree that people in part hold **ecocentric** values (Chapter 5), how can these

Ecocentrism An environmental ethical stance that argues that ecological concerns should, over and above human priorities, be central to decisions about right and wrong action (compare to anthropocentrism)

be extended to forest protection, management decisions, and more socially and ecologically desirable outcomes? How might we use ethical and legal tools *here and now* to rework society's relationship with trees?

This question has nowhere been more directly addressed than by legal scholar Christopher Stone, who asks whether trees should have actual legal rights and standing in court. He argues that the history of Western enlightenment and common law legal traditions is one in which things initially without rights are progressively granted such rights over time. For example, under Western law for hundreds of years, children did not have rights. They could be legally punished, worked, or married off at the discretion of the patriarch. Much the same can be said of a number of people and entities that enjoy legal rights now, including women in traditional patriarchy, black people under slavery, or non-landholders under feudalism. It would seem absurd to us now that these people would not have the same legal rights as others (specifically, as adult, white, landholding men), but for long periods this was the case. Slowly, Stone argues, legal tradition expanded the number of people and things recognized as having rights. Most dramatically, in most contemporary legal systems around the world, corporations actually now hold the legal standing and rights of individuals (though arguably few of the responsibilities).

What is it for something to have rights?

When Stone describes having "rights," he means it in the formal legal sense. This means, first, that if someone has a specific right (to vote, for example), some kind of public authoritative body (like a court) must be obligated to review any actions that might impinge on that person's right. Second, that person should have the ability to take legal actions (or for a guardian to take legal actions on behalf of that person) to defend these rights, and that a court must take injury to that person into account in their considerations. Generally, where something does not hold a legal right, moreover, it is typically considered the property of someone who does hold rights.

So as currently configured, trees definitely do not have rights. It is not in the interest of a tree to be cut down, for example, but no review is required for doing so as long as that action is taken by its owner. It might be the case that tree-cutting is reviewed by a court if it violates some kind of law (like the Endangered Species Act of the United States in the case where the tree was providing a place for a rare bird to live), but the review is not in defense of the right of the tree as an individual.

The same is true for natural beings and objects of all kinds. You cannot legally pollute a stream, for example, but the stream has no right to contest pollution of itself. Only people nearby who drink or use the water have that right. Moreover, if someone has to pay money damages for polluting a stream, they pay them to the people who live downstream, not to *the stream itself*.

What would the rights of trees look like?

Stone is quick to point out that a legal right for a tree would not make it universally illegal to cut down trees. After all, he insists, people have rights but they cannot exercise them everywhere all the time. Sometimes the rights of individuals are "executed" and constrained. Trees need not be exempt from removal or any form of harm. And not all rights apply to all things or people. Corporations cannot plead the Fifth Amendment, for example. Trees need not have the right to vote, therefore, or any number of other specific and inappropriate rights.

What it would mean instead, Stone insists, is that certain specific rights of natural objects might be outlined, based on current law. Guardians, or representatives, would be legally established to have the obligation and opportunity to take grievances against those imping-ing on the specific right of that object directly to court for review. This is already done for children and for those deemed not fully capable to represent their own interests in court (a corporation is so represented, as is an invalid). In sum, according to Stone there is nothing legal, practical, or ethically problematic about the extension of rights to trees, fish, oceans, rivers, or anything else.

It should be pointed out that this is an approach totally unlike a market perspective on the question of forests. A market approach to ameliorating deforestation might encourage reforestation by assessing the costs of deforestation to people and perhaps providing eco-nomic incentives to discourage forest-cutting. In a rights-based scenario, on the other hand, the damages of deforestation *to trees themselves* would have to be weighed and evalu-ated by a court in the calculation of harm.

So too, it differs dramatically from a political economy approach to deforestation. Such an approach would stress the unjust actions of large corporate and state interests, for example, that cause value to flow away from local producers. It might also perhaps point to the decline in the productive value of the forest in question, and call for direct political action in defense of the rights of local people. A rights-of-nature approach, conversely, would force the acknowledgment of the *exploitation of trees themselves* and mobilize legal mechanisms to protect both local people and trees themselves against depredation.

In a fundamental way, this is the approach that most acknowl-edges that forests are constituted by trees, living things with interests upon whom deforestation acts. As counterintuitive as it is from **anthropocentric** ways of thinking, it is one that perhaps has the best view of the trees through the forest.

> **Anthropocentrism** An ethical standpoint that views humans as the central factor in considerations of right and wrong action in and toward nature (compare to ecocentrism)

The Tree Puzzle

In this chapter we have learned that:

- The extent and composition of global tree cover has varied tremendously across global and human history.
- Humanity's complex and deeply emotional relationship to trees and forests has histori-cally enabled the destruction of forests in the past but also a sometimes overly single-minded fixation on forest recovery.

- Human activities in recent centuries have clearly been linked to a significant overall decline in forest cover.
- Forest cover is actually increasing in some areas and data tracking forest-cover change are not foolproof.
- Market approaches to the problem of deforestation stress the forest transition theory and the recovery of tree cover through economic growth and development.
- Political economy approaches to deforestation explain tree-cover decline as a result of the flow of value from forests, especially through commodity production.
- Ethics-based approaches to the problem might employ an extension of legal rights to natural objects to address rampant destruction of forests and trees.

This brings us back to the grove of oaks in Berkeley. Despite the heroic efforts of the protesters and the legal efforts of activist groups, these trees no longer exist. Could a forest transition occur in North American cities (like Berkeley) through some form of valuation of trees? Did the protest here fail because it was not explicit enough and sufficiently directed toward the more fundamental political and economic structural constraints that directed priorities toward athletic facilities rather than trees? Was legal action insufficient here because the rights of trees themselves cannot be considered in a court under current legal precedent?

Whatever the answer to these questions, the Berkeley protesters did know and prove something fundamental. Trees are one of the most persistent puzzles in the history of environment and society interactions. The traces of humanity on earth are most evident in the dramatic decline and recovery of forests. Getting between an ax and a tree is an extremely powerful way of getting someone's attention.

Questions for Review

1. Describe a forest passing from disturbance through succession to climax, as theorized (and idealized) by Frederic Clements.
2. What management implications arose from Clements' theory of succession? How has contemporary ecological theory altered these notions?
3. What, generally, does the forest transition theory predict? Should its predictions be received as unqualified good news?
4. What does it mean to say that forest clearance in the Global South is an extension of colonial relations with the Global North?
5. Does Christopher Stone's proposition establish a truly ecocentric basis for forest conservation and management? How so or why not?

Exercise 10.1   Trees and Institutions

In this chapter, we have reviewed how the puzzle of trees might be addressed by population, markets, political economy, and ethics. Is there room for an analysis or set of solutions to deforestation that relies on institutions, collective action, and common property theory? How are forests and deforestation a collective action problem? What would an institutional solution to forest-cover loss look like? What are the limits of viewing trees as common property?

Exercise 10.2   Are Plantation Forests Useful Forests?

Compare information on plantation forests from *Sinkswatch* (http://www.sinkswatch.org/plants.html), an organization that "tracks and scrutinises carbon sequestration projects," with information on plantations from *Green Resources* (http://www.greenresources.no/company.aspx), a company that manages plantations for carbon storage. Do you think plantation forests are a viable component of addressing global climate change (see Chapter 9)? What are the limits of plantation forests for replacing lost original forests? What advantages do they have over "pristine" forests, if any?

Exercise 10.3   Appreciating Trees

This video (http://www.youtube.com/watch?v=BickMFHAZR0) from the science videoblog Veritasium explains, with a little basic science, the incredible wonder of how trees can raise water to their highest parts, an amazing feat that otherwise appears to defy some basic facts about the physics of suction. Consider trees for a moment. What other characteristics are most notable, mysterious, or impressive? What qualities of trees might have stood out to people living in other eras or times in history? What makes trees such potent symbols of nature?

References

Cohen, S. E. (2004). *Planting Nature: Trees and the Manipulation of Environmental Stewardship in America*. Berkeley: University of California Press.

Delcourt, H. R. (2002). *Forests in Peril: Tracking Deciduous Trees from Ice-Age Refuges into the Greenhouse World*. Blacksburg, VA: McDonald and Woodward Publishing.

Grainger, A. (2008). "Difficulties in tracking the long-term global trend in tropical forest area." *Proceedings of the National Academy of Sciences of the United States of America* 105(2): 818–23.

McKinley, J. (2008). "Berkeley tree protesters climb down." *The New York Times*, September 10.

Owusu, J. H. (1998). "Current convenience, desperate deforestation: Ghana's adjustment program and the forestry sector." *Professional Geographer* 50(4): 418–36.

Ranganathan, J., R. J. R. Daniels, M. D. S. Chandran, P. R. Ehrlich, and G. C. Daily (2008). "Sustaining biodiversity in ancient tropical countryside." *Proceedings of the National Academy of Sciences of the United States of America* 105(46): 17852–4.

Richards, J. F. (1990). "Land transformation." In B. L. T. Turner, W. C. Clark, R. W. Kates, et al. (eds.) *The Earth as Transformed by Human Action*. Cambridge: Cambridge University Press, pp. 163–78.

Suggested Reading

Hecht, S., and A. Cockburn (1989). *The Fate of the Forest: Developers, Destroyers and Defenders of the Amazon*. London: Verso.

Shiva, V. (1988). *Staying Alive: Women, Ecology and Development*. London: Zed Books.

Tudge, C. (2005). *The Tree*. New York: Three Rivers Press.

Vandermeer, J., and I. Perfecto (2005). *Breakfast of Biodiversity: The Truth about Rainforest Destruction*, 2nd edn. Oakland, CA: Food First.

Williams, M. (2006). *Deforesting the Earth*. Chicago: University of Chicago Press.

11

Wolves

Source: Jim DeLillo/Shutterstock.

Chapter Menu

Keywords

- Anthropocentrism
- Apex predators
- Background extinction rate
- Biodiversity
- Conservation biology
- Ecocentrism
- Ethics/ethical
- Extinction crisis
- Masculinity
- Natural resource management
- NEPA
- Niche
- Reconciliation ecology
- Rewilding
- Stakeholders
- Sustainability
- Trophic cascades
- Trophic levels

Environment and Society: A Critical Introduction, Second Edition. Paul Robbins, John Hintz, and Sarah A. Moore.
© 2014 John Wiley & Sons, Ltd. Published 2014 by John Wiley & Sons, Ltd.

The Death of 832F

On December 6, 2012, a wolf known as "832F" was legally shot by a licensed hunter just outside the boundaries of Yellowstone National Park. Three days later, the *New York Times* ran a feature highlighting the controversy surrounding the wolf's death. After all, 832F (alphanumerically named by wolf biologists, the "F" is for the pack it belonged to) was Yellowstone's "best known wolf," a "tourist favorite," even a "rock star" (Schweber 2012). 832F was the alpha female of the Lamar Valley pack. Spending much of their time hunting and frolicking in the wide expanses of an open valley that is within view of one of the park's main thoroughfares, the Lamar Valley pack is Yellowstone's most-watched wolf pack (by scientists and tourists alike).

The controversy surrounding 832F's death is not just another manifestation of the ages-old hunting versus anti-hunting debate. This controversy goes far deeper than that. To begin to tap into the ideologies and emotions fueled by this debate, we have to backtrack to the morning of January 12, 1995. On what would otherwise have been a quiet winter morning, hundreds of people lined US Highway 89 to witness a celebrity motorcade traveling through the northwest entrance to the park. Within the trailer were eight wolves from Canada. Their destination, indeed, was Lamar Valley. Yellowstone's last wolf had been shot in the 1920s and they had been absent from this magnificent ecosystem since then, but the federal government was taking the bold step of reintroducing them to the park. Department of the Interior Secretary Bruce Babbitt, one of the many high-ranking officials on hand, called it a "day of redemption and a day of hope" (Fischer 1995: 161). The mood was triumphant, but the good vibes were quickly dampened, at least for a few hours.

The night before, the Wyoming Farm Bureau (representing agricultural interests, including livestock raisers) had filed an emergency appeal in federal court to halt the reintroduction. Standard practice is for judges to issue "stays" (temporary halting of actions) to give themselves time to review the appeal. The judge initially called a 48-hour stay on the reintroduction, meaning that the wolves could not be released into the park for two days. The judge, as it turns out, did not need two days to decide whether to grant the appeal; early that same evening the stay was lifted and the wolves were released from their pens into the Yellowstone snow. Environmentalists cheered. Yellowstone was, as many emotionally said, finally "whole" again. Ranchers and many other locals, however, greeted the event with mortification.

Since their reintroduction to the park in 1995 (and along with a second reintroduction a few hundred miles to the west), wolves have thrived in the Rocky Mountains of Yellowstone and the surrounding ecosystems. Over a thousand wolves now inhabit their former haunts in this region. Indeed, they have done so well that Rocky Mountain wolf populations were removed from the federal endangered species list beginning in 2009. As such, management of the wolves reverted to the states (who manage non-endangered wildlife) and all three states surrounding Yellowstone have subsequently initiated wolf hunting (and trapping) seasons (even though they cannot be hunted inside national parks). As did their reintroduction in 1995, the decision to renewal wolf hunting sparked controversy, but this time livestock interests cheered while many environmentalists cried foul. The fact that the most famous wolf in the world's first national park was killed during the first wolf hunting season in the state of Wyoming in almost a century did nothing but add fuel to the fire.

How and why, then, did it ever happen that wolves were intentionally eliminated from nearly their entire natural range, *even in national parks*? Moreover, what could explain both the fanatical support from many for wolves' continued protection as well as the deep feelings of opponents of the species?

A Short History of Wolves

The wolf (or the "gray wolf," more technically), *Canis lupus*, is the largest member of the Canidae, the dog family (Figure 11.1). Other canids include foxes, coyotes, jackals, African wild dogs, and domestic dogs. Domestic dogs are so genetically similar to wolves that they are now considered by most to be a subspecies of the wolf, *Canis lupus familiaris*. Many subspecies of the gray wolf have been identified and include the endangered red wolf (*Canis lupus rufus*), the Mexican wolf (*Canis lupus baileyi*), and the Iranian wolf (*Canis lupus pallipes*).

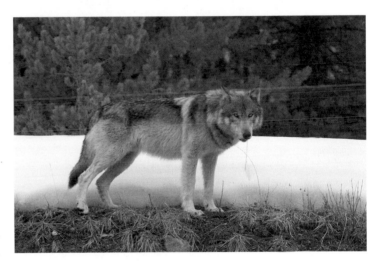

Figure 11.1 The gray wolf. *Source*: Al Parker Photography/Shutterstock.

The gray wolf evolved into something very close to its present form several hundred thousand years ago. Through successive ice ages (during which an ice bridge opened up between North America and Eurasia) the wolf spread throughout most of North America and Eurasia. An adaptable species, wolves occupy desert, grassland, forest, and tundra ecosystems. Adults range in size from around 45 pounds (the smallest subspecies is the Arabian wolf) to over 100 pounds (which would be a large northern gray wolf). Coat color varies widely, even within local populations, ranging from white-blond to every conceivable gray and brown to slate black. Most wolves feed primarily on ungulates – hoofed animals which include wild species such as elk, deer, antelope, and bison as well as domestic species such as cattle, sheep, and goats. Indeed, the ubiquity of domesticated ungulates is one of the primary reasons that the wolf has for so long been an object of concern and fear for human societies.

Despite conflict with humans, wolves still inhabit much of their historic range (Figure 11.2 and Table 11.1). Eurasian wolves live as far east as Eastern Siberia (Russian Federation), Mongolia, and parts of China. The largest Eurasian populations exist across Siberia southwest through the Central Asian Republics. Though critically endangered across the southern portion of their range, wild wolves still persist from Bangladesh across the Indian

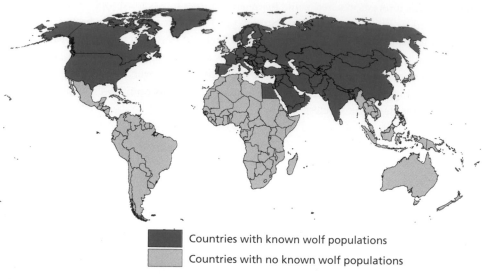

Countries with known wolf populations

Countries with no known wolf populations

Figure 11.2 World map of countries with known wolf populations. *Source*: Data from Mech and Boitani (2003) and International Wolf Center: http://www.wolf.org/.

Table 11.1 Countries worldwide with wolf populations of 2,000 or greater.

Country	Wolf population
Canada	52,000–60,000
Kazakhstan	30,000
Russia	25,000–30,000
Mongolia	10,000–20,000
China	12,500
United States	9,000
Kyrgyzstan	4,000
Tajikistan	3,000
Belarus	2,000–2,500
Spain	2,000
Ukraine	2,000
Uzbekistan	2,000

Source: Data from Mech and Boitani (2003).

subcontinent, west through the Arabian Peninsula (where very little is known about their distribution and numbers), even into Africa, where a small population of perhaps 50 individuals survives in Egypt. In North America, both Alaska and Canada have substantial populations, even though they were eliminated from nearly half of their North American range after the arrival of European settlement.

Wolves live in packs, extended families usually of about five to eight individuals. Most years, only one female per year per pack gets pregnant after copulating with one male member of the pack. Litters commonly consist of six to eight pups, but litters as small as one and as large as 14 have been noted by field biologists. Pups are raised by the entire pack. They are nursed exclusively for the first couple of weeks, after which pack members feed them regurgitated meat. Within a few months, pups are eating raw meat and their social activities have broadened beyond play. Within the first year, most are hunting with the pack. Young wolves will live as subordinate members within the pack for between one and four and a half years.

The social structure of the wolf pack is intimately tied to every facet of the pack's survival and reproduction. At least three hierarchies exist in every wolf pack: one for the females, one for the males, and a third non-gender-specific hierarchy that varies from season to season. The lead male and the lead female – often called the "alpha" wolves – are usually, but not always, the parents of the year's pups. Socially structured activities include raising young, play, territory defense, and hunting. Sound familiar? There exists a large literature on the parallels between wolf and human sociality.

The ecological role of the wolf

Ecosystems – geographical areas inhabited by assemblages of plants and animals interacting with their physical environment – contain multiple **trophic levels** which comprise the local food webs. Over-simply, these map out a food chain in which photo-synthesizing plants are consumed by herbivores, which are in turn consumed by predators. Wolves exist as **apex predators** (also commonly called "top carnivores") in that they have no natural, regular predators. Most ecosystems will have multiple apex predators. For example, in the Northern Rocky Mountains wolves, grizzly bears, lynx, wolverines, and golden eagles are all apex predators.

The **biodiversity** of a given ecosystem – the number of differ-ent species – is determined by a number of abiotic (non-biological) and biotic (biological) factors. Abiotic factors include availability of water, wildfires, storms, harsh winters, and the like. Biotic factors include limiting factors such as competition, disease,

> **Trophic Levels** Parallel levels of energy assimilation and transfer within ecological food webs; in terrestrial ecosystems, photosynthetic plants form the base trophic level, followed "up" the web by herbivores and successive levels of carnivores
>
> **Apex Predators** Also known as "top carnivores," the animals in any ecosystem occupying the top trophic level; apex predators do not have any natural predators
>
> **Biodiversity** The total variability and variety of life forms in a region, ecosystem, or around the world; typically used as a measure of the health of an environmental system

parasitism, and predation, as well as availability of food and habitat. Any change in the abundance of one species in an ecosystem affects other species and processes within the ecosystem as well (think of the well-worn ecological maxim *everything is connected*). Some changes are initiated from low trophic levels. Quite obviously, decline in a plant species in an ecosystem will affect the herbivores that rely on it, whose potential resulting decline would affect predators that rely on them. Species distribution and abundance within eco-systems is also regulated by changes initiated by high-trophic-level species. A decline in (or absence of) predators has effects on the distribution, numbers, and the behavior of prey species. As wolves are removed from an ecosystem, for example, their prey will increase in numbers (at least temporarily), but the effects invariably go well beyond that. Prey species freed from predation alter their feeding habits, which alters plant densities

Trophic cascades The effects on subsequent (higher or lower) trophic levels after the elimination or reduction in numbers of individuals in one trophic level

and distributions, which itself causes other changes, and so on. These destabilizing effects, known as "**trophic cascades**," course up and down through multiple trophic levels, usually resulting in a simplified (less diverse) ecosystem (Terborgh and Estes 2010).

Yellowstone National Park, site of a relatively recent elimination of wolves, followed several decades later by their reintroduction, provides a real-world laboratory of trophic cascades at work. Biologist Douglas Smith referred to Yellowstone after reintroduction as "the best chance we've ever had to figure out the difference between a wilderness system with wolves versus one without wolves" (Smith and Ferguson 2005: 118). One of the most prominent changes in Yellowstone since the reintroduction of wolves was the rapid recovery of willows. With fewer total elk (who feed on willows) more constantly on the move since wolf reintroduction, willows are not fed on as intensively. The renewal of willows has led to the reemergence of beavers, since beavers use willows for dams and lodges. Beaver ponds lead to a proliferation of reptiles and amphibians. Increases in eagles, magpies, and ravens have been noticed due to the wolf-kill carcasses left scattered about their feeding areas as well, with carcasses finally providing food for invertebrate species like beetles and decomposing in the soil, becoming food for detritus feeders and eventually becoming soil nutrients. The bottom line is simple: the Yellowstone ecosystem is a different place with wolves. So how was it that an iconic park like Yellowstone came to be bereft of wolves?

Three centuries of slaughter: Wolf eradication in the United States

When European Americans settled the New World, hundreds of thousands of wolves roamed across nearly the entire continent. By 1958, they had been extirpated from nearly all of the contiguous United States and Mexico (see Figure 11.3). So what, exactly, can explain the demise of such an intelligent, adaptable animal that existed in such abundance over such a large area? For over three centuries, wolves were subject to a systematic, and ultimately successful, extermination campaign.

Wolf bounties – moneys paid by the government to citizens who kill wolves – go back at least as far as 1630. The share of public revenue in the American colonies dedicated to wolf eradication is impressive. In Chester County, Pennsylvania, for example, 28 percent of taxes collected was spent paying out wolf bounties. Dozens of other counties and municipalities across the colonies spent 10 percent or more of their budget on wolf bounties into the eighteenth century (Fischer 1995). The eradication campaign was successful. By 1700 wolves were extinct throughout most of New England and by 1800 they were absent east of the Appalachian Mountains. In the nineteenth century, Midwestern states followed the colonial model and most quickly and efficiently eradicated their wolf populations.

After the Civil War, western expansion accelerated. With generous bounties paid by the federal government, "buffalo hunters" killed literally tens of millions of Great Plains bison (which were the primary subsistence base for many Native American tribes, as well as a primary food source for wolves). As livestockmen moved into the newly "opened" West, wolves became dependent on cattle and sheep. Predictably, a final campaign of

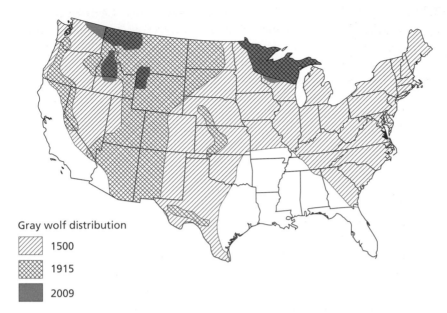

Gray wolf distribution

(hatched)	1500
(cross-hatched)	1915
(solid dark)	2009

Figure 11.3 Estimated range of gray wolves in the United States. *Source*: Adapted from data from the following sources: Current (2009) distribution: USFWS: www.fws.gov/midwest/Wolf/ archives/2006pr_dl/2006pr_dlsum.htm and Sightline.org: www.sightline.org/maps/maps/Wildlife -Wolf-CS06m/?searchterm=None; 1915 Distribution: Young and Goldman (1944), p. 58; 1500 Distribution: Mech (1970), p. 31.

shooting, trapping, and poisoning succeeded in eliminating wolves from all but the largest swaths of federally owned forests. Bounty hunters and forest rangers eliminated these remnant populations. The last confirmed wolves in Yellowstone were trapped and shot by park rangers in 1926 (Foreman 2004). All in all, thousands of wolves were killed in the United States by private hunters, cattlemen, and federal officers in the first few decades of the century. Fortunately (at least from the perspective of most environmentalists), the epic of wolf eradication was followed not too long after by the contemporary era of conservation. By the 1940s, nearing the end of their systematic elimination, wolves were slowly gaining advocates within the scientific and conservation communities. Wolves began to appear not as things that threatened the stability of nature, but instead as part of larger ecological processes and networks. Key pieces of landmark legislation would give legal teeth to endangered species conservation. CITES (Convention on International Trade in Endangered Species of Wild Flora and Fauna), signed in 1973, is an international agreement that bans or strictly regulates the international trade in plant and animal species threatened with extinction. Many wolf populations worldwide are listed under and regulated by CITES.

In 1973, the United States passed the Endangered Species Act (ESA), one of the most far-reaching and ambitious national environmental laws ever established (see Box 11.1). All existing populations of wolves outside of Alaska were included in the original list of endangered species covered by the ESA. Powerful environmental groups like Defenders of

Box 11.1   Environmental Solution? Wildlife Friendly Beef and Wool

One laudable recent example of **reconciliation ecology** (see Chapter 1) can be found in the Rocky Mountain Northwest, where livestock ranchers and conservationists are allying to simultaneously conserve wolves and maintain ranching as an economically viable livelihood. That this alliance even came about is notable, as ranchers and environmentalists have historically been rather adversarial parties. The source of a considerable amount of the tension between these two groups was the traditional "shoot on sight" mentality of many ranchers toward predators. Even though ranchers are far from solely responsible for the demise of predator populations, they nonetheless were vilified by many environmentalists, who often felt that predator conservation should override economic hardships of livestock producers.

Ranchers and environmentalists in some places, however, have moved beyond their differences to work toward a shared goal, the preservation of open space. The common enemy is exurban development. In places near rapidly growing cities and towns like Fort Collins, Colorado and Livingston, Montana, enormous portions of open range are being swallowed up by subdivisions, roads, and shopping malls. Many environmentalists saw ranchers as potential allies in the fight against this land-use transformation. Environmentalist–rancher alliances resulted in a substantial network of "conservation easements" in the region. In a typical easement, the rancher-landowner is granted some sort of tax break or other financial incentive in return for a guarantee that they will not sell and subdivide their land. The result is a win–win for both environmentalists and ranchers, preserving open space *and* livelihoods. Building on the productive relationships developed in the conservation easement movement, some ranchers and environmentalists have taken their alliance even farther. One of the more innovative ideas is "wildlife friendly" certification programs. The Seattle-based Wildlife Friendly Enterprise Network will certify beef and wool with their "wildlife friendly" stamp of approval if ranchers manage their herds using non-lethal methods. This might mean guard dogs instead of shotguns or poison, and it also might mean losing more livestock to predation. Ideally, the producers will be able to offset the higher costs of operation by selling to a customer base willing to pay a premium to know that their beef or wool was raised in a predator-friendly manner.

Reconciliation Ecology   A science of imagining, creating, and sustaining habitats, productive environments, and biodiversity in places used, traveled, and inhabited by human beings

Wildlife and the National Wildlife Federation pushed for aggressive programs to reestablish their presence throughout large parts of their former range (websites at: www.defenders.org and www.nwf.org), an effort that came to fruition in 1995, but whose outcome, as we have seen, remains contested almost two decades later.

The puzzle of wolves

This brief history of wolves provides insight into many facets of the relationship between nature and society. For one, it highlights that the relationships between humans and wild animals are complicated and change over time and across cultures. Wolves represent how particular "pieces" of non-human nature can be powerful symbols of broader aspects of the human–nature relationship. The history of the eradication and conservation of wolves shows how the very fate of the species is tightly tied to its cultural symbolic value. Wolves persist as a humbling (and hopeful) reminder of the difficulties of trying to live in the world without destroying its wildness.

Wolves are puzzles that force us to ask the following questions:

- Exploring our sometimes divisive relationships to one another – centered on wolves – how do we assert environmental priorities and govern our behavior in a way that is fair and democratic?
- Critically assessing our present relationship with wolves, *where* can we make room for wolves in a human-dominated world, and *how*?
- Assessing our historical relationship with wolves, what can explain both our persecution and subsequent celebration of this species?

Wolves present something of a window into humanity. When we look at wolves, we can see how science, industry, and emotion become entangled. Working to solve the puzzle of wolves, we may come a bit closer to forging a more sustainable relationship with non-human nature.

Ethics: Rewilding and Wolves

In Chapter 5 we established environmental issues as **ethical** dilemmas, problems of right versus wrong human actions toward nature. An ethics perspective is commonly applied to questions regarding the treatment of individual animals, both wild and domestic. Increasingly, ecological ethics also grapples with questions of right action toward species, entire ecosystems, and future generations of humans and non-humans alike. An ecological ethics perspective can have a good deal to say about solving the puzzle of wolf conservation.

Wanted: An ecocentric ethic of sustainability

An ethics of **sustainability** informs us that we have a moral obligation to sustain the quality and productivity of the environment for future generations. With this guidepost, we can critically assess current actions and ask, "Can such and such an action be continued more or less indefinitely? *Is it sustainable?*" If so, great! If not, then the *right* thing to do is to alter our actions so that they are sustainable. **Ecocentrism**, for its proponents, serves as a corrective to **anthropocentrism**. Seeing humans as part of nature, ecocentric ethics looks beyond narrow, human priorities to judge right and wrong actions within a broader, ecological context.

Even the deepest of ecologists, however, cannot really conform to a *solely* ecocentric ethic. We *must*, it seems, allow anthropocentric priorities to guide our environmental policy and planning, at least in part. For example, we need to divert some

Ethics/Ethical The branch of philosophy dealing with morality, or, questions of right and wrong human action in the world

Sustainable/Sustainability The conservation of land and resources so as to secure their availability to future generations

Ecocentrism An environmental ethical stance that argues that ecological concerns should, over and above human priorities, be central to decisions about right and wrong action (compare to anthropocentrism)

Anthropocentrism An ethical standpoint that views humans as the central factor in considerations of right and wrong action in and toward nature (compare to ecocentrism)

portion of the fresh water available in every ecosystem for use by humans. We should, in other words, simultaneously work to sustain the environmental conditions in which human and non-human communities can meet their needs.

There are some issues, moreover, that cannot be adequately judged through a strictly anthropocentric calculus. If you are a proponent of reintroducing wolves to New England or Scotland (two proposed wolf reintroduction locations), for example, it is difficult to make your case arguing along solely anthropocentric lines. Granted, wolf reintroduction in these regions might spark an ecotourism boom that could help revitalize rural communities, as it has for a handful of communities around Yellowstone. This is a thin line to walk, however, as it is difficult to predict the long-term economic impact that reintroduced wolves would actually have. Besides, what if economic projections show no economic benefits? Is that reason *not* to proceed? Most wolf supporters would answer with an emphatic "no," and as such, many environmentalists argue that issues like species reintroductions should be guided by ecocentric concerns.

This ecocentric spirit is most evident in the "**rewilding**" movement, which argues exactly along these lines, based in the philosophy of deep ecology and the science of **conservation biology** (Foreman 2004; Rirdan 2012). Deep ecology arms rewilding advocates with the philosophical tools to argue for an ethics of sustainability (*what to preserve, and why*) and conservation biology provides the scientific roadmap to get there (*what it will take to make it happen*).

Rewilding A practice of conservation where ecological functions and evolutionary processes, which are thought to have existed in past ecosystems or before human influence, are deliberately restored or created; rewilding often requires the reintroduction or restoration of large predators to ecosystems

Conservation Biology A branch of scientific biology dedicated to exploring and maintaining biodiversity and plant and animal species

Extinction Crisis The current era of anthropogenically induced plant and animal extinction, estimated to be between one thousand and ten thousand times the historical average, or background extinction rate

Background Extinction Rate Usually given in numbers of plant and animal species per year, the estimated average rate of extinction over long-term, geologic time, not counting mass extinction events

Rewilding, Part I: The ethical dimension

Every year, we lose a significant portion of the Earth's biodiversity. The magnitude of the **extinction crisis** is quite alarming. It is estimated that the current extinction rate is one thousand times or more the historical average or **background extinction rate**. There have been five historical major extinction events in the past half-billion years, the most famous of these also being the most recent. About 65 million years ago, dinosaurs and (less famously) many mollusks became extinct. As you likely learned in childhood, many scientists believe that this extinction event was kick-started by an asteroid impact. The difference between historic extinctions and the current crisis is that today's extinction crisis is an anthropogenic (human caused) event.

Anthropogenic causes of the current extinction crisis include: fragmentation of habitats, loss of ecological processes, invasions of exotic species, air and water pollution, and climate change (Hambler and Canney 2013). Concomitant with the extinction crisis, it is argued, is the impoverishment of genetic diversity upon which adaptation and evolution rest. The broader significance of the extinction crisis, therefore, lies in its potential irreversibility and longevity. Take tropical deforestation, another justifiably high-profile current environmental issue, for comparison (see Chapter 10). Even a tropical rainforest can rejuvenate itself given a century or two. In other words, when we destroy a rainforest, we are "undoing" a century or two's worth of ecological work. Compare this to the possible elimination of 50 percent (or more) of all living species on the planet, as the eminent biologist E. O. Wilson (2012) believes could happen *within this century*, and we have (some argue) something far more worrisome than a razed forest or depleted fishery. Rather, what we have is the undoing of tens of millions of years of the planet's biological heritage.

Considered in this light, it is no surprise that many holding a consciously ecocentric worldview place this issue – reversing the extinction crisis and renewing evolutionary processes – atop their list of environmental priorities.

Rewilding, Part II: How to get from here to there

Conservation biology is the scientific study of the biodiversity crisis. Many conservation biologists are also activists who promote rewilding. Rewilding advocates argue that "vast expanses of self-willed terrain [should] be protected and recovered" (Barlow 1999: 54). Central to rewilding is the ecological role of large predators.

Successes like the Yellowstone wolf reintroduction are a start, but supporters of rewilding acknowledge that if their broad goal of a global-scale renewal of biodiversity and evolution is to become a reality, areas outside of large parks and designated wildernesses require special attention (Sessions 2001). Indeed, there are many areas outside of formal wilderness where one might have "free nature," as Arne Naess, the founder of deep ecology, refers to it. Zones of free nature would be areas of sparse enough human habitation and intact enough natural ecosystems where the full complement of natural ecological-evolutionary processes could be restored and maintained (Nic 2003). Wolves would have to be reintroduced and managed on areas beyond government land, where people live, ranch, farm, and play.

Wary of the wild: Deep ecology and democracy

Which leaves us with "only" one small problem: How do we manage wolves once they are reintroduced to places where people live? Deep ecology may offer up ecocentrism as an appealing corrective to anthropocentric ethics and their attendant ecological destruction. Beyond giving us rather broad guideposts, however, deep ecology provides little help as to *how to make this happen all the while maintaining democratic forms of decision-making*. Some critics have even gone so far as to see deep ecology as leading to an *inherently authoritarian (or "eco-authoritarian") politics*. The potential of individual "self-realization" notwithstanding, when it comes down to managing real natures in real places, most proponents of deep ecology invariably fall back on *scientific* ecology as the final word for decision-making. Granting scientific ecologists sole responsibility for all management considerations regarding reintroduced wolves would be giving them literal authoritarian power; that is, decision-making control not subject to the checks and balances that constitute a democracy. This is a good part of the reason why proponents of, for example, "radical democracy" (a social movement dedicated first and foremost to maintaining decision-making power at all strata of society) are wary of calls for science (solely) guiding politics.

Happily, deciding "between" ecology and democracy is a false dilemma. It is possible to have our wild nature and our democracy, too. One of the more promising forms of such win–win ecologies arose out of this very puzzle, wolf management, in the North Woods of Minnesota.

Institutions: Stakeholder Management

Different people have different reasons to *positively or negatively* value wolves. Just to take a couple of easy examples: Livestock owners view wolves as a threat to their livelihoods, while (as discussed above) rewilding advocates see them as ecological necessities. This is part of what makes wolf management so vexing. It is not a matter of assessing how to divvy up a commonly valuable resource, like a patch of forest or an ocean fishery. Yet wolves are still common property resources. In Chapter 4, we reviewed the management of commons as problems often successfully solved through *institutions*, that is, "systems . . . leading to orderly and constrained use of natural resources." If wolves are to persist (at least without an authoritarian de-peopling of the landscape), environmentalists must *constrain* their "use" of the animals (i.e., they cannot be everywhere, their populations expanding indefinitely). Hunters and livestock owners, just the same, must constrain their traditional treatment of the wolf (i.e., shoot on sight). As such, people are experimenting with new institutional structures. The best hope for wolves, some say, is to get these so-called "**stakeholders**" together, and have them craft rules and responsibilities collectively.

Stakeholders   Individuals or groups with a vested interest in the outcome of disputed actions

Natural Resource Management   Both the academic discipline and professional field dedicated to the management of environmental conditions, goods, or services for social goals, which may range between instrumental human utility to ecological sustainability

NEPA   The National Environmental Policy Act of 1970 commits the US government to protecting and improving the natural environment; after NEPA, the federal government is required to write environmental impact statements (EIS) for government actions that have significant environmental impact

Public participation in resource management

Natural resource management in the United States was, for most of the modern era, a highly centralized, "expert" affair. The seeds of a more participatory management structure were sown in 1970 with the passage of the National Environmental Policy Act (**NEPA**), which among other innovations required "environmental impact statements" (EIS) for any government management action. Further, these statements required the inclusion of *public input and participation* in the process.

Many endangered species conservation plans, wolf reintroduction in Yellowstone included, are now vetted through the full EIS process. The reintroduction of wolves to Yellowstone suggests, however, that although wolf management priorities have changed over time (from eradication to conservation), it hardly marked a new era in management *style*. Locals had little voice in how (or if) the reintroduction was to be carried out. Indeed, Bruce Babbitt and Mollie Beattie – two high-ranking federal officials – literally carried the cage of the first wolf to be released into the snow. For some, this was a powerful (and negative) symbolic gesture: wolf reintroduction was a top-down, federally imposed action. As such, for many residents of Montana and Idaho, wolf reintroduction was perceived as business-as-usual: East Coast priorities imposed in their backyards. This was so much the case that some environmentalists feel reintroduction may have done as much harm as good, further polarizing opponents against proponents of environmental protection in the region (Fischer 1995). It was not until a few years later that a different model, one that moved from public *input* to a more truly *participatory* structure, would be tested in the highly volatile context of wolf conservation.

Stakeholders in Minnesota wolf conservation

In 1998, the state of Minnesota began implementing the first *stakeholder* model wolf management plan in the United States. Home to about 2,500 wolves, Minnesota was given more management autonomy by the federal government because it had the largest and most stable wolf population.

The process began with 12 informational meetings held throughout the state, in which attendees were informed of the state's plan, and additionally could provide comments and recommendations on the process. After the 12 meetings, a wolf management "roundtable" was convened. The roundtable included representatives from environmental groups (e.g., the Sierra Club), agricultural interests (e.g., the Minnesota Farm Bureau), wolf groups (e.g., HOWL – Help Our Wolves Live), hunting and trapping groups (e.g., Minnesota Deer Hunters Association), and tribal interests (there are 11 Native American reservations in Minnesota). These were joined by regional and scientific representatives.

The roundtable had a specific mandate to develop a management plan for the state's wolves, formed entirely through *consensus*; *every* member of the roundtable had to back the plan or it was back to the drawing board. After several meetings, including a marathon 10-hour final session, the roundtable voted unanimously on a management plan. Highlights of the plan included:

- The state's wolf population would be managed to expand its numbers and range.
- Landowners could kill wolves caught depredating on livestock or pets.
- No wolf hunting or trapping seasons would be considered for at least five years.
- Livestock and pet owners would be compensated for losses.
- The state would encourage non-lethal methods of livestock protection.
- A stiff fine of $2,500 for illegal wolf kills would be implemented.

After submitting its plan to the state department of natural resources, most roundtable members felt they had reached a reasonable consensus and most Minnesotans held a positive impression of the process. It became quickly apparent, however, that roundtable members had worked (tirelessly, and for months) under the false impression that their plan would be implemented as written. This proved to be far from the case. As it turned out,

Minnesota Wolf Management Zones

Legend
Wolf Management Zones
- Wolf Management Zones A
- Wolf Management Zones B
- Cities/Towns Dividing Wolf Zones A & B
- County Boundaries

Figure 11.4 Wolf management zones in Minnesota. *Source*: Data from http://wildlife.utah.gov/wolf/pdf/mn-wolf-plan-01.pdf, p. 45.

the Minnesota state legislature continued to hold final authority, and they initially proceeded by largely overlooking the group plan altogether and presenting their own, which included extensive hunting and trapping. Only after a public outcry did a revised plan emerge, representing something of a compromise. The revised plan implemented the stakeholder plan on 90 percent of the wolves' range (Figure 11.4), making the remaining 10 percent into an "agricultural zone" in which landowners have much more flexibility in killing wolves (Williams 2000).

Evaluating the results

As would have to be expected, there is mixed opinion on the merits of the roundtable and the resulting management plan. Supporters of the final outcome highlight that the roundtable group was able to forge a consensus plan that was deemed biologically sound by state scientists. Supporters also point to the significance of the *process* of the roundtable, in that it built bridges and opened lines of communication that will make future wolf (and other) management issues more easily resolvable.

Critics still abound, however. Some in the environmental community felt that the final plan was too much of a compromise and did not represent a true commitment to wolf recovery. Most pro-wolf critics of the plan most vociferously opposed the splitting of the state into two management zones. Which is the fairest assessment? Certainly, the process was not perfect, and the stakeholder team should have been aware of their limited power from the start. But a decade-plus into the implementation of the plan, results are encouraging. Wolf numbers in the state are up, to around 3,000. Like in the Rocky Mountain states, Minnesota recently instituted its first wolf hunt since delisting. Not everyone was pleased with this (HOWL, for example, howled in protest), but many environmentalists and biologists see the hunt as a pragmatic and reasonable management action. Wolf protection advocates may in the end have gotten more than they realize. According to veteran wolf biologist David Mech, one nearly sure route to failure in wolf recovery is to *overprotect* them, allowing them to become "pests" to livestock owners. Indeed, this is exactly what happened in Poland: *three times* wolves were reintroduced with full protection and no leeway for control, and all three times they were all shot by landowners (Emel 1998). So, in the case of Minnesota, by including livestock owners, hunters, and trappers in the decision-making process, perhaps the agri*cultural* attitude toward wolves in Minnesota will change from a "shoot on sight" mentality to one where living with wolves is viewed as the best goal for all concerned. If, via the new institution of stakeholder management, Minnesota turned that corner, then its wolves would probably stand a much better chance of long-term recovery than they would have otherwise. But changing human views of wolves, for either environmentalists or for ranchers, is no easy affair, because of the powerful *social constructions* of the wolf among differing communities.

Social Construction: Of Wolves and ~~Men~~ Masculinity

In Chapter 8 we introduced the social construction of nature. Viewing nature not as some preexisting entity but rather as a social construction – a product and process arising from human images, stereotypes, and cultural norms – can be a productive exercise in a number of ways. In the puzzle of wolves, a social constructivist analysis can help shed light on the connections between dominant representations of the wolf and our treatment of and attitudes toward these animals.

Man as righteous hunter, wolf as evil hunter

The fact that European Americans exterminated the wolf across so much of its native range is tragic, but not particularly surprising. After all, early American settlers carried with them a culture that feared the wild creatures that inhabited the "wilderness" (see Chapter 8). Moreover, wolves were a *practical* problem for agrarian settlers. Wolves may not have killed people, even if Western wolf mythology might lead one to believe so (think "Little Red Riding Hood"), but they did (and *still do*) kill livestock. But can these two factors – a disdain toward the wild and an agrarian mode of production – really explain the fanaticism of the killing? Can these factors explain the gruesomeness and carelessness of some of the techniques used to kill wolves? Does this explain the use of poisons so deadly that they affected literally thousands of non-targeted species – including many overtly desirable – just to rid the land of every wolf? What about the public torturing and/or burning of trapped wolves? Or killing all but one of a litter of wolf pups, and then tying the pup by its leg to a tree so that its cry would bring back its mother (to be shot) (Figure 11.5)? As the geographer Jody Emel ponders:

Figure 11.5 An early twentieth-century government wolf trapper. *Source*: Unknown photographer.

> *What is this all about?* It is not solely about protecting livestock, because . . . the slaughter went on long after the economic threat ended. It continues to this day. (Emel 1998: 201, emphasis added)

An examination of constructions of **masculinity** during this era can help us more fully understand its causes and learn

Masculinity The socially agreed-upon characteristics of behavior associated with men in any society; these may vary significantly between cultures, locations, and periods of history to avoid repeating history. First clues come from one of the masculine stereotypes of the day: the gentleman hunter. In turn-of-the-twentieth-century America, the gentleman hunter was the pinnacle of manhood. He embodied all the qualities of the idealized rugged, independent American. He was a survivor, wise in the ways of nature, thriving in solitude that would strike fear in lesser men. Yet he was selective and restrained, only ever killing as much as he could use.

The wolf, too, is a hunter. Such a good hunter, perhaps, that for many men, there may have been some envy at work. Moreover, wolf-as-hunter fell short of cultural standards of "the hunt." First off, wolves hunt in packs. This appeared cowardly when compared to the idealized solitary huntsmen. Wolves also sometimes kill more than they need, leaving "wasted" flesh strewn about kill sites. Of course, most predators do this, a practice that opens up ecological **niches** for scavengers, which are integral to terrestrial and marine ecosystems everywhere. But this is not how wolf kills were viewed. In contrast to the *humane* gentleman hunter, which treated his game with *mercy*, the wolf was viewed as savage or merciless. This attitude is typified by turn-of-the-twentieth-century natural historian William Hornaday: "There is no depth of meanness, treachery, or cruelty to which [wolves] do not cheerfully descend" (Hornaday 1904: 36). If there was to be any hope of bringing light to the wilderness (see Figure 8.2), these creatures had to be done away with.

> **Niche** In ecology, the location of an organism or species within a larger ecosystem, typically fulfilling an ecological function

Clearly, the man for the job was the wolves' opposite: a righteous, gentleman hunter, bringing order to the wilderness. Wolf hunters were *heroic*. It is difficult if not impossible to assess exactly how much causality to place on the contrasting constructions of hellish wolf and righteous hunter. It is also difficult to untangle all the seemingly double standards at work in American society at that time. For example, how did society reconcile these constructions of the evil wolf while at the same time witnessing (*subsidizing* even) the merciless mass-slaughter of bison on the Great Plains? And even as we can never hope to conclusively answer these questions, we can recognize the power of constructions in guiding our actions and our notions of acceptable versus unacceptable actions. For centuries, negative constructions of wolves fueled an extreme hatred toward them, and this hatred was manifest in a terrible slaughter that went nearly unquestioned by society as a whole.

Wolves save the wilderness, but for whom?

A critical constructivist analysis of wolves should not, however, stop at the turn-of-the-twentieth-century anti-wolf attitudes; it must be brought to bear on their opposite. Wolves are no less powerfully constructed today than they were a century ago. Wolves have become, in North America at least, nearly synonymous with "wilderness," but as reviewed in Chapter 8, wilderness itself is far from an innocent social construction. While wilderness is (currently) typically constructed as land outside human control, actual wilderness areas are, rather, marked by formal sets of rules that dictate their use. The ecological utility of wilderness is a relatively recent justification for its preservation. Even as late as the 1960s, the overriding official justification for wilderness was recreation. This is codified in the Wilderness Act of 1964, the legislation that formalized the US system of designated wilderness areas. As went the typical language of the day, "man" needed a place for solitude, a respite from modern urban civilization.

As such, the allowed uses of wilderness are non-motorized, low-impact activities like canoeing, backpacking, and fishing. These are all activities that are quite literally exclusive, in regards to both gender and class. The wilderness was, and to a good degree still very much is, the domain of middle-class men. It takes time and money to, say, take the famous six-day float trip down the Salmon River through the Selway-Bitteroot Wilderness in Idaho. Gendered exclusivity exists on many levels as well. For example, how many working-class women with children at home have the freedom to head off for a week (or an afternoon for that matter!) of quiet recreation in the wild? Viewed in this manner, debates over wilderness areas are not arguments over using versus not using a piece of land as much as debates over who gets to use them and in what manner.

But the era of protecting wilderness for the respite of the white man has (justifiably) waned. Today, justifications for land preservation rest more commonly on ecological grounds. Enter the wolf. Today, the presence of wolves *makes* (read: constructs) a "rewilded" land, a *wilderness*. Regardless of formal "Wilderness" designation, getting wolves onto the land – *constructing wilderness* – favors some land uses (and some land *users*) over others. Wolves in northern Vermont could, for example, give weight to opponents of snowmobilers, as wolves tend to avoid areas of high snowmobile use. It might make it easier if they can argue that affluent bed-and-breakfast patrons are visiting the area to listen to wolves howling and not snowmobiles humming.

Wolf reintroduction would also spur a local growth-industry in conservation biology research. By arguing for wolf reintroduction, scientists are arguing for personal and somewhat exclusive access to the land (now constructed as the "ecosystem"). Granted, it would be unfair and cynical to argue that this is *the* motivation behind their advocacy. But it is undeniable that scientists have something to gain, personally and professionally, from successful reintroduction. It is also undeniable that, like earlier dominant uses of the wilderness, the backwoods "muddy boots" fieldwork of large carnivore science is an overwhelmingly white and well-educated affair. Perhaps the reticence toward ambitious rewilding efforts like wolf reintroduction held by many rural residents in Minnesota, Vermont, and elsewhere is fueled less by some archaic disdain toward wolves but rather the recognition that they may be the ones asked to make significant changes for the sake of conservation.

The Wolf Puzzle

In this chapter we have learned that:

- Wolves are an evolutionarily successful, adaptable species.
- Humans have a long history of intimate interactions with wolves, dating back thousands of years to their domestication, through to the more recent era of systematic programs of eradication, to the even more recent trend of wolf conservation.
- Novel institutional models of wolf conservation offer more democratic and possibly also more effective methods of ensuring the species' long-term health and survival.

- Ecocentric ethics suggests that we need to think well beyond the bounds of human usefulness if we are to allow significant spaces for wolves to thrive.
- Conservation biology suggests that the fate of the wolf may be linked to the broader fate of global biodiversity and evolutionary processes.
- Social constructions of the wolf have changed through time, and these constructions are inextricably tied to societal norms and stereotypes.
- Social constructions of the wolf have effects; they are tied to the way in which we treat these magnificent animals (note: the irony of this statement is not lost on us; we realize that wolves-as-magnificent-animals itself is a construction, reflecting our culture, and having real effects).

This brings us back to Yellowstone, with its thriving wolf population. With wolves now the objects of hunts as well as the gazes of tourists, the next decade of wolf conservation *around* (if not so much *in*) Yellowstone will be a telling reflection of 1) shifting social-environmental priorities, 2) competing socio-environmental discourses, and 3) increasing enviro-institutional experimentation.

Globally, calls for wolf recovery will increase. What will be the fate of the wolves of India? Of Egypt? Of Denmark? Will wolves be reintroduced to the Highlands of Scotland, as some have proposed? The answers will, no doubt, vary from place to place, from population to population. Hopefully, we can learn from the past and sort through the complex spaces of our mutual interaction. Wolves are, to be sure, one of the more difficult, persistent, and intriguing puzzles of nature and society.

Questions for Review

1. List a species from each trophic level (producer through apex predator) in a food web somewhere near your home. (The food web can be terrestrial or aquatic.)
2. How has the reintroduction of wolves affected the ecosystem in and around Yellowstone National Park?
3. Write an ethics-based argument in favor of *or* against reintroducing wolves into the northeastern United States.
4. Contrast the role of local citizens in the Minnesota wolf "roundtable" and the Yellowstone reintroduction process.
5. Explain the following statement: The presence of wolves helps construct a wilderness.

Exercise 11.1   Wolf Conservation and Human Population Growth

In this chapter, we have reviewed how the puzzle of wolves might be addressed by ethics, institutions, and social construction. Explain how you might understand this problem using a population-centered framework (as described in Chapter 2). How might human population growth affect existing populations and habitats of wolves and pose challenges for wolf conservation? What are the limits of a population-based approach to wolves?

Exercise 11.2   The IUCN "Red List" of Threatened and Endangered Species

The International Union for the Conservation of Nature and Natural Resources (usually referred to by its truncated acronym "IUCN") catalogs endangered and threatened plant and animal species worldwide on its "Red List." Research and write about three species that are listed as either "critically endangered" or "endangered" on the IUCN "Red List." (The IUCN Red List is on the web at www.iucnredlist.org.) For each species, write/describe:

1. a basic description of the plant or animal species;
2. where it lives: include both (a) its preferred type of habitat as well as (b) where, geographically on Earth, the species lives (you are encouraged to add a map for each species);
3. the threats to the species (e.g., habitat loss, pollution, overhunting, etc.).

Exercise 11.3   Examining the Wolf Hunting Debate

As discussed in the opening of this chapter, since many wolf populations have recently been removed from the Endangered Species List, many US states have instituted legal hunting seasons on wolves. Several environmental groups (e.g., Defenders of Wildlife, Earthjustice) have been openly critical of the rush to hunt wolves and launched online activism campaigns opposing them. Find such a campaign on the web and summarize it *critically*. Explain the rationales used to oppose the hunts (Are they population-centered, based in ethical arguments, market-based economic arguments, etc?). Additionally, write about how wolves and nature in general are *socially constructed* to make their pleas work.

References

Barlow, C. (1999). "Rewilding for evolution." *Wild Earth* 9(1): 53–6.

Emel, J. (1998). "Are you man enough, big and bad enough? Wolf eradication in the US." In J. Wolch and J. Emel (eds.) *Animal Geographies*. New York: Verso, pp. 91–116.

Fischer, H. (1995). *Wolf Wars: The Remarkable Inside Story of the Restoration of Wolves to Yellowstone*. Helena, MT: Falcon Press.

Foreman, D. (2004). *Rewilding North America*. Washington, DC: Island Press.

Hambler, C., and S. Canney (2013). *Conservation*. Cambridge: Cambridge University Press.

Hornaday, W. (1904). *The American Natural History*. New York: Scribner's Sons.

Mech, D. (1970). *The Wolf*. Garden City, NY: Natural History.

Mech, L. D., and L. Boitani (eds) (2003). *Wolves, Behavior, Ecology, and Conservation.* Chicago, IL: University of Chicago Press.

Nie, M. A. (2003). *Beyond Wolves: The Politics of Wolf Recovery and Management.* Minneapolis: University of Minnesota Press.

Rirdan, D. (2012). *The Blueprint: Averting Global Collapse.* Louisville, CO: Corinno Press.

Schweber, N. (2012). "'Famous' wolf is killed outside Yellowstone." *New York Times,* 6 December.

Sessions, G. (2001). "Ecocentrism, wilderness, and global ecosystem processes." In M. E. Zimmerman, J. B. Callicott, G. Sessions, et al. (eds.) *Environmental Philosophy: From Animal Rights to Radical Ecology.* Upper Saddle River, NJ: Prentice Hall, pp. 236–52.

Smith, D. W., and G. Ferguson (2005). *Decade of the Wolf: Returning the Wild to Yellowstone.* Guilford, CT: Lyons.

Terborgh, J., and J. Estes (2010). *Trophic Cascades: Predators, Prey, and the Changing Dynamics of Nature.* Washington, DC: Island Press.

Williams, T. (2000). "Living with wolves." *Audubon* 102(6): 50–7.

Wilson, E. O. (2012). *The Social Conquest of Earth.* New York: Liveright.

Young, S. P., and E. A. Goldman (1944). *The Wolves of North America, Part I.* London: Constable.

Suggested Reading

Lopez, B. (1978). *Of Wolves and Men.* New York: Scribner.

Mowat, F. (1963). *Never Cry Wolf.* Toronto: McClelland and Stewart.

Walker, B. L. (2005). *The Lost Wolves of Japan.* Seattle, WA: University of Washington Press.

Wildlife Friendly certification website: http://wildlifefriendly.org/, accessed August 8, 2013.

Yochim, M. (2013). *Protecting Yellowstone: Science and the Politics of National Park Management.* Albuquerque: University of New Mexico Press.

12

Uranium

Source: © RGB Ventures LLC dba SuperStock/Alamy.

Chapter Menu

Environment and Society: A Critical Introduction, Second Edition. Paul Robbins, John Hintz, and Sarah A. Moore.
© 2014 John Wiley & Sons, Ltd. Published 2014 by John Wiley & Sons, Ltd.

Keywords

- Carbon footprint
- Conditions of production
- Depleted uranium
- Discourse
- Externality
- Fallout
- Manhattan Project
- Nuclear chain reaction
- Nuclear fission
- Nuclear power
- Nuclear proliferation
- Primary sector
- Radwaste
- Risk assessment
- Risk communication
- Spent nuclear fuel

Renaissance Derailed?

In early 2011, proponents of nuclear power and firms in the uranium mining sector were feeling optimistic. Memories of the 1986 meltdown at the Soviet Chernobyl nuclear reactor were fading. Uranium mining and processing output worldwide were rising. China – the world's largest consumer of energy – was planning to build 30 new nuclear power plants. To help meet an expected rise in demand for nuclear fuel, the United States opened its first new uranium enrichment plant in 30 years. All signs appeared to point toward what industry boosters were calling a "nuclear renaissance," an economic rebirth to an industry that had been crippled and stagnant since accidents at Three Mile Island, Pennsylvania in 1979 and Chernobyl in 1986. And then, in the spring of 2011, disaster struck again.

The morning of March 11, 2011 was like any other at the Fukushima Daiichi nuclear power plant, located along the northeast coast of Japan. Three of the six reactors at the plant were online and producing electric power, while the other three were shut down and undergoing planned, routine maintenance. But at 2:46 in the afternoon, a magnitude 9.0 earthquake struck the ocean floor just 70 kilometers off the coast. As soon as the earthquake was detected, the plant went into emergency shutdown. To keep the radioactive fuel at a safe temperature, backup diesel generators pumped cooling water to the reactors. Less than an hour later, a tsunami (which had been triggered by the quake) flooded the plant. The generators failed, the cooling water to the cores was shut off, and the reactors began to overheat.

Within days, the plant had experienced multiple "core meltdowns," wherein the molten fuel becomes fugitive, causing structural damage and superheating water and steam. Owing to the meltdowns and resulting hydrogen explosions, tremendous amounts of radioactive pollution were released into the surrounding air and water, causing widespread environmental damage. Villages close to the plant may be permanently uninhabitable. Unsafe levels of radioactivity have been detected in milk and vegetables grown as far as 200 miles away. Months after the disaster, fish caught 12 miles off the Fukushima coast registered levels of radioactive contamination over 250 times levels considered safe. Understandably, many Japanese citizens began to question whether the benefits of nuclear power outweigh the risks.

Bowing to popular unrest following the disaster, the Japanese government tentatively agreed to phase out nuclear power by 2040 (only to backpedal from that self-imposed deadline five days later). The Fukushima disaster has affected commodity markets far away from Japan as well. Germany has committed to abandon nuclear power altogether, and support has waned in other countries as well. Uranium prices, as of October 2012, were at a two-year low, barely a third of what they were five years prior. Calls for a nuclear renaissance, it seems, may have been premature.

When and how did we discover uranium's unique properties? Why do we continue to utilize it, despite its terrifying capacity to do harm? How is it that some people urge us to increase our extraction and use or nuclear power (some even justifying these arguments *on environmental grounds*)? By examining the puzzle of uranium, we can shed considerable light on persistent and confounding aspects of the society–environment relationship.

A Short History of Uranium

Uranium is a metallic element, number 92 in the periodic table. It is the heaviest naturally occurring element. Uranium is formed from supernovae – massive stellar explosions that expel energy and matter into space. The uranium in Earth's geosphere (about 2–4 parts per million in the crust), captured at the birth of the solar system, has been there for the entire 4.6-billion-year life of our planet.

More significant than its atomic weight, violent history, or ancient age, however, is uranium's property of radioactivity. Radioactive elements are unstable, emitting particles and energy until they are reduced to a more stable, lighter element. Given enough time, any sample of uranium will decay into lead. The process, however, is incredibly slow. Depending on the isotope (more on that in a moment), the half-life of uranium decay is between 700 million and 4.5 billion years. For example, a mineral sample containing four grams of uranium would take many millions of years for half of the uranium to decay (through unstable elemental intermediaries) to lead, at which point the sample would still contain two grams of (still-decaying) uranium.

Probing into nature's atomic secrets

In 1789, the German chemist Martin Klaproth discovered uranium, naming it after the then-recently discovered planet Uranus. A century later, the French chemist Henri Becquerel discovered radioactivity almost by accident, when he noticed fogging around uranium salt on photographic plates that had not been exposed to light.

Becquerel's discovery piqued the interest of the Parisian physicists Marie Sklodowska (later Curie) and Pierre Curie. After five years of experimenting (mostly via the element radium, one of the unstable decay products of uranium), Marie and Pierre Curie and Becquerel received the Nobel Prize for Physics in 1903. The Curies were both suffering from what we now call radiation sickness, and their condition delayed the Nobel lecture by two years. When Pierre delivered the Nobel address, he maintained a modicum of optimism, but was clearly troubled by what they had discovered. "Is it right to probe so deeply into nature's secrets?" he mused. "The question must here be raised whether [radioactivity] will benefit mankind, or whether the knowledge will be helpful" (Zoellner 2009). It might be argued that over a century later – even acknowledging that **nuclear power** accounts for 16 percent of global electric production (IAEA 2007) – this question is still difficult to answer.

The 1932 discovery of the neutron was a watershed for nuclear physics. By 1938, German chemists had successfully bombarded uranium nuclei with neutrons and witnessed a remarkable result. The resulting particles were barium atoms, an element about half as heavy as uranium. They correctly concluded that the uranium atoms had effectively been split in half, and named the newly discovered process binary fission (now known as **nuclear fission**).

Nuclear Power   electric power produced from a nuclear power plant, utilizing induced nuclear fission to generate heat, steam, and electricity

Nuclear Fission   a process through which the nucleus of an atom is split into two lighter nuclei, producing two lighter atoms and releasing energy; nuclear particles (e.g., neutrons) are also often released in the process

Nuclear Chain Reaction   when a single nuclear fission or fusion event triggers a self-propagating sequence of nuclear fission or fusion reactions

Manhattan Project   the highly secretive nuclear research and engineering program of the United States (and allies) during World War II that developed the first nuclear bombs

Fallout   airborne radioactive pollution caused by a nuclear weapon or an explosion at a nuclear power plant or other such facility

Along with the "new" atoms, induced (i.e., artificial, as opposed to geological) fission also releases energy and free neutrons. A "**nuclear chain reaction**" occurs when the free neutrons penetrate nuclei of other unstable heavy atoms, which then split, producing more energy, atoms, and more neutrons, and so forth in a cascading fashion. If this process could be catalzyed, the energy produced could be captured (for nuclear power production) or released (for a nuclear bomb).

The Manhattan Project and the power of nuclear technology

The threats of Nazi Germany and Imperial Japan in World War II provided the United States with the impetus to provide the billions of dollars (as well as the incredibly elaborate security infrastructure) necessary to build a nuclear engineering facility from the ground up. This undertaking, which would eventually be named "**The Manhattan Project**," was launched in 1939. By 1942 the Manhattan Project operated at over two dozen research sites, most notably Oak Ridge, Tennessee and Los Alamos, New Mexico.

To create a nuclear chain reaction required "enriching" uranium to make it more fissile (i.e., easily split). The issue is that of the two commonly occurring isotopes of uranium, only one is fissile. All atoms of any given element have the same number of protons, but different isotopes have different numbers of neutrons. Isotopes are designated by the element's chemical symbol followed by the sum of the number of protons and neutrons. Uranium ore is over 99 percent U^{238}, the common isotope containing 92 protons and 146 neutrons. U^{238}, however, is not fissile. Much scarcer is the highly fissile U^{235} isotope (still with 92 protons but with 143 neutrons). Less than 1 percent of the atoms in uranium ore are U^{235}. Enrichment is the process of separating the U^{235} from U^{238} atoms, then rebundling them into pure uranium with a higher concentration of U^{235}. In 1944, at the Oak Ridge nuclear laboratory, engineers successfully enriched a sample of uranium to 15 percent U^{235}, plenty "rich" enough, it proved, to sustain a nuclear chain reaction. Samples were sent to Los Alamos, where luminaries such as Enrico Fermi and Robert Oppenheimer engineered the world's first nuclear weapons.

On August 6, 1945, the United States dropped a nuclear bomb on Hiroshima, Japan. The blast and the resulting radioactive **fallout** killed upwards of 150,000 people. While the necessity and wisdom of the Hiroshima and subsequent Nagasaki bombings are (to put it mildly) highly debatable, it is undeniable that these events tragically ushered in a new, nuclear era.

After World War II, the nuclear focus split in two directions. One was the continued development of nuclear arms, but much of the new nuclear research went into "peaceful" applications, mostly notably, developing viable nuclear power plants. In 1954, the Soviet Union became the first country to open a nuclear power plant that fed electricity onto the power grid.

Nuclear power production expanded quickly in its first few decades. Worldwide nuclear power production rose over 100-fold between 1960 and 1980. For countries with significant financial resources yet limited fossil fuel resources, like France and Japan, nuclear power was seen as a logical sector to rapidly develop. Over 430 nuclear power plants now operate in 30 countries. Many proponents of the technology argue (despite the accidents at Three Mile Island, Chernobyl, and Fukushima) that nuclear power has a relatively positive safety history and that its benefits (e.g., reliable power, relatively low carbon emissions) far outweigh its problems. By contrast, opponents of nuclear technologies argue the opposite: that the dangers inherent in the technologies are so profound and various and so long-lasting that nuclear power production (and, less controversially, nuclear weapons) should be phased out as quickly as is reasonably possible. Opponents are not just weary of worst-case scenarios, such as nuclear war or Fukushima-scale meltdowns. Hazards are present along every link of the "nuclear fuel chain."

The nuclear fuel chain

To fully appreciate the complexity of turning mined uranium into electricity – and, just as importantly, to understand the many problems inherent in the utilization of this technology – we must examine the "nuclear fuel chain" (Figure 12.1). This perspective highlights the entire cradle-to-grave life cycle of mined uranium and all of its by-products.

The nuclear fuel chain begins with exploration and mining. Three countries – Canada, Australia, and Kazakhstan – account for over half of all uranium mining worldwide, but the ore is also mined in Russia, several African countries, China, the United States, and

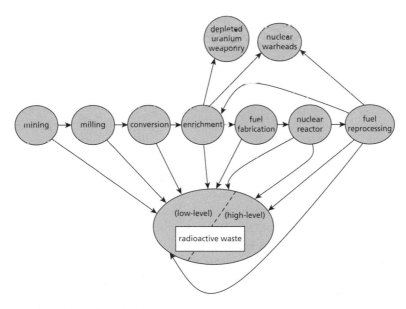

Figure 12.1 The nuclear fuel chain.

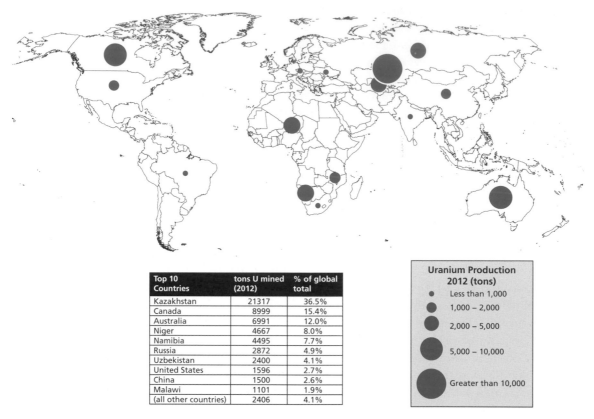

Top 10 Countries	tons U mined (2012)	% of global total
Kazakhstan	21317	36.5%
Canada	8999	15.4%
Australia	6991	12.0%
Niger	4667	8.0%
Namibia	4495	7.7%
Russia	2872	4.9%
Uzbekistan	2400	4.1%
United States	1596	2.7%
China	1500	2.6%
Malawi	1101	1.9%
(all other countries)	2406	4.1%

Uranium Production 2012 (tons)

- Less than 1,000
- 1,000 – 2,000
- 2,000 – 5,000
- 5,000 – 10,000
- Greater than 10,000

Figure 12.2   World uranium production, 2012. *Source*: Data from World Nuclear Association, http://www.world-nuclear.org/info/Nuclear-Fuel-Cycle/Mining-of-Uranium/World-Uranium-Mining-Production/#.UXahukrNl8E.

few other countries (**see** Figure 12.2). Whether extracted from open pit mines, underground mines, or using a newer technology known as "in situ" mining, it is simply not possible to extract uranium (or any other) ore from underground without impacting the surrounding land, air, and water.

The second "link" in the chain is the initial processing or "milling" of the ore, in which the uranium is chemically separated from the surrounding rock, producing a substance called "yellowcake." To get from yellowcake to nuclear fuel requires three more links in the fuel chain. Yellowcake (U_3O_8) must first be converted into uranium hexafluoride gas (UF_6). The "conversion" process can release highly toxic gases if plants are not operated under the strictest safety procedures. Indeed, the sole conversion facility in the United States (located in Illinois) was shuttered for 12 to 15 months for safety upgrades after the US government found the facility potentially unsound (Elk 2012).

Converted uranium must then be "enriched" at a separate facility (as described above). One troublesome by-product of uranium enrichment is "**depleted uranium**," the leftover pure

Depleted Uranium   a by-product of uranium enrichment; dense, pure uranium comprised of nearly 100% non-fissile U^{238} atoms; used in armor and weapons, which may leave behind radioactive contamination when discharged uranium that is composed of nearly 100 percent non-fissionable U_{238} atoms. Depleted uranium is incredibly dense and is used in some countries in armor and ammunition. The United States armed forces, for example, used depleted uranium ammunition to destroy Iraqi tanks in both the 1991 and 2003 wars with Iraq. Despite claims by US military officials that depleted uranium poses no human health or environmental hazard, there is widespread controversy over the dangers of lingering toxicity in Iraq (and other countries) in areas where depleted uranium munitions were used (Peterson 2003).

Finally, enriched uranium is processed into fuel pellets in a process known as fuel "fabrication." A nuclear power plant operates similarly to a conventional gas or coal plant, where fuel produces heat, which turns water into steam, which is forced under pressure through turbines, which are connected to a generator, which then distributes electricity onto the grid. Inside the reactor "core," fission releases neutrons (and heat). Some free neutrons split other atoms (releasing more neutrons and more heat), and so on. "Control rods," which capture some of the free neutrons, are raised and lowered between the fuel rods to maintain the desirable rate of fission (and heat production).

In addition to electricity, nuclear power plants produce dangerously radioactive waste products. These can be broken down into "high-level waste" and "lower-level waste." High-level waste, comprised mostly of spent nuclear fuel, is dangerously radioactive and remains so for thousands of years. Lower-level waste is everything else that has become radioactively contaminated to the point where it cannot simply be disposed of in a solid waste landfill. This category includes concrete and metal from power plants, protective clothing worn in the plant, used control rods, and decommissioned nuclear reactors (which usually operate for 40–80 years). Different types of low-level waste require different methods of disposal, few of which are without risk and controversy. The waste, once stored (out of sight, if not out of mind), brings us to the end of the nuclear fuel chain.

Even considering the energy inputs of the entire fuel chain, nuclear power has a lower **carbon footprint** than fossil fuels. As such, some nuclear proponents (including a few environmental luminaries like *Gaia Hypothesis* author Paul Hawken) argue that nuclear power is integral to any sincere attempt to mitigate global warming.

> **Carbon Footprint**   the total amount of greenhouse gases (carbon dioxide, methane) produced by a given individual, group, economic sector, or commodity production process

The puzzle of uranium

Uranium presents a vexing puzzle. Perhaps no other substance produces such obvious utility and embodies such terrifying harm. Like Icarus, are we "flying too close to the sun" with our continuing reliance upon nuclear technologies? In this short history, we learned about both the promise and danger inherent in nuclear technologies:

- Nuclear power plants produce a significant amount of the world's electricity, and do so *relatively* cleanly (when all goes well).

- Producing nuclear fuel is a cumbersome process, with risk, pollution, and toxic-waste products produced at every step in the chain, and the threat of worst-case scenario accidents is frightening.

With such seemingly self-evident arguments for and against it, it is easy to see why nuclear power has such vociferous boosters as well as critics. Assessing the puzzle of uranium through three analytical lenses, we gain a finer appreciation for the complexity of the issue and better equip ourselves to answer difficult questions, such as: Who benefits, and who loses, from our continued reliance on uranium? What is the long-term solution to the nuclear waste problem? Does nuclear power present a wise path forward?

Box 12.1   Environmental Solution? Energy-Efficient Buildings

Nuclear power plants produce about 16 percent of the world's electricity. Coal contributes closer to 40 percent. Neither of these technologies is particularly attractive from an environmental perspective (as you should well understand by this point in the book). One way that we could reduce the need to produce so much electricity would be to reduce demand, that is, lower the total amount of electricity used (this holds at whatever scale the "solution" is sought : local, national, global, etc.). You notice we did not say that "we could *simply* reduce demand." Acknowledging that – all other things being equal – reduced demand will also result in reduced prices for electric power, which could in turn result in usage increases (a theoretical market bind known as "Jevons Paradox"), it is not implausible to imagine institutions (see Chapter 4) that could be crafted to offset the "market problem" of reducing demand. These not-insignificant digressions aside, the bottom line is that it is much easier to envision crafting sustainable futures that include more efficient use of any and all resources.

One of the most straightforward ways that we could decrease overall use of electricity is by designing and building more energy-efficient buildings and retrofitting existing buildings with energy-efficiency improvements. In the United States, for example, nearly 40 percent of all *energy* usage (not just electricity) is from residential and commercial buildings (the other two sectors that gobble energy are transportation and industry). Updating buildings for higher energy efficiency results in an average total energy-use reduction of 30 percent per building. Typical improvements include energy-efficient lighting (e.g., compact fluorescent or light-emitting-diode (LED) bulbs and on-demand lighting), improved insulation (including energy-efficient windows), improvements in heating and cooling systems (including usage of fans, programmable thermostats, and heat pumps), and energy-efficient appliances and electronics. Bear in mind, too, that this 30 percent energy-use reduction figure does not even figure in reductions that would result from tweaking thermostats a bit lower in the winter and a bit higher (or even "off") in the summer.

Doing the math, we can see (by reducing the 40 percent figure by 30 percent) that around 12 percent of the total electricity usage in the United States could be saved through energy-efficient building updates. That's the equivalent of over half the electricity produced by the entire network of nuclear power plants in the United States. Let us stress that we are not oversimplifying this solution and implying that we could simply go out and retrofit buildings and follow that up by shuttering 60 percent of the nuclear power plants in the country. Rather, these figures are intended to be illustrative devices. But even through this heuristic example alone, it is clear that the old idea of "doing with a little less" is not so radical, and would not require giving up all the comforts of our modern age.

Risk and Hazards: Debating the Fate of High-Level Radioactive Waste

Nuclear power is, in a word, *risky*. Meltdowns. Weapons proliferation. Pollutants with multi-thousand-year toxicities. Every discussion of the pros and cons of nuclear power is, to one degree or another, a discussion about risk. After all, who couldn't appreciate the *benefits* of nuclear power? (From the humble to the magnificent: Who doesn't cherish being able to flick the switch on an electric light-bulb to read a good book? Who could fail to marvel at the spectacular Kuala Lumpur skyline or the Sydney waterfront at night?) By contrast, it is the *risks* of nuclear power that worry everyday citizens, bedevil the growth of the industry, and make the management of nuclear technologies such a challenge.

In Chapter 6, we discussed decision-making from a risk assessment perspective. Such a framework is a well-worn method in nuclear technology planning and assessment, nowhere better illustrated than in the long-running debates over storage of high-level nuclear waste.

High-level radioactive waste: Hazardous for a long, long time

As discussed in the short history above, high-level radioactive waste, comprised mostly of **spent nuclear fuel**, remains dangerously radioactive for a very long time. Strontium-90 (one of the decay products of spent fuel), for example, emits a particularly toxic form of radiation that physiologically behaves like calcium and has been linked to bone cancer and leukemia (US NRC 2012). Strontium-90 remains dangerous for a few hundred years. Other decay products emit harmful levels of radioactivity for tens to even hundreds of thousands of years. Consider: humans have been an "industrial" species (utilizing steam power, metal machining tools, factories, and the like) for around 250 years or so. We are now knowingly creating highly dangerous pollutants that will be around for that amount of time *multiplied one hundred times or more*. So what do we do with the roughly 12,000 metric tons of spent fuel that is discharged every year from nuclear power plants worldwide?

> **Spent Nuclear Fuel** nuclear fuel that is no longer fissile enough to sustain a nuclear chain reaction
>
> **Radwaste** radioactive waste products generated from nuclear technologies such as nuclear power and nuclear weapons production; commonly classified into high level wastes (more radioactive and longer-lasting) and lower level wastes (less radioactive and shorter-lived). Also commonly known as "nuclear waste"
>
> **Nuclear Proliferation** the spread of nuclear weapons around the world

Four prominent options exist for handling high-level radioactive waste (we will use the recognized abbreviated term "**radwaste**" from here out). Two of these are onsite at power plants. The first of these is storing the waste in onsite cooling pools that require constant inputs of energy, only ever a temporary solution. A second option, onsite "dry cask" storage, has a good safety record, but it is very expensive and therefore not favored by utilities. A third option is reprocessing spent fuel, which can then be used in other types of nuclear reactors. As promising at that sounds, reprocessing is not only incredibly expensive, but more significantly it produces a plutonium isotope that can be used in nuclear weapons. So those who want to minimize **nuclear proliferation** are strongly opposed to increasing reprocessing.

Which leaves us with the fourth and final option, deep-geological storage: an underground repository in a geologically stable location where large amounts of radwaste could be stored (more or less) "permanently." Bear in mind throughout this discussion that no such high-level radwaste repository is yet in operation (although one is under construction in Finland). We turn our attention now to one well-known *proposed* deep-geological storage site, in Yucca Mountain, Nevada, called by some "the most studied piece of real estate on the planet" (US Senate 2006).

Yucca Mountain and risk-assessment site selection

In 1982, with the passage of the Nuclear Waste Policy Act (NWPA), the United States federal government was directed to construct a permanent deep-geological repository for high-level radwaste with a timetable of a little over a decade. The goal was to find a location that would maximize *isolation* of radwaste from the surrounding environment. Two criteria were paramount: First, the site needed to be free from groundwater intrusion, which could corrode storage containers, causing leakage into subsurface water supplies. Second, the site needed to have minimal seismic activity (e.g., earthquakes), which could jeopardize the structural integrity of the facility.

Initial studies located potentially suitable sites in seven states, including some in the more densely populated Eastern United States. Politics, however, soon infiltrated what was intended to be an objective, scientific process. In 1987, politicians from densely populated areas of the Eastern United States forced passage of an amendment to the NWPA that listed Yucca Mountain as, by fiat, *the only potential site to receive further study*. Not surprisingly, this amendment became known colloquially as the "Screw Nevada bill" (Fialka 2009).

Risk Assessment The rigorous application of logic and information to determine the risk – possibility of an undesirable outcome – associated with particular decisions; used to so reach more optimal and rational outcomes

Once Yucca Mountain had been named the sole potential site for a high-level radwaste repository, numerous **risk assessment** studies were conducted by the Department of Energy (DOE). Congress directed the Environmental Protection Agency (EPA) to establish acceptable risk thresholds on radioactivity release from the site and a time frame over which the release limits would apply. The EPA settled on limits of 15 millirems of radioactivity per resident per year over a period of 10,000 years (US EPA 2012).

After assessing the DOE's many risk-assessment studies in light of the EPA standards, in 2002 the DOE recommended approval of the Yucca Mountain site to then President George W. Bush. Even acknowledging the remote possibilities of volcanoes, earthquakes, and water seepage, the DOE assured that a Yucca Mountain repository would be safe for at least 10,000 years (Walker 2009). Over the opposition of then Governor of Nevada Kenny Guinn, Bush sent the recommendation to Congress, which voted to approve the site.

Critiques of the Yucca Mountain risk assessment

Just as soon as it looked like the NRC might come close to its target date of 2010 for opening the Yucca Mountain repository, things quickly started to unravel. One major stumbling

Table 12.1 Comparison of predicted and actual radioactive contaminant migration at Maxey Flat Low-Level Radioactive Waste facility, Kentucky (US), 1962.

Maxey Flat, Kentucky low-level waste repository, 1962	Time frame	Distance of pollutant travel
Model prediction (used in site selection risk assessment)	24,000 years	½ of one inch
Actual pollutant migration	10 years	2 miles

block came in 2004, when a federal appeals court ruled that the 10,000-year standard was arbitrary and weak, and ordered the EPA to set release limits out *one million years* from the date of the closure of the facility!

Numerous critics had long argued that the Yucca Mountain risk estimations from the suitability studies were fraught with problems. The time-frame of predictions was high on the list of concerns. In an exhaustive critique of the site selection process, Kristin Shrader-Frechette argues that long-term risk assessments of geological repositories are problematic from the start because they rely on geological models that are speculative and scientifically unverifiable. Geology, she argues, is an explanatory rather than a predictive science, citing a notorious 1962 case as a dubious precedent. Maxey Flats, Kentucky was chosen as a lower-level nuclear waste disposal site based on predictive geological modeling similar to that later used in the Yucca Mountain risk assessments. The Maxey Flats study predicted it would take 24,000 years for buried plutonium to migrate one-half of an inch, and that there was no chance it could migrate off-site in any foreseeable time frame. The site was approved and built, yet after only *ten years* of operation, plutonium was found to have migrated *two miles* off-site (Table 12.1). The plutonium migration discovery forced the closure of the site and $50–85 million in cleanup costs (Shrader-Frechette 1993).

Proponents of the Yucca Mountain repository have had a very difficult time conveying mollifying **risk communication**. Appeals to geological models can only go so far when it can be shown that these models are by nature speculative. Appeals to the "obvious" safety of siting the facility in such an arid climate pale the more we learn about the fluctuating nature of climate over time (precipitation predictions from the original study were based on *40 years* of rainfall data). Is it any wonder, then, that the residents of a state with no nuclear power plants would be weary

> **Risk Communication**   A field of study dedicated to understanding the optimal way to present and convey risk-related information to aid people in reaching optimal and rational outcomes

of receiving and storing all of the most dangerous waste from 43 other states? Is it fair to ask this of them? At present, opponents of the plan are savoring victory. In 2010, President Barak Obama (with the urging of Nevada Senator Harry Reid) shelved Yucca Mountain planning and construction.

In the following section, we backtrack to the other end of the nuclear fuel chain – uranium mining – and examine an even more egregious case of one population bearing the burden of benefits that they themselves would never realize.

Political Economy: Environmental Justice and the Navajo Nation

In Chapter 7, we discussed how capitalist commodity production can produce crises and injustices. In this section, we will examine through the lens of political economy the uranium mining boom that began in the 1940s on the Navajo Indian Reservation, exposing one of the great cases of environmental injustice (see Chapter 7) of the twentieth century.

Laboring in Navajo mines

At the end of World War II, the largest known uranium reserve in the United States was along the Colorado Plateau region of the desert Southwest. Some of the largest accessible uranium deposits there were on the Navajo Indian Reservation. Into the early twentieth century, most Navajo tribal members lived as they had for generations: raising horses, sheep, and goats across wide swaths of the desert and raising the traditional crops of corn, melon, and squash on what little land would support them. By 1945, circumstances had changed and the reservation would quickly and profoundly be opened up to the outside world. A 1919 law had opened Indian lands to mineral exploration. World War II was over and the nuclear age had begun. The Cold War kept demand for uranium high for decades. By the early 1950s, dozens of large uranium mines had opened on Navajo land.

Primary Sector   economic activities that involve the direct extraction of resources from the environment, such as mining, forestry, and marine fishing

Conditions of Production   In political economic (and Marxist) thought, the material or environmental conditions required for a specific economy to function, which may include things as varied as water for use in an industrial process to the health of workers to do the labor

Externality   The spillover of a cost or benefit, as where industrial activity at a plant leads to pollution off-site that must be paid for by someone else

In **primary sector** activities (such as mining, fishing, and forestry), capitalists secure access to the **conditions of production** (the saleable natural resources) and hire wage laborers to extract the resources, which are sold as commodities. Capitalists make profits by paying laborers less than the value they add to the commodity. Capitalists will attempt to keep labor costs low, because cheaper labor means higher profits. They will also attempt to keep non-labor costs low. One way of doing this is by practicing environmentally unsound practices that result in environmental **externalities**, such as preventable off-site pollution.

As mining is by its very nature a hazardous occupation and a polluting enterprise, governments attempt to keep capitalist excesses in check by passing regulations aimed at ensuring safe working conditions and environmentally sound practices. The Navajo Reservation, existing as something of a country within a country, offered up an opportunity for a high rate of labor exploitation and negligent environmental practices, an avenue that many capitalists (and bureaucrats) were content to travel.

The arrangement for uranium prospectors on the Navajo Reservation was easily exploited. Anyone could prospect on the reservation, but only Navajos could apply for mine permits. Typically, white prospectors would find a reserve, pay English-speaking and well-connected Navajos to apply for the permit, then pay them a 2 percent royalty once the lode started paying off. One troublesome aspect of this system was that most rural Navajo herders – the ones living and working the land to be mined; the ones that would be displaced by mining operations – spoke only Navajo and did not understand what was happening to their land (Eichstadt 1994). They were granted the same choice given countless times to rural, subsistence people living in the way of progress: either work in the mines or move somewhere else.

Predictably, Navajo mines harbored a typical colonial division of labor: white managers, engineers, and foremen, and Navajo miners and hourly employees (cleaning, transporting materials, etc.) (Figure 12.3). Hourly employees were (at best) paid minimum wage, while the miners were paid an industry-substandard $1.50–2.00 per hour. The pittance paid to Navajo mineworkers, however, was far from the most egregious component of the colonial relationship between the US government, its mining-corporate intermediaries, and the Navajo Tribe.

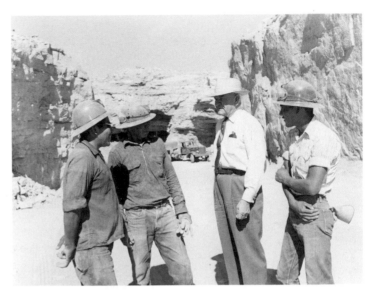

Figure 12.3 Colonial division of labor in the Navajo uranium mines. Denny Viles (third from left), executive with the Vanadium Corporation of America, in shirt, tie, and soft-sided hat; the other three men in the picture are hard-hatted Navajo mineworkers. *Source*: Photo courtesy of Fort Lewis College, Center of Southwest Studies.

Cancer comes to the Navajo Reservation

In the 1950s, cancer was almost unheard of among Navajo tribal members. So much so, in fact, that a physician documented the Navajo's seeming imperviousness to cancer in a 1956 scientific peer-reviewed journal article (Pasternak 2011). Owing to decades of uranium mining on the reservation, however, that trend would soon make a harrowing reversal.

By the time uranium mining began in earnest on the reservation, the link between uranium mine work and cancer (usually lung cancer) was well established. The cause was mineworkers' long-term exposure to radon gas and "radon daughters" (short-lived decay products of radon). The daughters are solids that can become easily airborne and breathed into the lungs.

A tragic combination of high profits and bureaucratic inertia allowed for terrible mine safety conditions for over three decades. Four supposedly independent federal agencies had different and often conflicting mandates for mining on Indian lands, while strong pressure to maximize uranium output led to a culture of looking the other way. Simple things like providing respirators for miners, wetting down (radon-daughter loaded) dust in mine shafts, properly venting shafts: none of these routine precautions were common in Navajo mines. The toll paid by Navajo miners was tremendous. A study of Navajo former-mineworkers in the 1980s found lung cancer rates to be 56 times the national average (several other types of cancer also were manifesting at dozens to hundreds times the national average).

As explained in Chapter 7, a political economy approach uncovers the power-laden relationships that structure society–environment relations. In this case, the US government drove up demand for uranium under the auspices of the Cold War. Tremendous amounts of money were there for the taking. Well-paid and high-level jobs (in government and the private sector) depended on continuously expanding uranium mining. Under these circumstances, from a capitalist's perspective, the Navajo Reservation proved to be the ideal location to find the largest uranium deposit in the country. Regulations could be skirted owing to the government's mismanagement of Indian lands, and the tribal members themselves – mired in poverty, mostly illiterate, and most not even speaking English – were easily exploited as low-paid workers knowingly placed directly in harm's way. The Navajo uranium era, as such, represents a classic and tragic case of environmental injustice – where unhealthful or dangerous conditions are disproportionately proximate to minority communities.

One chapter of this sad history perfectly illustrates the scale (and the racism at the root) of these injustices. In the 1950s and 60s, on uranium mines across the Colorado Plateau, mining companies had long taken to giving away the "tailings" – the uranium-laden rubble that remained after processing. As bad luck would have it, uranium tailings make fine mortar and bricks, and over the years people in mining areas of Colorado, Utah, and New Mexico carted away tailings and used them to add onto their homes or even construct new homes. This was particularly appealing to Navajos, many of whom lived in dwellings with bare earthen floors.

In 1968, the federal government sent a Public Health Service worker to inspect buildings in (nearly all white) Grand Junction, Colorado that had been constructed using radioactive tailings. The inspections returned frightening results – buildings emitting 100 times or more the radioactivity expected for the area. The government wasted no time cleaning up Grand Junction. Beginning in 1971, $250 million of public money was spent demolishing and rebuilding 4,000 buildings.

Despite a similar pattern of tailings used for home construction on the Navajo Reservation, no such federally funded remediation took place there. This negligence cannot be placed solely on faceless bureaucratic inertia, either. A 1975 EPA inspection of Navajo houses reported dozens of dangerously radioactive dwellings and recommended government-funded cleanup and remediation. The recommendation was rejected twice by two separate federal agencies, including the *Indian Health Service*! Navajos continued to live in (and be sickened by) radioactive houses for another two decades, a full 30 years after the federal government had gone out of its way to clean up Grand Junction to better-than-new condition (Pasternak 2011).

The stories told here are just snippets of the human health and environmental damage wrought by decades of uranium mining on the Navajo Reservation. Detailed histories include promised but never-delivered Navajo royalties, men and women Navajo ranchers (and their livestock) sickened by drinking uranium-laced water near mines, and surface and groundwater pollution from poorly constructed tailings pile spill (including the notorious 1979 liquid tailings spill at Church Rock, which to this day remains the largest ever release of radioactive materials into the environment in US history). In 2005, the Navajo tribal government unanimously passed a permanent ban on all uranium mining and processing on tribal lands. In a land of very little economic development, the Navajo have decided the costs or uranium extraction far outweigh the benefits.

The Social Construction of Nature: Discourses of Development and Wilderness in Australia

Half a world away from the Navajo Reservation lies the sparsely populated, tropical Northern Territory of Australia. Like the Navajo Reservation, this area is home to valuable deposits of uranium. In this section, we will shift our theoretical lens to the *constructions* that helped forge the evolution of land use in the area. In Chapter 8, we discussed the notion of "**discourses**," statements and concepts that become taken for granted, but at the same time *do work in the world*. We will examine how discourses of "development" and "wilderness" worked to inscribe notions of what constitutes appropriate and inappropriate uses of the land.

> **Discourse** At root, written and spoken communication; thicker deployments of the term acknowledge that statements and texts are not mere representations of a material world, but rather power-embedded constructions that (partially) make the world we live in

Four pillars mark the analysis presented in this section. First, it is an assessment of the development of uranium resources in Australia, a country with no nuclear power plants that exports nearly 100 percent of the uranium mined within its borders. Second, the Ranger Mine assessed here is the second largest producing uranium mine in the world, in the end accounting for close to 1 percent of the world's total electricity production. Third, the mine is surrounded on all sides by Kakadu National Park, the largest terrestrial national park in Australia (at nearly 20,000 square kilometers, it is nearly half as large as Switzerland). Finally, this land has been occupied by indigenous people (known in Australia as Aboriginals) for tens of thousands of years.

Terra Nullius: The British settlement of a peopled, but "unowned" land

The modern country of Australia, it could be said, was founded on a social construction. British settlement in the late eighteenth century was justified through the common law doctrine of *terra nullius*, meaning land belonging to no one. Lands deemed unowned could be claimed through the simple act of occupation. But when the British arrived in (we do not want to say "discovered") Australia in the 1780s, like Columbus in the Caribbean three centuries earlier, they did not find an "empty" land. Indeed, near present-day Kakadu National Park, British settlers met Aboriginals who had been engaged in trading with neighboring islanders for a century or more. The only thing that made Australia "unowned" was the fact that the indigenous locals did not have modern conceptions (*constructions*) like private property or a hierarchical, social system in which exclusive ownership of land would even make sense.

By 1849 most British settlements in the wet, mosquito-ridden Northern Territory had been abandoned. The remaining herds of Asian water buffalo that had been introduced by the British were set free. The only settlements left were geopolitical settlements on the coast left to stave off Dutch colonial expansion into Australia from the north. Into the twentieth century, white settler activity in the northern interior consisted mostly of scattered "buffalo camps," where now-feral buffalo were hunted and the skins and meat sold for export. Skilled as skinners, horsemen, and hunters, many Aboriginals were employed in this industry. After this and short-lived markets in crocodile hides and gold mining collapsed, the area was being eyed by (white) Australians for two kinds of development, as a national park and for uranium extraction.

Repeating the pattern of colonial history that rendered the indigenous people of this region invisible, local Aboriginals were not initially consulted by proponents of either land-use plan. By the late 1970s, however, landmark legislation mandated an Aboriginal voice in land-use decision-making. The Aboriginals, legally, had *arrived* (even though they had always been there!). No longer *terra nullius*, a new set of constructions was needed to justify uranium mining in the Northern Territory.

Development in the Northern Territory

Proponents of uranium mining at the Ranger deposit deployed rationalist discourses of "development" to justify their plans. The benefits of developing the Ranger deposit were explained to the Aboriginals in what must have seemed rather abstract terms of projected value of the deposit, total jobs forecasted, and tax revenues that would accrue to the Northern Territory – this being explained to scattered, subsistence and semi-subsistence local dwellers, of whom most spoke no English, but all of whom were by then well aware of the long and brutal history of white oppression of Aboriginals.

Perhaps unsurprisingly, "economic development" and "the national interest" overrode Aboriginal opposition, and the mine proposal was approved (Banerjee 2000). The Ranger Mine, which would quickly become one of the world's largest producing uranium mines, began producing uranium ore in 1980 (Figure 12.4).

It may sound cynical to critique the idea that this area and the Aboriginals – monetarily poor as they were – were underdeveloped. But should the history of (even modern) "development" be viewed as a colonial and imperial history itself? Such a narrative has been put forth by many "critical" development scholars: Western development in indigenous regions worked to normalize all aspects of society along Western ideals, not so much for the betterment (the "development") of the indigenous people, but rather for the expansion (the "development") of capitalist profiteering (Banerjee 2000; Escobar 1995).

Does this general critique of Western development apply to this manifestation of development, the opening of the Ranger Mine in the Northern Territory? Aboriginals living in the Northern Territory do receive per capita payments based on mine revenues, but the $450–700 per person per year has done little to address the dire poverty of rural Aboriginals, whose income still averages almost 40 percent less than rural non-Aboriginals. Aboriginals comprise 25 percent of the population of the Northern Territory but only constitute 7 percent of the mining workforce, most of which are minimum-wage, unskilled

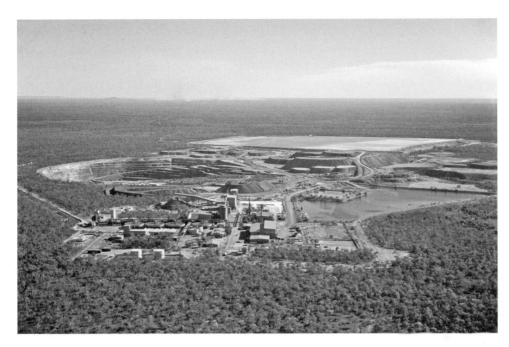

Figure 12.4 The Ranger Uranium Mine and Mill, Northern Territory, Australia. *Source*: G. Bowater/Corbis.

jobs (Banerjee 2000). Is it any wonder, then, that there was widespread Aboriginal opposition to expanding uranium mining in the region when a second, nearly adjacent uranium mega-mine was proposed two decades after the Ranger Mine opened? Not all white Australians, as we have noted, thought that uranium mining was the best use of this land. Many felt that it deserved protection as a national park. But the discourses that rationalized park protection, as well, would clash with Aboriginal understandings of life on the land.

Kakadu National Park: Saving a (socially constructed) wilderness

At the same time that the fate of the Ranger uranium deposit was being debated, a large swath of land surrounding the Ranger deposit was being put forth as a proposed national park. A loose, strategic alliance quickly formed between Aboriginals and conservation-minded white Australian proponents of park designation. Even as these indigenous and non-indigenous Australians held in common an opposition to uranium mining, there were many ways in which the white conservationists and the Aboriginals failed to see eye to eye. Principal was the conservationists' notion that the land deserved protection because it was a "wilderness."

The Eurocentric nature of this discursive construction is exemplified in a 1976 article in the magazine *National Parks Journal* titled "Farewell Wilderness: Uranium Mining vs. Nature Conservation" (Colley 1976). As discussed in Chapter 8, when a land is constructed as a wilderness, it has the effect of de-peopling the land, often stripping the voice from the (usually indigenous) people who live and work there. The *Parks Journal* essay, constructing the park as a "wilderness remnant," does just this. Nowhere in the article is the presence of Aboriginals noted. Framing the conflict as a choice between "nature" and "uranium," the article *at best* places the indigenous dwellers *within* the "nature" under threat from uranium mining. At worst, through this act of omission, the journal is silent to the possibility that park protection could potentially deny local Aboriginals traditional use of their land. Per the course, it is (white) conservationists and Western-modeled parks protection that are offered as the saviors.

Most Aboriginals in the area have supported the national park designation since the inception of the proposal and continue to do so today, and most still remain opposed to uranium mining. Park status, after all, provides an additional buffer of legal protection from land-use changes that most Aboriginals oppose, such as expanded resource extraction or resort tourism. Local Aboriginals understand that framing the park as a wilderness is part of what established and maintains the park's political and popular support. But they also realize the potential disenfranchisement that comes with codifying the park as, *most fundamentally*, a wilderness.

The Aboriginals have no interest in protecting the park as some sort of "remnant" landscape, a slice of nature frozen in time. Rightly so, they insist on retaining in perpetuity their rights to forage, hunt, fish, and *live* in the park. The Aboriginals, in tandem with environmentalists, by the 1990s had successfully established formal, legal redefinitions of wilderness in the management plans for this park. As such, Aboriginals, and lately many environmentalists as well, are deploying "wilderness" in a more pragmatic fashion, as a deliberately *constructed* land management designation. Environmentalists, no doubt, will continue to do so as long as they see it as effectively protecting the park's famous biodiversity and scenic landscapes, and keeping uranium mining expansion at bay. Local Aboriginals will as well, as long as it helps them retain their autonomy and livelihoods. If Kakadu-as-wilderness fails to achieve these objectives, however, the "wilderness" may be discarded for a new set of constructions that will guide understandings, and use, of the land.

The Uranium Puzzle

In this chapter, we have learned that:

- Scientists sensed soon after its discovery that uranium held both promise and danger.
- Nuclear weapons were commissioned long before any nuclear power plant ever went online.
- Nuclear power plants produce about 16 percent of the world's electricity (about the same as hydropower).
- Nuclear accidents, such as the meltdowns at Fukushima, Japan, can cause severe, widespread, and long-lasting damage.
- Producing nuclear fuel is a cumbersome process, with risks, pollution, and toxic-waste products produced at every step in the chain.

- Nuclear fuels emit fewer tons of greenhouse gases than do fossil fuels.
- Nuclear waste products – for which we have no clear long-term disposal solution – remain dangerously radioactive for an almost unimaginably long time period. Risk assessments are a necessary, but partial, component in tackling this problem.
- A political economy of uranium mining demonstrates that the people who have borne the greatest burden of harm from uranium extraction are often not the same people who have reaped its benefits.
- Constructivist analysis shows that discourses were critical components of imperial expansion, but it also illustrates how discourses are just as critical to those still resisting colonial repression.

Uranium stands as one of the more vexing environment–societies puzzles. With 430 nuclear power plants operating worldwide (not to mention global stockpiles of nuclear weapons!), we are already "on the hook" for dealing with this issue for the next *few thousand years*! Whether to expand the sector (optimistic that we can one day finally solve the safety and disposal issues) or, on the contrary, deciding how fast and what degree to scale back: no options are without their difficulties and downsides.

Questions for Review

1. Describe the processes known as induced nuclear fission and a nuclear chain reaction.
2. Unlike coal, uranium ore is not usable as nuclear fuel. Why is this so, and what must be done to produce nuclear fuel out of uranium ore?
3. How is most high-level radioactive waste disposed of currently? What other prominent method has been proposed, and what are some of the problematic aspects of this approach?
4. Why did the Navajo tribal government vote to ban uranium mining on their reservation in 2005?
5. Why are Aboriginals in Australia's Northern Territory weary of embracing notions of both economic development and wilderness preservation?

Exercise 12.1   Debating the Future of Nuclear Power

On the internet, find one pro-nuclear argument made from an institutional or markets perspective, and one anti-nuclear argument from an ethics perspective. Use credible sources (avoid personal blogs). Think critically about how the positions are justified. Having done this, imagine yourself occupying *both* sides of a fictional debate where the question posed is "Countries worldwide should work together to phase out nuclear power as quickly as possible." Write two one-paragraph summary answers to this question (one "agree" answer and one "disagree" answer). Finally, write an explanation of which argument you think is stronger, and why.

Exercise 12.2   Should Australia Move Ahead with the Jabiluka Mine

In addition to the Ranger deposit, a second uranium deposit lies under land completely surrounded by Kakadu National Park. This deposit could potentially yield more uranium (and more revenue) than the Ranger Mine. Your assignment is to research and write about this debate, answering the following questions: When was this deposit discovered? What key events in the Jabiluka debate transpired in 1998? What is the current status of the deposit? What is *your opinion* on whether the Jabiluka mine should be opened for operation? (Support your answer.)

Exercise 12.3   Uranium Mining in the Global South

This chapter focused mostly on uranium mining in the United States and Australia, yet a significant amount of uranium is mined in less-developed countries in the Global South. Write a short essay on the uranium sector in Niger, Namibia or Uzbekistan (choose one). What percentage of your chosen country's GDP does uranium extraction account for? What are the primary export markets for the uranium mined there? Does your country have any domestic nuclear power plants? From what you found, does it appear that there are prominent (social and/or environmental) controversial aspects to uranium mining?

References

Banerjee, S. (2000). "Whose land is it anyway? National interest, indigenous stakeholders, and colonial discourses." *Organization and Environment* 13(1): 3–38.

Colley, A. (1976). "Farewell wilderness: Uranium mining vs. nature conservation." *National Parks Journal*, February.

Eichstadt, P. (1994). *If You Poison Us: Uranium and Native Americans*. Santa Fe, NM: Red Crane Books.

Elk, M. (2012). "Honeywell shutters uranium plant, lays off more than 200 workers." *In These Times* [online edition], July 20. Retrieved October 31, 2012:, from http://inthesetimes.com/working/entry/13551/honeywell_shutters_uranium_plant_lays_off_over_200_workers/.

Escobar, A. (1995). *Encountering Development: The Making and Unmaking of the Third World*. Princeton, NJ: Princeton University Press.

Fialka, J. (2009). "The 'screw Nevada bill' and how it stymied U.S. nuclear waste policy." *New York Times*, May 11. Retrieved November 5, 2012, from http://www.nytimes.com/cwire/2009/05/11/11climatewire-the-screw-nevada-bill-and-how-it-stymied-us-12208.html.

IAEA (2007). "Nuclear Power: Status and Outlook, A Report from the IAEA." Vienna: International Atomic Energy Association. Retrieved October 22, 2012, from http://www.iaea.org/newscenter/pressreleases/2007/prn200719.html.

Pasternak, J. (2011). *Yellow Dirt: A Poisoned Land and the Betrayal of the Navajos*. New York: Free Press.

Peterson, S. (2003). "Remains of toxic bullets litter Iraq." *Christian Science Monitor*, May 23.

Shrader-Frechette, K. S. (1993). *Burying Uncertainty: Risk and the Case Against Geological Disposal of Nuclear Waste*. Berkeley: University of California Press.

US EPA (Environmental Protection Agency) (2012). "Radiation protection: About Yucca Mountain standards." Retrieved November 8, 2012, from http://www.epa.gov/radiation/yucca/about.html.

US NRC (United States Nuclear Regulatory Commission) (2012). "Backgrounder on radiation protection and the 'tooth fairy' issue." Retrieved November 1, 2012, from http://www.nrc.gov/reading-rm/doc-collections/fact-sheets/tooth-fairy.html.

US Senate (2006, March). "Yucca Mountain: The Most Studied Real Estate on the Planet." Report to the Senate Chairman. Retrieved November 9, 2012, from http://epw.senate.gov/repwhitepapers/YuccaMountainEPWReport.pdf.

Walker, S. (2009). *The Road to Yucca Mountain*. Berkeley: University of California Press.

Zoellner, T. (2009). *Uranium: War, Energy, and the Rock that Shaped the World*. New York: Viking.

Suggested Reading

Ferguson, C. (2001). *Nuclear Energy: What Everyone Needs to Know*. Oxford: Oxford University Press.

Keuletz, V. (1998). *The Tainted Desert: Environmental and Social Ruin in the American West*. New York: Routledge.

Lawrence, D. (2000). *Kakadu: The Making of a National Park*. Carlton South, Victoria, AU: Melbourne University Press.

Lupinacci, J. (2000). "Creating corporate value and environmental benefit with improved energy performance." *Environmental Quality Management* 10(2): 11–17.

Mahaffey, J. (2010). *Atomic Awakening: A New Look at the History and Future of Nuclear Power*. New York: Pegasus.

Makhijani, A., L. Chalmers, and B. Smith (2004). "Uranium Enrichment." Takoma Park, MD: Institute for Energy and Environmental Research.

Pineda, C. (2012). *Devil's Tango: How I Learned the Fukushima Step by Step*. San Antonio, TX: Wings Press.

Randolph, J., and G. Masters (2008.) *Energy for Sustainability: Technology, Planning, Policy*. Washington, DC: Island.

Rhodes, R. (2012). *The Making of the Atomic Bomb: Twenty-Fifth Anniversary Edition*. New York: Simon and Schuster.

Shrader-Frechette, K. S. (1995). "Environmental risk and the iron triangle: The case of Yucca Mountain." *Business Ethics Quarterly* 5(4): 753–77.

Williams, T. (1992). *Refuge: An Unnatural History of Family and Place*. New York: Vintage Books.

13

Tuna

Source: Ugo Montaldo/Shutterstock.

Chapter Menu

Keywords

- Animal rights
- Bycatch
- Conditions of production
- Consumer boycott
- Dolphin safe tuna
- Exclusive economic zones (EEZs)
- Fordism
- Green consumption
- Maximum sustainable yield
- Moral extensionism
- Post-Fordism
- Purse-seine fishing
- Relations of production
- Second contradiction of capitalism
- Social construction
- Sustainability
- Transnational corporations
- Utopian

Environment and Society: A Critical Introduction, Second Edition. Paul Robbins, John Hintz, and Sarah A. Moore.
© 2014 John Wiley & Sons, Ltd. Published 2014 by John Wiley & Sons, Ltd.

Blood Tuna

The 2006 film *Blood Diamond* was not your standard international action film, with a fantastical plot, far removed from the comfortable lives of viewers in the West. Rather, for many viewers, the diamond jewelry they owned implicated them in the violence they witnessed on screen. *Blood Diamond* brought to light (albeit in rather over-the-top, Hollywood fashion) the human bloodshed that is part and parcel of the international trade in West African diamonds. Shocked viewers realized that, through their diamond purchases, they may have unwittingly funded a pointless and ruthless war, with all of its attendant killing, rape, smuggling, torture, and illegal incarcerations. Exposure of this violence resulted in some real changes in global diamond markets. Many consumers were now demanding – and were soon able to purchase – certified "cruelty free" or "conflict free" diamonds. Diamonds, of course, are not the only natural resource whose troubling history gets hidden within commodities.

Eighteen years earlier, another film had produced similar reactions and results. The 1988 film, however, was no Hollywood production, but rather footage from low-budget handheld movies filmed by Sam LaBudde aboard the Panamanian tuna fishing boat *Maria Luisa*. LaBudde was a spy of sorts. A biologist by training, he had gotten a job as a galley cook aboard the *Maria Luisa*, but with the hidden intent of filming the slaughter of dolphins. Dolphins, for reasons still unknown to biologists, school above tuna in some parts of the world's oceans. In one part of the Pacific Ocean, for about 30 years, fleets of tuna boats had been targeting the easily spotted dolphins to locate the tuna that schooled beneath them. In three decades over six million dolphins were tangled in the massive tuna nets and killed, most drowning before they could be released (Gosliner 1999).

LaBudde got what he came for. The film – which included graphic images of dead and dying dolphins – was shown in pubs, independent cinemas, and on college campuses across the United States and then around the world. Shocked filmgoers cringed to think that this seemingly innocuous commodity – canned tuna – could have left such a trail of blood in its wake. As they later would for diamonds, consumers responded in force to this saga of "blood tuna," a commodity far more humble and far more common.

Indeed, few wild-caught food products are as ubiquitous as tuna. *Annual* catches for some species of tuna are in the *billions* of pounds! Yet, like most animal products, tuna arrives in our kitchens with little visible evidence of its natural history or the human labor that got it from sea to table. What does a tuna even look like? How and where are they caught? And by whom? Are tuna overfished? In this chapter, we will examine these questions through the lenses of markets, political economy, and ethics. By closely examining the puzzle of tuna, we learn a great deal about the problem facing the world's marine ecosystems, about the massive impact of food consumption on the environment, and about the awkward relationship between ethics and economics.

A Short History of Tuna

"Tuna" is an informal designation referring to a suite of similar fish species, all belonging to the family Scombridae. All tuna share a similar morphology. They are largest in the

Figure 13.1 The sleek, powerful, bluefin tuna. The bluefin are the largest of the tuna (the largest one ever caught weighed 1,496 pounds). *Source*: Brian J. Skerry/National Geographic/Getty Images.

middle and smoothly tapered toward both front and back, with a powerful and distinctive crescent-shaped tail (Figure 13.1). One physiological adaptation in particular gives them much of their power. Tuna are endothermic, or warm-blooded, which means they get more oxygen, more quickly, to their muscles than they would otherwise (Whynott 1995).

Tuna are some of the fastest swimmers in the ocean (tuna have been clocked swimming at nearly 70 miles per hour). They have stamina, too. Tuna travel on some of the longest migrations of any animal, many with seasonal migrations of four thousand or more miles. Not only is this undeniably impressive, but it has socioeconomic implications as well. Because of their far-ranging nature, only truly global efforts will prove successful for the long-term conservation of these fish (Greenberg 2010).

Tuna is a versatile food fish. It is eaten raw (as "sashimi," which means thinly sliced raw seafood). Tuna filets have become popular cooked as "steaks" on outdoor grills. Tuna is popular in soups and chowders in many different cuisines worldwide. And, of course, as many American schoolchildren come to know it as "tuna fish," tuna comes in a can. The most commercially important species of tuna are bluefin, yellowfin, bigeye, albacore, and skipjack. Each has different markets, with bigeye tuna eaten mostly fresh in Japan and Korea, for example, and albacore consumed as canned "white" tuna in the United States (Ellis 2008).

In the sections that follow, we will discuss the bluefin and yellowfin. These varieties are emblematic, first because they are both objects of familiar consumption to us, but also because they represent a crisis of overfishing in the world's oceans (especially bluefin), and because they raise issues of collateral damage to other species in their harvesting (especially dolphins in yellowfin fisheries).

Bluefin tuna: From horse mackerel to ranched sushi

Bluefin are the largest tuna (often, in fact, called "giant bluefin"), with individuals commonly weighing over 1,000 pounds. Despite their great size, for most of the modern era bluefin were not a commercially valuable catch. In the first decades of the twentieth century, when bluefin was known commonly in North America as the "horse mackerel," its flesh was considered unfit for human consumption and was sold as an ingredient in commercial pet food. It was, and remains, an elite sport fish (Ellis 2008: 84).

The fate of the bluefin changed dramatically in the 1960s. Sushi has been central to the Japanese diet since at least the seventeenth century. However, popular demand for bluefin (especially "toro," the marbled red belly meat of the bluefin) is a recent phenomenon. In the 1960s, Japan built a fleet of refrigerated tuna freighters that could remain at sea for weeks, pursuing previously inaccessible giant bluefin fisheries. The demand for maguro, as soon as it was widely available, increased faster than the fish could be caught. Quickly, non-Japanese fishers – from the United States and Canada to the Mediterranean – jumped into what has remained an incredibly lucrative market (one recreational angler, for example, caught a single giant bluefin off the coast of Nova Scotia in November 2012 projected to sell at auction in Japan for over $32,000 (Johnson 2012)). The money to be made unsurprisingly resulted in an increasingly heavy and unsustainable harvest.

One of the latest ways that fishers have tried to maximize bluefin production is by "ranching" them. In South Pacific and Mediterranean fisheries, entire schools of young bluefin are caught in "**purse seine**" nets; so-called because after the net encircles the school, the bottom of the net is drawn together like the strings of a purse. The enormous nets are towed to nearshore waters where the tuna are raised for a few months in pens before being harvested and exported, mostly to Japan.

> **Purse-Seine Fishing**   An effective fishing method for species that school near the surface; a large net is encircled around the targeted catch, after which the bottom of the net is drawn tight like the strings of a purse, thus confining the catch in the net

Distressingly, tuna ranching has further decimated wild bluefin tuna stocks. Tuna caught for ranching do not count against legal catch quotas (even though they are being permanently removed from wild populations), but they do not fall under aquaculture regulations either (because they are not reared in captivity). The practice, therefore, goes almost completely unregulated. Bluefin ranching deleteriously affects the age structure of wild populations. Prior to ranching, the heaviest fishing pressure was on the largest tuna. Now, more juvenile bluefin are being removed from wild stocks. Bluefin populations are losing the very fish that will be needed to replenish their numbers in the future.

Bluefin tuna are overfished; meaning simply that more fish are being caught than are regenerating. The ramifications are as social as they are ecological. Overfishing results in considerable hardship in fishing-dependent communities. In many cases, "artisanal" (small-scale) fishers suffer first and most. When a local fishery becomes overfished, large boats owned by multinational corporations simply relocate to another fishery, but this is not an option for small-scale artisanal fishers. Many well-known fish species that are readily available at supermarkets are actually severely overfished species (Table 13.1).

The Eastern Tropical Pacific yellowfin tuna fishery

Yellowfin tuna are smaller than bluefin but still quite large, some exceeding 400 pounds. One of the most commercially valuable and historically most heavily fished tuna fisheries in the world is the yellowfin tuna fishery in the Eastern Tropical Pacific (ETP) Ocean. The ETP stretches south from southern California along the coast of South America, covering some 18 million square kilometers. The valuable southern portion of the fishery (off Central and South American coasts) was first exploited by US boats in the 1930s, when improvements in refrigeration enabled boats to stay out at sea longer and venture farther offshore.

Table 13.1 Severely overfished marine species.

Fish species	Fishing method	Interesting facts
Atlantic cod	Bottom trawling; pole and line	Officially closed as a commercial fishery in Canada since 1992, Georges Bank population shows no signs of rebounding
Atlantic halibut	Longlines; pole and line	Overfished for centuries; may become extinct in the wild
Orange roughy	Bottom trawling	Can live to be over a hundred years old; population reduced by 70% in only 30 years of fishing
Ocean Perch	Mostly bottom trawling	Slow growing fish species reproduces at an unusually late age
Scalloped hammerhead shark	Longlines	Population reduced by over 80%; bycatch includes albatrosses and endangered sea turtles

Source: Data from Blue Ocean Institute: www.blueocean.org; Consortium for Wildlife Bycatch Reduction: http://www.bycatch.org.

Since cotton nets (as used in cooler waters off California) degraded quickly in the warmer southern waters, the southern ETP boats switched to pole and line fishing (Gosliner 1999).

Pole and line fishing was considerably more labor-intensive than purse-seine fishing, but remained profitable until the 1950s, when US markets were inundated with cheap, imported tuna. The pole and line ETP yellowfin fishery quickly became unprofitable, but was saved two technological innovations. One was synthetic (nylon) nets that held up in the warmer waters. The other was a larger, more powerful power block that could haul in once-unimaginably large nets. The reconversion of the southern ETP fleet to purse-seine fishing was rapid. Within a few years the fishery was more productive and profitable than ever (Joseph 1994).

Unlike skipjack tuna, which (as their name suggests) "skip" along the surface and are therefore easily spotted from boats or spotter planes, yellowfin swim at depth, which makes them difficult to spot. For reasons still unknown to ecologists, ETP yellowfin (and, strangely, not yellowfin elsewhere) often swim below schools of dolphins, allowing fishermen to target schools of tuna by searching first for easily spotted dolphins. By 1960, this had become the primary method for finding yellowfin. Once a dolphin school was spotted, a fleet of speed-boats would "corral" the dolphins to concentrate them. After this was accomplished, a boat would drag a huge nylon purse-seine net around the dolphin school, simultaneously trapping yellowfin beneath. The main boat (utilizing a new, large power block) would then haul in the catch (and most of the dolphin). The innovations that had "saved" the commercial viability of this fishery also doomed millions of ETP dolphins.

Bycatch Non-targeted organisms incidentally caught by commercial fishing operations, including many fish species, but also a large number of birds, marine mammals, and sea turtles

In the early years of the purse-seine dolphin method, little effort was made to reduce dolphin **bycatch** mortality. A few dolphins would breach over the net and escape, but most would be

Box 13.1   Environmental Solution? Open Ocean Aquaculture

Aquaculture (the raising of aquatic organisms for harvest) has grown exponentially in the past few decades. The production of farmed aquatic species now almost matches the total global wild-caught tonnage. Consistent with our tales of tuna in this chapter, the potential demand appears nearly bottomless. But even as it might intuitively seem like marine aquaculture would be environmentally preferable to harvesting wild fish from stressed populations, most current marine aquaculture practices are far from ecologically benign. Many of the problems stem from the fact that nearly all existing marine aquaculture facilities operate in easily accessible and relatively sheltered nearshore environments.

Farm-raised salmon, for example, are usually raised in bays or inlets. They are also raised very intensively, with individual nets or pens sometimes holding tens of thousands of salmon. That many fish produce incredible amounts of waste. Since their surrounding environment is one of relatively calm water, this waste does not readily dilute and disperse and can easily become a significant local pollutant. The cramped salmon are often treated with antibiotics to reduce the spread of infectious disease. Pesticides are even used in the pens. As such, synthetic chemicals are being directly applied to marine ecosystems. The ecological problems associated with marine aquaculture do not stop at salmon. Shrimp farming, for example, has recently become the largest cause of coastal mangrove deforestation globally.

Proponents of new forms of marine aquaculture say that it may be time to start "thinking outside the bay." If most of the ecological problems associated with marine aquaculture stem from where it is practiced, why not move it farther offshore? Offshore fish farms would not just provide a medium for the dilution and dispersal of the waste produced, but the "real estate" available for such facilities is, for all practice purposes, nearly infinite. Offshore fish farms could also (in theory) house more fish in less confined conditions. Offshore farms could relieve pressure on nearshore ecosytems, enabling rehabilitation of their full suite of ecosystem functioning and services. But there are, of course, problems. Building offshore farms that can withstand the tumultuous open ocean environment is proving to be an incredible engineering challenge. Costs of operating and maintaining offshore facilities will be higher. Investors have not exactly beaten down the doors of budding offshore aquaculture firms. And the ecological considerations do not just magically disappear as fish farms move offshore, either. Pollutants are still produced. Diseases can still spread to wild populations. These (and other issues) are lessened in the offshore environment, but not eliminated. And this is all without mentioning the unforeseen ecological consequences that invariably arise anytime we undertake a food production revolution on the scale proposed by many proponents of open ocean aquaculture.

Source: Upton and Buck 2010

hauled aboard in the nets and die before they could be thrown back in the water. The numbers of dolphin deaths associated with this fishery during the 1960s are staggering (Figure 13.2). When these figures went public in 1968 through the media, there was an immediate public outcry and political response. The "tuna–dolphin problem" (like the problem of overfishing of bluefin today) became the order of the day, creating a human/environment puzzle with global implications.

The puzzle of tuna

This overview of tuna sheds light on some of the seemingly intractable problems bound within the rapidly changing relationship between people and the world's oceans. The review

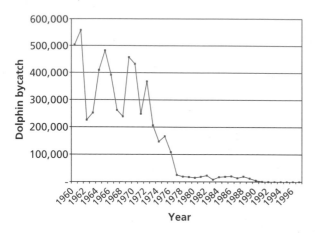

Figure 13.2 Dolphin mortality at the hands of US fishing vessels using purse-seine tuna technology in the Eastern Tropical Pacific, 1960–97. *Source*: Adapted from data from Gosliner (1999), p. 124.

shows us how changes over time in society – including evolving tastes, technological developments, and evolving ideas of right and wrong – have all radically changed the way we harvest and eat tuna. Tuna are a kind of puzzle when we acknowledge that:

- Tuna are valuable. The demand for tuna seems to have no ceiling, yet wild stocks of tuna are an undeniably finite resource.
- Tuna is everywhere! Its ubiquity (for example, on store shelves) masks the declines of wild populations.
- The puzzling relationships between tuna and other sea creatures (like dolphins) make it very difficult to heavily harvest tuna without impacting other species as well.

Tuna provide a window through which we can see the effects on nature of our tastes, trends, technologies, and cultures. As such, tuna present an important puzzle: Can the global community make agreements that will preserve wild tuna stocks? Viewing the ETP tuna–dolphin controversy through the lenses of markets and commodities, political economy, and ethics, we see that different perspectives paint very different pictures and point us toward different types of solutions.

Markets and Commodities: Eco-Labels to the Rescue?

We began the discussion of markets and commodities in Chapter 4 by asking the strange question: "*Can using more stuff lead to the availability of more stuff?*" Can this same logic apply to overexploited marine resources? Stated more baldly: Can the free market save the very resources it has depleted? Intuitively, it would seem like it would not, yet a slight tweaking of the question cuts to the heart of one of the most ambitious and widespread recent conservation efforts. So, in this case, perhaps we might ask: *Can consuming the right fish save our oceans?*

This is the bet on which many scientists, government officials, environmentalists, and seafood corporations have recently put their money. Despite centuries of overexploitation of ocean resources that continue to the present day, our best chance at reversing this trend, some say, is by harnessing the forces of the market through informed and enlightened **green consumption**. In this section, we review the campaign for "**dolphin safe**" labeling of canned tuna, often touted as one of the great success stories of the green consumption movement.

Green Consumption Purchasing of products that are purportedly environmentally friendlier or less harmful than their alternatives; a model of environmental protection that relies on consumer choices to change the behavior of firms or industries rather than regulation

Dolphin Safe Tuna Tuna caught without killing dolphins as bycatch

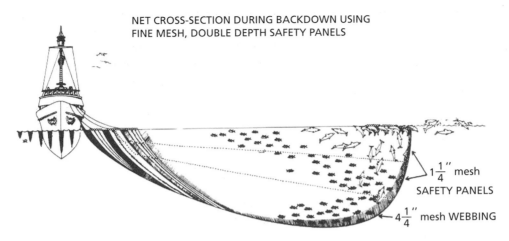

NET CROSS-SECTION DURING BACKDOWN USING
FINE MESH, DOUBLE DEPTH SAFETY PANELS

$1\frac{1}{4}''$ mesh
SAFETY PANELS

$4\frac{1}{4}''$ mesh WEBBING

Figure 13.3 The "Medina panel, " one of a few technological and operational changes made by purse-seine tuna fishers in attempts to reduce dolphin mortality. *Source*: Food and Agriculture Organization of the United Nations (FAO).

Attempts at solutions through legislation

Largely in response to the public outcry over dolphin deaths at the hands of ETP yellowfin purse seiners, in 1972 the US Congress passed the Marine Mammal Protection Act (MMPA). The MMPA prohibited the killing, selling, importing, and exporting of marine mammals or marine mammal parts, but included confusing and even conflicting exceptions for ETP dolphins. Indeed, the legislation proved vague enough and contained enough loopholes that dolphin mortality continued in high numbers for years after passage of the MMPA (Figure 13.2).

Amendments to the MMPA in 1976 led to a substantial decline in dolphin mortality. Boats were required to corral dolphins over and out of the nets before hauling the nets aboard. The nets also now had to be fitted with a fine-meshed "Medina panel" that reduced the number of dolphins ensnared underwater (Figure 13.3). Even with these changes, however, dolphins continued to die. The original MMPA goal of movement toward zero dolphin mortality remained elusive. Indeed, 1984 amendments to the MMPA allowed the US fleet (which was by this time no longer the only country catching ETP tuna with purse-seine fishing) to kill 20,500 dolphins annually, a testament to the persistence of the problem (Joseph 1994).

Consumer activists to the rescue

Many environmentalists remained outraged that a dozen years after the MMPA, dolphin mortality was still considered acceptable. The regulatory route was proving unsatisfactory. In the late 1980s, the environmental nongovernmental organization Earth Island Institute (EII) organized a **consumer boycott** of canned

Consumer Boycott A method of protest that aims to pressure corporations into changing their practices by urging people to forgo purchasing products associated with the targeted corporations tuna, urging consumers to forgo purchasing canned tuna until producers could show that their product did not result in the deaths of dolphins. The boycott was substantial, yet it was not until 1988 that the LaBudde film – as told in the opening story of this chapter – gave the campaign the needed shot in the arm. After the film was shown nationwide, the boycott grew in strength, tuna sales declined, and environmentalists launched a massive letter-writing campaign to tuna producers and politicians. A coalition led by EII started promoting the idea of labeling tuna caught without targeting dolphins as "dolphin safe."

In 1990, the campaign celebrated when the three largest US tuna brands (StarKist, Chicken of the Sea, and Bumblebee), which comprised 90 percent of the US market, agreed to purchase only "dolphin safe" tuna (Baird and Quastel 2011). The federal government soon passed a law requiring canners using the "dolphin safe" label to adhere to standards as defined by the EII consortium. Informed US consumers understood, then, that any tuna purchased with the "dolphin safe" label did not involve the pursuit or capture of dolphins. Congress also passed a trade embargo against the importation of tuna from any countries that could not prove their tuna fishing practices were "comparable" to US regulations (Bonanno and Constance 1996: 6). This effectively shut out Mexico, Venezuela, and Panama (the countries with the largest ETP tuna fleets still targeting dolphins) from their largest export market.

The label stays intact

Coalitions of Latin American states have since filed lawsuits against the United States on charges of discriminatory protective measures in violation of free trade agreements, but have repeatedly failed to gain access to US markets for their purse-seine tuna fishers. Internal pressure (from Democratic and Republican administrations) to water down the "dolphin safe" standards in support of free trade was also brought to bear. Despite the domestic and international political pressure, however, the original "dolphin safe" standards as defined by EII have so far remained intact.

From many angles, the campaign for dolphin conservation in the ETP appears to represent an unqualified success of market forces put to work in the cause of conservation. Dolphin mortality has declined steadily since the activist campaign was launched, down close to *99 percent* from its peak in the 1960s. Most American consumers, no doubt, now go away feeling good about their tuna purchases, knowing their sandwich is not soaked in the blood of dolphins. Similar labeling campaigns have since sprung up in many European countries, Australia, and New Zealand (although not all "dolphin safe" labels worldwide adhere to the same standards).

But the success also could lead one to question the overall impact of the practice. We might wonder, for example: How many consumers see "dolphin safe" and understand its definition? How many assume that "dolphin safe" equals "eco-friendly" writ large? This, in fact, would be a dubious assumption (as will be discussed in the environmental ethics section that follows). As green labels proliferate, is it really possible for the average consumer to track the legitimacy and regulations associated with every "green" certification? Undoubtedly not, but the rise of green certification does mark a change in power on the commodity production landscape. With the aid of a political economy perspective, we can assess this transformation of power for "dolphin safe" tuna and "green" seafood more broadly.

Political Economy: Re-regulating Fishery Economies

In Chapter 7, we stated that it is impossible to understand our relationship with nature without bringing the economy into the picture. Moreover, we showed how and why the economy is never separate from politics (hence: "political economy"). Unlike a perspective that seeks out solely market-based solutions when problems arise (for example, the previous section on green labels), political economy takes a converse approach, analyzing the ways in which capitalist production, no matter how many patches are applied, can never escape its own crises and contradictions, whether on land or in the sea.

In the case of the ETP yellowfin tuna fishery, we can, for example, see the **second contradiction of capitalism** at work. As soon as tuna fishers started targeting schools of dolphins, they were degrading the ecosystem on which they relied for their livelihood. Even though ETP yellowfin tuna have not been overfished per se, the means of production (boats and nylon purse-seine nets) that expanded over the decades through cutthroat competition caused ecosystem degradation (dolphin slaughter) that disrupted and ultimately derailed the production process. The contradiction, therefore, is still clear: the tuna industry was unable to continually increase production without befouling its **conditions of production**.

It could be argued that, moreover, in the absence of cutthroat, global capitalism, the changes in fishing methods (from pole and line to purse-seine mega-nets) would never have taken place. The transition, after all, was made to increase harvests at lower cost. Hundreds of fishers were laid off as the yellowfin fishery transitioned from a labor-intensive (pole and line) to a capital-intensive (purse-seine) means of production. During the pole and line ETP tuna fishing era (pre-1959), the fishermen and deckhands were *mere* workers, paid for their labor, onto which a premium was added as profit for the owners of the operations. From a capitalist's perspective, they were expendable.

Imagine alternative **relations of production**, where the workers owned and controlled the boats, refrigeration, and processing equipment – and were able to maintain their domestic market by, for example, keeping cheaper imported tuna from coming into the country. In such a system, there would have been no incentive for them to have moved to larger nets, and eventually to a wholesale reliance upon dolphins to land their catch. Put another way, they would not have put themselves out of work. They would have, ideally, worked to maintain both their livelihoods and the ecological conditions necessary to

Second Contradiction of Capitalism In Marxist thought, this describes the tendency for capitalism to eventually undermine the environmental conditions for its own perpetuation, through degradation of natural resources or damage to the health of workers, etc., predicted to eventually lead to environmentalist and workers' movements to resist capitalism, leading to a new form of economy. Compare to the first contradiction of capitalism

Conditions of Production In political economic (and Marxist) thought, the material or environmental conditions required for a specific economy to function, which may include things as varied as water for use in an industrial process to the health of workers to do the labor

Relations of Production In political economic (and Marxist) thought, the social relationships associated with, and necessary for, a specific economy, as serfs/knights are to feudalism and workers/owners are to modern capitalism

Utopia/Utopian   Imaginary, idealized social conditions arising from socio-political systems that facilitate cooperation over competition

Maximum Sustainable Yield   The largest seasonal or annual amount of any particular natural resource (e.g., timber, fish) that can be harvested indefinitely

Exclusive Economic Zones (EEZs)   Usually extending 200 nautical miles off the coasts of sovereign states, EEZs are sea-zones within which states claim ownership over fishery and mineral resources

Sustainable/Sustainability   The conservation of land and resources so as to secure their availability to future generations

Fordism   Relations of production dominant in many industrialized countries in the first several decades of the twentieth century; marked by large, vertically integrated corporations, high wages and rates of consumption, and considerable state power

sustain them. Retrospective speculations like these may be somewhat **utopian**, but they nevertheless provide glimpses of how alternative social relations could have concrete ecological advantages.

Geopolitics of tuna

Another strength of a political economy approach to nature–society puzzles is the insight it provides in explaining the way resources are exploited and regulated. Beginning in 1949, US and Latin American tuna fishing nations, in an effort to maintain the ETP yellowfin fishery, agreed on annual tuna harvest quotas based on projections of **maximum sustainable yield**. The catch limits, however, were applied on a first-come, first-served basis. Once each season's quota was reached, the fishery was closed. This encouraged a reckless "race to harvest" with bigger boats and bigger nets (Bonanno and Constance 1996: 131).

In 1976, Mexico and other Latin American countries with Pacific coasts extended their "**exclusive economic zones**" **(EEZs)** – their sea-zone ownership jurisdictions – out 200 miles from their coasts, following the lead of the United States, which had been the first nation to do this. The Mexican government began seizing US boats for fishing without permission in its EEZs. As a result of this and other factors, including El Niño years causing tuna number declines, boats switching from US to Mexican flagging, and US boats leaving the ETP for the Western Pacific, the US ETP fleet shrank dramatically during this period.

Even after the exodus of the US fleet, however, Mexican tuna boats were shut out of US markets owing to the MMPA trade embargo. Would the embargo have been enacted had the US fleet not lost access to the most productive ETP tuna fishery? Even as we can never know for sure, one thing is clear: Environmental regulations are just as often the product of geopolitical struggles to control natural resource production and profits as they are institutions most fundamentally aimed at **sustainability**. At the same time, changes in systems of production may also lead to new forms of regulation.

From a Fordist to a Post-Fordist fishery

The early era of US dominance in the ETP yellowfin fishery from the 1950s to the 1980s typifies what political economists call "**Fordism**." Named after Henry Ford and the early Ford Motor Company production model, Fordism refers to relations of production that combine high wages, mass production, and mass consumption. Fordism is typified by vertically integrated domestic corporations (where firms own or control the production chain from bottom to top) and forms of state power that favor tariffs against low-cost foreign competition, sustaining continued profitability for large firms.

The large tuna consuming countries in the 1950s to early 1980s (namely, the United States and Japan) were also the largest tuna catching and processing countries. US tuna boats sold their tuna to US canners, who sold to US customers. Some tuna boats were even owned by tuna processing firms, typifying the vertically integrated Fordist corporation. The state maintained the profitability of the industry by securing and maintaining US dominance in the ETP (and later, away from it, as described above).

The state could only forestall broader trends from affecting the US fleet for so long, however. As Fordism morphed into new relations of production referred to as "**post-Fordism**," the locus of power shifted away from the state to **transnational corporations (TNCs)**. The 1980s saw a restructuring of the global tuna industry, typified by the dismantling of vertically integrated US tuna firms. The trend was kick-started by a combination of factors, including the rise of increasingly cheap, factory farmed (Chapter 4) beef and poultry, which led to a decrease in consumer demand for tuna and a growing crisis of overproduction spurring continued price declines (see Chapter 7). As a result, the old system broke apart, with formerly vertically integrated corporations divesting significant portions of their operations. The large US tuna brands were eventually absorbed by Asian TNCs. Most of the fishing,

> **Post-Fordism** Arising in the last decades of the twentieth century, the current relations of production in most industrialized countries; marked by decentralized, specialized, and often subcontracted production, the prominence of transnational corporations, and diminished state power
>
> **Transnational Corporations (TNC)** Corporations operating facilities in more than one country; also commonly called multinational corporations (MNCs)

canning, and processing is now secured through subcontracting. Thus, the familiar tuna "company" is now merely a "brand" owned by a large TNC that searches the globe for the least expensive materials and labor to assemble its products. This transition to a post-Fordist global tuna industry is now complete, with implications for regulation of the world's fisheries.

Post-Fordist regulation: The Marine Stewardship Council

With a decentralized, global tuna production system, traditional modes of regulation (based within nation states) become less tenable, leaving space for new ones to emerge. In 1997, the World Wildlife Fund and agro-food mega-TNC Unilever established the Marine Stewardship Council (MSC). The mission of the MSC is to provide market-based incentives to corporations for the production of "sustainably" harvested seafood. If a fishery meets MSC guidelines, its associated seafood products can gain the MSC seal of approval (Figure 13.4). In a similar spirit to the "dolphin safe" label, consumers are urged to be part of the solution by sending their seafood dollars to firms that are "doing the right thing." Though an attractive model for green consumption, there are reasons that consumers might want to be wary of granting this trend a full embrace.

Figure 13.4 A label from a can of Alaska salmon bearing the Marine Stewardship Council stamp of approval. (MSC label blown up to show detail.) This was one of only three MSC-certified products we could find at our local chain supermarket; all were canned Alaska salmon.

From a social justice perspective, the MSC is receiving troubling reviews from small fishers throughout the Global South, who are shut out from MSC certification owing to not having the connections and capital to even begin the certification process. As large companies move into waters previously fished by poorer nations, locals there are locked out of markets in wealthy countries by apparently "green" labels, thus exacerbating the loss of jobs and opportunities in the poorest parts of the world. In this way, producers from poorer nations are bearing a disproportionate share of the "shock" that accompanies the "opening up" of the world to free markets (Klein 2007). As such, green labels appear to (somewhat ironically) favor large-scale, corporate, and conglomerated firms over small craft producers.

Environmentalists and social justice activists, informed by this political economy perspective, should critically evaluate new environmental regulations and regulatory bodies in terms of the degree to which they add more voices or more balance to governance and accountability. New forms of post-Fordist regulation like the MSC, increasingly corporatized and supranational in scale, are often even more inaccessible to citizens (except as consumers!) than the Fordist state regulations they replace. From this point of view, we would be well served to check what lies behind the labels. This is especially true if we begin to consider the complex ethical tradeoffs that differing forms of regulations entail, for individual species, and the ecosystem more generally.

Ethics: Saving Animals, Conserving Species

> *"Tuna is a fun food. If it's associated with the harassment and killing of a noble creature like the dolphin, that's not right. Hopefully, in a few years, the safest place for tuna will be swimming underneath a dolphin."* (Ted Smyth, Vice President of Heinz Foods, which at the time owned the StarKist tuna brand (United States Fish and Wildlife Service 2008))

Why were so many people so moved to action by the images in the LaBudde film? Why has the picture of tuna boat deckhands slinging a dead dolphin overboard become such an icon of environmental wrongdoing? All the while the tuna boycott gained momentum, countless other ocean fisheries were increasingly overfished. Is there some irony that tuna – some of the most unsustainably harvested ocean fish – have become nearly conflated with dolphin conservation? One way to view the success of the dolphin safe tuna campaign and simultaneous failure of ocean fisheries conservation (tuna included) is as a victory of **animal rights** over ecological ethics.

Animal Rights   An ethical position and social movement that states that non-human animals, particularly intelligent mammals, should be granted rights as ethical subjects on par or at least similar to human beings

Rights for "noble creatures": The case against dolphin-setting

When speaking of "conservation" or "ecology," most discussions of right and wrong actions deal with the plight of *species*. The United States, for example, passed the Endangered

Species Act (ESA) in 1973 to stop plant and animal species from going extinct. Once-endangered species that stand as ESA success stories include the peregrine falcon and the American alligator. Through federal legislation, society deemed it *wrong* to allow species to go extinct due to human action. However, the ESA laid down no ethical mandate concerning the treatment of *individual* alligators, peregrine falcons, or animals of any other species. Such legal measures, as such, are expressions of ecological ethics but *not* statements regarding animal rights. However, questions of environmental ethics, Singer argues, need not stop at the level of species.

As reviewed in Chapter 5, Peter Singer (1975) argues for **moral extensionism**: that we should extend our moral concern to all creatures that have interests. Dolphins are intelligent, highly evolved animals that easily fit highly into Singer's (and no doubt any animal rights activist's) hierarchy of interests. It is straightforward, therefore, to make a case that it is *wrong* to drown hundreds of thousands of dolphins a year in tuna nets. For that matter, the argument can be (and was) made that it is wrong to kill *any* dolphins in tuna nets. It is no wonder that so many people were so appalled by the images from the LaBudde film – images of obviously sentient creatures meeting rather horrible fates.

> **Moral Extensionism** An ethical principle stating that humans should extend their sphere of moral concern beyond the human realm; most commonly, it is argued that intelligent or sentient animals are worthy ethical subjects
>
> **Social Construction** Any category, condition, or thing that exists or is understood to have certain characteristics because people socially agree that it does

Tuna, unlike dolphins (and whales), do not sit highly in most people's hierarchy of interests. (Indeed, bestselling author Zane Grey described yellowfin tuna as "stupid pigs" in his 1925 high-seas adventure book *Tales of Fishing Virgin Seas* (Safina 2001: 185).) Imagine the outcry if mutilated tuna at market (Figure 13.5) were dolphins. Granted, this treatment of tuna is anathema for some radical animal rights activists. For most people, however, this is simply a picture of fish for sale. As such, the dolphin safe campaign can be chalked up more as a victory for animal rights than for ecological ethics (as, for example, the success of the campaign did little to stem overharvesting of marine species). It might also be said that it is the **social construction** (see Chapter 8) of dolphins as charismatic species with interests, relative to tuna and other fish, that makes this distinction, and its confusing ethics, possible.

Figure 13.5 Does a tuna have rights? Mutilated tuna rest on pallets at a seafood wholesaler in Tokyo. The image accompanied a "treehugger.com" article about overfished tuna stocks. No mention was made of the tunas' rights or their dignity being violated, either before or after catch. *Source*: (© 2008) P. Y. Yee, Singapore.

Can a rights victory produce an ecological defeat?

Reading the dolphin–tuna controversy as one involving two sometimes conflicting types of environmental ethics, animal rights and ecological ethics, we gain clues as to why ocean conservation lags so far behind marine mammal protection. Unlike dolphin and whale conservation efforts, which (usually) aim to minimize or even eliminate mortality, fish conservation efforts customarily aim for maximum sustainable yield. The drive to maximize harvests invariably overrides considerations of the maintenance of ocean ecology.

This is not to say that society lacks an ecological ethic of the sea. Rather, the dominant ethic (with notable exceptions, see Exercise 13.3 below) is that it is *right* to manage fish for harvest while protecting marine mammals from harvest. This ethic has failed to produce a paradigm shift toward conservative (or *precautionary*) approaches to fisheries management, and, as such, could be argued to be only a slight improvement over the earlier era of unregulated "tragedy of the commons" overexploitation of the oceans. This would support the common, broader argument made by many ecological ethicists that, until society develops a truly ecological ethic, the increasingly unsustainable exploitation of nature will continue.

What implications does this have for the oceans? Consider this: tuna sales in the United States are at all-time highs. Moreover, *every* can of tuna sold in the United States carries the dolphin safe label. Which begs the question: What happened to all the boats that were setting on dolphin in the ETP when the "dolphin safe" campaign drastically reduced demand for their product? One thing is for sure. They did *not* simply revert to pole and line fishing. While this would have reduced stress on the yellowfin, eliminated dolphin mortality, and resulted in new jobs for fishers, it was not a cost-effective option for boat owners and thus not even considered a realistic option (see the section on political economy above).

The purse seiners, rather, did one of two things. Some boats remained in the ETP, but switched from setting on dolphins to setting their purse seines around logs and other floating objects, under which (like dolphin schools) yellowfin tend to aggregate. The problem is, yellowfin schools under dolphin tend to be much "cleaner" catches than those under logs; meaning that nets set on logs "can entail hundreds of times the bycatch that netting around dolphins does" (Bloomberg Newswire 2008: 436). Considering that 30–40 percent of all bycatch is dead before it is thrown back, increasing bycatch by two or three orders of magnitude could be viewed as a substantial ecological tradeoff for the lives of individual dolphins.

Still more ETP purse seiners, however, simply moved to the Western Tropical Pacific (WTP), where dolphin bycatch is not a problem. The resulting, massive increase in WTP yellowfin harvests has resulted in stocks that are now either fully fished or overexploited. Indeed, some Pacific yellowfin stocks are so severely depleted that eight Pacific Island nations, concerned about collapse of the fishery, have called for an international moratorium on tuna fishing in an area the size of Alaska (Back et al. 1995).

Many consumers see the "dolphin safe" label and assume it means they are purchasing an eco-friendly product. Consumers have been given the *green* light to purchase canned tuna and feel good about doing so. And, granted, thousands upon thousands of dolphins *were* spared thanks to the campaign. However, significant *ecological* problems continued or even intensified: (non-dolphin) bycatch increased and overfishing just moved west. Is there something *wrong* with that?

The Tuna Puzzle

In this chapter, we have learned that:

- Tuna exist in almost unimaginably large numbers in the sea, yet nearly everywhere they exist, they are being unsustainably harvested.
- Wild tuna stocks have suffered from multiple new fishing technologies (purse seiners, tuna ranching) as each technology has allowed us to pull more fish out of the sea.
- Unlike humans (but like the rest of non-human nature), tuna respect no political boundaries. Yet their fate is inexorably tied to geopolitical decisions.
- Tuna fetch a high price; as usual, when there is big money to be made, ecological considerations can get put on the backburner.
- In the ETP, schools of large yellowfin tuna swim below easily spotted schools of dolphins, so for many years dolphins died so that consumers could get cheap canned tuna.
- Green consumer campaigns have successfully re-regulated tuna production through "dolphin safe" labeling, suggesting that through markets, consumer advocacy can move corporations to "do the right thing."
- Political economy approaches, conversely, urge us to view market based solutions with a critical eye, closely assessing the altered sites and scales of power that accompany each market-based success story, even "green" ones.
- Ethics approaches show us that, at least in the ocean, our ecological ethics has yet to catch up with our support for animal rights.

Tuna are only one small node in the complex network of relationships that are the world's oceans. Large-scale overfishing of many other species, massive marine pollution, global warming, and numerous other impacts are radically transforming the seas, well beyond the tangle of dolphins in nets. Nevertheless, tuna remain one of the clearest avenues to help us understand the power our individual consumption choices exert on global ecosystems, while simultaneously underlining the deeply structured way the seas are incorporated into global trade. To the degree that reforms of tuna fisheries have occurred, there may be precedent for new ways of dealing with the global crisis facing the oceans. To the opposite degree, however, that massive efforts to restrain extraction have resulted in only nominal ecological changes, the case of tuna points to the long swim ahead.

Questions for Review

1. How valuable was bluefin tuna meat a century ago? How about today? How has this change affected their harvest?
2. Describe and contrast pole and line and purse-seine fishing. How and why did the US eastern Pacific yellowfin fishery evolve from purse seine to pole and line and back to purse seine? Be sure to include the political economic factors as well as the geography of this shift.

3. Who launched a consumer boycott to save ETP dolphins? Was it successful? Explain.
4. From a fishery management perspective, what is different about marine fisheries located within 200 miles of coasts compared to open ocean fisheries located farther offshore?
5. Of tuna and dolphin, which are more common recipients of moral extensionism? Why is this so?

Exercise 13.1   Eco-Labeling and Certification

Tuna are only one of countless products labeled for "green" or "sustainable" consumption. But who are the organizations that oversee the certification of these products? What procedures do they use? Where competing labels exist, how do they differ? Find an eco-labeled product and try your best to answer the following questions: 1) What does the label assure? 2) Have the characteristics of the product assured by the label improved or changed environmental practices of the companies making the product? What do the words on the label mean (for example: "natural"). 3) Who oversees that certification process; are they "third parties" (people or groups apart from the company)? 4) What procedures does the product undergo to claim the label and how is that confirmed?

Now consider the following: how much time and labor did it take for you to confirm (or deny) that the label in question is reliable and does what it says? What would it take to do so for all such products you consume, assuming you wanted to? How much *trust* must be placed in labels? Do you feel it is well placed?

Exercise 13.2   Contemporary Commercial Fishing (and Overfishing)

Purse-seine fishing with once-unimaginably large nets is not the only modern commercial fishing technique that threatens has the potential to wipe out fisheries around the world's oceans. Other techniques that can and do often lead to overfishing include longlining and drift-netting (sometimes called gill nets).

For this assignment, choose one modern, intensive commercial fishing method (purse seine, longlining, gill netting, bottom trawling, or another that you find on your own) to research. In a one-page essay, describe the technique and three ocean fisheries (species and location) in which this technique is commonly applied. Additionally, describe whether or not these fisheries are being fished sustainably and how, if at all, catch limits in these fisheries are regulated.

Exercise 13.3   Scientific Whaling

One of the most well-known slogans of the environmental movement is "Save the Whales!". Rubber dinghies manned with Greenpeace or Sea Shepherd Society activists ramming whaling ships is an iconic image of "direct action" environmental activism. The international whale conservation movement has become so popular, indeed, that very few countries worldwide harvest any whales from the world's oceans, and most haven't for decades. A few countries, however, engage in a practice known (by its proponents) as "scientific whaling." What is scientific whaling? What countries engage in this practice? How is it rationalized? What groups (and nations) are opposed to it, and why? Read up on this topic, and explain whether opponents of scientific whaling make arguments based primarily in animal rights ethics or ecological ethics (or, perhaps, some of both).

References

Back, W., E. R. Landa, et al. (1995). "Bottled water, spas, and early years of water chemistry." *Ground Water* 33(4): 605–14.

Baird, I., and N. Quastel (2011). "Dolphin-safe tuna from California to Thailand: Localisms in environmental certification of global commodity networks." *Annals of the Association of American Geographers* 101(2): 336–55.

Bloomberg Newswire (2008, June 16). "Pacific nations ban tuna boats to stop stock collapse." Retrieved April 11, 2009, from www.bloomberg.com/apps/news?pid=20601101 &sid=aqOdnFHygH1k.

Bonanno, A., and D. Constance (1996). *Caught in the Net: The Global Tuna Industry, Environmentalism and the State*, Lawrence: University of Kansas.

Ellis, R. (2008). *Tuna: A Love Story*. New York: Knopf.

Gosliner, M. L. (1999). "The tuna–dolphin controversy." In J. R. Twiss Jr. and R. R. Reeves (eds.) *Conservation and Management of Marine Mammals*. Washington, DC: Smithsonian Institution, pp. 120–55.

Greenberg, P. (2010). *Four Fish: The Future of the Last Wild Food*. New York: Penguin.

Johnson, S. (2012). "Anyone for sushi? Fisherman catches 1,000lb tuna (that'll make 20,000 servings with rice)." *Daily Mail*, November 25. Retrieved January 3, 2013, from http://www.dailymail.co.uk/news/article-2238284/Anyone-sushi-Fisherman-catches-1-000lb-tuna-make-20-000-pieces-delicacy.html.

Joseph, J. (1994). "The tuna–dolphin controversy in the Eastern Tropical Pacific: Biological, economic and political impacts." *Ocean Development and International Law* 25: 1–30.

Klein, N. (2007). *The Shock Doctrine: The Rise of Disaster Capitalism*. New York: Metropolitan.

Safina, C. (2001). "Tuna conservation." In B. A. Block and E. D. Stevens (eds.) *Tuna: Physiology, Ecology and Evolution*. San Diego, CA: Academic Press, pp. 413–59.

Singer, P. (1975). *Animal Liberation: A New Ethics for Our Treatment of Animals*. New York: New York Review (distributed by Random House).

United States Fish and Wildlife Service (2008). *Factsheet: American Alligator: Alligator mississippiensis*. Arlington, VA: Author.

Upton, H., and E. Buck (2010). "*Open Ocean Aquaculture*." Washington: Congressional Research Service. Retrieved August 8, 2013, from http://www.cnie.org/NLE/CRSreports/10Sep/RL32694.pdf.

Whynott, D. (1995). *Giant Bluefin*. New York: Farrar, Straus & Giroux.

Suggested Reading

Mansfield, B. (2004). "Neoliberalism in the oceans: 'Rationalization,' property rights, and the commons question." *Geoforum* 35: 313–26.

Rogers, R. A. (1995). *The Oceans Are Emptying: Fish Wars and Sustainability*. Cheektowaga, NY: Black Rose.

Sharpless, A., and S. Evans (2013). *The Perfect Protein: The Fish Lover's Guide to Saving the Oceans and Feeding the World*. Emmaus, PA: Rodale.

14

Lawns

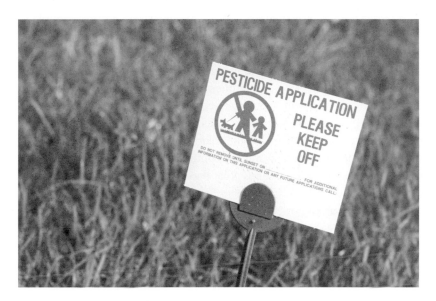

Source: Suzanne Tucker/Shutterstock.

Chapter Menu

Keywords

- Affect
- Agrodiversity
- Columbian Exchange
- Commodity chain
- Eutrophication
- Ideology
- Monoculture
- Narrative
- Overaccumulation
- Pull marketing
- Risk
- Risk perception
- Social construction
- Spatial fix
- Urban heat island effect

Environment and Society: A Critical Introduction, Second Edition. Paul Robbins, John Hintz,
and Sarah A. Moore.
© 2014 John Wiley & Sons, Ltd. Published 2014 by John Wiley & Sons, Ltd.

How Much Do People Love Lawns?

Suzanne had a dilemma. An average American home owner with whom one of the authors spoke a few years ago, she described a problem she had with her dog. As she explained: "One of our dogs was very allergic to the [lawn chemical] treatment. In the spring when they would start to fertilize, his paws would just get raw and bleed. . . . So, for a couple of days after we had the grass done we would put these little booties on the dog. Otherwise it would really hurt him, and he would just bite and chew at his paws and they would bleed all over the place. We felt so badly for him" (Robbins 2007: 1). Remarkably, when confronted with the very real suffering of her dog, rather than ceasing to apply chemicals to her turfgrass yard, Suzanne chose to put booties on her dog instead.

Suzanne is an educated professional. She understands the risks associated with pesticide and fertilizer use, and even acknowledges that the treatments are probably not good for the environment or the health of her family. But she continues to pay a service to treat her lawn heavily, every few weeks, all summer long. What drives her to do something that she seems basically opposed to?

The answer lies in the tremendous power of the turfgrass lawn, a landscape maintained by hundreds of thousands of people around the United States and many other countries, and a multi-billion-dollar business worldwide. The lawn is a remarkable cultural phenomenon.

But it is also an environmental phenomenon. Probably the largest irrigated crop in America, lawns demand tremendous inputs of water. To maintain its perfect "green" look, moreover, they demand significant inputs of insecticides and herbicides, along with care and cutting using fuel-demanding equipment: weed-eaters, edgers, mowers. The ecological footprint of lawns is felt downstream, where the fertilizers that run off their surfaces wash into streams and lakes, causing blooms of growth from algae, leading to the sterilization of freshwater habitats. The chemicals used to maintain them include some of the more potent cocktails familiar from intensive industrial agriculture; lawn treatments are almost always followed by the planting of signs warning children and pets to stay away.

In this way, lawns are a fascinating environment–society problem. They are fully "natural" in the sense that they are formed from the fabric of vigorous perennial grass species, which grow aggressively as they have evolved to do over hundreds and thousands of years. They are wholly "unnatural" in the sense that their maintenance requires exhaustive discipline on the part of people, and the use of fully artificial chemical inputs. To what degree are lawns an expression of our instinct to live in, and tend to, the environment? To what degree do they represent the reverse urge to control, and expel wild nature from the world around us? Why do people cultivate them so intensely, even though they know such efforts may be bad for the environment?

A Short History of Lawns

Lawns as we know them today are not actually a very old cultural phenomenon, although the grasses that grow in them are a deep part of human history. Grasses grown in lawns are perennial ones, meaning that they do not die off from season to season. Grasses that are most common in lawns today were originally domesticated from their wild ancestors by people thousands of years ago for livestock raising. Because they grow *rhizomatically* – through shoots that grow laterally underneath the surface of the soil – they tend to thrive under conditions of grazing. Cattle chew off the top of the plant, usually before it is allowed to seed, but the plant continues to grow, expand, and widen in a dense mat near the surface of the soil. These qualities make turfgrass species good for forming wide open pastures, but it means they do best when clipped frequently.

Turfgrasses as part of human economic history

These turfgrasses were brought to the New World as part of the **Columbian Exchange**, the ecological transformation of the world by the movement of plants and other species back and forth from the Americas shortly after their discovery. The 10 most important lawn grass species in the United States, including the ubiquitous Kentucky Bluegrass (*Poa pratensis*), are all native to Europe, Asia, and Africa and not to the Americas.

> **Columbian Exchange** The movement of species across the Atlantic Ocean, from the New World to the Old World and vice versa, and the resulting ecological transformations
>
> **Agrodiversity** The number and range of species in cultivated areas. Higher agrodiversity is typically associated with the robustness of a farming system and its ability to withstand weather and disease (ant. Monoculute)

Turfgrasses were cultivated in America, during the seventeenth and eighteenth centuries, as they had always been, mostly for cattle and sheep raising, and typically grew in pastures mixed with numerous other species, like clover (*Trifolium* species). In this sense, lawn grasses were long part of a system of **agrodiversity**: a complex mix of species on which farming systems were based in the period before industrialization.

The shift to maintaining lawns for aesthetic purposes would come much later. Cultivated turfgrass open spaces are ancient, of course, and large medieval estates in Europe had huge lawns, managed by servants and peasants. The intensive, well-manicured front yard lawn of today, however, is probably not much older than the middle twentieth century. This is largely because 1) there were insufficient private yard spaces necessary for making lawns in the period before World War II and 2) because the machinery, chemicals, and nutrient inputs required to make lawns look as smooth and emerald-green as we know them today were not widely available to the public before 1950.

Prior to the twentieth century, those people who were not living in rural areas (where turfgrass was grown for pasturing) lived in densely populated urban centers, where little or no space was given over to open yards. As automobiles began to change the urban landscape, however, new lands around the urban fringe were available for settlement. The suburbs began to form in the early twentieth century and then expanded enormously in the 1940s and 1950s. In this period, a new class of entrepreneurs emerged, real estate developers who had a strong incentive not only to plot new lands for housing, but to plot and sell off as much land as possible, converting it from agricultural uses to domestic ones (Jackson 1985). The growth of suburban housing was therefore accompanied by large swaths of open space in the front and back yard. The square footage of housing did not increase much in this period, but the size of lots ballooned, with most houses built on parcels more than double the size of the home. The large areas were quickly given over to the growing of turfgrass, a simple landscape choice that allowed a clear view of the home for sale: curb appeal. In this way, the lawn is an artifact of a change in the way cities were settled and real estate was plotted, marketed, and sold in North America.

The chemical revolution

These lawns emerged precisely at the right time for maintenance through intensive chemical controls. Chemicals for lawn treatment in the period before 1950 were numerous, but crude and extremely dangerous. These included carbon tetrachloride, mercury bichloride, kerosene, and one of the most potent and common toxins of the time: lead arsenate (Figure 14.1). This product, adopted from commercial agricultural production, is a highly potent insecticide, but also a serious toxic substance. Both lead and arsenic can be toxic; arsenic exposure can lead to numerous forms of cancer, while lead exposure in children affects the nervous system, leading to impaired brain development. Nasty stuff.

These dangerous and cumbersome chemicals were swept away practically overnight, however, by the arrival of a new generation of pesticides, especially including the insecticide dichlorodiphenyltrichloroethane: DDT. DDT was developed in the late 1930s and played a critical role in WWII by controlling malarial mosquito populations. After the war, the chemical became widespread in both commercial and household use. Much cheaper and apparently safer than other chemicals, people managed their homes, lawns, and gardens with DDT, which became a normal part of American life.

Figure 14.1 Lead arsenate – most popular pesticide prior to DDT. *Source*: Joe Hoffman.

Problems with DDT became apparent early on, but it wasn't until the publication of the now-classic environmental book *Silent Spring* by Rachel Carson in 1962 that people began to fully realize the environmental impact of the chemical. Toxic to freshwater and marine life and devastating to bird populations, DDT was eventually banned in the United States in 1972. Nevertheless, many other chemicals were introduced in the 40 years since to take the place of DDT and these all have known and suspected health and environmental risks associated with them. The herbicide 2-4,D is a suspected carcinogen. The herbicide glyphosate is known to have impacts on ecosystems. Popular organophosphate chemicals cause neurological damage. Fertilizers that assure rapid growth and green color have major impacts on water quality and degrade lakes and streams through the process of **eutrophication**: the loading of waterways with nutrients, leading to explosive algal blooms, and ultimately resulting in starvation of dissolved oxygen. Lawns can be kept and maintained without chemical inputs, of course, but not if they are to be a **monoculture**, devoid of weeds or differing grasses, and to have the clean green look desired by most home-owners. Sales of these products have only increased in the decades since *Silent Spring*, and lawn applications are now more than a $10 billion annual chemical business.

> **Eutrophication** A process where water bodies (and sometimes soils or habitats) become very high in nutrients, resulting in frequent algal blooms, swings in dissolved oxygen concentrations, and overall degradation
>
> **Monoculture** A single crop cultivated to the exclusion of any other potential species or harvest

The explosion of lawns

The growth in this industry is predicated on the overall expansion of the coverage of lawns. One recent study showed that lawns cover as much as 23 percent of land cover in Franklin County, Ohio, the location of the very average suburban city of Columbus (Robbins and Birkenholtz 2003). A more expansive study, using satellite remote sensing, concludes that there are 128,000 square kilometers of turfgrass in the United States (Figure 14.2), making lawns the single largest irrigated crop in America, outpacing soybeans, corn, and any other major industrial crop (Milesi et al., 2005). Lawns are also blossoming internationally. With

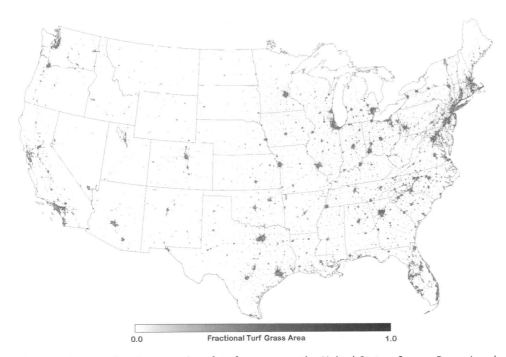

0.0   Fractional Turf Grass Area   1.0

Figure 14.2 Map showing quantity of turfgrass across the United States. *Source*: Reproduced with permission from http://earthobservatory.nasa.gov/IOTD/view.php?id=6019 and NASA.

new housing markets and growing affluence in many parts of the world, lawns can now be seen in places as far-flung as South Africa, Australia, and India.

The environmental impacts of all this turfgrass are extensive. As noted above, chemical inputs and fertilizer runoff are bad for surrounding ecosystems. Many of these chemicals also have impacts on human health. Water demands for lawns are extremely high, especially during the summer, making lawns a major part of the urban water budget.

Urban heat island effect Warming experienced by cities that occurs through the absorption and re-radiation of heat from buildings and sidewalks. Vegetation in urban areas reduces this effect

Of course, lawns have some benefits. The presence of green cover is far preferable to bare concrete in terms of the **urban heat island effect**, that warming of the city that occurs through the absorption and re-radiation of heat from buildings and sidewalks. Growing grass also absorbs carbon (see Chapter 9), contributing in a small way to offsetting global warming, therefore.

The puzzle of lawns

Nonetheless, the maintenance of green lawns is economically and ecologically expensive. They are also viewed by many of the people who create them (think of Suzanne above) as hazardous and problematic. These people maintain lawns nonetheless. Lawns, in short, are a puzzle. In this short history we have reviewed the emergence of turfgrass lawns and concluded the following:

- Turfgrasses are evolved to be grazed or mown and grow rhizomatically, making them therefore ideally suited for creating expansive lawn landscapes.
- Monocultural home lawns are not very old, however, and awaited the booming of the post-World War II real estate market and the emergence of modern insecticides and herbicides.
- Chemicals and other inputs into lawns have inherent hazards associated with them, along with impacts on the surrounding ecosystem.
- Lawns have expanded in coverage across the United States and around the world, however, often in the face of information suggesting the problems associated with turfgrass monoculture.

This raises some basic questions about human environmental behaviors. Why do people do things that may be hazardous? Is it that they don't know or that they don't care? What influences their decision-making? How are social norms and economic patterns implicated in such decision-making?

Risk and Chemical Decision-Making

As long as an emerald-green, well-kept, monocultural yard is desired by homeowners, there are some inevitable hazards associated with the contemporary lawn, as well as some environmental impacts including chemical externalities and water demands. It would be reasonable to assume that people who keep such lawns are making a kind of rational **risk** calculation. As you will recall from Chapter 6, risk is the known or estimated probability of harm from a hazard-related decision. In this regard, it might be predicted that, given that the prevalence of lawn chemical use remains very high in the United States and elsewhere, people are insufficiently aware of the hazards to take them into account. That is, the **risk perception** of chemical hazards may be impeded by lack of education or critical information about what pesticides can do to children's health, what herbicides can do to local biodiversity, or what fertilizers might do to nearby aquatic ecosystems.

> **Risk** The known (or estimated) probability that a hazard-related decision will have a negative consequence
>
> **Risk Perception** A phenomenon, and related field of study, describing the tendency of people to evaluate the hazardousness of a situation or decision in not-always-rational terms, depending on individual biases, culture, or human tendencies

Is chemical use irrational or uninformed?

Working from this assumption, it would be reasonable to advocate for better risk communication strategies, including product labeling, consumer education, and other outreach activities. By providing consumers with reliable information about the hazards associated with specific products, we might expect a difference in their environmental behaviors.

Such an interpretation does not hold well with the facts, however. A national survey of homeowners conducted in the early 2000s (Robbins 2007) reveals several things. First among them, it concludes that those people who use insecticides, herbicides, and fertilizers on their lawns are statistically *more* likely to claim that chemicals are bad for the environment, their children, and human health than those who *do not* use them. In short, people who hire lawn chemical companies or who directly purchase and apply these inputs are better informed about the hazards of these chemicals than their non-chemical-using counterparts. They also tend to be wealthier and better educated. Minimally, this means that people are reading the bags, warning labels, and company disclaimers that come with these products. More significantly, it suggests that merely educating people about hazards may not have much influence on their behavior.

Chemicals as economically (or socially) rational

But thinking with risk provides us with alternative hypotheses as well. It is possible, most notably, that people who use chemicals, being well aware of their risks, rationally see benefits that outweigh those costs. The range of potential economic benefits that come with lawn chemical usage may enter into decision-making. Realtors in typical markets, for example, suggest that lawns improve "curb appeal" of properties significantly, perhaps as much as $10,000 worth of enhanced sale value of properties. In theory, therefore, lawn chemical users are accepting degradation of ecosystems, risk to their children's development and their own health as a tradeoff for a value increase of several thousand dollars for their property. Whether or not you or I consider such a tradeoff a reasonable one, it may be driving some consumer environmental behaviors.

Many homeowners surveyed as part of the study described above did indeed mention economic benefits of chemical inputs for property. Thirty-four percent of those surveyed claimed that whatever their neighbors were doing in maintaining their properties, these behaviors had a negative effect on water quality. Half of those surveyed, however, said that these behaviors improved property values. In this sense, there seems to be some feeling among respondents that people's input decisions were good for property values even if they were sometimes bad for the environment. As one resident told interviewers about a time his lawn went dead: "People wanted to know, what the hell are you doing? You are decreasing our property values!" (Robbins 2007: 112).

Here again, however, the evidence is muddled. Though many surveyed and interviewed people mentioned economic incentives for lawns, a great many more weighed the benefits in more intangible ways. If only half of those surveyed identified economic benefits, a vast majority (a full 73 percent) pointed to "neighborhood pride" as a main benefit of chemical

Box 14.1   Environmental Solution? Organic Lawn Inputs

Given the hazardousness of lawn chemical inputs and their often environmentally undesirable impacts, many consumers have turned to alternative lawn care products and services to meet their needs. The range of these products is large but they come in a few categories. The first is fertilizers from non-petroleum sources (e.g., ground corn, alfalfa, cottonseed, or blood and feather meal). Another is the application of beneficial nematodes, tiny predators that kill insect parasites (like grubs) in lawns, without the need of chemical insecticides. The demand for this range of products is growing, so much so that traditional chemical formulator and service companies have entered the organic market. Consider Organic Choice™, an organic fertilizer regime marketed under the largest brand name in the lawn chemical industry (Scotts LawnService®).

To be sure, the choice of organic inputs over inorganic ones does represent an alternative to intensive petroleum-based chemical inputs. On the other hand, many of these green commodities are surprisingly unnecessary. For example, nematodes marketed as part of a "natural" regime for lawn care actually occur naturally in soils, as long as they are allowed to, by letting soil health recover. In plain terms, organic companies are selling things people can make for themselves, stressing again the ongoing drive for surplus value built into the lawn economy.

Many non-commodity options also exist, including cultivating personal patience for a diverse lawnscape that may have multiple species and change its look and color over the growing season. Such an approach, what Bormann et al. (2001) call a "freedom lawn," chiefly entails letting a lawn go its own way and learning to live with it. This has numerous advantages. Most notably, a reduction in nutrient fertilizer inputs means that the lawn will grow less aggressively and so will need to be cut less often, resulting in the use of less fossil fuel and the production of less lawn waste. By the same token, letting clover grow in your lawn replaces the needs for fertilizer inputs because clover naturally fixes nitrogen. Doing nothing, in this sense, is better than doing anything else.

The more radical choice is to replace one's lawn altogether, a decision many homeowners make, where social and legal pressure allows them to do so. Groups across North America, including an organization called the "Wild Ones," provide information on native species, ecological restoration, and planting and maintenance that encourage people to put indigenous and historically local species back into their front yards, mimicking the landscapes that came before settlement. Even if these lawns are no less artificial than turfgrass ones, they have very different ecological functions and play host to all sorts of biodiversity, possibly making the best alternative to high-input lawns . . . no lawn at all.

usage. Clearly, the use of chemicals is driven by more than simple economic motivations. People enjoy a collective or social benefit from chemical usage. Accepting their acknowledged risk associated with that behavior, this choice must also be seen as "rational," even though the benefit is one rooted in **affect** (see Chapter 6): an emotional experience (like pride). Seen from the point of view of risk analysis, therefore, lawn chemical usage appears to operate through a kind of logic, but one that is as deeply social as it is economic.

> **Affect** Emotions and unconscious responses to the world that influence decision-making
>
> **Narrative** A story with a beginning and end; environmental narratives such as "biological evolution" and "the tragedy of the commons" aid our comprehension and construction of the world
>
> **Ideologies** Normative, value-laden, worldviews that spell out how the world is and how it ought to be
>
> **Social Construction** Any category, condition, or thing that exists or is understood to have certain characteristics because people socially agree that it does

Social Construction: Good Lawns Mean Good People

This is because much of the value that people who keep well-groomed lawns get for their efforts is not economic, but instead comes in the form of social status and a feeling of responsibility. Returning to research on lawn chemical behaviors, people who use lawn chemicals share many other qualities. They are more likely to say they are "interested in knowing what's going on in the neighborhood" and they can name more of their neighbors than people who do not use these kinds of inputs. Perhaps most importantly, people who use lawn chemicals are statistically more likely to do so if their neighbors also use lawn chemicals.

A well-maintained lawn, for the people who maintain them in any case, says that you are a good citizen. As one homeowner told interviewers, "I know this neighborhood has a certain status, a certain look. I surely wouldn't want to ruin it for anybody" (Robbins 2007: 111). Such a value is not consumed in a strictly individual way, but in a more collective or communal way. In this sense it is a social good. Conversely, poor lawn management behavior is viewed as a sign of bad character. "If you don't cut twice a week you are a communist!" one homeowner told interviewers, "It's like, oh man!" (Robbins 2007: 111). These negative feelings are often far more important than positive ones, since avoiding stigma or poor social status drives many of our behaviors.

Landscape as text

So a lawn is more than an amenity; it is really a form of **narrative**, a story about a community and the people who live there. It says that the people in the area who keep lawns are connected to one another, that they are responsible in their behaviors to one another, and that their actions are about mutual benefit and community. The lawn landscape is, in a way, a kind of text, which people write together. It also seems that the lawn carries with it a kind of **ideology** – a normative worldview about how the world is and ought to be. In this worldview, people have responsibility to behave in a particular way and owe some amount of effort to one another. In this sense, the lawn is a **social construction** (as per

Chapter 8). This does not mean merely that it is a socially invented ecology, which it quite obviously is, but rather that it is a landscape filled with agreed-upon *meaning*. A lawn maintained meticulously through frequent cutting and use of chemical inputs signals pride-of-place, respect for neighbors, responsible civic action, and willingness to do things for others.

Viewed as a social construction, some possible avenues for changing behaviors become available. If a certain kind of social solidarity leads to the use of inputs, can a sense of solidarity be mobilized to guide people to non-chemical alternatives? There is evidence that this may be the case. As noted above, people are more likely to use chemicals if their neighbors do. As a result, when people use different kinds of landscaping, they may set a precedent for new behaviors in a community. In many cases, for example, individual homeowners may choose to replace their lawn with native vegetation. This might be native prairie grasses in some regions, or cactus and thorn scrub in others, depending on climate and local conditions. In either case, by breaking the monoculture of the community with alternatives, individuals may make it easier for other neighbors to later follow suit. A social-environmental problem, in this sense, may have a social solution.

Social and ecological anxiety

Unsurprisingly, individual efforts to change landscaping are often initially viewed with hostility by some neighbors. It has been the case, for example, that households that choose alternative landscaping over lawns are actually *sued* by one or more of their neighbors (Crumbley 2000). Such an eventuality is only limited where municipal laws explicitly state that people are protected from lawsuits if their landscaping choices are safe and legal (Rappaport 1993).

These laws are the exception, however, rather than the rule, and many people remain motivated to keep high-input lawns and maintain their chemical input behaviors as part of their civic responsibility. The fact that these very same landscapes and behaviors may cause harm to neighbors, their children, and the environmental conditions in which neighborhoods sit is either pushed out of the minds of residents, or accepted as an inevitable price to pay for these benefits. The resulting contradiction is one that is not lost on people. Many lawn chemical users continue to maintain their properties as their neighbors do, but express an underlying anxiety about doing so.

When confronted with a die-off of local ducks, one resident told interviewers, "I'm thinking geez, you know there are some really horrible environmental effects here. . . . It says that on the bag, but you know you don't pay too much attention to that. Still, it goes down the drain. I want a nice looking lawn, but I don't want to endanger any [wildlife]" (Robbins 2007: 104). In this sense, there is often an offsetting or undermining feeling of concern or guilt associated with lawn care.

In the face of this general ill-feeling and temptation to change behaviors, how and why is widespread use of inputs for lawns maintained? The answer to this may lie outside the realm of social pressure and belong more to the larger political and economic pressures that drive lawn chemical manufacture and sales.

Political Economy: The Chemical Tail Wags the Turfgrass Dog

This is because many of the key elements of the lawn chemical system are driven by large-scale economic interests. Including all sectors of turfgrass care (i.e., services, equipment, inputs, etc.), the US turfgrass industry generated $57.9 billion total revenue in 2002 (Haydu et al. 2006). Lawn chemicals are only a part of that industry, but a large and important component, $10 billion or more. It is necessary, therefore, to think about the lawn through the lens of political economy. For consumers, after all, the lawn is only a single household choice, while for chemical companies it is a major sector for sales, marketing, and the engine of a multi-billion-dollar industry.

The lawn chemical economy has several components (Figure 14.3), including:

- retail sellers (like "big box" hardware stores);
- lawn services (who provide full lawn services);
- distributors (who resell and bundle chemical packages for applicators);
- formulators (who take raw chemicals and combine them into brand name products);
- manufacturers (who mass produce raw herbicide, insecticide, and fertilizer chemicals).

Figure 14.3 The lawn chemical commodity and knowledge chain. *Source*: Adapted from Robbins (2007, Figure 5.1)

Pressures on the lawn chemical commodity chain

Beginning with manufacturers, raw chemicals are produced by major multinational companies (with familiar names like Dow Chemical Company). Most of these chemicals are dedicated to the agricultural market. Producers typically use raw petrochemical inputs to make a range of herbicides, insecticides, and fertilizers commonly used on corn, soybeans, and other global commodities. A fraction of these manufactured chemicals find their way to formulators, those companies who bundle the raw chemicals into household brands (with familiar names like Scotts®). Formulators do a great deal of direct marketing to households and work closely with distributors and retail sellers. Most consumers come into contact with lawn inputs either at a retail outlet (including familiar stores like Home Depot) or through a lawn service company (like TruGreen®). Each of these players along this **commodity chain** between the consumer and the raw product has a vested interest in maintaining and increasing the flow of value along the way, since each takes only a marginal share of the profits in the sale and resale of value-added materials.

Commodity Chain The path along which raw materials are turned into finished products and eventually consumed, with each link or node in the chain being a site for increasing added value and opportunity for profit

This is all the more true as the industry faces increasing constraints. Each sector in this industry is under increasing pressure and faced with challenges to its revenue stream. For manufacturers, the cost of inputs (especially petroleum) is constantly increasing, causing margins on sales to fall. Increasing efficiency by farmers, moreover, including the use of crops requiring fewer pesticides (e.g., BT potatoes – see Chapter 16), results in constrained markets, and the need to find new buyers. Formulator companies that have grown greatly in recent years are beginning to compete for a limited number of buyers. Increasing regulation of the pesticide industry also means that the costs for testing and marketing products is rising, again cutting into profits. Retailers are faced with increasing consolidation, the tendency of large-box stores to expand in number as the number of retail companies falls, leading to falling retail prices and fierce competition. Finally, increasing consumer concern (or "chemophobia" as it is called in the industry!) has cut into the customer base for both chemical retailers and applicator companies.

These together might be viewed as symptoms of **overaccumulation** (see Chapter 7), a condition where highly successful periods of growth are followed by stagnation owing to the concentration of wealth and a slow decline in consumer power, leading to an economic crisis of underconsumption. After growing a highly successful and highly integrated chemical manufacturing and supply system, the market for lawn inputs may have begun to top out. As a result of all these pressures, all parts of the lawn chemical industry have a single common objective: to get chemical-using consumers to use more inputs and to increase the number of households that buy and consume chemicals and services.

> **Overaccumulation** In political economy (and Marxism), a condition in the economy where capital becomes concentrated in very few hands (e.g., wealthy individuals) or firms (e.g., banks), causing economic slowdown and potential socioeconomic crisis
>
> **Pull Marketing** A strategy to increase demand for products or services by reaching consumers directly and convincing them they have a previously unknown need or problem that can be solved by a specific product

Marketing strategies: Manufacturing demand

One of the most evident signs of the stress on this system is the aggressive innovations that have been made in marketing over recent decades. Chemical formulators, in particular, have become enormously creative in trying to accelerate consumption of lawn chemical products. Most successful in this regard has been the shift from "push" to **pull marketing**. Historically, in "push" marketing, companies would "push" product out the door to retailers, including small hardware or home and garden stores. Consumers would maintain their lawns, occasionally see a problem (a brown spot or gap, for example), and then consult a hardware store to ask for a pesticide remedy or fertilizer treatment, the one "pushed" by the formulator company. By comparison, "pull" marketing goes directly to the consumer and tells them about a problem they might have, figuratively "pulling" them into the store. This more aggressive approach is designed, in essence, to create demand rather than simply wait for it and to imbue in consumers a perception of the lawn landscape that inspires them to take action through the use of inputs (Robbins and Sharp 2003).

Another radical innovation by formulator companies has been to expand into markets outside of the traditional domain of the United States and Canada. Lawn chemical companies work tirelessly to find (and create) new markets in Australia, South Africa, India, and China. By finding places in the world that might yet be untouched by the lawn economy and developing an enthusiasm and aesthetic for well-kept lawns in consumer populations, the industry is again seeking to create demand. This **spatial fix** (see Chapter 7) represents a temporary safety valve for an industry like lawn chemicals, which faces stagnant or declining local revenues and works to globalize both its consumption and production systems.

> **Spatial Fix** The tendency of capitalism to temporarily solve its inevitable periodic crises by establishing new markets, new resources, and new sites of production in other places

In sum, a political economy view of the lawn chemical question highlights how little choice individual consumers may actually have and the disproportionate power of the chemical industry in influencing demand. It also shows that the industry itself is under constant and ongoing pressure, which further limits and structures its decision-making. A political economy approach, in short, presents chemical behaviors as deeply structured. While the demands of the turfgrass dog should wag the chemical input tail, it appears to be the reverse case: demand for lawns is manufactured by the industries that maintain them.

For this reason, some regulations have been introduced, which move beyond the individual consumer, to begin to address the problem at a larger scale. In New York State, for example, many pesticide products may not be applied legally to grass and turf areas within 100 feet of lakes, ponds, rivers, streams, or wetlands. Whole municipalities in Canada have banned "cosmetic" (i.e., consumer lawn) pesticides entirely, removing them from the market and local stores. The overall environmental impact of these kinds of legal innovations is not fully known yet, but they mark a significant change in the way both producer and consumer environmental decisions are regulated.

The Lawn Puzzle

In this chapter, we have learned that:

- Turfgrasses are plant species that have evolved alongside people and grazing pressure.
- Lawns are a recent cultural artifact.
- Emerald-green manicured monocultural lawns typically require some chemical inputs.
- Many lawn chemical inputs are hazardous to humans or ecosystems.
- People use these inputs even though they acknowledge the associated risks.
- Social influences for maintaining lawns are high, as lawn care is associated with good citizenship and neighborliness.
- There may be social opportunities for decreasing the use of chemicals.
- The lawn industry is a global multi-billion-dollar one with many components.
- Pressures on the lawn economy force companies to seek to expand lawn chemical usage.
- Innovations in marketing and global business strategy seek to make up for crises in the chemical industry, maintaining pressure on consumers to keep intensive lawns.

In this way, lawns are not an entirely a unique socio-ecology. As a hazard that we appear to impose upon ourselves, lawns raise questions about what is or is not "natural" as well as questions about whether or not we can or cannot make free "choices."

Which brings us back to Suzanne, who continues to use a fertilizer treatment that causes obvious suffering to the dog she loves. Is she so different than the rest of us, who may drive a fuel-inefficient pickup truck or SUV even though we know it is probably not good for the environment or who buys a bottle of water knowing that this "healthy" choice is one that may not be good for the environment? Even when we are concerned about these choices, we make them as part of our day-to-day lives. This is because our choices are at least somewhat influenced by the social and economic conditions around us. More than this even, the lawn offers us an opportunity to ask whether we choose to maintain an ecological system like turfgrass monoculture or, instead, whether the turf of the lawn *causes us to behave in a way that maintains it.*

Questions for Review

1.   Describe the way turfgrasses grow. What has influenced their evolution and what implications does this have for how we maintain them?
2.   What is a monoculture and how does it differ from ecologies more typically found in the environment? What does that mean for maintaining lawns?
3.   What parts of lawn chemical decision-making might be classified as strictly "rational" and intentional? What other influences are there on homeowner decision-making?
4.   What does the phrase "landscape as text" mean and how does it apply to turfgrass lawns?
5.   List some of the pressures that act on the lawn chemical industry. How has the industry responded and to what effect?

Exercise 14.1   What is a "Weed"?

The term weed is a subjective one, which simply means a plant growing in a place where it is not wanted. Some plants may be very valuable in one context but a nuisance in others. The goal of monocultural lawn management is to remove all weeds, of course. Is anything of value lost in the process? Go to the internet or other source and list four or five species that are typically considered weeds, in lawns or other contexts. Do these species have any value? What benefits or uses might they be put to? Do they have historical value? Who might have used them in the past and for what? Is the word "weed" simply a social construction or does it have some utility in real terms?

Exercise 14.2   The War over Pesticides

Browse the websites of Dow Agrosciences Turf division (http://www.dowagro.com/turf/), an important producer and innovator of chemical inputs, and that of Beyond Pesticides (http://www.beyondpesticides.org/), a non-profit dedicated to the elimination of all pesticides. How does each represent chemical inputs? How does each use and understand the meaning of words like "safety" and "sustainability"? How are hazards and risks framed for visitors to these sites?

Exercise 14.3   Responsibility for Environments: Do Objects Make You a Subject?

Lawns are only one example of objects in the world around us for which we may have responsibility to maintain (consider: pets, cars, etc.). List two or three objects, landscapes, or ecologies you maintain as part of your routine. What specific actions must you take to do this? Are there associated environmental costs or externalities? Does the maintenance or management of these things in the environment have an impact on how you think or feel? Do you think your relationship to these objects helps to make you into a certain kind of person, citizen, neighbor, or member of a community?

References

Bormann, F. H., D. Balmori, G. T. Geballe, and L. Vernegaard (2001). *Redesigning the American Lawn: A Search for Environmental Harmony*. New Haven, CT: Yale University Press.

Crumbley, R. (2000). "Neighbors sue over high grass." *Columbus Dispatch*, October 19.

Haydu, J. J., A. W. Hodges, and C. R. Hall (2006). "Economic Impacts of the Turfgrass and Lawncare Industry in the United States." University of Florida Institute of Food and Agricultural Sciences.

Jackson, K. T. (1985). *Crabgrass Frontier: The Suburbanization of the United States*. New York: Oxford University Press.

Milesi, C., S. W. Running, C. D. Elvidge, J. B. Dietz, B. T. Tuttle, et al. (2005). "Mapping and modeling the biogeochemical cycling of turf grasses in the United States." *Environmental Management* 36: 426–38.

Rappaport, B. (1993). "As natural landscaping takes root we must weed out the bad laws: How natural landscaping and Leopold's Land Ethic collide with unenlightened weed laws and what must be done about it." *The John Marshall Law Review* 26.

Robbins, P. (2007). *Lawn People: How Grasses, Weeds, and Chemicals Make Us Who We Are*. Philadelphia: Temple University Press.

Robbins, P., and T. Birkenholtz (2003). "Turfgrass revolution: Measuring the expansion of the American lawn." *Land Use Policy* 20: 181–94.

Robbins, P., and J. Sharp (2003). "Producing and consuming chemicals: The moral economy of the American lawn." *Economic Geography* 79: 425–51.

Suggested Reading

Jenkins, V. S. (1994). *The Lawn: A History of an American Obsession*. Washington, DC: Smithsonian Institute Press.

Steinberg, T. (2006). *American Green: The Obsessive Quest for the Perfect Lawn*. New York: W. W. Norton.

15

Bottled Water

Source: Jason Keith Heydorn/Shutterstock.

Keywords

- Commodity
- Common property
- Desalinization
- IPAT
- Life cycle analysis
- Overproduction
- Primitive accumulation
- Risk assessment
- Risk communication
- Risk perception

Chapter Menu

Environment and Society: A Critical Introduction, Second Edition. Paul Robbins, John Hintz,
and Sarah A. Moore.
© 2014 John Wiley & Sons, Ltd. Published 2014 by John Wiley & Sons, Ltd.

A Tale of Two Bottles

Luisa Guzman climbs the steps of a makeshift street on the outskirts of Tijuana, Mexico carrying a five-gallon bottle of water, a more than 40-pound load. The winding alley is steep and runs with sewage, part of a labyrinth of recently made roads that snake along the hilly flanks of one of the fastest-growing cities in the world. Luisa carries her heavy load through the streets of this *colonia* – an informal, unplanned, squatter settlement – toward her home on the high hills. This encumbered walk is a daily task in her household, where these bottles are the sole source of drinking water for her family.

The underfunded Comisión Estatal de Servicios Públicos de Tijuana, an agency charged with supplying water to this city of five million people, is incapable of connecting most of these settlements to the municipal water supply. Perhaps 25 percent of Tijuana residents live "off the grid," therefore, with no running water coming from their taps. As a result, city residents are incredibly creative in securing access to water. Luisa harvests water from her roof and stores it in large plastic barrels. Her neighbors nearby, with equal inventiveness, have indirect access to water by illegally tapping nearby municipal pipes. All of these households use these water sources for critical household purposes like bathing, and then reuse the bath water for multiple loads of laundry, finally discharging the remainder to their gardens. In this way, Tijuana residents, and people like them throughout Mexico, are among the most efficient users of water in the world.

But drinking water poses an exceptionally difficult problem, so most households depend exclusively on bottled water. These five-gallon plastic jugs are sold off of trucks throughout the city by water vendors. At 10 pesos for five gallons (around US$1), this is a modest but critical part of Luisa's household budget, and it is a standard expense not only for *colonia* dwellers throughout the city, but wealthier households as well. The sources of the bottles vary, but in most cases, they are filled directly from the municipal supply, making the bottled water business a lucrative trade for those who sell the state-provided commodity to citizens like Luisa who have not been linked to basic services.

A mere few miles north across the US border in the city of San Diego, Carlos Perez turns his Prius, off of Harbor Drive, into the parking lot of a 7–11 convenience store facing the sea. Entering the store, he walks to the back refrigerator, pulls a 16-ounce bottle of Dasani water from the case, and brings it to the register. He pays $1.49 (approximately $60 for five gallons at this rate) and drives home.

Like almost all San Diegans, Carlos is connected to a municipal water and sewer supply that provides tap water around the clock, every day of the week. Nevertheless, he will consume roughly 30 gallons of bottled water in a year, near the national average, spending hundreds of dollars annually for a product provided by his tax money for free. Certainly, he likes the taste of the water he buys in the store, and he feels safer with water that has undergone "reverse osmosis." Even so, like Luisa's water, Carlos' is nothing more than treated local tap water, indeed, the very same Colorado River water that supplies Tijuana. But unlike bottled water in Tijuana, that sold in San Diego is wrapped with a slick blue label by the Coca-Cola Company and sold at a price 60 times higher than its Mexican counterpart, and hundreds of times more expensive than its tap water source, which costs fractions of a penny per gallon.

How did a ubiquitous, free-flowing, fundamental building block of all life on Earth come to be a commodity that is captured, marketed, and distributed around the world? To what degree does the marketing of water reflect a real state of scarcity, a plausible response to a health risk, or merely the clever gimmick of a marketing executive? And with what different implications for Luisa and Carlos, for Mexico, the United States, and the rest of the world?

A Short History of Bottled Water

Water as a marketed commodity, specifically bottled for resale and consumption at distant sites, is a relatively recent phenomenon. The earliest markets for bottled water were rooted in the perceived health benefits of "spa waters," sourced in hot springs throughout Europe. Perceived to have medical value, these were captured and sold around the world as early as the 1700s. Later advances in chemistry led to a decline in the sale of these waters, as many of their purported benefits were debunked in the 1800s. The persistent perception that bottled *mineral* waters are healthful and scarce, on the other hand, helps sustain bottled water drinking in the present day (Beverage Marketing Corporation 2009).

By the beginning of the twentieth century, "artesian" spring waters and other water from natural sources had entered a new market phase. Many brands familiar today (Poland Springs,

Figure 15.1 The Poland Spring "Spring House" in 1910. Like other naturally occurring springs, these water sources had become elite destinations in the 1800s. Markets for their waters were associated with luxury, health, and opulence. They were not a typical household expense, however, for working people who were only then beginning to receive regular water delivery through modern plumbing. *Source*: Photograph provided courtesy of the Poland Spring Preservation Society.

for example) were first established in the middle of the 1800s. These waters were still typically associated with spring waters simultaneously operating as therapeutic retreats and baths. Such bottled products were therefore somewhat elite, certainly expensive, and not in any way typically consumed by average American, British, and European people who were just then beginning to receive reliable modern municipal tap water (Figure 15.1).

In other parts of the world, bottled water sales during this period were entirely unheard of, and would likely have seemed bizarre. For the average agrarian producer or rural-dweller in India, Mexico, Egypt, or China in 1900, pure water sources were available in the

Common Property A good or resource (e.g., bandwidth, pasture, oceans) whose characteristics make it difficult to fully enclose and partition, making it possible for non-owners to enjoy resource benefits and owners to sustain costs from the actions of others, typically necessitating some form of creative institutional management

form of local wells or tanks, and a significant labor input (typically by women) would have been dedicated to drawing freely available water from these common areas (Figure 15.2). Even today, in much of the world, water is considered a free good and part of the **common property** of communities.

Beginning in the 1970s, however, elite international brands of waters, including Evian and Perrier, began to make their way into consumer markets. By the 1990s, an incredible acceleration of bottled water consumption had begun around the world, with continued acceleration until the present.

Figure 15.2 Women draw water from a communal well in Rajasthan, India. Though groundwater declines threaten these rural water supplies, villagers depend on freely available communal water sources for survival, and upon the significant women's labor require to draw, carry, and dispense water every day. *Source*: Courtesy of Dr Trevor Birkenholtz.

The current global state of the bottled water market

By 2009, an enormous range of bottled water products had become available to consumers. These products are very different, and treated somewhat differently under national and international laws. Specifically, bottled waters include:

- *Spring water and "artesian" spring water.* This is water drawn from a single underground water source. In the case of "artesian" water, this merely represents groundwater from a confined aquifer where the water source flows to the surface.
- *Mineral water.* To be considered real mineral water, the water must contain 250 parts per million of minerals, and they must occur naturally and be derived from the water source.
- *Purified water.* By far the most common form of bottled water, this is water that may come from surface water sources (like rivers and streams) but often comes from a municipal source. The water is treated, but this is not much more than expensive tap water and represents the vast majority of the bottled water market.
- *Fortified products.* This includes a range of new bottled waters with additional nutritional additives, like vitamins or electrolytes.

Between 2002 and 2007, global consumption of bottled water of all kinds grew from 34 billion gallons annually to 49 billion, representing a 7.6 percent annual increase over the period. The leading consumer nations of bottled water are diverse and represent tremendous differences in the types of markets for this commodity. In overall consumption, the

United States leads the world, consuming nearly nine billion total gallons of bottled water annually, followed by Mexico at 5.8 billion gallons. In terms of per capita use, the world leader is the United Arab Emirates (UAE), followed by Mexico, a number of European countries, and the United States. The average person in Mexico consumed 68 gallons of bottled water in 2007. In the United States, each person consumed almost 30 gallons in that year. People around the world are clearly drinking more bottled water every year (Landi 2008) (Figures 15.3 and 15.4).

This represents a massive growing economy. In 2007, sales of bottled water in the United States amounted to more than 11 billion dollars. This puts bottled water in the current number two sales position for all beverages marketed in the United States, behind only carbonated soft drinks.

In part, the rise of bottled water consumption, in both poorer and wealthier countries, arises from a perception (both justified and unjustified, as we will see below) that traditional and municipal water sources are compromised. Recent outbreaks of water-borne disease, nitrogen alerts, and other crisis events have certainly contributed to consumer concern over water quality. This

Figure 15.3 US per capita consumption of bottled water from 1988 to 2007. The steady increase in US bottled water consumption shows no signs of abatement. Consumption has quadrupled in the past 20 years. *Source:* Adapted from Landi (2008).

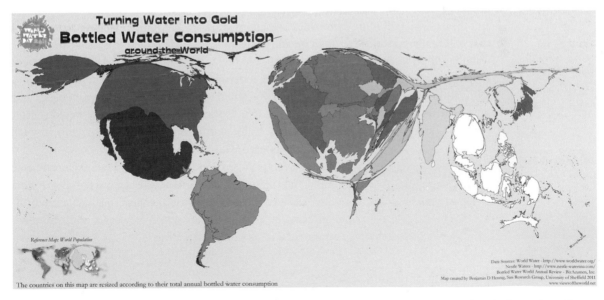

Figure 15.4 Cartogram of bottled water consumption worldwide. *Source:* Reproduced from http://www.viewsoftheworld.net/wp-content/uploads/2011/03/BottledWaterConsumption.jpg. CC BY-NC-ND 3.0.

is tied to a less coherent, but no less persuasive, feeling among consumers in wealthy countries that bottled water is "natural," a social construction that associates bottled water with healthy and environmentally friendly living. And to be sure, relative to corn-syrup-laden soft drinks that otherwise dominate the market, bottled water is probably an improvement in this regard.

In countries like Mexico, India, and Egypt, on the other hand, the water system has been dramatically transformed in recent years, driving demand for bottled water in both rural and urban areas. In part, this demand has been a result of significant urbanization where, as in our introductory story, the capacity of municipal services to keep up with demand has been outstripped by growth. On top of this, however, has been a change in the way water is owned and managed around the world. In many countries water services have been privatized, often as a result of poor state management, and the distribution of water has come to be governed through water markets. In such cases, the purchase of water, in bottles or directly from tanker trucks, is a fact of daily life.

Environmental impacts of bottled water

Contradicting the warm "green" feelings often associated with bottled water (and its typical labels depicting pristine mountain streams), bottled water has unquestionable environmental costs. Consider first the package itself. Water bottles are made from plastic (PET or polyethylene), a product that is itself derived from petroleum; for every kg of bottle, roughly two kilos of petroleum are required. Second, consider the energy and material impacts of simply moving water around. While it is true that most bottled water comes from regional sources (often the city tap water in the town where it is sold), it must nevertheless be bottled, trucked, or shipped from place to place, requiring the consumption of petroleum and the expulsion of more carbon dioxide, adding further environmental costs to a product that is actually very close at hand for most consumers. Finally, the life cycle of the typical water bottle ends in a landfill, with the associated costs and impacts of garbage management more generally. These include the costs and environmental impacts of hauling, as well as the land demands for garbage disposal. More than 30 million tons of plastic entered the municipal solid waste stream in 2007, less than 7 percent of which was recovered (Päster 2009). Certainly water bottles are recyclable. But only a small proportion of bottled water containers ever are.

Life Cycle Analysis   The rigorous analysis of the environmental impacts of a product, service, or object from its point of manufacture all the way to its disposal as waste; also known as cradle-to-grave assessment

The total footprint for a bottle of water depends enormously on brand and location, so a full **life cycle analysis** of the product remains elusive. Weighed against the near negligible environmental costs of a glass of tap water, however, bottled water's environmental footprint is staggering.

The puzzle of bottled water

This brief review of the history of bottled water suggests several things about the relationship between environment and society. First, it is a relatively recent phenomenon, meaning

Box 15.1   Environmental Solution? Filling Stations for Reusable Bottles

The enormous hidden costs of bottled water have several components. Producing the bottle requires both petroleum and water. Every bottle may require as much as twice the amount of water in its production as it contains. Transportation of water also requires fossil fuels. One well-informed calculation for the most exotic of all bottled waters – Fiji brand – suggests a staggering total. Fuel demands are estimated at 160 grams of fossil fuels to produce the bottle in China, 2 grams to deliver it to Fiji, and 81 grams to get it to a store in Europe or America (Hunt 2004). Leaving aside the tragic irony that perhaps in excess of one-third of the Fijian population goes without clean potable water, both the bottle and its transportation have a high impact.

Buying bottled water from generic – and probably local – sources brings the footprint of bottled water down dramatically. But since most bottled water is treated tap water, it might be easier to simply drink from the tap. Consumer behavior studies have repeatedly shown, however, the preference people have for portability and the usefulness of bottles. So what to do?

One simple option is the installation of refilling stations that are built to accommodate refillable bottles. Built into the existing network of water fountains and delivery, these can be installed relatively cheaply. The water supply represents already-treated municipal water and so introduces no extra steps in processing.

A life cycle assessment of refillable bottles, compared with conventional recycling and purchased bottled water, shows the enormous potential of this technology. Drinking from public water supplies or the household tap (whether the source is groundwater or surface water) is an improvement over "one-way" bottled water in almost every regard, including the impact on waste generation, energy demand, climate change, consumption of abiotic resources, and eutrophication (Nessi et al. 2012).

These devices have been in use in many public institutions (especially schools) over the last several years and show promise. In high-traffic areas where fountains are heavily used, some institutions report savings in the number of discarded or recycled bottles to number into the tens of thousands every year. Coupled with campus bans on the sale of bottled water, there has been an adoption of the technology by a majority of students and other users.

Of course, this sort of solution is only feasible in places that are relatively wealthy, in global terms, and already endowed with effective and well-funded municipal water treatment plants. While good for places like malls and universities, it has limited applicability in underdeveloped contexts. Nor does it constrain the bottled water industry in any way, except by undermining its market somewhat. Nonetheless, by making it as easy as possible for people to get access to water without making unnecessary resource demands, refillable water stations represent a simple and ingenious alternative to bottled water markets.

---

that it is a product that can only be explained with reference to specifically current changes in human life. Second, it is a case of a product that, despite being wrapped in an image of good health and clean living, has negative environmental implications.

This review stresses several things about bottled water that make it a specific kind of *puzzle*:

- Bottled water has been associated historically with rarified health benefits and elite patterns of consumption, making people's desire for the product more than a merely rational choice.

- Increases in bottled water consumption in industrialized nations exploded in the last decade as a result of a combination of perceived health risks from public supply and a marketed "lifestyle" choice associated with affluence.
- In "underdeveloped" or poorer nations, on the other hand, bottled water use is on the increase as traditional community supplies have become scarcer, more polluted, and increasingly privatized.
- In both industrialized and poorer nations, water has become more expensive, and consuming bottled water has increased human environmental impacts associated with its production, transportation, and landfilling.
- All of this points to the strange case in which – in a few short years – a freely available, ecologically innocuous, and historically communal resource has become an environmentally detrimental privatized commodity.

Bottled water therefore provides lessons for understanding the evolution of human resource use over time under very different development conditions, but it also presents a *puzzle*: given its rapid turn toward a commodity, does bottled water represent the solution to a problem of water scarcity, a rational response to risks associated with declining water quality, or, rather, an artificial market cleverly engineered to sustain profits? As with other objects explored in this book, differing perspectives provide differing insights into these questions, again with highly contradictory answers.

Population: Bottling for Scarcity?

It is commonly observed that water on the Earth is both ubiquitous and terrifically scarce. A quick look at the global water budget confirms that there is plenty of water, though not in the places and forms most needed by people. Of the Earth's roughly one and a half billion cubic kilometers of water, approximately 97 percent is the saline water of the oceans. Much of the rest is in glaciers and groundwater, leaving 0.01 percent of the total water in lakes, rivers, and circulating in the atmosphere. In this sense, water is absolutely scarce. In quickly growing underdeveloped countries, moreover, roughly a quarter of the population goes without access to safe drinking water. This is a significant problem given that water-borne disease accounted for three and a half million deaths worldwide in 1998 alone (Rogers 1996). With population continuing to grow over the past 20 years at a rapid pace (see Chapter 2), and the total amount of available water essentially fixed, one might reach the conclusion that bottled water is a solution to the increasing scarcity imposed by dwindling available resources.

Looked at another way, however, the scarcity of water is really quite relative; a great deal of freshwater exists on Earth (approximately 55,000 cubic kilometers), though it is not equally distributed or efficiently utilized. The total amount of freshwater available in sub-Saharan Africa, for example, is around 6,000 cubic meters per person. People living in the region utilize barely 2 percent of that for agriculture, industry, and domestic purposes combined. In Canada and the United States, on the other hand, people use at least a quarter

Table 15.1   Freshwater usage around the world. The total average withdrawals of freshwater per person vary enormously around the world, as do the proportions of those dedicated to domestic use.

World region	Per capita annual withdrawals (m³)	Agricultural withdrawals (%)	Industrial withdrawals (%)	Domestic withdrawals (%)	Domestic withdrawals (m³)
North America	1,663	38	48	14	233
Oceania	900	72	10	18	162
Central America & Caribbean	603	75	6	18	109
South America	474	68	12	19	90
Europe	581	33	52	15	87
Middle East/North Africa	807	86	6	8	65
Asia	631	81	12	7	44
Sub-Saharan Africa	173	88	4	9	16

Source: Adapted from World Resources Institute, Earth Trends Data Tables.

of the water available. Table 15.1 describes the usage of renewable freshwater resources around the world (meaning the use of surface water and groundwater), as well as the percentage of water use in different sectors and the average quantity used domestically every year.

Notable here is the relative degree of use in differing sectors, across differing regions. While Europe uses about a third of its water for agriculture, Asia dedicates a full four-fifths to that usage. Also outstanding are the staggering differences in domestic usage between regions, with North Americans each using almost 15 times as much water as their sub-Saharan African counterparts. If bottled water usage is rising in some underdeveloped countries – like Mexico, for example – it is at least in part because available water is not directed to domestic use (owing to poor infrastructural development).

Broken down further, the average American's domestic water usage is also revealing. As is clear from Table 15.2, much domestic water usage is dedicated to water-demanding toilets and other conveniences. So too, these are all highly amenable to technological improvements and conservation measures (5 percent of household use comes from toilet leakage!). If water is a product of scarcity in the United States, then it is a scarcity that results largely from inefficiencies.

Who drinks bottled water?

When we compare these usage estimates against the countries where bottled water has a large and growing market, the picture becomes even more complicated. Table 15.3 shows a selection of the countries who lead the world in bottled water consumption, including the top three countries, the UAE, Mexico, and Italy. Starting with the case of the UAE, we

Table 15.2   Domestic US water use. A family of four uses 400 gallons of water daily, 300 of which are used indoors.

Water use	%
Toilets	26.7
Clothes washer	21.7
Shower	16.8
Faucet	15.7
Leaks	13.7
Other	5.3

Source: Adapted from http://www.epa.gov/WaterSense/pubs/indoor.html.

Table 15.3   Selected leading per capita consumer nations of bottled water, 2007.

Rank	Countries	Bottled water consumption per capita 2007 (liters)[1]	Actual renewable water resources per capita (m³)[2]	Population density 2002 (people per km²)[2]	Per capita GDP 2008 est. (US$)[3]
1	UAE	259.7	49	32	40,000
2	Mexico	204.8	4,357	52	14,200
3	Italy	201.7	3,336	191	31,000
5	France	135.5	3,371	108	32,700
9	USA	110.9	10,333	30	47,000
15	Croatia	92.0	23,890	82	16,100
18	Thailand	89.3	6,459	125	8,500

[1] *Source*: Adapted from Beverage Marketing Corporation (2009);
[2] *Source*: World Resources Institute, Earth Trends Data Tables;
[3] *Source*: CIA World Factbook.

see an extremely high annual rate of bottled water consumption. This country (really a federation of princely states) is not a heavily populated one, indeed it is tiny, but it consists of wealthy oil states located in a desert with almost no freshwater resources at all. Extensive consumption of bottled water is unsurprising here. Hydrology and climate tell us little, on the other hand, about the situation in Mexico, where freshwater resources abound. Here, water access is especially problematic in rapidly urbanizing areas with little infrastructural capacity to meet citizen needs. Under conditions of considerable poverty and large-scale informal urban settlement (as described in the opening of this chapter), the adoption of bottled water is also unsurprising, though for dramatically different reasons. Much the same might be said of Croatia and Thailand.

For Italy, France, and countries like them (including the United States), neither of these explanations appears compelling. Here are nations with modest overall populations, well-developed infrastructures, and relatively abundant natural water sources. And yet they sustain significant bottled water markets. As we shall see, some proportion of this consumption is driven by the perception in these places that, while public water may be abundant, its quality may be questionable.

While increasing the number of people on Earth clearly marginally increases the stress on the global water system, therefore, the immense variability in global conditions means that the wealth of countries and their infrastructural technology certainly play the key role in determining water use, as per the **IPAT** formula laid out in Chapter 2. In this formulation, you will recall, the *impact* of people on the environment is the result of a combination of factors, taken to include the overall quantity of human *population*, but exacerbated or mediated by the *affluence* of that population and the available *technology* they use to live. As noted above, water use technologies profoundly influence the proportion of water available for household use and for human consumption. Similarly, water treatment infrastructure – and its notable absence in many underdeveloped settings – heavily impacts the real need for a treated supply of bottled water. Put this way, drinking water scarcity driven by human population stress alone does not explain the explosion of bottled water consumption around the world.

> **IPAT**   A theoretical formula holding that human Impact is a function of the total Population, its overall Affluence, and its Technology; this provides an alternative formulation to a simple assumption that population alone is proportional to impact
>
> **Desalinization**   A technology that removes salts and other minerals from water, especially sea water; prohibitively expensive in most contexts, current techniques are highly energy demanding

Still, some sort of relative scarcity is at work, through highly variable sets of local conditions and human expectations. One can conclude that bottled water is best viewed as a response to scarcity, therefore, but clearly of at least three different kinds: hydrological scarcity, techno-economic scarcity, and perceptual scarcity. In the first case (hydrological scarcity), some unique combinations of climate, affluence, and human population, as in the oil-rich Gulf States most notably, present a hydrological regime where bottled water is an almost inevitable response. Such places are also the ones most likely to turn to other capital- and energy-demanding water solutions, including **desalinization** of sea water.

In the second case (techno-economic), we find conditions of underdevelopment exacerbated by swiftly urbanizing populations moving into burgeoning municipalities. Combined with slipshod water distribution and treatment facilities in these cities, a form of scarcity emerges where we might predict the occurrence of large-scale bottled water markets. Potable water here is scarce, even though natural water supplies are plentiful.

In the final case, even where water and water treatment are widespread, a perception that bottled water is safer or healthier may account for a kind of scarcity (perceptual scarcity), where affluent consumers turn to an alternative for a widely available staple resource, like water.

Risk: Health and Safety in a Bottle?

Leaving aside the problems of underdeveloped safe water supplies in the poorer parts of the world (to which we will return shortly!), it is possible to ask whether consumers in developed countries are making a kind of risk assessment when they choose to drink bottled water. In this case, when relatively wealthy consumers with plenty of available tap water turn to Dasani and Evian, questions arise about people's perception of water quality. Ignoring for a moment issues surrounding the taste of bottled and tap water (see the next section for more on this), it is likely that a significant proportion of bottled water drinkers purchase the product for health and safety reasons. Though survey results on this question vary, many consumers – as many as half – report either that bottled water is a "healthier option" or that tap water is "riskier" than bottled water (Napier and Kodner 2008).

This makes bottled water an extremely interesting puzzle to which we might apply insights from the field of risk analysis and risk perception (Chapter 6). As you will recall, these approaches to environment and society issues examine the world in terms of hazards. These fields examine the role of risk – a probability of harm – not only in terms of how risky certain decisions are, but also why people assign levels of risk to actions and behaviors that may be far higher or lower than experts would suggest.

For water, we can reasonably ask what, if any, actual risks are associated with tap water – a **risk assessment**. If the actual risks of tap water are not comparable to the ones people imagine, we might also consider the problem of **risk perception**, that not-always-rational, socially and culturally influenced, cognitive process where people come to evaluate the risk of a product or behavior. To the degree that people perceive the risks of their tap water in a way that may be misleading, we might finally consider techniques in **risk communication**, which seek to convey technical information (about trace elements in water, for example) in an intuitive way, and so lead to better informed decisions.

> **Risk Assessment**   The rigorous application of logic and information to determine the risk – possibility of an undesirable outcome – associated with particular decisions; used to so reach more optimal and rational outcomes
>
> **Risk Perception**   A phenomenon, and related field of study, describing the tendency of people to evaluate the hazardousness of a situation or decision in not-always-rational terms, depending on individual biases, culture, or human tendencies
>
> **Risk Communication**   A field of study dedicated to understanding the optimal way to present and convey risk-related information to aid people in reaching optimal and rational outcomes

Risk assessment: Is bottled water "healthy" or "less risky"?

The earliest bottled waters were spa waters touted for their health benefits, deriving mostly from ideas about their mineral content. Research on mineral waters, however, is highly inconclusive, because the contents of each source vary enormously. This is also true of tap water around the world, making any health claim for choosing bottled water over tap water generally untenable. Given that many bottled waters *are* tap water, this comparison becomes all the more fruitless. What's in the bottle is probably no better for you than what comes out of your garden hose (Landi 2008).

Of course, compared to other available beverages, water is always a pretty good option. The bottled water industry – which defends this position vociferously – has a strong argument here. Over the past few decades the growth in bottled water consumption appears to have come in part at the expense of soft drink consumption. In a country like the United States, adult onset diabetes is on the rise, typically caused by high-sugar diets over the course of a lifetime. A switch from cola and root beer to bottled water would probably be beneficial for many people.

The converse question, whether bottled water is safer than tap water, is also amenable to risk assessment. Certainly, in places where the water supply is poorer overall, and during periods of obvious declared water emergencies, bottled water is undeniably less risky than tap water.

But further investigation of bottled water raises real questions about whether or not it is really any safer than other daily sources, especially municipal treated water. Most notable is a revolutionary 1999 report from the National Resources Defense Council (NRDC), which tested bottled water extensively in the United States. This study concluded that about a third of all bottled waters were simply packaged municipal water, and that of those bottled waters that were effectively tap water, many were not treated any further (Napier and Kodner 2008).

Of course, municipal tap water is already heavily treated. This is because the water that comes to your tap is derived from a huge range of sources, including lakes, rivers, and groundwater, all of which are exposed to a lot of different pollutants, ranging from live bacteria to viruses and metals. It is understandable that municipal water is strictly regulated (in the United States by the Safe Drinking Water Act) and treated extensively. Typically, water is pumped from the source through screens and put in tanks for flocculation and coagulation, where chemicals (like alum) are added to help fine suspended matter drop out. This usually destroys 99 percent of viruses or other contaminants. The resulting water is then filtered through sand and gravel. The water is fluoridated at this point (fluoride is added), and sometimes chlorinated. Ozonation might follow, where ozone gas is introduced to eliminate any possible remaining microbes. In some cases, ultraviolet (UV) radiation might also be applied. Tap water and any bottled water derived from tap water are pretty safe as a result.

The NRDC results concluded, however, not only that bottled waters were no safer than tap waters but in some cases they were *less safe*. US tap water, the study emphasizes, must meet rigorous standards set by the US Environmental Protection Agency, whereas bottled water is regulated by the Food and Drug Administration, which often provides exemptions and loopholes for bottled waters. More recent research has raised further concerns, and some bottled spring water sources, for example, may have trace minerals (like arsenic) with negative health implications (Doria 2006).

Working under the understanding, therefore, that bottled water is not generally healthier than tap water and by no means any safer, rational risk analysis does not appear to be at the core of growing consumer water purchases in countries like the United States and United Kingdom, where tap water is ubiquitous and highly regulated. We would do better, therefore, to think of this as a problem of *risk perception*. In this regard, what do people think about bottled water, and why do they think it?

Risk perception and the limits of risk communication in water quality

Research suggests that a proportion of the population consistently thinks tap water represents some kind of health and safety risk. Bottled water users are similarly most likely to cite health and safety as their leading reason for not drinking from the tap. Indeed, some proportion of bottled water drinkers (as much as a quarter) typically believes that bottled water is entirely free of contaminants (Napier and Kodner 2008).

These views are not surprising if we consider some of the general trends discovered in risk perception science. As you will recall from Chapter 6, people tend to have an inflated distrust of phenomena over which they do not have direct control, relative to things they do control. Drinking water quality, and the complex systems of treatment public water undergoes, definitely is not under the direct control of most people. It is also the case that given the invisibility of water quality risks, there are few objective ways for the average person to directly know the quality of their water. As a result, people tend to base their judgments on taste or color. Poor taste in public water, however, is not a good indicator of water quality or safety. As a result, people consistently and irrationally overestimate the hazards of public tap water (Anadu and Harding 2000).

Most tap water is regulated and safe, and a lot of bottled water is merely tap water. Can biased perceptions be overcome through clearer information about our water supplies? Specifically, decision scientists assert that, when it comes to water, the public is increasingly interested in side-by-side comparisons of their tap water to that of other towns and utilities, as well as to bottled water. These comparisons, it is believed, will help allay consumer fears about perfectly good tap water, which have in the past caused them to mistakenly report their own water supply as worse than that of other utilities or of bottled water.

Early experiments in this area are promising. Side-by-side "blindfold" comparisons have been conducted in communities where municipal tap water quality is in fact comparable to bottled water quality. Presented with the study results that show that they are unable to consistently distinguish between the two sources, people have become far less likely to under-rate their water supply. Put simply, people can learn to overcome their tendency to dislike their tap water. This new perception, however, has not been demonstrated to actually affect people's behavior, especially their purchase of bottled water. People who have seen such side-by-side comparisons of their water with bottled water have come away complaining less about their municipal supply, but they still continue to buy bottled water that is no healthier or safer (Anadu and Harding 2000).

This final finding suggests the intractability of the bottled water market to improved risk communication. It hints at the limits of a risk/hazards approach to explaining people's actions. Despite the optimistic hope that better information leads to more rational behaviors, something more deeply rooted may be going on. The view from a political economy perspective, conversely, points to more stubborn forces propelling the bottling of water. Instead, political economy might suggest, bottled water is part of a larger insidious privatization of public goods that both steals from poorer people and imposes itself as a false commodity on wealthier ones.

Political Economy: Manufacturing Demand on an Enclosed Commons

For thousands of years, drinking water has been a classic common property good, typically drawn from wells and rivers and managed through informal community rules (or institutions, as per Chapter 4). Indeed, in many parts of the world, people's access to water remains free, though important restrictions protect community water supplies against overexploitation or pollution. Where large cities have risen over the centuries, these informal mechanisms have typically given way to larger-scale, state dictated and managed systems of municipal water supply. Modern water grids and the sophisticated water treatment facilities that go with them are centuries-old products of city planning. Development worldwide has largely been synonymous with municipal and national governments providing safe drinking water to citizens.

The rise of the water commodity

During the 1980s and 1990s, however, these systems were challenged by new ways of thinking about water. Public utilities increasingly became "enterprise" units, who were expected to cover their costs by becoming more efficient and setting water fees/prices at appropriate levels. Some utilities were replaced altogether by private companies and water vendors. In cities like Buenos Aires, Argentina and Jakarta, Indonesia, municipal control over water sources and distribution have been surrendered entirely to private firms. In other cases, areas that were inconvenient or difficult to supply privately continued to be serviced by the government, while easier, more lucrative parts of cities were increasingly "cherry-picked" and turned over to private vendors. Throughout all of these changes, the benefits of efficiency and market logic were widely touted (Bakker 2004; Grand Rapids Press 2007; and see Chapter 3).

The rise of bottled water, while not an explicit part of the privatization of water services, coincides with this process. Bottled water, like privatization of city water, reflects an overall shift toward private responsibility and corporate profit in water provision. From the point of view of political economy, this trend is seen as largely detrimental and part of a larger set of discouraging trends. Specifically, from this vantage, a shift to bottled water (among other kinds of water privatization) turns water into a **commodity**, a thing marketed for profit. This process embodies two foundational concepts from political economy: **primitive accumulation** and **crisis of overproduction** (see Chapter 7 for further discussion).

Bottled accumulation: Selling back nature

In the first case, it is clear that water sources around the world, which have been historically freely available, are increasingly controlled privately. In the case of bottled water, concessions to private companies have repeatedly occurred. The Nestlé company, for example, pumps 218 gallons of groundwater per minute from an aquifer in Michigan, based on a 99-year lease from the state. This water otherwise feeds local lakes and streams. Nestlé, who essentially pumps the water for free and received significant tax breaks to locate the company at this site, bottles the water under

Commodity   An object of economic value that is valued generically, rather than as a specific object (example: pork is a commodity, rather than a particular pig). In political economy (and Marxist) thought, an object made for exchange

Primitive Accumulation   In Marxist thought, the direct appropriation by capitalists of natural resources or goods from communities that historically tend to hold them collectively, as, for example, where the common lands of Britain were enclosed by wealthy elites and the state in the 1700s

Overproduction   In political economy (and Marxism), a condition in the economy where the capacity of industry to produce goods and services outpaces the needs and capacity to consume, causing economic slowdown and potential socioeconomic crisis the brand name "Ice Mountain." The company has faced down community opposition that insists that this water rightfully flows to nearby Osprey Lake and local wetlands (Marketing Week 2005). In essence, public water is made private and then sold back to consumers from whom it has been expropriated.

Throughout the developing world, the connection of bottled water to appropriated public sources is more complex, but no less evident. Many water vendors in India, for example, take control of publicly piped water either legally (through contracts) or illegally (through bribes), and then sell it to households or to marketers. The case of Tijuana, described earlier, is compelling evidence of the way publicly held resources, in this case municipal water, are bottled for free and sold at significant markups to people whose connection to municipal services is increasingly denied.

From a market-oriented perspective, it can certainly be argued that capitalists are merely filling a need here. The failure of Tijuana to make provision for its citizens provides an unfortunate gap into which innovative entrepreneurs enter to help poorer people and make a modest profit, from this angle. But given that the state actually provisions and treats the water at taxpayer expense, the seizure and exploitation of public goods as private commodities might also be viewed as a kind of basic theft. This primitive accumulation of water supplies provides businesses with free profits, drawing directly on natural water sources previously held by communities. These are sold back to the public in bottles.

Bottled overproduction: Producing demand

On the other hand, in places like San Diego, with fairly complete and still publicly available water supplies, the problem is less supply but instead *demand*. In a culture with far more soda, beer, and juice choices than could possibly be consumed by the population, it is difficult to increase the demand for beverages. This presents a limit for capital accumulation for firms and for investors seeking profits by buying into major multinational companies like Pepsi, Coca-Cola, or myriad others. Beverages, a multi-billion-dollar industry, would appear to be reaching a maximum, raising the specter of stagnating markets.

The only solution to this problem is to *create* demand, that is, to make people want your product. In the case of bottled water, the lion's share of investment in bottled water goes into packaging and marketing. The total number of separate, albeit effectively indistinguishable, bottled water brands underlines this point. The Nestlé corporation alone sells no fewer than *15* different brands of bottled water. The expansion of this bottled water market is aimed at eating away at whatever non-commodity goods remain in people's lives (i.e., tap water). This represents the only real possible expansion of markets and economic growth, staving off the grim prospect of flat sales.

To do so, the industry is attempting to expand and cement consumption habits among younger consumers and children, and establish long-term brand loyalty. As one marketing trade journal complained, because people are becoming *too confident* in their tap water, new, less well-informed consumers must be found:

> The increasing consumer confidence in tap water and in asking for it at restaurants and bars may well prove to be the key in effecting further rises in both penetration and volume

consumption per head among adults. But the attitudes and behavior of children, carried into adult consumption patterns, may well counter this trend and prove to be more significant in the long run. (National Petroleum News 2007: 34)

And this is only the trade journal for the industry making the bottles!

In political economic terms, this effort to get people to pay money for something they already receive for free is a symptom of a larger problem: overproduction. In this view, the capacity of firms to produce consumer goods far outstrips the desire or capacity for them to be consumed, especially by working people who live off the limited wages provided by these same firms. This leads to a crisis of underconsumption, where the economy cannot digest goods (like beer and soft drinks) fast enough to maintain profits. Force-feeding such an economy demands that new needs be created, preferably essential rather than optional ones. Bottled water is a perfect fit.

Taken together then, from a political economy point of view, there are two linked trends in bottled water: 1) In poorer regions and countries, there is a trend toward expropriating community water supplies, and marketing that water back to residents in bottles. 2) Among wealthy consumers and in well-developed areas, there is a simultaneous effort to create demand for bottled water even where plenty of clean water is already available. Critically, these are both part of the same system.

The Bottled Water Puzzle

In this chapter, we have learned that:

*   Bottled water consumption has exploded around the world in the past two decades, coming to compete with and replace other sources of drinking water.
*   The production, packaging, and transportation of water in a bottle means that it is not an environmentally benign way to get and consume water.
*   Meeting human water needs is increasingly difficult in a rapidly growing and urbanizing world, but bottled water may only be viewed as a response to scarcity by acknowledging differing kinds of scarcity: hydrological, socioeconomic, and perceptual.
*   One of the central drivers behind bottled water consumption is the perception that other water supplies are less safe or less healthy.
*   Risk assessment shows no significant advantages of bottled over tap water, raising questions about human biases in risk perception.
*   The simultaneous growth of markets for bottled water in underdeveloped countries as well as wealthier ones suggests that a common economic driver – commoditization of nature – may be behind water privatization.

This brings us back to our water consumers in Tijuana and San Diego. Does bottled water represent the most efficient and safe way to provision drinking water in the twenty-first century to rich and poor alike? Or does it instead suggest a surrender of the environment to private ownership? Can and should municipal water (or clean air, garbage collection, parks . . .) be made available to the world's poor through social provisioning instead of markets? Can better risk communication allow consumers to make better informed judgments about the risk and threats of water (or spinach or peanuts or toys . . .)? To what degree does allowing firms to control the sources and distribution of water (or public space, conservation areas, trees . . .) increase efficiencies in delivery, and to what degree does it inflate unnecessary consumption and lead to a loss of public control over the environment?

Bottled water is a puzzle that shares a lot, therefore, with an enormous range of natural goods and environmental services. The revolutionary and rapid growth of bottled water around the world is either the leading edge of a desirable consumer revolution or a warning sign about the decline of our responsibility to one another and the Earth.

Questions for Review

1. "Dasani" and "Aquafina" are two of the bestselling brands of bottled water in the United States. Who owns and markets these brands? Where do they get the water that goes into the bottles?
2. How (and why) has the recent and rapid urbanization in countries like Mexico, India, and Egypt affected the demand for bottled water?
3. Discuss the three discrete types of scarcity that are combining to drive global water consumption steadily upward.
4. In the United States, are municipal drinking water and bottled water held to the same regulatory standards? Explain.
5. What does it mean to say that many places worldwide have recently witnessed the "accumulation" of their freshwater supplies?

Exercise 15.1   Thinking with Life Cycle Assessment

As described in this chapter, a life cycle assessment is a highly quantitative and rigorous way to trace the environmental impacts of a product, service, or object from its point of manufacture to its disposal as waste. Take the case of bottled water or some other object you interact with daily that is accessed somewhere across the globe and purchased and consumed where you live. Tracing the life of the product in your imagination, list all of the possible impacts that this product has on the environment at every step along the way. What are some of the most hidden costs or externalities of this production? Remember to consider access to the resources, manufacturing of any components, and the ultimate fate of the product. What alternatives might there be for any of these steps or hidden costs?

Exercise 15.2   Social Construction of Bottled Water

In this chapter, we have reviewed how the puzzle of bottled water might be addressed in terms of population, risk, and political economy. Explain how you might understand this problem using a social construction framework (as described in Chapter 8). You may want to consider, in particular, the way bottle labels actually *look*. What images and text are utilized? What ideas of nature, geography, and history do they invoke? How does this matter to the way consumers think about themselves and the product? With what implications for the environment?

Exercise 15.3   A Bottled Water Taste Test

Perform a blind taste test of water from the tap and one or two brands of bottled water (yes, we are asking you to buy water; but this is for science). Can you tell the difference in taste between them? What do you think the taste differences, if you can tell, reflect? If possible, go to the website for your municipal water provider. What is in your water and in what qualities? How, if at all, does this differ from the contents of the bottled water you sampled? Does knowing any of this encourage you or discourage you from really buying or consuming bottled water?

References

Anadu, E. C., and A. K. Harding (2000). "Risk perception and bottled water use." *Journal of the American Water Works Association* 92(11): 82–92.

Bakker, K. (2004). *An Uncooperative Commodity: Privatizing Water in England and Wales*. Oxford: Oxford University Press.

Beverage Marketing Corporation (2009). *Beverage Marketing's 2007 Market Report Findings*. International Bottled Water Association 2009 [cited April 3, 2009]. Retrieved April 3, 2009, from www.bottledwater.org/public/statistics_main.htm.

Doria, M. F. (2006). "Bottled water versus tap water: Understanding consumers' preferences." *Journal of Water and Health* 4(2): 271–6.

Grand Rapids Press (2007). "Ruling dampens challenge to water rights; Group can't sue over Nestlé's private land, court says." *Grand Rapids Press*, July 26, p. A1.

Hunt, C. E. (2004). *Thirsty Planet*. New York: Zed Books.

Landi, H. (2008). "Bottled water report." *Beverage World* 127(4): S12–14.

Marketing Week (2005). "Profits flow in from bottled-water market." *Marketing Week* 24.

Napier, G. L., and C. M. Kodner (2008). "Health risks and benefits of bottled water." *Primary Care* 35(4): 789–802.

Nessi, S., L. Rigamonti, and M. Grosso (2012). "LCA of waste prevention activities: A case study for drinking water in Italy." *Journal of Environmental Management*, 108, 73–83.

Päster, P. (2009). "Exotic bottled water." Retrieved April 3, 2009, from www.triplepundit.com/pages/askpablo-exotic-1.php.

Rogers, P. (1996). *America's Water*. Boston, MA: MIT Press.

Suggested Reading

Gleick, P. H. (2011). *Bottled and Sold: The Story Behind Our Obsession with Bottled Water*. Washington, DC: Island Press.

Opel, A. (1999). "Constructing purity: Bottled water and the commodification of nature." *The Journal of American Culture* 22(4): 67–76.

Royte, E. (2008). *Bottlemania: How Water Went on Sale and Why We Bought It*. New York: Bloomsbury USA.

Senior, D. A. G., and N. Dege (eds.) (2005). *Technology of Bottled Water*. Oxford: Wiley Blackwell.

Wilk, R. (2006). "Bottled water: The pure commodity in the age of branding." *Journal of Consumer Culture* 6(3): 303–25.

16

French Fries

Source: johnfoto18/Shutterstock.

Keywords

- Anthropocentrism
- Columbian Exchange
- Conservation
- Ecocentrism
- Genome
- Globalization
- Hazard
- Monoculture
- Preservation

Chapter Menu

Environment and Society: A Critical Introduction, Second Edition. Paul Robbins, John Hintz, and Sarah A. Moore.
© 2014 John Wiley & Sons, Ltd. Published 2014 by John Wiley & Sons, Ltd.

Getting Your French Fry Fix

You are driving down the interstate, on your way home from school on vacation. You think you packed enough food for the trip. But, the more exits that whiz by, the more the roadside restaurants call to you. Golden arches lure you with the promise of hot, crispy French fries – just the thing to get you through the next couple of hours on the road (and more attractive than the sandwich you managed to pack in your post-exam haze). Try as you might to avoid it, you soon find yourself in the McDonald's drive-through, waiting with a dozen other cars. Unfortunately, you've managed to stop right at lunch hour.

Lucky for you, though, as is true of most stores in the mega-brand, this particular McDonald's has one person on fry duty for the whole lunch rush. For 90 minutes or more, your counterpart on the inside pours the required amount of perfectly cut, almost uniform, frozen fries into the fry basket and drops them in hot vegetable oil. After a couple of minutes, when the timer rings and the fries are just the right color, the basket is removed from the oil and the fries are dumped into the adjacent warming area, where they are sprinkled with a generous dose of salt. From there, the fries are scooped into a range of differently sized packets – medium, large, and the one you ordered, supersized. This process is repeated hundreds of times during a typical lunch hour.

The line has moved efficiently and before long, you've paid the cashier and driven to the second window. Here, you are handed a white bag with a familiar logo on it containing your supersized order of fries, some packets of ketchup and salt, and a few napkins. As you drive away, you wrestle with a system for salting and putting ketchup on your fries one-handed, while keeping your eyes on the road and one hand on the wheel. When you are finally able to take the first bite, you find the fries to be just as you imagined them – hot, crispy, salty – yummm!

You, and the millions like you, who consume French fries every day have become part of the billions served. Not just in the United States, but around the world. Sure, the particulars change – in England you order chips and get salt and vinegar to eat them with, in Mexico, you can get a side of jalapeno salsa to put on your *papas fritas* – but the fries themselves are reliably, dependably, the same.

What does it take to produce this uniformity around the world? How does your super-sized bag of fries connect you, not only to millions of consumers across the globe, but also to the environment? These are the questions that will be answered in this chapter. First, you will learn the history of the French fry, from the lowly and much maligned potato to the mass-produced perfectly formed treat of today. Next, by applying what you learned in Chapters 5, 6, and 7, you will gain an understanding of how the puzzle of the modern fry might be examined using a risk approach, a political economy approach, or an ethics approach.

A Short History of the Fry

To understand the French fry as an environmental puzzle one must first understand its most important raw material – the potato. Today the potato is the world's fourth largest crop, after corn, wheat, and rice; in 2005, more than 323 million tonnes of potatoes were produced worldwide. Most of this production is for food. While fresh potatoes are still consumed around the globe, much of the world's potato production is used for frozen potato products, a high percentage of which are the fries supplied to restaurants. About 10 million tons of frozen fries are consumed in the world each year. Fries are the top exported US potato product; more than half of the potatoes grown in the United States are exported as fries and in 2009, more than 3 billion pounds of frozen French fries were exported.

Wild potatoes are inedible, bitter, and toxic – a far cry from the Russet Burbank used for French fries today. In this section, we will trace the history of the potato from the many varieties that were dietary staples of the indigenous people of South America, to the domesticated **monoculture** of the industrial potato of today. Along the way, the journey of the potato highlights a history of colonization, the emergence of industrial agriculture, **globalization**, and an increasing distance between food production and food consumption.

> **Monoculture**   A single crop cultivated to the exclusion of any other potential harvest
>
> **Globalization**   An ongoing process by which regional economies, societies, and cultures have become integrated through a globe-spanning network of exchange
>
> **Columbian Exchange**   The movement of species across the Atlantic Ocean, from the New World to the Old World and vice versa, and the resulting ecological transformations

What a long, strange trip it's been: Cultivation and use of *Solanum tuberosum*, from the New World, to the Old, and back again

The potato was first domesticated 7,000 years ago on the Andean altiplano where several varieties grew wild. There were blue potatoes, red potatoes, yellow and orange potatoes in myriad shapes, which ranged in flavor from bitter to buttery to sweet. Andean peoples developed a spud to suit each environment, encouraging variety and increasing the heartiness of the crop. In addition to purposeful cross-cultivation, domesticated potatoes continued to be hybridized with local weed potatoes.

When the Spanish arrived in South America, they acquired not only silver, gold, and dyes, but also many new foodstuffs that were then introduced to Europe, as part of what is called the **Columbian Exchange**, the movement of species from the New World to the Old World across the Atlantic and vice versa, with all the ecological transformations that this entailed (Figure 16.1).

The potato's first significant foothold in Europe was Ireland, where it arrived in 1588. Though adapted to the climate, the potato carried with it a load of cultural baggage that discouraged its spread into other European countries for the next century. The new food was suspected of causing leprosy and encouraging immorality. The fact that it grew underground was also viewed as suspicious, along with the fact that it had come from "backwards" uncultured tribes in the Americas. Racist assumptions associated with the experience of colonialism left traces on food. Moreover, the colonization of Ireland by England during the nineteenth century meant that, once again, the potato was associated with the history of a people constructed (see Chapter 8) as inferior to the English. On the other hand, the potato also allowed the Irish to support themselves, rather than having to rely on their more powerful and economically dominant colonizers. The potato was easy to grow and

Figure 16.1 Transfer and spread of the potato after the Columbian Exchange.

to maintain. It did not have to be grown in straight rows (like the cereal crops popular on the continent), and could grow in marginal environments, the kinds to which Irish cultivators were relegated by English colonialism.

The potato continued to spread to continental Europe as some cereal crops began to fail. Despite initial resistance to the crop among the elite and the peasants alike, European royalty began to see the potato as a way to keep their subjects fed. In Germany, Frederick the Great forced peasants to grow them, as did Catherine the Great in Russia. In 1794, the wheat crop across Northern Europe failed and the use of the potato as a fill-in was considered. After a series of debates about the foodstuff, the practical need to keep people fed won out and the English did adopt the potato.

Meanwhile, Irish dependence on the potato, or more precisely, on a single cultivar, commonly known as the lumper, proved to be fatal. In the late summer of 1845, and again in 1847 and 1848, a disease caused by the pathogen *Phytophthora infestans* arrived on the island and devastated the potato crop, which was made especially vulnerable owing to the monoculture of a single variety. One million people died, and thousands more were ill over the three years. This resulted in a massive outmigration from Ireland to the United States.

The Irish had already brought potatoes (back!) to the Americas in the century before the potato famine. The potato was not, however, widely grown or eaten in America until after 1872. In that year, American horticulturalist Luther Burbank (1849–1926) developed what we recognize as the standard Idaho spud, the Russet Burbank potato. Burbank, improving on the varieties that had been brought to the United States by Scotch Irish settlers, developed a potato with a russeted skin that was more resistant to disease. In the 1900s, the Russet Burbank was a widespread crop in Idaho. The total value of the potato market in Idaho in 1882 was $250,000. Just over 20 years later, in 1904, the value of the potato crop in Idaho came in at over $1.3 million.

The advent of the fry and the American century

Despite the slow spread of the potato, long viewed as a lowly and possibly poisonous food, methods of cooking the potato had been developed and refined throughout Europe. There is a longstanding debate over whether the French or the Belgians were the first to fry potatoes. In either case, it was not until the early twentieth century, when American soldiers back from serving in Europe in World War I demanded them, that the fried potato became popular in the United States.

At the time that war veterans demanded them, frying potatoes was a task better undertaken in a restaurant with sufficient equipment to do it. It is at this point, therefore, that the history of the French fry becomes irrevocably entangled with the emergence of new types of dining experience: drive-through and fast-food restaurants. The first drive-through restaurant opened in Dallas in 1921 (Plummer 2002) and the growing number of automobiles on the road in this period fueled the trend, which exploded after World War II.

In 1951, milkshake salesman Ray Kroc went to Richard and Maurice McDonald, owners of a fast-food emporium in San Bernadino, California, with a proposal. In 1955 the first McDonald's outlet opened in Des Plaines, Illinois on the outskirts of Chicago. A second and then a third outlet quickly followed. By 1965 there were 700 McDonald's restaurants across the United States.

In the following decades, frozen French fries, pioneered by McDonald's, became wildly popular in the United States. In 1960 consumers in the United States ate about four pounds of frozen French fries per year and about 81 pounds of fresh potatoes. Four decades later, in 2000, they ate about 30 pounds of frozen fries a year and 50 pounds of fresh potatoes (Schlosser 2001). McDonald's today is still the largest buyer of potatoes in the United States. This is not surprising given that trade sources estimate that 90 percent of the potatoes consumed in the United States today are sold by fast-food franchises. Nor is this a phenomenon particular to the United States. Worldwide exports of frozen potato products (of which 90 percent are fries) were valued at almost 2 billion dollars in 2000 (Yen et al. 2007).

The demands of the Russet Burbank and contemporary frozen French fry production

The increasing popularity of fast food and the need for a constant supply of frozen potatoes have been a boon for the Russet Burbank. Though, as discussed above, the Russet Burbank is a relatively recent cultivar, only one of countless potato varieties domesticated in the Andes and bred around the globe in the centuries since, it is now the dominant potato throughout the world.

Despite its popularity, the Russet Burbank is not easy to grow. Or, at least, it is not easy to produce specimens appropriate to the frozen fry industry, which requires uniformity in size and shape. Mass production of the Russet Burbank for the frozen fry industry requires multiple inputs, including water, chemicals, and energy (Table 16.1).

Table 16.1   Energy inputs and costs of potato production per hectare in the United States.

Inputs	Quantity	Kcal	Costs ($)
Labor	35 hours	1,964,000	350.00
Machinery	31 kg	574,000	300.00
Diesel	152 L	1,735,000	31.92
Gasoline	272 L	2,750,000	78.88
Nitrogen	231 kg	4,292,000	142.60
Phosphorus	220 kg	911,000	121.00
Potassium	111 kg	362,000	34.41
Seeds	2408 kg	1,478,000	687.00
Sulfuric acid	64.8 kg	0	73.00
Herbicides	1.5 kg	150,000	13.50
Insecticides	3.6 kg	360,000	14.40
Fungicides	4.5 kg	450,000	180.00
Electricity	47 kWh	135,000	3.29
Transportation	2779 kg	2,307,000	833.70
Total		17,470,000	2863.70
Potato yield	40,656 kg	23,296,000	Kcal input/output 1:1.33

Source: Data from Pimentel et al. (2002).

Consider the steps one potato farmer listed in Michael Pollan's *Botany of Desire: A Plant's Eye View of the World* (2001). First, he applies a soil fumigant that kills all microbial life in the soil. Next, during planting a systemic insecticide is added. Third, when the plant is six inches tall, it gets an herbicide. After this, the plant receives weekly cycles of chemical fertilizers. This is followed by a fungicide when the rows begin to close. Often, the next step is to use crop dusting to protect against pests like aphids. During all of this, of course, the crop also requires from 500 to 700 mm of water (Food and Agriculture Organization). Though this is not as much water as many cereal crops need, it still averages about six gallons of water to produce one serving of French fries. Add to this the cost of irrigation and energy and the average cost per acre to the commercial potato farmer is $1,950. Fast-food companies will pay $2,000 for the 20 tons of potatoes that are produced on each acre. Given this very slim margin, it is hard for farmers to get off of the input "treadmill." Even if farmers would like to switch to other varieties, they cannot because fast-food suppliers demand that they produce Russet Burbanks, so they are forced to do what they can to make this work. They have little choice but to keep adding more and more chemicals, water, and energy, even if it produces only marginally better results.

The puzzle of French fries

French fries are ubiquitous. As such, they represent an object that certainly seems straight-forward. Take a potato, cut it, fry it, voilà! But, as we have seen in the above socio-natural history, there is much more to the fry than meets the eye (or the mouth!). Several major characteristics, then, of the French fry as an environmental puzzle must be taken into account:

- Not just any potato can become a fry. The mass production and consumption of the French fry demands a select breed of potato that can stand up to industrial production and that behaves the way that we expect when we slice and fry it. This leads to a virtual monoculture of a single variety of potatoes around the world.
- Russel Burbank production is tied to increasing intensification of cultivation, with widespread environmental implications, including high inputs of water, fertilizer, and pesticides.
- The French fry is a cultural phenomenon, one whose immense popularity is wrapped up with the advent of the car and fast food, and the homogenizing processes of globalization.
- The expectation of such homogenous "French fries" leads to heavy processing of the potato in fast-food production.

The environmental puzzle of the French fry is therefore that its universal success in diverse contexts (from Slovenia to Guam) has led to a system of production that is anything but diverse. This allows us to think about the connection between how we make what we eat and how we remake the environments in which we must live. In the following sections, we consider the implications of this puzzle, beginning with French fry consumption as a matter of food choices. Here, we can begin to understand how what we put in our body is often tied to a complex process of risk assessment. These individual choices, though, take place in a context of consumption and production on a societal and global scale. Therefore, the socio-environmental puzzle of French fries may also be approached through political economy frameworks. Finally, we consider how the need to produce more and more mass-marketed food products like French fries presents us with difficult questions about the ethics of food production.

Risk Analysis: Eating What We Choose and Choosing What We Eat

In Chapter 6, we discussed how socio-environmental puzzles might be explained in a framework of hazards and risks. In this section, we consider how such a framework sheds light on efforts to mitigate the impacts of the French fry on the human body. McDonald's was sued in 2005 by the group Ban Trans Fats (BTF). They claimed that the fast-food chain had not followed up on promises it made to consumers in 2002, when the company promised to reduce the use of trans fats (the common name for a type of unsaturated fat containing trans-isomer fatty acids – also called partially hydrogenated vegetable oil) in its products. The company settled the suit and donated 1.9 million dollars to the American Heart Association (AHA; see the archives of the organization at www.bantransfats.com for a history of the movement).

Why was there so much pressure on this and other fast-food restaurants to switch from trans fats to more healthy fats to fry their food? Because, increasingly, the use of trans fats became an unacceptable risk to individual consumers of fast food, and at an aggregate level, a burden on people's health.

Dietary and nutrition sciences have long addressed the role of food in human health and our understanding of the effects that food has on human bodies has changed throughout the centuries. Notably today, our assessment of the health risks (the possible negative consequences) of consuming certain foods is increasingly shaped by different understandings of food and nutrition. Nutritional information, and our access to it, has influenced some consumers' willingness to eat certain foods.

In the case of trans fats, how has the level of risk involved in eating French fries been established by scientists and communicated to the public? How do people, given this type of information, make decisions about what they eat? And, if there are risks associated with food choices, whose responsibility is it to mitigate those risks?

The science of good and bad fats

Hazard An object, condition, or process that threatens individuals and society in terms of production or reproduction

While trans fats may not be what we think of as a typical environmental **hazard** (like a tsunami or nuclear accident, for example – as discussed in Chapter 6), they are a possible threat to human health. Trans fats come from a process of hydrogenization. Hydrogenization is a process of using pressure to force hydrogen atoms into unsaturated fatty acids such as vegetable fats and oils. Partial hydrogenization is the process of adding hydrogen atoms until a food is at a desired consistency. The process was first developed in the 1890s by a French chemist, who was later awarded the Nobel Prize. The use of hydrogenization to produce stable cooking oils was developed and patented in 1902 by Wilhelm Normann. Soon after, trans fats became the first *human-made* fats to enter the food supply. In 1911, Procter and Gamble began selling Crisco, the first widely available trans fat product in grocery stores. At first, Crisco and its competitors (e.g., margarine) were not widely used. It was not until the rationing of butter during World War II that margarine and other trans fat products were widely adopted.

In 1957, the AHA declared that saturated fats, like those in butter and other animal products, were a factor in heart disease. This meant that, in terms of human health, trans fats were positioned as a less risky alternative. Acting on this information, in 1984 consumer advocacy groups were successful in getting fast-food restaurants, many of which used beef tallow in their fryers, to switch to trans fats instead. The use of such oils skyrocketed. Given the ever-increasing popularity of fast food, trans fats became a significant part of the typical American, and to some extent the European, diet.

But, even though many people argued that trans fats were the healthier alternative, several scientific studies in the early 1990s associated the use of trans fats with a rise in what we now call bad (LDL – low density lipoprotein) cholesterol. Increased levels of LDL were associated not only with heart disease, but also with diabetes and a host of other serious ailments. Before the decade was over, legislation was proposed in the United States to make food producers list the amount of trans fats on nutrition labels. This was not passed. In 2003, however, Denmark went a step further than requiring labeling. They actually put a cap on the amount of trans fats in certain foods. That same year, due to continued consumer activism, the US Food and Drug Administration began requiring that manufacturers list trans fats on nutrition labels. While many food manufacturers and restaurants, including fast-food chains, reduced their use of trans fats, not all did so to the satisfaction of lobbying groups like BTF. This resulted in law suits, like the one that opened this section.

Better information, healthier choices?

As information about the health risks of dietary choices changed, individuals adjusted their behavior to account for these. One source of this information is the AHA, who started a "Face the Fats" consumer education campaign in April of 2007. To assess the success of this and similar campaigns, the AHA commissioned a study to track people's understandings and perceptions of trans fats and the impact that these had on eating behaviors. The study, undertaken by a group of medical doctors, nutrition experts, and marketing researchers, concluded that awareness about trans fats among the American public increased. Researchers found that between 2006 and 2007, consumer concerns over both total fat content and the types of fat in foods increased (Figure 16.2). During the same period, news coverage of trans fats doubled, from 516 articles to 1,138. The percentage of people who identified trans fats as a potential contributor to heart disease also increased, with 73 percent of people responding that this fat source increases one's risk of heart disease. In this case, increased information and awareness also changed respondents' behaviors. Significantly more people said that they reviewed trans fat information before making purchases, looked for "zero trans fat" labels, and substituted zero or low trans fat products.

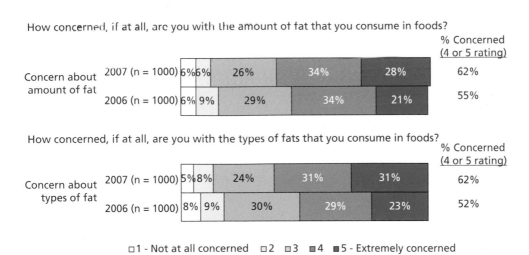

Figure 16.2 Concern over amount and types of fat. *Source*: Reprinted from *Journal of the American Dietetic Association*, 109:2, Eckel, R. H., P. Kris-Etherton, et al., Americans' awareness, knowledge, and behaviors regarding fats: 2006–2007, 288–96, Copyright (2009) with permission from Elsevier and the American Dietetic Association.

At the same time, more people knew which common foods contained trans fats. French fries, in this case, were most often identified as containing trans fats. People were beginning to think about trans fats and French fries, in a big way.

Risk, choice, and regulation

Knowledge does not always lead to changes in behavior, however. For example, one study of midsized cities indicated that certain groups of women identified fast-food restaurants as hazards in their neighborhood (Colapinto et al. 2007). That study also found, though, that despite knowing the risks that fast-food consumption poses to their health, people still choose to eat in these restaurants. The long-term risks are not significant, or immediate, enough to outweigh the convenience of these foods for many people. Unlike a salmonella infestation, a melamine contamination, or a food allergy – all risks that typically produce immediate, noticeable behavioral changes in consumers – the negative consequences of a diet high in French fries and other fast foods are experienced long after that food is consumed. So, even though better information is available, the risks posed by fry consumption do not always produce the immediate (gut reaction!) responses.

While it is easy to blame people for their eating behaviors, and more recently to vilify heavier people for everything from lower productivity to strains on the health care system (Guthman and DuPuis 2006), the social, economic, and political contexts in which food choices are made represent a significant influence that cannot be ignored. In the study on trans fats mentioned above, for example, even though awareness of the health effects of such fats increased overall, neither this awareness nor associated behavioral change was evenly distributed across all groups. They were more concentrated among women, 45 or older, who have at least some college education, incomes of $75,000 or higher, and who live in the Northeast or the South.

So, what is to be done? Given the proven risks of eating a diet high in French fries and other fast food and the public health concerns over the "epidemic" of obesity, how do we make decisions about who should eat what? Should individual choice and free markets determine eating behavior? Or, is an aggregate level of public health enough of a reason to ban important components of such fast-food staples as French fries? While many would argue the former, as of 2008 approximately 20 states and local jurisdictions had proposals for reducing trans fats in restaurants or schools and 11 cities and counties had adopted regulations to restrict trans fats in restaurants. One reason that many people turn to regulation to control such hazards and mitigate the risks associated with them is that often, we do not *really* have a choice about the foods we consume. Rather, our selections are driven by political-economic contexts outside of our direct control. In other words, a political economy of food, in this case the fry, is at work. We will examine this in the next section.

Political Economy: Eat Fries or Else!

In Chapter 7, we discussed the insights that a political economy framework can provide in thinking about environmental puzzles. One key to this framework is to think about how socio-environmental objects are wrapped up in the drive for the creation of surplus value in a capitalist system. This process of surplus value production and circulation holds true as much for the food we consume as it does for the tennis shoes we buy. In this section we will see how, if we frame the environmental puzzle of the French fry as a problem of political economy, we could ask questions not only about the food choices that people make, but also about how those are related to broader socioeconomic conditions, including fast-food marketing, the concentration of fast-food restaurants in marginalized communities, the globalization of fast-food restaurants, and the food production system itself.

You want what we say you want – marketing and food choices

Whenever you walk into a fast-food restaurant, chances are someone asks you "What would you like?" Some places even let you "have it your way." And, whether you answer immediately (fries and a shake, please!) or it takes you a while (um, well, I guess I'll have the Value Meal with chicken strips and a cola), the choice is yours. Darn the consequences – I'll have that apple pie! Or – wait, I'm going to the beach next week – better make that a diet cola! But, is it really so simple? Is it just that you've *weighed* your options and made the appropriate choice? Or, is something else going on? What makes us choose the food we do?

Of course, dieticians, nutritionists, medical doctors, weight loss counselors, gym trainers, psychologists, and beauty magazine editors all espouse theories accounting for people's behaviors. Psychological conditions (stress!), nutrient deficiency, lack of exercise, overabundance of certain hormones, or peer pressure, many sources argue, get in the way of making rational food choices. All individuals need to do is make more *rational* choices.

But, to what degree are such choices individual in the first place? Are your food choices shaped by marketing, including not just commercial advertisements, but other subtle selling points, like portion sizing?

The development of fast food was an exercise in branding. Early fast-food restaurants were identified by the distinctive shape of their buildings, as they are today. When you see golden arches on a road sign, you know what to expect. This is true because with this branding comes standardization of products. Chances are you know the difference between a Quarter Pounder with Cheese, a Whopper, a Junior Deluxe, and a Double Double without giving it much thought. But, what makes you choose one over the other, or over different options? Not surprisingly, advertising exposure and acceptance are key determinants in who eats fast food, and where they eat it. Knowing this, fast-food restaurants spend a lot of money on advertising each year. They must do this, because competition among different firms leads to lower surpluses, unless a business can somehow compensate for the potential loss of customers. In many cases, companies can maintain surpluses by cutting labor costs. But, branding allows firms to try to maintain a loyal customer group by differentiating their products from others that are basically the same.

Once the restaurant has lured you in, it may find other, sometimes more subtle ways to ensure profits. What, for example, ever happened to the small-sized fry? The much-discussed practice of supersizing is often used to increase profit margins. As this practice has become more widespread (even though it was condemned in the popular movie *Super-size Me*), our own notions of portion size change. There is some evidence that children exposed to fast-food advertising begin to view these super-portions as the norm (Schlosser 2001). Good, perhaps, for the bottom line, but not the waistline. Well, all's fair in business, you might say. Even if advertising influences our choices, we can still opt for healthier food if we really want or need to. Of course you can, *unless*, by dint of where you live and work, you have no healthier choices.

Demand or supply: The geography of fast food

According to Eric Schlosser, author of *Fast Food Nation: The Dark Side of the All-American Meal*, Americans spent six billion dollars on fast food in 1970 and more than 110 billion in 2000. The French fry is the most widely sold foodservice item in the United States. Almost half of the money spent on food in the United States today is spent in restaurants, mostly fast-food restaurants. None of this is particularly surprising. What might be more surprising to some is that the availability of fast food (and especially healthier alternatives) varies greatly by where people live. Numerous studies have shown that not only does fast-food advertising get concentrated in certain places, but also that the actual restaurants themselves have patterns to their locations.

Many poor neighborhoods exhibit a high density of fast-food restaurants, meaning that the number of restaurants located in that area is higher than the number of such restaurants in other communities of the same size. In a review of the available literature on restaurant density, socioeconomic indicators, and obesity rates, Larson et al. (2009) found that neighborhood residents who have better access to supermarkets and limited access to convenience stores tend to have healthier diets and lower levels of obesity. Conversely, there was evidence that residents with limited access to fast-food restaurants have healthier diets and lower levels of obesity. Further, residents of low-income, minority, and rural neighborhoods were most often affected by poor access to supermarkets and healthful food, while the availability of fast-food restaurants and energy-dense foods has been found to be greater in lower-income and minority neighborhoods. From these data, the authors concluded that policy intervention is necessary to assure equitable access to healthy foods (Apple 1996; Larson et al. 2009). So, what may appear as individual choices about food consumption are directly related to political and economic factors.

We need more fries!!!

Whether we believe that our individual decisions are influenced by psychology, marketing, or the spatial distribution of choice, what is clear is that what we put in our bodies has repercussions, not just for us, but for society and environment at a global scale. In a book called *Education, Identity, and Cheap French Fries*, Michael Apple (1996), an expert in critical pedagogy, tells the sad story of one such effect. He is visiting a friend and colleague in what he calls a "remote Asian country." They are driving through heat, humidity, and glaring sun, down a two-lane road. He is jarred from his internal musings over higher education by a familiar sign on the side of the road. The sign, for him, is too familiar. It is

Box 16.1   Environmental Solution? Slow Food

A typical meal in the United States may last only a few short minutes. Ironically, the length of time and distance over which the components of the food probably come is likely far larger. Indeed, the average lunch might be a heavily imported affair; consider that food imports to the United States include not only vegetables and fruits but also poultry, beef, seafood, and dairy. That lunch is also probably a heavily processed event, with the food likely worked over with fillers, treated for preservation, frozen, and then reconstituted, heated, and served. The convenience of this kind of food is undeniable, but its costs are harder to measure, on health (preservatives are not always good for you), on the environment (every road mile food travels requires carbon emissions), and on your psyche (can you really fully enjoy a meal like that?).

Founded in the 1980s to counter the trend toward this kind of eating and living, the Slow Food movement was established based on the principle that a meal should be: "Good," in the sense of its quality as food and experience, "Clean," in the sense that it should have a light environmental footprint in terms of the way it was both grown and prepared, and "Fair," in the sense that it promotes socially just food economies.

In terms of the personal and experiential part of the meal, Slow Food should be patiently waited for, and consumed at a leisurely pace. It therefore represents a change in the pace of typical modern lifestyles, drawing the brakes on the reckless momentum of our daily lives.

More radically, Slow Food proposes a totally new food economy, favoring the preservation of many disappearing local varieties of foods, from rare apples to special regional cheeses, and the defense of small-scale, local markets and craft farmers, rather than supermarkets and factory farms. It also stresses local preparation in small restaurants and kitchens. Though it began in Italy and thrives in Europe, the movement is making great inroads in the United Kingdom and the United States.

A possible criticism of the Slow Food movement, at least as it has been advanced so far, is that it can be elitist. United States federal law does not actually require breaks for workers, though it does require that any such breaks be compensated. Lunch breaks for the average worker last 30 minutes and are uncompensated. Organic foods are often more expensive than more generally available varieties. Many poor people do not even live within a short drive of a grocery store. Who can afford the time and money for Slow Food, one might ask? A new food economy, therefore, will have to address fundamental problems of wealth and work time around the world as it tackles the way we eat.

Even so, Slow Food's growing popularity suggests that people are increasingly interested in reclaiming not only environmental sustainability but also simple joys in their daily lives, pointing to a possible happy convergence of new kinds of societies and environments in the future.

Source: Petrini and Padovani (2006)

the iconic symbol of an American fast-food restaurant that he is careful not to name. Surprised and confused, he asks his friend, a local fellow, what the sign is doing there. Surely there is no such restaurant around here. But, his friend is also surprised; he says to him "Michael, you don't know what these signs signify? . . . These signs signify exactly what is wrong with education in this nation" (p. 2).

His friend then describes how the country, in an effort to lure foreign investment, had offered large tracts of land to international agribusinesses. The land they were driving through had been bought up cheap by a potato grower and supplier of French fries for the restaurant whose signs they had passed. The company, of course, had jumped at the chance to grow potatoes cheaper. There was only one problem – hundreds of people lived on that

Table 16.2   World potato production, 1991–2007.

Countries	1991	1993	1995	1997	1999	2001	2003	2005	2007
	Million tonnes								
Developed	183.13	199.31	177.47	174.63	165.93	166.93	160.97	159.97	159.89
Developing	84.86	101.95	108.50	128.72	135.15	145.92	152.11	160.01	165.41
Total	267.99	301.26	285.97	303.35	301.08	312.85	313.08	319.98	325.30

Source: Reproduced from www.potato2008.org/en/world/index.html (Data from FAOSTAT).

land. The government pushed the people, few of whom had formal deeds, despite having lived there for hundreds of years, off the land. Progress, in the form of intensive potato production, had come to the region. But, this progress had costs beyond the loss of subsistence farming on which hundreds of people had depended. Because the company was given tax breaks as incentives to locate potato production there, there was no money to attend to public services like utilities or schools. "Michael," his friend concluded, "there's no schools because folks like cheap French fries" (p. 4).

The need, on the part of fast-food companies, to continue to extract surplus value required the internationalization, not only of fry consumption, but also of its production. Internationally, more potatoes are now produced in the developing world than in the developed (FAO 2008) for the first time in several centuries (see Table 16.2). While some of this is for local consumption, many of the potatoes grown in these places are meant for the frozen fry market. As we see in Apple's example above, this can be a driving factor in landscape change.

As smallholders and subsistence growers are pushed off the land to make room for factory farming, the countryside switches from a landscape of diversity to one of large-scale monoculture. As we have seen above, monocultural potato production for the French fry market requires numerous inputs, including chemical fertilizers, pesticides, water, and energy. The amount of inputs required also increases when the crop is not indigenous to the area in which it is being grown. So, imagine the experience of the Idaho potato farmer on the input treadmill (described above) being replicated across the globe. While some might argue that this can be addressed by markets and contracts (Chapter 3), a political economist would see this as a problem of environmental justice. Is it fair that people in a small Asian country lose their livelihoods and find their soils and streams polluted so that other people can have cheap fries?

Such questions of justice, while the purview of political economic approaches, might easily be thought of in ethical terms, especially if they are extended to the condition of the non-human world. In this case, how has the French fry's transformation of agriculture led to changes in environments around the world, and what are human responsibilities, especially concerning global biodiversity, in the wake of the Russet Burbank revolution? When we feed the world, what do we owe the planet? In the next section, we will explore these issues by considering the socio-natural puzzle of the French fry through the lens of an ethics approach.

Ethics: Protecting or Engineering Potato Heritage?

In Chapter 5, we discussed ethical approaches to environmental issues. This approach raised questions about environmental values and how we might measure and attempt to balance them against human demands. A large part of debates over these issues centers on the value of species and species diversity. In this section we will emphasize the ethical questions, especially regarding biodiversity, that may surround the French fry.

Agrodiversity

An ethical approach to the puzzle of the French fry might begin by taking us back to the Andes and the many varieties of potatoes domesticated there. As the potato made its journey to Europe and then back to the Americas, new varieties were developed, but more were lost. The Irish lumper potato was once dominant across the globe. Now, it has virtually disappeared while today's most prevalent potato species, the Russet Burbank used in the frozen fry market, has reached a level of dominance that is virtually unprecedented (Pollan 2001).

This holds ecological implications. We discussed monoculture and the intense inputs it requires. These inputs are necessary, not only to produce a consistent specimen, and thus to satisfy commercial demands, but also *to protect the species from its own success*. The more a species is encouraged to exist on its own, and the less biodiversity and crop diversity allowed in its production system, the more susceptible it is to widespread disease and other forms of crop failure. By planting vast monocultural and input-intensive tracts of Russet Burbanks, we have aided in the elimination of other crop species and created environmental conditions that are often bad for surrounding ambient ecosystems (a violation of an **ecocentric** approach to environmental ethics). We have also doomed our crops to potential failure, however, endangering food supplies for human populations (a violation of an **anthropocentric** valuing of nature). Remember, after all, that the Irish lumper suffered from *Phytophthora infestans* as a monoculture; one million people died, and thousands more fell ill.

> **Ecocentrism** An environmental ethical stance that argues that ecological concerns should, over and above human priorities, be central to decisions about right and wrong action (compare to anthropocentrism)
>
> **Anthropocentrism** An ethical standpoint that views humans as the central factor in considerations of right and wrong action in and toward nature (compare to ecocentrism)

Whether we define our environmental ethics in ecological or anthropocentric terms, it is clear that we face a question of right action. How do we think about and remedy the decline in agrodiversity engendered by the global corporate agriculture of French fries? While there are a number of possible avenues, we will focus on two, both of which present further questions of their own. First, while international potato production is driven by the need for frozen fries and dominated by one species, groups in some areas are trying to recover species diversity, largely through local innovation and the search for alternative agricultural networks. Conversely, other interests are using controversial biotechnology to protect the Russet Burbank itself from disease, often trying to reduce the need for other inputs at the same time.

Rescuing diversity: Back to the future?

In the Andean mountains of Peru, where our story of the potato began, we can today find four species of potato under extensive cultivation by farmers, three of which are only found in the immediate region. In 2008, the government created a national potato registry to store genetic material from local varieties. This was done in response to concern over the threat to many indigenous species and varieties from commercial growing for urban and international populations. In addition to this, other steps toward species conservation have been taken.

Lino Mamani, a member of the Sacara farming community, has come together with people from five nearby communities to create a 12,000-acre potato park. They were able to do this with assistance from the International Potato Center. According to Mamani, there are about 1,000 varieties of potatoes in the park, 400 of which had to be planted from material from the International Potato Center. These potatoes are dispersed throughout the park to allow them to grow in the altitude to which they most easily adapt. Much like the ancient Incan farming system, each variety is allowed its own niche, but the varieties are allowed to grow side by side with their wild relatives. This enhances the resilience of the potato park. On the United Nations page for the Year of the Potato, Mamani describes it this way: "Our native varieties live well with their wild relatives, which you will find all around here. They have a good relationship, like a family. But our potatoes don't live well with modern varieties. The potatoes you see here belong to us. They came to us from our ancestors and will go on with our children" (Sullins 2001). He goes on to describe the many inputs required by commercial potatoes and the havoc they wreak on the local environment.

Projects like this one address the concern over species and varietal diversity, by bringing native species back to their original home. And, many people would argue that this is a good thing. But, such projects have their limits. To reproduce a "native" environment, many would argue that you must pick a moment in time to "go back to." True **preservationists** would look for a pristine nature from which all human activity should then be excluded. Such a preservationist ethic would say that this park might be a step in the right direction, but that it does not go far enough because it allows human use of the land and harvest.

> **Preservation**   The management of a resource or environment for protection and preservation, typically for its own sake, as in wilderness preservation (compare to conservation)
>
> **Conservation**   The management of a resource or system to sustain its productivity over time, typically associated with scientific management of collective goods like fisheries or forests (compare to preservation)

On the other hand, an argument from a **conservationist** also might not clearly fit. Here, while human use of land might be encouraged, this kind of park does not set as its goal either the maximization of the land's utility or the assurance of its future productivity for human use.

As a middle road, the establishment of a potato park might reflect a *land ethic* like that proposed by Aldo Leopold (see discussion in Chapter 5). Leopold's land ethic is between conservation and preservation and supports ideas of what we might call today sustainable agriculture. In this way, a potato park might be seen as a responsible solution to the environmental problem of species loss. The trick comes when you consider Leopold's famous maxim: "A thing is right when it tends to preserve the integrity, stability, and beauty of the biotic community. It is wrong when it tends otherwise." Who, in this case, gets to decide what is right and what is wrong? How do we measure the effect of species reintroduction on the "integrity, stability, and beauty of the biotic community"?

Whether you believe in preservation, conservation, or something in between (or none of the above, for that matter), we face different ethical questions when we consider what right action might be when people can, not just protect, but actually create and alter species.

Biotechnology

As a variety, it should be clear that Russet Burbank potatoes require a lot of inputs to produce those predictable uniform fries we all love. They are also susceptible to something called net *necrosis*, a potato disease that threatens to wipe out whole crops. But, because so much of the potato market is now in frozen potatoes, destined for fast-food chains, individual potato producers have little choice but to keep growing the Russet Burbank. In an attempt to make this variety a little more farmer (and environmentally) friendly, companies have turned to biotechnology. The result is genetically modified (GM) potatoes.

One example of this is the New Leaf potato, a now defunct variety developed by Monsanto. The New Leaf is basically a Russet Burbank, genetically engineered to produce its own pesticide. This is intended to stave off the Colorado potato beetle, which is a threat to commercial potato crops. The New Leaf produces bacteria (*Bacillus thuringiensis* or BT) which ward off pests, within the plant itself. The spud is itself actually registered as a pesticide with the Environmental Protection Agency (Pollan 2001).

The advantages here are potentially enormous. Fewer pesticides are necessary when growing this variety, making it a boon for both farmers (who are exposed to fewer chemicals) and the surrounding ecosystem as well.

There is uneasiness provoked, however, by the idea of producing and consuming such GM organisms (GMOs). Because these organisms have been developed and created by a person in a lab, companies patent them to limit their free spread. On the one hand this might be considered a good thing as the GMOs are not allowed to "contaminate" other species, but they often do get loose, as was the case with GM corn in southern Mexico. Here, despite assurances to the contrary, GMOs may actually present a threat to native, wild, or even other commercially grown species. Moreover, because these plants are patented, the farmer is not free to replant from his own stock year after year. He or she is legally required to continue buying new seeds and plants from the company, in this case Monsanto.

While humans have modified plants for a long time (native Andeans mixed strains of domesticated potatoes), new biotechnologies are now allowing us to do that at the level of the **genome**. From an ethical perspective, we can ask: Is this the right thing to do? We might be modifying potatoes and other crops to help us feed more people more efficiently, but how do we weigh this against our valuation of the natural world? Who decides what new species get to exist, and for what purposes? How do these new socionatural objects impact the rest of the physical world?

> **Genome** The complete set of genes of an organism, species, etc.

Although other BT species (like cotton) have met with more success, the New Leaf itself did not last long. McDonald's, one of the first promoters and large-scale buyers of this GM potato, was forced to abandon plans to use it in 2002, owing to consumer concerns. Apparently, that's one line consumers are not yet willing to cross to satisfy their hunger for cheap fries.

The French Fry Puzzle

In this chapter we have learned that:

- Frozen French fries, just like other foods, have a history that spans centuries and continents.
- Mass French fry production is intimately tied to the boom and spread of the fast-food industry from about the 1950s on.
- Not just any potato can become a fry. Mass production of frozen French fries demands a species that can be widely planted and that responds well to the conditions of commercial agriculture. When grown with significant inputs, including chemicals, water, and energy, the Russet Burbank is the perfect fry potato.
- Risk approaches to understanding the environmental puzzle of the French fry could focus first at the scale of the human body. What we put in our bodies is, in part, dependent on what, if any, negative consequences we might associate with it. Our assessment of risk is often influenced by larger societal contexts, including but not limited to the production of scientific knowledge.
- A political economy framework helps us to understand that fry consumption is not always as much as an individual choice as it seems. It is tied instead to broader political economic processes that influence the consumption and production of foods, often at a global scale.
- An ethics approach emphasizes the costs to biodiversity of the dominance of Russet Burbank potatoes over other varieties less suitable to mass commercial production. We might be able to protect ecological systems by reintroducing lost potato species. On the other hand, we may be able to make the Russet Burbank better through biotechnology, a controversial tool that allows us to change and create new species.

Questions for Review

1. The potato arrived in Europe via the "Columbian Exchange." Explain.
2. Describe some of the environmental costs of our voracious consumption of French fries.
3. Trace, from 1957 to the present, the "rise and fall" of trans fats.

4. How does the growing "McDonaldization" of developing countries spell more bad news for their small farmers? (This, despite the fact that all the new restaurants will, of course, be buying plenty of agricultural products grown on farms.)

5. Why (perhaps) should it concern us that, every year, the total global potato production is concentrated into increasingly fewer varieties of potatoes? Discuss the actions being taken in Peru in the face of this trend.

Exercise 16.1   Health Knowledge or Food Fads?

Trans fats became popular in the United States in the twentieth century as a *healthy* food alternative to dietary fats from animals, especially butter and beef tallow. Now we know trans fats to be potentially very harmful. Given that health information is always changing and being updated in the face of new information, what is the best way to assess *risk* in foods and make healthy food choices? What sources of information do you feel are most reliable? Why? What are the strongest influences on the kinds of information that are available to people? When faced with competing claims about food-related risks (from internet sites, for example), what is the most rational way to reconcile them?

Exercise 16.2   Market Solutions for Agrodiversity?

In this chapter, we have reviewed how the puzzle of French fries might be addressed in terms of risk, ethics, and political economy. Starting from the notion that markets can be harnessed for social and environmental good (as described in Chapter 3), how might we understand this problem differently? Specifically, consider the problem of crop diversity. Read this short example of the case of rice varieties (http://news.bbc.co.uk/2/hi/science/nature/7753267.stm) and answer the following: Are there market opportunities or pressures that might increase, rather than decrease the numbers of varieties of crops in the world? To what degree is there unmet demand for other kinds of foods and food production systems? How might supply be unleashed?

Exercise 16.3   What Makes French Fries So Cheap?

Consider the French fry from its inception as a potato plant to its eventual destination in your body. Try to list all the costs, paid and unpaid, along the line of production, transportation, and consumption that are incurred in making French fries (consider things like labor, environmental impacts, and so on). Once you have a produced an exhaustive list, consider who pays the cost of each. Is it the consumer, the retailer, the farmer? What costs go "unaccounted" and are externalized onto the public? Which costs are the most "hidden" or hardest to track or measure? If these costs were included in the price of French fries, how expensive do you imagine they might be?

References

Apple, M. W. (1996). *Education, Identity and Cheap French Fries*. New York: Teachers College Press.

Colapinto, C. K., A. Fitzgerald, et al. (2007). "Children's preference for large portions: Prevalence, determinants, and consequences." *Journal of the American Dietetic Association* 107(7): 1183–90.

Food and Agriculture Organization (FAO) (2008). "International Year of the Potato." Retrieved April 2009, from www.potato2008.org/en/perspectives/mamani.html.

Guthman, J., and M. DuPuis (2006). "Embodying neoliberalism: Economy, culture, and the politics of fat." *Environment and Planning D: Society and Space* 24(3): 427–48.

Larson, N. I., M. T. Story, et al. (2009). "Neighborhood environments: Disparities in access to healthy foods in the US." *American Journal of Preventive Medicine* 36(1): 74–81.

Petrini, C., and G. Padovani (2006). *Slow Food Revolution: A New Culture for Eating and Living*. New York: Rizzoli.

Pimentel, D., R. Doughty, C. Carothers, S. Lamberson, N. Bora, et al. (2002). "Energy inputs in crop production in developing and developed countries." In R. Lal, D. O. Hansen, N. Uphoff, and S. A. Slack (eds.) *Food Security and Environmental Quality in the Developing World*. Boca Raton, FL: CRC Press.

Plummer, C. (2002). "French fries driving globalization of frozen potato industry." *Frozen Food Digest* 18(2): 12–15.

Pollan, M. (2001). *The Botany of Desire: A Plant's Eye View of the World*. New York: Random House.

Schlosser, E. (2001). *Fast Food Nation: The Dark Side of the All-American Meal*. Boston, MA: Houghton Mifflin.

Sullins, T. (2001). *ESA: Endangered Species Act*. Chicago, IL: American Bar Association.

Yen, I. H., T. Scherzer, et al. (2007). "Women's perceptions of neighborhood resources and hazards related to diet, physical activity, and smoking: Focus group results from economically distinct neighborhoods in a mid-sized US city." *American Journal of Health Promotion* 22(2): 98–106.

Suggested Reading

Crosby, A. W. (1986). *Ecological Imperialism: The Biological Expansion of Europe, 900–1900*. Cambridge: Cambridge University Press.

Goodman, D., and M. Watts (2002). *Globalising Food: Agrarian Questions and Global Restructuring*. New York: Routledge.

Guthman, J. (2004). *Agrarian Dreams: The Paradox of Organic Farming in California*. Berkeley: University of California Press.

Kloppenburg, J. (1988). *First the Seed: The Political Economy of Plant Biotechnology*. Cambridge: Cambridge University Press.

Schlosser, E. (2002). *Fast Food Nation*. New York: Penguin.

17

E-Waste

Source: © Andrew McConnell/Panos.

Keywords

- Capital accumulation
- Commodity
- Environmental justice
- Externality
- Pollution haven hypothesis
- Spatial fix
- The Basel Convention
- Uneven development

Chapter Menu

Environment and Society: A Critical Introduction, Second Edition. Paul Robbins, John Hintz, and Sarah A. Moore.
© 2014 John Wiley & Sons, Ltd. Published 2014 by John Wiley & Sons, Ltd.

Digital Divides

Standing over a hotplate, the young men burn the plastic casing from copper wire. They smile and invite the group over for a closer look. Reticently, the visitors approach the smoking hotplate, cameras in hand. The young men explain simply that they are recovering the valuable materials from electronic waste – a task undertaken by many here in what has become known as the "digital dumping ground" of Agbogbloshie. (Figure 17.1) In this informal settlement northwest of Accra's central business district, millions of tons of e-waste are processed each year. The 40,000 or so residents are poor refugees from the northern part of Ghana, or from the rural areas of the country closer to this capital city. On this overcast day, the study-abroad students and faculty touring the area stand awkwardly, watching the men and asking polite questions about their work and lives. They are surrounded by organized chaos. Plastic children's toys – mini versions of supermarket carts – are piled separately from portable stereos with CD players and removable speakers, still in their original packaging. Younger children appear to be playing with the toys. On second glance, though, the children are, in fact, breaking the toys apart – their contribution to the work of processing wasted or excess consumer goods marketed to people who are, sometimes literally, on the other side of the world.

In the late 1990s, efforts had been made to bridge the digital divide between Ghana and more developed countries. Donation programs provided functional second-hand computers from the United States and Europe to Ghanaians for one-tenth the price of new ones.

Figure 17.1 In Agbogbloshie, Accra, Ghana. *Source*: Andrew McConnell/Panos.

Despite the good intentions of many of these programs, as consumers in the United States and Europe bought increasing numbers of personal computers (PCs), and disposed of old ones at a faster rate, stockpiles of non-functional units sneaked into these donations. By labeling broken electronics as second-hand goods, exporters have exploited loopholes in anti-dumping regulations meant to prevent poorer countries from receiving a dispropor-tionate share of potentially hazardous waste. Rather than usable computers that might help Ghanaians cross the digital divide, places like Agbogbloshie have been overrun with broken PCs and other discarded electronics.

Here, as in many informal settlements in China, India, and other parts of Africa, young men with no safety equipment perform risky labor, industriously turning wasted electron-ics into raw materials that can be sold for further production. While middlemen who amass copper or aluminum collected by many individuals can earn up to US$6 per day, most workers receive only a very small fraction of that. Further, this income is earned at sub-stantial cost to the public and environmental health of the area. Toxic chemicals are released in the burning of plastic coatings and metals used in electronics. Nausea, headaches, and respiratory ailments are the immediate results, while high exposure to carcinogens poses longer-range health concerns. High levels of toxins remain in the soil and seep into the water supply in this former wetland. Instead of remedying the digital divide, electronics production and disposal have only exacerbated differences in income and working condi-tions between consumers and "recyclers" of these items. The United States is the leading exporter of waste to Ghana, while the United Kingdom, Germany, Korea, Switzerland, and the Netherlands contribute smaller amounts. A new digital divide is thus emerging – one based not on access to electronic goods (or the information that they may help one acquire), but rather on the ability or inability to distance oneself from discarded electronics.

When cell phones, computers, televisions, and other electronics are discarded, they become electronic waste (e-waste or WEEE   Waste Electrical and Electronic Equipment). In recent estimates, up to 50 million tons of post-consumer e-waste are discarded each year. E-waste poses a unique socio-environmental puzzle. It is not a natural product, but it is one whose management greatly impacts the environment and public health, as is evident in the case of Agbogbloshie. It also stands uneasily between waste and commodity, risk and resource. In this chapter, we will explore these facets of the e-waste puzzle by first defining e-waste and tracking its emergence as a significant environmental challenge over the past several decades. We will then consider e-waste through the lenses of risk, markets, and political economy.

A Short History of E-Waste (2000)

The category of e-waste comprises household and corporate machines that are at their end of life (EOL). Major categories of these include televisions (both flat-screen and older cathode ray tube (CRT) models); personal desktop and portable computers and peripherals (printers, fax machines, copiers); monitors; and cell phones and other mobile devices. While electronics make up under 2 percent of municipal solid waste (MSW) flows in the United States and other developed countries (and less in lesser developed countries), they are an area of concern for environmental groups since their impacts are disproportionate to their volume in landfills. For example, it is estimated that in the United States, 70 percent of the heavy metals in landfills comes from discarded electronics. Further, it is a very rapidly growing part of the waste stream, so the effects of these products are anticipated to increase rapidly in the next couple of decades.

Because these products are made with materials that are hazardous to dispose of and process, they are often considered hazardous waste. Like other wastes, reliable statistics on the production and disposal of e-waste are difficult to attain and to compare. This is in part because countries, states or provinces, and municipalities categorize items differently and use varying methods for measuring or estimating the amounts of waste they manage. It is also due to lack of regulatory oversight in many places. In recent years, despites these difficulties, several international and national organizations and regulatory bodies have made attempts to better monitor the amount of e-waste generated and disposed of in different countries, in part because they view this waste stream as one with both acute and mounting environmental challenges.

The United States is the largest producer of e-waste in the world, disposing of about 3 million tons a year. This, of course, is the flip side of the United States being one of the world's largest consumers of electronics. According to the United States Environmental Protection Agency (EPA), 440 million electronic products were sold in the United States in 2010. This represented a doubling of such sales from the year 1997. This increase was driven mostly by a ninefold increase in the sale of mobile devices. Total sales of other devices, in fact, declined slightly. In 2010, mobile device sales accounted for approximately 53 percent of sales across all categories, while in 1998 they accounted for only 12 percent. While the total numbers of electronic products sold have increased over time, the overall weight of e-waste has decreased in some places owing to a change in the composition of the waste stream. For example, the switch from heavier CRT televisions and monitors to flat screens has decreased the tonnage of electronic goods disposed of each year (though this is partially offset by ever-larger screen sizes). At the same time, cell phones and other mobile devices, which are lighter, now account for a larger proportion of e-waste. China is the second largest national producer of global e-waste, disposing of 2.3 million tons of it in 2010 (Schluep et al. 2010). Other countries, like India, with growing middle classes likely to purchase cell phones and computers might see their e-waste increase by 500 percent in the next decade (Schluep et al. 2010).

A world of TV viewers?

While many discarded home appliances, like refrigerators, can be counted as e-waste, this chapter focuses mainly on discarded televisions, computers and peripherals, and mobile devices. The first of these to be mass-produced and sold was the television. The British company, Baird, was the first to sell a mass-produced television called the "Televisor." It sold about 1,000 units between 1930 and 1933. This product was initially designed to work in conjunction with another popular household appliance of the period – the radio, but later models worked independently. Telefunken, a German company, manufactured the first commercially available electronic televisions with CRTs in 1934, followed by other makers in France (1936), Britain (1936), and the United States (1938). About 19,000 electronic televisions were made in Britain, and approximately 1,600 in Germany before World War II; between 7,000 and 8,000 sets were made in the United States before it entered the war in late 1941. US production was halted from April 1942 until the late summer of August 1945, when demand for and production of televisions skyrocketed owing to postwar prosperity, increases in leisure time, network expansion, and technological advances that made sets cheaper to produce and buy. While only 0.5 percent of US households had a television in 1946, 55.7 percent had one in 1954, and 90 percent by 1962. In Britain, there were 15,000 television households in 1947, 1.4 million in 1952, and 15.1 million by 1968. Today, the global TV market comprises about 1.2 billion households and about 50 million televisions are purchased each year. North American consumers purchase a new television every seven years and the average household owns 2.8 televisions. While North American and European viewers constitute about 70 percent of the TV revenue market share, viewership and TV purchases are growing in Asia-Pacific (21 percent), Latin America (8 percent) and Africa and the Middle East (2 percent).

Until the early 2000s, the dominant technology used in television displays, and later in computer monitors, was CRTs. These contain high amounts of lead (four to eight pounds per tube!) and posed problems for landfill managers. In the United States, many states started to ban the disposal of CRTs beginning in 2000. Instead of disposing of CRT-based devices in landfills, consumers and waste managers were encouraged to recycle this leaded glass. New recycling companies emerged to take advantage of the new market, but as technologies for producing televisions and monitors changed, fewer companies worldwide accepted used CRTs that could be broken up and re-formed into new tubes. In 2013, only two such companies remained – both in India. This has led to what some officials call a "glass tsunami" that overwhelms the warehouses of companies that have collected stockpiles of the now-useless material. In turn, several "recycling" companies have been cited for violating environmental regulations in the United States and elsewhere. Nor are current technologies much more environmentally friendly. CRTs have been replaced by flat panels that use fluorescent lights containing highly toxic mercury. These also have little recycling value, so many collectors end up dumping these in landfills.

Personal computers and mobile phones

The world's first PC to be successfully commercially marketed appeared in 1977. Sales of PCs grew moderately over the following decade in countries like the United States. By the 1990s, sales had increased and the time in use of computers and peripherals began to drop. In 2000, global computer sales were about 135 million units, with 46 million units being sold in the United States. By 2011, those numbers had more than doubled to 355 million and 95 million, respectively. While the United States is still the largest global purchaser of computers (comprising about 40 percent of the market), its proportion of sales is dropping slowly as the rest of the world purchases more units. Currently, 25 percent of the market is in Europe and about 12 percent is in the Asia-Pacific region.

Cell phone ownership and use lagged behind PC use for the last couple of decades of the twentieth century, but overtook it in the first decade of the twenty-first century. The first non-car-based cellular phone call was made between competing corporate innovators (from Motorola to Bell industries) in the United States in 1973. However, the Japanese were the first to launch a commercial cellular phone system. It was initiated in Tokyo in 1979. A year later, the city of Chicago, Illinois was the first city in the United States to run a pilot program that provided cellular phones and service to 1,000 households. In 1982 the Federal Communications Commission (FCC), the branch of the US government in charge of regulating inter- and intra-state communications, changed regulations, allowing for the use of cellular networks on a broad scale in the United States. From 1990 to 2011, worldwide mobile phone subscriptions grew from 12.4 million to over 6 billion, penetrating about 87 percent of the global population. The world's top cell-phone-using countries in 2011 in total numbers of cell phones were 1) China (1,150,000,000), 2) India (861,660,000), 3) the United States (327,577,529), 4) Brazil (263,040,000), and Russia (256,117,000). When comparing the units in use with the population of each country, though, these rankings shift a bit. Russia, with over 1.5 cell phones per person, becomes number one, followed by 2) Brazil (1.37); 3) the United States (1.04); 4) China (0.85); and 5) India (0.70).

In the United States, 2.37 million short tons (each 2,000 pounds) of e-waste were ready for EOL management in 2009, representing a 120 percent increase over the number in 1999. CRT products represent 47 percent of that number. An additional five million short tons of products were estimated to be in storage in the United States in the same year, with CRT-based products (televisions and monitors) representing the highest rate of storage. Approximately 141 million mobile devices were ready for EOL management in 2009, more than any other type of product, yet by weight, they represent less than 1 percent of discarded electronics. In the United States, 25 percent of electronics were collected for recycling, with computers collected at the highest rate (38 percent).

The histories of television, PCs, and cell phones' consumption and use point to important factors to consider when thinking about the puzzle of e-waste. First, technological innovation leads to the consumption of novel goods, often without consideration for how those goods will be safely disposed of. Second, while the United States, Europe, and developed countries in other regions are the primary consumers of such goods, consumption in other areas is growing. As these products reach their EOL, we can anticipate that the overall amount of e-waste produced globally will also rise. Third, technological innovation also leads to shorter life spans for electronic goods (Figure 17.2) as consumers scramble to get the newest products or the ones that work best with current software and operating systems. This planned obsolescence also leads to a growing burden of e-waste globally. Fourth, while new technologies often phase out the use of particular hazardous chemicals, they are often made with other materials that may also include toxins. The shift from CRT to flat-screen TVs, for example, may reduce the amount of lead in landfills, but may increase the presence of mercury. In the following sections we will consider the e-waste puzzle through the lenses of risk, markets, and political economy.

Risk Management and the Hazard of E-Waste

As discussed above, e-waste often contains toxic materials such as lead, mercury, PCBs, asbestos, and CFCs, and is therefore a hazard to public and environmental health. The three

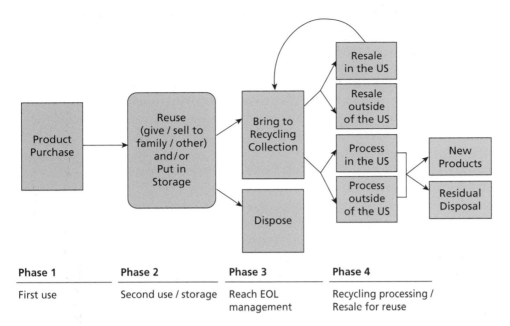

Phase 1	Phase 2	Phase 3	Phase 4
First use	Second use / storage	Reach EOL management	Recycling processing / Resale for reuse

Figure 17.2 Life-cycle flow chart for electronic products. *Source:* United States Environmental Protection Agency: Electronics Waste Management In The United States Approach 1. http://www.epa.gov/osw/conserve/materials/ecycling/docs/app-1.pdf.

main ways that e-waste poses a hazard are: 1) from the products themselves (lead and mercury from CRTs or flat screens, which may leach into soil and water sources when landfilled); 2) due to substandard processing (chemicals released in burning and smelting); and 3) due to reagents used in the recycling process (cyanide and other strong leaching agents). The hazards presented by the disposal of e-waste are not exactly like those presented by "natural" phenomena like drought or flooding, but they must still be managed. Environmental regulators manage these hazards in part by assessing the risk that certain materials pose when disposed of in specific ways. In Chapter 6, risk was defined as the probability that a certain decision or action will have a negative consequence. Risk assessments and related decisions are influenced by the degree of access to information, as well as other factors like culture. Information and managerial cultures change over time, however, and often, perfect knowledge does not exist. The question, then, for environmental managers is how best to proceed in the present to minimize *known* risks. This type of decision-making can have unexpected outcomes.

Take the case of CRTs in the United States. A CRT is a vacuum tube that contains an electron gun and florescent screen used to view images. The face of a CRT is usually made up of a thick lead to protect its interior and block X-ray emissions. As consumers accumulated and then disposed of more CRT-based products, like television sets and computer monitors, evidence began to mount that toxins, most notably lead, were leaching from these wastes into landfills, with potentially hazardous effects on nearby water and soil quality. This prompted concern by landfill managers in the United States and elsewhere by the 1980s, but became the focus of disposal bans in the 2000s. In October of 2001, the United

States Environmental Protection Agency (EPA) created rules stating that CRTs had to be taken to special recycling facilities, rather than disposed of in landfills. Just over a year later, the EPA began fining companies that disposed of CRTs in landfills or through incineration. This contributed to an increase in companies that offered recycling services for CRTs to municipalities and consumers. A similar process occurred in Europe where CRTs are managed under the provisions of the WEEE directive, which became law in 2003.

When many of these bans came into effect, firms who collected CRTs were able to sell them to a dozen companies in the United States and 13 more around the world who would melt down the tubes to make new ones or to provide raw materials for other products. In the past decade, however, demand for these as materials for production has decreased dramatically. Television and computer companies have switched to flat-screen versions that rely on other technologies, like light-emitting-diode display (LED), liquid crystal display (LCD, the most common type), and plasma. Since the early 2000s, most of the plants that recycled CRTs have closed or changed their processing. There are only two firms, both in India, who still reprocess CRTs. While in 2004 recyclers were paid more than US$200/ton for these materials, in 2012, *they had to pay* about that amount for someone to take CRTs. Local recycling firms in the United States, who had collected large numbers of CRT products, then found themselves in possession of stockpiles of essentially worthless items. Reactions ranged from illegal dumping to abandoning warehouses full of leaded glass. Because of this, in September of 2012, California passed an emergency measure that allowed companies to send CRTs to hazardous waste landfills through 2014. In this case, California regulatory agencies made a decision based on limiting risk. Abandoned warehouses, which are not equipped for high volumes of hazardous waste storage, could become highly polluted industrial sites. Dumping CRTs in hazardous waste landfills, while not ideal, is a less risky option.

This is not the only risk calculation that regulators and other environmental decision-makers were faced with. CRTs are being replaced with other technologies that contain less lead, but more mercury. The EPA estimates that CRTs contain 25 times more lead than LCDs, but also points out that mercury may have greater impacts in solid and hazardous waste landfills given mercury's toxicity to both human and environmental health. Because LCD and other flat-screen displays have less recycling potential under current technology, these are more likely to end up in landfills. Technological change often means the trading of one problem for another, and this results in a situation where risk assessments made under current best knowledge are inadequate to managing contemporary and future risks. Further, the EPA's management strategies falter in the face of market fluctuations that they may not be able to anticipate. In the following section, we consider what happens to our understanding of e-waste when we focus, not on risk, but on these fluctuating markets.

E-Waste and Markets: From Externality to Commodity

A markets approach to the puzzle of e-waste must first consider how e-waste comes to be an important commodity that is traded, often internationally. Second and relatedly, it must also consider how the nature of this commodity might be thought of differently depending upon the fate of the waste. E-waste can be shipped from one place to another for disposal *or* for recycling. Each of these presents a separate piece of the e-waste puzzle that will be discussed below.

Pollution havens

In the 1970s and 1980s, companies from the Global North saw the disposal costs of hazardous materials multiplied by a factor of 25. This led to a multi-billion-dollar industry in the hazardous waste trade, including increasing amounts of e-waste. In environmental economics, it is argued that insufficient environmental policies in some countries could distort the market and make the international hazardous waste trade more harmful to the environment and to public health (Rauscher 2001). This is commonly known as the **pollution haven hypothesis**.

The "pollution haven hypothesis" holds that some countries might voluntarily reduce environmental regulations in order to attract foreign direct investment. Even if producers are not inclined to relocate production to places with fewer environmental regulations and lower labor costs, they might still decide to export the negative externalities of their production (like hazardous waste) to places where disposal is cheaper. To prevent uneven, unjust, and potentially dangerous transboundary waste shipments, trading partners were forced into international agreements such as the Basel Convention, which came into effect in 1992. **The Basel Convention** prevents richer countries from exporting their hazardous wastes to poorer countries. It has been ratified by 172 nations. The United States signed the agreement in the early 1990s but has yet to ratify it, which poses a significant difficulty for tracking electronic and other hazardous waste, given that the United States is the world's largest producer of both. Since the Convention came into effect, many firms and countries have shifted from exporting e-waste for disposal to exporting e-waste for recycling.

> **Pollution Haven Hypothesis**   A theory that holds that some countries might voluntarily reduce environmental regulations in order to attract foreign direct investment
>
> **The Basel Convention**   Formally known as the Basel Convention on the Control of Transboundary Movements of Hazardous Wastes and Their Disposal, Basel is an international treaty that entered into force in 1992, and is designed to prevent wealthier countries from dumping hazardous waste on less developed countries

Recycling e-wastes

In terms of international environmental economics, it has been suggested that in a "first-best" world of equal trade relationships, international trade in hazardous waste could be beneficial to all countries involved. Indeed, such logic was echoed in the late 1990s by the EPA who argued that one reason to export hazardous waste was that in some cases, "hazardous wastes constitute 'raw' material inputs into industrial and manufacturing processes. This is the case in many developing countries where natural resources are scarce or non-existent" (US EPA 1998).

While posing significant hazards for the environments and people near where it is disposed of, e-waste also contains valuable materials that may be "mined" for resale and future production. These include iron, aluminum, copper, gold, silver, platinum, palladium, indium, gallium, and rare earth metals. Up to 60 elements can be found in e-waste. And, given enough volume, the quantities and value of materials can be significant. According to StEP (Solving the E-waste Problem, a group from the United Nations Environmental Program; 2009), one ton of mobile phones (about 6,000 units) contains about 3.5 kilograms of silver, 340 grams of gold, 140 grams of palladium, and 130 kg of copper. Additionally, cell phone batteries contain about 3.5 grams of copper. Together these materials can be valued at 15,000 current USD. Moreover, one could argue, it is easier and has less impact on the environment to reprocess e-waste than to mine for new materials. Another benefit of recycling e-waste is the potential for new jobs. In this case, it is estimated that 296 jobs each year are created for every 10,000 tons of material that are reprocessed rather than simply disposed of.

Externality The spillover of a cost or benefit, as where industrial activity at a plant leads to pollution off-site that must be paid for by someone else

Waste, including hazardous and electronic waste, is often considered a negative **externality** of the production process. Fees for disposing of waste have traditionally been thought of as the price of doing business. Throughout the history of capitalist production, manufacturers have sought ways to reduce expenditures by increasing efficiency and by reducing labor and other input costs. In addition, many firms have sought the cheapest way to dispose of the externalities of production. Wastes, though, are also equally an effect of the consumption process. Rather than being externalities that firms have to deal with, therefore, they are often part of household practices and municipal and other levels of management. In an effort to keep such materials out of local landfills, waste managers have sought to gauge and exploit the willingness of consumers to pay for greener or more sustainable practices based in recycling. This is a fairly difficult sell for many waste managers given that consumers must be willing to pay, not for the presence of an amenity, but rather for a more abstract notion of harm reduction. Because consumers are often not exposed to, or even aware of, the effects of e-waste disposal, it is often hard to convince them to participate in such recycling programs. Even if consumers participate in the free "recycling" programs sponsored by Best Buy, Staples, Verizon, or a number of other stores or in cities like Seattle, Washington, they still incur transaction costs – time and energy to engage in the "proper" disposal of e-waste, rather than the more expedient option of simply dumping it in household solid waste. Further, as we will see in the next section, it is unclear how much of the e-waste managed by such programs is, in fact, recycled, rather than dumped. Groups like the Basel Action Network (BAN) have tried to solve this problem through certification programs (see Box 17.1).

Though e-waste represents an important export market, recent trends suggest that the growing value of products within the waste have made retaining and re-purposing products in their country of origin increasingly attractive. According to a United States International Trade Commission study in 2013, of the $20.6 billion in reported (legitimate) transactions of used electronic products (UEP) in the United States, a full $19.2 billion were destined for domestic sales; exports represented only $1.45 billion, or 7 percent of sales. What this suggests is that a formal market for used products has developed in developed countries, and that some significant part of the e-waste stream is reprocessed domestically in its country of origin. Indeed, the study suggests that some historic import sites for waste – like

Box 17.1   Environmental Solution? The E-Waste Stewardship Project

The Basel Action Network is a non-profit, nongovernmental charitable organization that developed in the wake of the Basel Convention. This organization is dedicated to confronting "global environmental injustice and economic inefficiency of toxic trade (toxic wastes, products and technologies) and its devastating impacts." The Network focuses on several areas of hazardous waste dumping, including the highly toxic shipbreaking industry (in 2012 European ship-owners dumped 365 toxic ships on South Asian beaches!) and the ongoing problem of international hazards shipment. Among its signature campaigns, however, is one dedicated entirely to fostering a responsible way to deal with e-waste: The E-Waste Stewardship Project (EWSP).

EWSP is a program that certifies companies in the recycling and asset recovery industries, if they comply with what are known to the best practices for handling and recycling e-waste. These best practices are both social and environmental, and include: prohibition of toxics from e-waste being dumped in landfills; compliance with international laws on imports and exports of waste; prohibition of the use of prison labor in recycling electronics; and protections for recycling workers, who are often gravely exposed to toxins. Companies that comply with these rules receive certification as "E-stewards" and consumers and retailers are encouraged to do business with them.

The EWSP campaign is skewed toward improving practices in the United States, a country that produces a tremendous quantity of e-waste. Because the United States never ratified the Basel Convention, it operates outside the restrictions of the Convention and has therefore become a focus for action using other mechanisms. By enrolling companies directly into a program that requires them to comply with international regulations, EWSP, in effect, enforces Basel Convention improvements on companies in the United States, a country that does not fall under the law.

This approach to the e-waste problem is an interesting hybrid between a regulatory framework, since the certification only goes to those who comply with the laws, and a market mechanism, since it relies wholly on people and businesses voluntarily contracting only with firms that operate under these restrictions. It relies on major retailers, in particular, to contract with these recyclers to help green their images. For example, Staples – a major electronics and office products retailer – became a licensed "e-Stewards® Enterprise company" in 2013, by pledging to use only certified e-Stewards Recyclers. This assures that more than 1,500 stores in the United States follow these rules.

There are limits to such an approach, of course. Being entirely voluntary, the program can do little to reach companies who simply choose to work with non-certified recyclers, whose bids and prices may be considerably lower than their more ecologically responsible counterparts. Moreover, consumers with little or no knowledge of what retailers are or are not enrolled are unlikely to improve the business of companies who comply. The EWSP reflects the great strengths and inherent weaknesses of market-based certification schemes.

the community of Guiyu in China, a notorious e-waste processing area – have begun to depend more heavily on local materials (i.e., e-waste from China) as exports have declined.

Of course, this fact should not distract for some important realities. First, much of the e-waste trade remains illegitimate, under-reported, or unreported. The worst exports, in other words, are not tracked. So too, recycling and reuse of material may occur in the country of their origin, but this does not rule out that the waste from recycling (which often contains some of the most hazardous materials) is often resold, exported, or dumped internationally. Waste processing is not free of waste. Finally, just because e-waste is being processed in its country of origin, this does not mean that workers are free from risk and exposure, that further dumping doesn't occur in the country of origin, or that disenfranchised or poorer populations will not to be exposed to processing facilities, air quality emissions problems, or other related externalities of recycling and reprocessing. Avoiding dumping on poor countries does not assure that there is no dumping on poor people.

E-Waste and Environmental Justice: The Political Economy of E-Waste

While a market approach emphasizes the ways in which certain economic incentives can be used to make e-waste management more sustainable, a political economy approach to understanding the puzzle of e-waste focuses on **uneven development** and **accumulation**, as well as questions of labor and the circulation of value. In this section, we discuss these aspects of the e-waste puzzle and then focus on questions of environmental justice.

The history of e-waste discussed above demonstrates the way that e-waste is an anthropogenic hazard – a by-product of the spread of mass consumption. This phenomenon is partly due to increases in global wealth in the decades following World War II. New technologies also made goods cheaper and more accessible. At the same time, though, firms have worked to create and sustain desire for their products through marketing and planned obsolescence. The capitalist economy depends on the expansion of markets – which means either finding new consumers or getting existing consumers to buy existing products. The history of e-waste demonstrates that global consumption of electronic products has spread over the past 60 years, but that far and away people in the United States and other wealthier nations still buy many more of these goods than anyone else. By continually updating televisions, cell phones, and computers, companies ensure that more products will be consumed. They also ensure that older products will either be stored (to enter the e-waste flow in the future) or discarded to make room for the new.

While richer countries are still the largest consumers of electronic products, they also enjoy the privilege of being largely distanced from the inevitable result of this consumption – waste. In the 1970s and 1980s, firms and waste managers from wealthier nations employed a **spatial fix** – sending hazardous wastes to other regions – to overcome increasing disposal costs. As discussed in the above section on markets, international agreements like the Basel Convention have been enacted to curtail this practice. As restrictions on the export of waste grew, waste management firms developed "recycling" programs as an alternative e-waste trade. These post-consumer recyclables, along with some pre-consumer e-waste being dumped from warehouses, often end up in landfills in countries with fewer environmental regulations or less oversight. The recycling programs discussed above are often greenwashing – ways to get around import quotas on used or discarded electrical equipment. Despite regulations, many

Uneven development The geographic tendency within capitalism to produce highly disparate economic conditions (wealth/poverty) and economic activity (production/consumption) in different places

(Capital) Accumulation The tendency in capitalism for profits, capital goods, savings, and value to flow toward, pool in, and/or accrue in specific places, leading to the centralization and concentration of both money and power

Spatial Fix The tendency of capitalism to temporarily solve its inevitable periodic crises by establishing new markets, new resources, and new sites of production in other places environmental nongovernmental organizations (ENGOS) suggest that as much as 50 to 80 percent of e-waste that is slated for recycling in Canada and the United States is actually exported internationally (Lepawsky and McNabb 2010; Basel Action Network 2002).

From a political economic perspective, recycling programs are opportunities to overcome barriers to accumulation. In addition to the fact that capitalism has solved a longstanding problem by making waste into a **commodity**, it should also be noted that this type of commodification is not just an inevitable outcome of economic progress. By putting waste back into capitalist circulation, wasted value that might just sit there gets redeployed, offering new opportunities for accumulation and capitalist expansion.

When e-waste recycling is done legally by firms in accordance with environmental and labor regulations, it usually involves a formal labor relationship where workers are paid a wage to take apart and process products. This may involve safety practices and equipment. Of course, it is true that even in these cases, wageworkers are paid less than the true value of their labor so that firms can accumulate capital. But, in the case of gray market or illegal dumping, the recovery of resources is more dangerous, and for most "workers" less remunerative. The results of this are evident in the story of Agbogbloshie from the beginning of the chapter. In the remainder of this section we will discuss the continued unevenness of the trade in e-waste and the **environmental justice** issues that this raises.

> **Commodity**   An object of economic value that is valued generically, rather than as a specific object (example: pork is a commodity, rather than a particular pig). In political economy (and Marxist) thought, an object made for exchange
>
> **Environmental Justice**   A principle, as well as a body of thought and research, stressing the need for equitable distribution of environmental goods (parks, clean air, healthful working conditions) and environmental bads (pollution, hazards, waste) between people, no matter their race, ethnicity, or gender. Conversely, environmental injustice describes a condition where unhealthful or dangerous conditions are disproportionately proximate to minority communities

Global e-waste/global environmental justice

Global flows of e-waste are hard to track and measure, particularly because the United States, the world's largest producer of e-waste, has not ratified the Basel Convention and is therefore not subject to the kinds of tracking that many other countries are. Nevertheless, several scholars have made attempts to track e-waste shipments internationally and many more have visited e-waste disposal sites to collect information about the lives of people in these places.

While some e-waste is disposed of or recycled locally in North America and Europe, there is evidence that there is a "systematic relationship between countries with lower GDP per capita and their status as net importers of e-waste" (Lepawsky and McNabb 2010).

According to geographers Josh Lepawsky and Chris McNabb, who studied the global flows of e-waste tracked by the United Nations, by 2006 Asia had become the dominant recipient of e-waste exported from other countries (Figure 17.3). This represented a quantitative change from 2001. That year, Asia was the destination for over 50 percent of exports from the Americas and Europe, about 80 percent from Oceania and all of the exports from the Middle East. By 2006, Asia received slightly less waste from the Middle East (98 percent), but much more from the Americas (96 percent), and Oceania (99 percent). Lepawsky and McNabb also found that much legally traded e-waste moves between countries

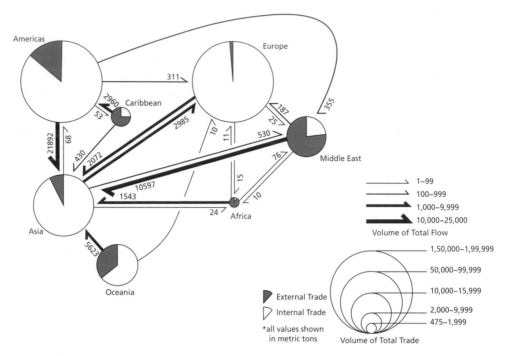

Figure 17.3   Global trade in e-waste, 2006. *Source*: Lepawsky and McNabb (2010, Fig. 2). Data from: UN Comtrade.

in the same region. This proportion grows as countries experience relative increases in wealth over time. By 2006, over 10 percent of Africa's e-waste trade was internal compared with 20 percent in the Caribbean and Middle East and 60 percent in Oceania. It is important to note that these figures account only for legal trade, while much of the e-waste trade is illegal. Greenpeace reports, for example, that inspections of 18 European seaports in 2005 found that perhaps 47 percent of waste (including e-waste) destined for export was illegal and went to the Far East, India, Africa, and China. It is estimated that anywhere from 50 to 80 percent of waste collected for recycling in the United States is disposed of similarly.

While many cases of e-waste dumping have been noted by nongovernmental organizations (NGOs) like Greenpeace around the world, only a handful of sites have been well documented. In addition to Agbogbloshie, one of the most famous of these is Guiyu in Guangdong Province, China, which is sometimes referred to as the e-waste capital of the world. It is estimated that of the 150,000 people in this area, tens of thousands work in informal e-waste recycling, a phenomenon first documented by the BAN (see Box 17.1) in 2003 in a film called *Exporting Harm*. One and a half million pounds of discarded computers, cell phones, and other electronics are processed in Guiyu each year. Studies have revealed that high levels of heavy metals like lead, copper, and zinc have polluted air and water supplies in the area and contaminated food products. Like other countries, mainland China took steps to ban the import of e-waste in 2000, but that has not prevented the continued shipment of wastes to that area. Similar conditions are faced by people in many parts of Africa, including port towns in Nigeria as well as Malaysia, and several cities in India.

Places like Guiyu and Agbogbloshie demonstrate the continued unevenness of economic development globally – a digital divide separating consumers of electronic products from the people who live and work with e-waste. In some cases, domestic consumption of e-waste by a growing middle class (as in India) is contributing to the problem, but in all cases it is still true that poor and marginalized populations, living informally on marginal lands, bear the public and environmental health burdens of increasing global consumption.

These are not passive victims, however. Informal e-waste processing is a dangerous task, as well as one that takes skill and initiative. It is also a way of making do – of eking out a living with whatever is available to you. In some places, like Agbogbloshie, middlemen work hard to continue to bring in e-waste to be reprocessed and others work extended hours to mine copper and other minerals to provide for themselves and their families. Through the arduous labor of informal recyclers around the world, waste is being transformed into valuable raw materials for continued economic expansion. Despite these facts, though, an environmental justice perspective would point to the larger political and economic processes that produce situations in which marginalized communities are continually exposed to toxic substances that producers and consumers of commodities are not. Further, it would point to the extreme surplus value being extracted from the labor of informal recyclers. In many ways, these people are supplementing capitalist firms by providing extremely cheap materials, while at the same time providing an environmental service for localities that would otherwise have to find ways to manage growing piles of e-waste.

The E-Waste Puzzle

In this chapter, we have learned that

- E-waste is an anthropogenic hazard that has increased in volume over time with the advent and increased consumption of goods like televisions, PCs, and cell phones.
- E-waste products pose different and often unforeseen risks to environmental and public health, depending on the technologies used in its production and processing.
- Markets in e-waste fluctuate with demand for certain products and the raw materials that can be mined from them.
- Regulation has been necessary to prevent large-scale dumping of e-waste in poorer countries.
- Some companies have found ways to change e-waste from an externality to a commodity.
- Despite regulation, shadow recycling programs have grown alongside legitimate ones so that e-waste and its hazards are unevenly distributed around the world.
- This uneven distribution exacerbates environmental justice issues.

In these ways, e-waste is like much hazardous waste. It is a by-product of mass consumption societies in which technological advances combine with planned obsolescence to encourage demand. For some, it is a resource and for others a hazard. It must be managed with an eye toward current risk assessments, but these are inadequate in that they do not account for changes in technology and subsequent fluctuations in market value that may affect how firms dispose of e-waste.

Questions for Review

1. What is e-waste and what factors account for the growing amounts of e-waste over time?
2. How do environmental managers make decisions about e-waste using risk assessment? What are the problems with doing so?
3. What is the pollution haven hypothesis and what is its importance for explaining the global trade of e-waste?
4. How does the geography of the global production of e-waste compare to the geography of e-waste disposal? Which places produce the most e-waste and which countries accept the largest amounts of e-waste for disposal or recycling?
5. What are living conditions like for many informal e-waste recyclers?

Exercise 17.1   The Secret Life of Cell Phones

Watch the video "The Secret Life of Cell Phones" (http://www.youtube.com/watch?v=UkbpiL9UsY8), a video created by INFORM Inc. (an environmental NGO). How many phones have you owned in your life? How often do you replace them? What happens to your old phones? If you turn your phone over to a company (phone company or retailer), do you know what practices their recycler uses? How would you find out? What ways might we encourage people to recycle phones? Who profits and benefits from the recycling of phones?

Exercise 17.2   What Does Your School (or Company) Do with E-Waste?

What does your college/university (if you are a student) or company (if you are an employee) do with its e-waste, old computers from labs, for example? How easy is it to find out and confirm what happens to these materials? Is there an office or division charged with managing or contracting e-waste disposal? How does it operate and at what cost to the institution?

Exercise 17.3   What Do We Really Know About Waste Flows?

Visit the infographic produced by UNEP/GRID (http://www.grida.no/files/publications/vital-waste2/VWG2_p34and35.pdf). This graphic and the accompanying maps reflect the *official waste trade*, as reported under the Basel Convention. What does it show about waste export and import? What are the limits of the data used to track these flows? What important flows might be missing from the data and not represented on the maps? Given problems with these data, what kinds of research might be necessary to find the real extent of e-waste flows (and hazardous waste flows more generally) internationally? How can we get a full accounting of where waste comes from and goes to?

References

Basel Action Network (2002). *Exporting Harm: The High-Tech Trashing of Asia.* Seattle, WA: Basel Action Network.

Lepawsky, J. and McNabb, C. (2010). Mapping international flows of electronic waste. *The Canadian Geographer//Le Géographe canadien* 54: 177–95. doi: 10.1111/j.1541-0064.2009.00279.x.

Rauscher, M. (2005). "International trade, foreign investment, and the environment." In K. G. Mäler and J. R. Vincent (eds) *Handbook of Environmental Economics*, 1st edn, vol. 3. Amsterdam: Elsevier, ch. 27, pp. 1403–56.

Schluep, M., C. Hagelueken, R. Kuehr, F. Magalini, C. Maurer, et al. (2010). *Recycling: From E-Waste to Resources.* United Nations Environment Programme.

StEP (Solving the E-waste Problem) (2009) *Recycling – From E-Waste to Resources*, United Nations Environmental Program. Retrieved from http://www.unep.org/PDF/PressReleases/E-Waste_publication_screen_FINALVERSION-sml.pdf.

United States Environmental Protection Agency (1998). *International Trade in Hazardous Waste: An Overview*. EPA Brochure 305-K-98-001, November.

United States Environmental Protection Agency (2008). *Electronics Waste Management in the United States, Approach 1*. Retrieved April 30, 2013, from http://www.epa.gov/osw/conserve/materials/ecycling/docs/app-1.pdf.

Glossary

Acid Rain Deposition of rain or snowfall with unusually high acidity, resulting from the emission of sulfur dioxide and nitrogen oxides into the air, typically from industrial emissions. This form of precipitation is harmful for plant life and aquatic ecosystems

Affect Emotions and unconscious responses to the world that influence decision-making

Agrodiversity The number and range of species in cultivated areas. Higher agrodiversity is typically associated with the robustness of a farming system and its ability to withstand weather and disease (ant. Monoculute)

Animal Liberation Named after Peter Singer's groundbreaking 1975 book, a radical social movement that aims to free all animals from use by humans, whether those uses are for food, medical testing, industry, personal adornment, entertainment or anything else

Animal Rights An ethical position and social movement that states that non-human animals, particularly intelligent mammals, should be granted rights as ethical subjects on par or at least similar to human beings

Anthropocene A metaphoric term sometimes applied to our current era, when people exert enormous influence on environments all around the Earth, but where control of these environments and their enormously complex ecologies is inevitably elusive

Anthropocentrism An ethical standpoint that views humans as the central factor in considerations of right and wrong action in and toward nature (compare to ecocentrism)

Apex Predators Also known as "top carnivores," the animals in any ecosystem occupying the top trophic level; apex predators do not have any natural predators

Background Extinction Rate Usually given in numbers of plant and animal species per year, the estimated average rate of extinction over long-term, geologic time, not counting mass extinction events

The Basel Convention Formally known as the Basel Convention on the Control of Transboundary Movements of Hazardous Wastes and Their Disposal, Basel is an international treaty that entered into force in 1992, and is designed to prevent wealthier countries from dumping hazardous waste on less developed countries

Biodiversity The total variability and variety of life forms in a region, ecosystem, or around the world; typically used as a measure of the health of an environmental system

Environment and Society: A Critical Introduction, Second Edition. Paul Robbins, John Hintz, and Sarah A. Moore.
© 2014 John Wiley & Sons, Ltd. Published 2014 by John Wiley & Sons, Ltd.

Birth Rate   A measure of natural growth in a population, typically expressed as the number of births per thousand population per year

Bycatch   Non-targeted organisms incidentally caught by commercial fishing operations, including many fish species, but also a large number of birds, marine mammals, and sea turtles

Cap and Trade   A market-based system to manage environmental pollutants where a total limit is placed on all emissions in a jurisdiction (state, country, worldwide, etc.), and individual people or firms possess transferable shares of that total, theoretically leading to the most efficient overall system to maintain and reduce pollution levels overall

Capital Accumulation   The tendency in capitalism for profits, capital goods, savings, and value to flow toward, pool in, and/or accrue in specific places, leading to the centralization and concentration of both money and power

Carbon Cycle   The system through which carbon circulates through the Earth's geosphere, atmosphere, and biosphere, specifically including exchanges between carbon in the earth (e.g., as petroleum) and the atmosphere (as CO_2) through combustion and back again through sequestration

Carbon Footprint   the total amount of greenhouse gases (carbon dioxide, methane) produced by a given individual, group, economic sector, or commodity production process

Carbon Sequestration   The capture and storage of carbon from the atmosphere into the biosphere or the geosphere through either biological means, as in plant photosynthesis, or engineered means

Carrying Capacity   The theoretical limit of population (animal, human, or otherwise) that a system can sustain

Climax Vegetation   The theoretical assemblage of plants arising from succession over time, determined by climatic and soil conditions

Coase Theorem   A thesis based in neoclassical economics, holding that externalities (e.g., pollution) can be most efficiently controlled through contracts and bargaining between parties, assuming the transaction costs of reaching a bargain are not excessive

Collective Action   Cooperation and coordination between individuals to achieve common goals and outcomes

Columbian Exchange   The movement of species across the Atlantic Ocean, from the New World to the Old World and vice versa, and the resulting ecological transformations

Command-and-Control   Forms of regulation that depend on government laws and agencies to enforce rules, including such things as regulated limits on pollution or fuel efficiency standards; contrasts with market-based or incentive-based approaches

Commodification   The transformation of an object or resource from something valued in and for itself, to something valued generically for exchange. In Marxist thought, the rise of the exchange value of a thing, over its use value

Commodity Chain   The path along which raw materials are turned into finished products and eventually consumed, with each link or node in the chain being a site for increasing added value and opportunity for profit

Commodity   An object of economic value that is valued generically, rather than as a specific object (example: pork is a commodity, rather than a particular pig). In political economy (and Marxist) thought, an object made for exchange

Common Property   A good or resource (e.g., bandwidth, pasture, oceans) whose characteristics make it difficult to fully enclose and partition, making it possible for non-owners to enjoy resource benefits and owners to sustain costs from the actions of others, typically necessitating some form of creative institutional management

Concept   A single idea, usually captured in a word or a phrase

Conditions of Production   In political economic (and Marxist) thought, the material or environmental conditions required for a specific economy to function, which may include things as varied as water for use in an industrial process to the health of workers to do the labor

Conservation   The management of a resource or system to sustain its productivity over time, typically associated with scientific management of collective goods like fisheries or forests (compare to preservation)

Conservation Biology   A branch of scientific biology dedicated to exploring and maintaining biodiversity and plant and animal species

Constructivist   Emphasizing the significance of concepts, ideologies, and social practices to our understanding and making of (literally, *constructing*) the world

Consumer Boycott   A method of protest that aims to pressure corporations into changing their practices by urging people to forgo purchasing products associated with the targeted corporations

Co-production   The inevitable and ongoing process whereby humans and non-humans produce and change one another through their interaction and interrelation

Cultural Theory   A theoretical framework associated with anthropologist Mary Douglas that stresses the way individual perceptions (of risk, for example) are reinforced by group social dynamics, leading to a few paradigmatic, typical, and discrete ways of seeing and addressing problems

Death Rate   A measure of mortality in a population, typically expressed as the number of deaths per thousand population per year

Deep Ecology   A philosophy of environmental ethics that distances itself from "shallow" or mainstream environmentalism by arguing for a "deeper" and supposedly more truly ecologically-informed view of the world

Demographic Transition Model   A model of population change that predicts a decline in population death rates associated with modernization, followed by a decline in birth rates resulting from industrialization and urbanization; this creates a sigmoidal curve where population growth increases rapidly for a period, then levels off

Depleted Uranium   a by-product of uranium enrichment; dense, pure uranium comprised of nearly 100% non-fissile U^{238} atoms; used in armor and weapons, which may leave behind radioactive contamination when discharged

Desalinization   A technology that removes salts and other minerals from water, especially sea water; prohibitively expensive in most contexts, current techniques are highly energy demanding

Discourse   At root, written and spoken communication; thicker deployments of the term acknowledge that statements and texts are not mere representations of a material

world, but rather power-embedded constructions that (partially) make the world we live in

Disturbance   An event or shock that disrupts an ecological system, thereafter leading either to recovery of that system (e.g., through succession) or movement of the system into a new state

Dolphin Safe Tuna   Tuna caught without killing dolphins as bycatch

Dominion Thesis   Arising from the Book of Genesis, the dominion thesis states that humans are the pinnacle of creation; as such, humans are granted ethical free rein to use nature in any way deemed beneficial

Ecocentrism   An environmental ethical stance that argues that ecological concerns should, over and above human priorities, be central to decisions about right and wrong action (compare to anthropocentrism)

Eco-feminism   Any of a number of theories critical of the role of patriarchal society for degrading both the natural environment and the social condition of women

Ecological Footprint   The theoretical spatial extent of the Earth's surface required to sustain an individual, group, system, organization; an index of environmental impact

Ecology   The scientific study of interactions among organisms and between organisms and the habitat or ecosystem in which they live

Ecosystem Services   Benefits that an organic system creates through its function, including food resources, clean air or water, pollination, carbon sequestration, energy, and nutrient cycling, among many others

Environmental Justice   A principle, as well as a body of thought and research, stressing the need for equitable distribution of environmental goods (parks, clean air, healthful working conditions) and environmental bads (pollution, hazards, waste) between people, no matter their race, ethnicity, or gender. Conversely, environmental injustice describes a condition where unhealthful or dangerous conditions are disproportionately proximate to minority communities

Ethics/Ethical   The branch of philosophy dealing with morality, or, questions of right and wrong human action in the world

Eutrophication   A process where water bodies (and sometimes soils or habitats) become very high in nutrients, resulting in frequent algal blooms, swings in dissolved oxygen concentrations, and overall degradation

Exclusive Economic Zones (EEZs)   Usually extending 200 nautical miles off the coasts of sovereign states, EEZs are sea-zones within which states claim ownership over fishery and mineral resources

Exponential Growth   A condition of growth where the rate is mathematically proportional to the current value, leading to continued, non-linear increase of the quantity; in population, this refers to a state of increasingly accelerated and compounded growth, with ecological implications for scarcity

Externality   The spillover of a cost or benefit, as where industrial activity at a plant leads to pollution off-site that must be paid for by someone else

Extinction Crisis   The current era of anthropogenically induced plant and animal extinction, estimated to be between one thousand and ten thousand times the historical average, or background extinction rate

Factory Farms   Intensive animal-raising agricultural operations; factory farms attempt to maximize production by raising as many animals in as little space as possible, often resulting in significant air and water pollution

Fallout   airborne radioactive pollution caused by a nuclear weapon or an explosion at a nuclear power plant or other such facility

Fertility Rate   A measure describing the average number of children birthed by an average statistical woman during her reproductive lifetime

First Contradiction of Capitalism   In Marxist thought, this describes the tendency for capitalism to eventually undermine the economic conditions for its own perpetuation, through overproduction of commodities, reduction of wages for would-be consumers, etc., predicted to eventually lead to responses by workers to resist capitalism leading to a new form of economy. Compare to the second contradiction of capitalism

Fordism   Relations of production dominant in many industrialized countries in the first several decades of the twentieth century; marked by large, vertically integrated corporations, high wages and rates of consumption, and considerable state power

Forest Transition Theory   A model that predicts a period of deforestation in a region during development, when the forest is a resource or land is cleared for agriculture, followed by a return of forest when the economy changes and population outmigrates and/or becomes conservation-oriented

Game Theory   A form of applied mathematics used to model and predict people's behavior in strategic situations where people's choices are predicated on predicting the behavior of others

Genome   The complete set of genes of an organism, species, etc.

Globalization   An ongoing process by which regional economies, societies, and cultures have become integrated through a globe-spanning network of exchange

Green Certification   Programs to certify commodities for the purposes of assuring their ecological credentials, such as organically grown vegetables or sustainably harvested wood products

Green Consumption   Purchasing of products that are purportedly environmentally friendlier or less harmful than their alternatives; a model of environmental protection that relies on consumer choices to change the behavior of firms or industries rather than regulation

Green Revolution   A suite of technological innovations, developed in universities and international research centers, which were applied to agriculture between the 1950s and 1980s and increased agricultural yields dramatically, but with a concomitant rise in chemical inputs (fertilizers and pesticides) as well as increased demands for water and machinery

Greenhouse Effect   The characteristic of the Earth's atmosphere, based on the presence of important gases including water vapor and carbon dioxide, to trap and retain heat, leading to temperatures that can sustain life

Greenwashing   The exaggerated or false marketing of a product, good, or service as environmentally friendly

Hazard   An object, condition, or process that threatens individuals and society in terms of production or reproduction

Holism   Any theory that holds that a whole system (e.g., an "ecosystem" or the Earth) is more than the sum of its parts

Ideologies   Normative, value-laden, worldviews that spell out how the world is and how it ought to be

Induced Intensification   A thesis predicting that where agricultural populations grow, demands for food lead to technological innovations resulting in increased food production on the same amount of available land

Institutions   Rules and norms governing collective action, especially referring to rules governing common property environmental resources, like rivers, oceans, or the atmosphere

Intrinsic Value   The value of a natural object (e.g., an owl or a stream) in and for itself, as an end rather than a means

IPAT   A theoretical formula holding that human Impact is a function of the total Population, its overall Affluence, and its Technology; this provides an alternative formulation to a simple assumption that population alone is proportional to impact

Kuznets Curve (Environmental)   Based in the theory that income inequality will increase during economic development and decrease after reaching a state of overall affluence, this theory predicts that environmental impacts rise during development, only to fall after an economy matures

Life Cycle Analysis   The rigorous analysis of the environmental impacts of a product, service, or object from its point of manufacture all the way to its disposal as waste; also known as cradle-to-grave assessment

Manhattan Project   the highly secretive nuclear research and engineering program of the United States (and allies) during World War II that developed the first nuclear bombs

Market Failure   A situation or condition where the production or exchange of a good or service is *not* efficient; this refers to a range of perverse economic outcomes stemming from market problems like monopoly or uncontrolled externalities

Market Response Model   A model that predicts economic responses to scarcity of a resource will lead to increases in prices that will result either in decreased demand for that resource or increased supply, or both

Masculinity   The socially agreed-upon characteristics of behavior associated with men in any society; these may vary significantly between cultures, locations, and periods of history

Maximum Sustainable Yield   The largest seasonal or annual amount of any particular natural resource (e.g., timber, fish) that can be harvested indefinitely

Means of Production   In political economic (and Marxist) thought, the infrastructure, equipment, machinery, etc. required to make things, goods, and commodities

Monoculture   A single crop cultivated to the exclusion of any other potential species or harvest

Monopoly   A market condition where there is one seller for many buyers, leading to perverted and artificially inflated pricing of goods or services

Monopsony   A market condition where there is one buyer for many sellers, leading to perverted and artificially deflated pricing of goods or services

Moral Extensionism   An ethical principle stating that humans should extend their sphere of moral concern beyond the human realm; most commonly, it is argued that intelligent or sentient animals are worthy ethical subjects

Narrative   A story with a beginning and end; environmental narratives such as "biological evolution" and "the tragedy of the commons" aid our comprehension and construction of the world

Natural Resource Management   Both the academic discipline and professional field dedicated to the management of environmental conditions, goods, or services for social goals, which may range between instrumental human utility to ecological sustainability

Naturalistic Fallacy   A philosophically invalid derivation of an ethical "ought" from a natural "is"

Nature   The natural world, everything that exists that is not a product of human activity; often put in quotes to designate that it is difficult if not impossible to divvy up the entire world into discrete natural and human components

Neo-Malthusians   Present-day adherents to a position – established by Malthus in the nineteenth century – that population growth outstrips limited natural resources and presents the single greatest driver of environmental degradation and crisis

NEPA   The National Environmental Policy Act of 1970 commits the US government to protecting and improving the natural environment; after NEPA, the federal government is required to write environmental impact statements (EIS) for government actions that have significant environmental impact

Niche   In ecology, the location of an organism or species within a larger ecosystem, typically fulfilling an ecological function

Nuclear Chain Reaction   when a single nuclear fission or fusion event triggers a self-propagating sequence of nuclear fission or fusion reactions

Nuclear Fission   a process through which the nucleus of an atom is split into two lighter nuclei, producing two lighter atoms and releasing energy; nuclear particles (e.g., neutrons) are also often released in the process

Nuclear Power   electric power produced from a nuclear power plant, utilizing induced nuclear fission to generate heat, steam, and electricity

Nuclear Proliferation   the spread of nuclear weapons around the world

Overaccumulation   In political economy (and Marxism), a condition in the economy where capital becomes concentrated in very few hands (e.g., wealthy individuals) or firms (e.g., banks), causing economic slowdown and potential socioeconomic crisis

Overproduction   In political economy (and Marxism), a condition in the economy where the capacity of industry to produce goods and services outpaces the needs and capacity to consume, causing economic slowdown and potential socioeconomic crisis

Photosynthesis   The process through which plants use the sun's energy to convert carbon dioxide into organic compounds, especially sugars that are used to build tissues

Political Ecology   An approach to environmental issues that unites issues of ecology with a broadly defined political economy perspective

Pollution Haven Hypothesis   A theory that holds that some countries might voluntarily reduce environmental regulations in order to attract foreign direct investment

Post-Fordism   Arising in the last decades of the twentieth century, the current relations of production in most industrialized countries; marked by decentralized, specialized, and often subcontracted production, the prominence of transnational corporations, and diminished state power

Preservation   The management of a resource or environment for protection and preservation, typically for its own sake, as in wilderness preservation (compare to conservation)

Primary Sector   economic activities that involve the direct extraction of resources from the environment, such as mining, forestry, and marine fishing

Primitive Accumulation   In Marxist thought, the direct appropriation by capitalists of natural resources or goods from communities that historically tend to hold them collectively, as, for example, where the common lands of Britain were enclosed by wealthy elites and the state in the 1700s

Prisoner's Dilemma   An allegorical description of a game-theoretical situation in which multiple individuals making decisions in pursuit of their own interests tend to create collective outcomes that are non-optimal for everyone

Production of Nature   In political economic thought, the idea that the environment, if it ever did exist separate from people, is now a product of human industry or activity

Pull Marketing   A strategy to increase demand for products or services by reaching consumers directly and convincing them they have a previously unknown need or problem that can be solved by a specific product

Purse-Seine Fishing   An effective fishing method for species that school near the surface; a large net is encircled around the targeted catch, after which the bottom of the net is drawn tight like the strings of a purse, thus confining the catch in the net

Race   A set of imaginary categories distinguishing types of people, typically based on skin color or body morphology, which varies significantly between cultures, locations, and periods of history

Radwaste   radioactive waste products generated from nuclear technologies such as nuclear power and nuclear weapons production; commonly classified into high-level wastes (more radioactive and longer-lasting) and lower-level wastes (less radioactive and shorter-lived). Also commonly known as "nuclear waste"

Reconciliation Ecology   A science of imagining, creating, and sustaining habitats, productive environments, and biodiversity in places used, traveled, and inhabited by human beings

Relations of Production   In political economic (and Marxist) thought, the social relationships associated with, and necessary for, a specific economy, as serfs/knights are to feudalism and workers/owners are to modern capitalism

Relativism   Questioning the veracity of universal truth statements, relativism holds that all beliefs, truths, and facts are at root products of the particular set of social relations from which they arise

Rewilding   A practice of conservation where ecological functions and evolutionary processes, which are thought to have existed in past ecosystems or before human influence, are deliberately restored or created; rewilding often requires the reintroduction or restoration of large predators to ecosystems

Risk Assessment   The rigorous application of logic and information to determine the risk – possibility of an undesirable outcome – associated with particular decisions; used to so reach more optimal and rational outcomes

Risk Communication   A field of study dedicated to understanding the optimal way to present and convey risk-related information to aid people in reaching optimal and rational outcomes

Risk Perception   A phenomenon, and related field of study, describing the tendency of people to evaluate the hazardousness of a situation or decision in not-always-rational terms, depending on individual biases, culture, or human tendencies

Risk   The known (or estimated) probability that a hazard-related decision will have a negative consequence

Scientism   Usually deployed as a term of derision; refers to an uncritical reliance on the natural sciences as the basis for social decision-making and ethical judgments

Second Contradiction of Capitalism   In Marxist thought, this describes the tendency for capitalism to eventually undermine the environmental conditions for its own perpetuation, through degradation of natural resources or damage to the health of workers, etc., predicted to eventually lead to environmentalist and workers' movements to resist capitalism, leading to a new form of economy. Compare to the first contradiction of capitalism

Secondary Succession   The regrowth of vegetation and return of species to an area cleared or reduced by disturbance, as where a forest recovers its "climax vegetation" cover after a fire

Signifying Practices   Modes and methods of representation; the techniques used to tell stories, introduce and define concepts, and communicate ideologies

Social Construction   Any category, condition, or thing that exists or is understood to have certain characteristics because people socially agree that it does

Social Context   The ensemble of social relations in a particular place at a particular time; includes belief systems, economic relations of production, and institutions of governance

Social Ecology   A school of thought and set of social movements, associated with the thinker Murray Bookchin, asserting that environmental problems and crises are rooted in typical social structures and relationships, since these tend to be hierarchical, state-controlled, and predicated on domination of both people and nature

Social Reproduction   That part of the economy, especially including household work, that depends on unremunerated labor, but without which the more formal cash economy would suffer and collapse

Spatial Fix   The tendency of capitalism to temporarily solve its inevitable periodic crises by establishing new markets, new resources, and new sites of production in other places

Spent Nuclear Fuel   nuclear fuel that is no longer fissile enough to sustain a nuclear chain reaction

Stakeholders   Individuals or groups with a vested interest in the outcome of disputed actions

Stewardship   Taking responsibility for the property or fate of others; stewardship of land and natural resources is often used in a religious context, such as "caring for creation"

Succession   Ecologically, the idealized tendency for disturbed forest areas to recover through stages of species invasion and growth, progressing from grassland, to shrubs, and eventually back to tree cover

Superfund   The environmental program established to address abandoned hazardous waste sites in the United States

Surplus Value   In political economic (and Marxist) thought, the value produced by underpaying labor or over-extracting from the environment, which is accumulated by owners and investors

Sustainable/Sustainability   The conservation of land and resources so as to secure their availability to future generations

Transaction Costs   In economics, the cost associated with making an exchange, including, for example, drawing a contract, traveling to market, or negotiating a price; while most economic models assume low transaction costs, in reality these costs can be quite high, especially for systems with high externalities

Transnational Corporations (TNC)   Corporations operating facilities in more than one country; also commonly called multinational corporations (MNCs)

Trophic Cascades   The effects on subsequent (higher or lower) trophic levels after the elimination or reduction in numbers of individuals in one trophic level

Trophic Levels   Parallel levels of energy assimilation and transfer within ecological food webs; in terrestrial ecosystems, photosynthetic plants form the base trophic level, followed "up" the web by herbivores and successive levels of carnivores

Uncertainty   The degree to which the outcomes of a decision or situation are unknown

Uneven Development   The geographic tendency within capitalism to produce highly disparate economic conditions (wealth/poverty) and economic activity (production/consumption) in different places

Urban Heat Island Effect   Warming experienced by cities that occurs through the absorption and re-radiation of heat from buildings and sidewalks. Vegetation in urban areas reduces this effect

Utilitarian   An ethical theory that posits that the value of a good should be judged solely (or at least primarily) by its usefulness to society; following the eighteenth–nineteenth-century philosopher Jeremy Bentham, usefulness is equated with maximizing pleasure or happiness and minimizing pain and suffering

Utopia/Utopian   Imaginary, idealized social conditions arising from socio-political systems that facilitate cooperation over competition

Wilderness   A natural parcel of land, more or less unaffected by human forces; increasingly, wilderness is viewed as a social construction

Zero Population Growth   A condition in a population where the number of births matches the number of deaths and therefore there is no net increase; an idealized condition for those concerned about overpopulation

Index

Note: page numbers in italics denote illustrations or figures

Environment and Society: A Critical Introduction, Second Edition. Paul Robbins, John Hintz,
and Sarah A. Moore.
© 2014 John Wiley & Sons, Ltd. Published 2014 by John Wiley & Sons, Ltd.